im
Great Priest Imhotep

3

MAKOTO
MORISHITA

Great Priest Imhotep

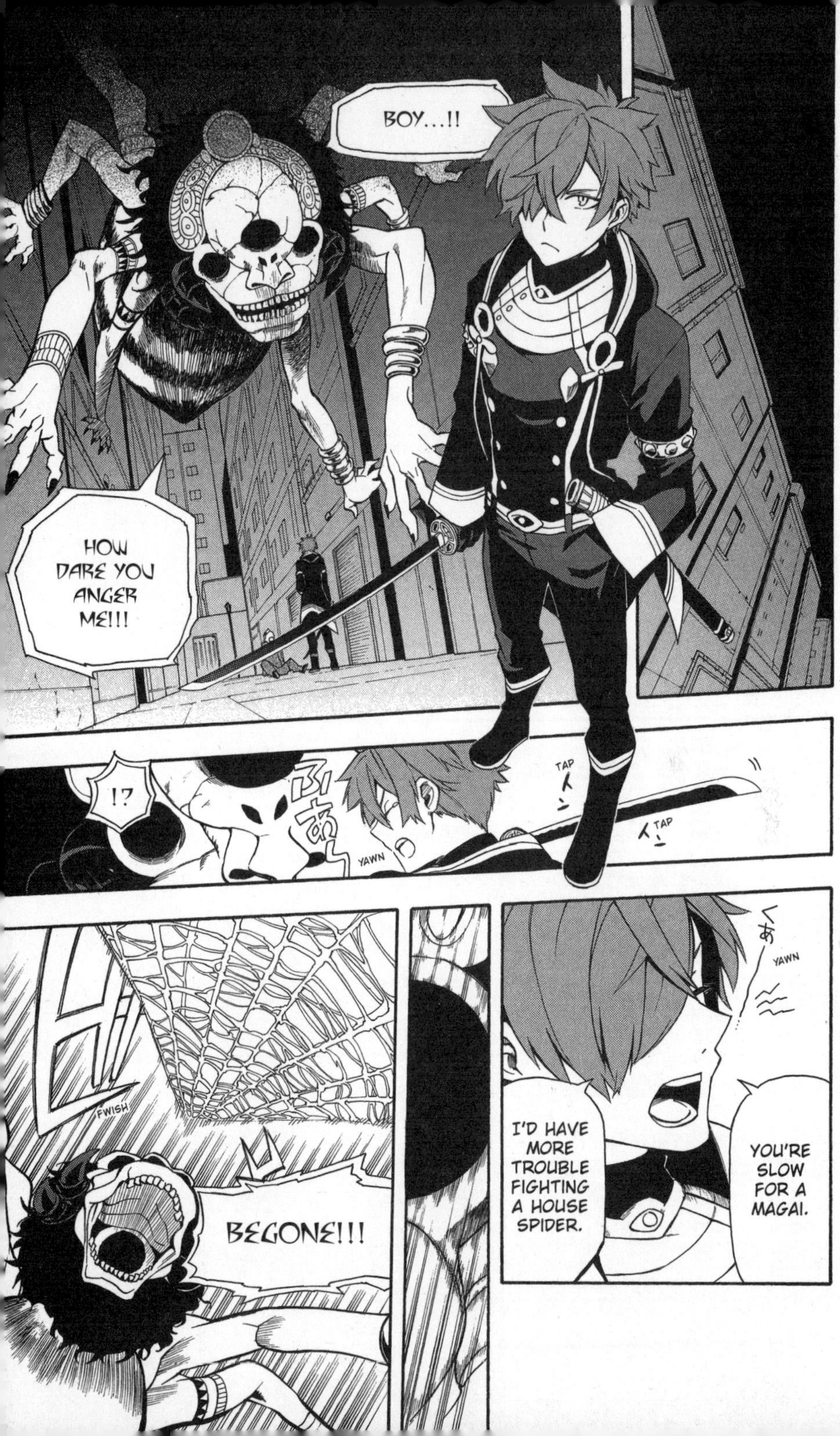
BOY...!!
HOW DARE YOU ANGER ME!!!
TAP
TAP
YAWN
!?
YAWN
YOU'RE SLOW FOR A MAGAI.
I'D HAVE MORE TROUBLE FIGHTING A HOUSE SPIDER.
FWISH
BEGONE!!!

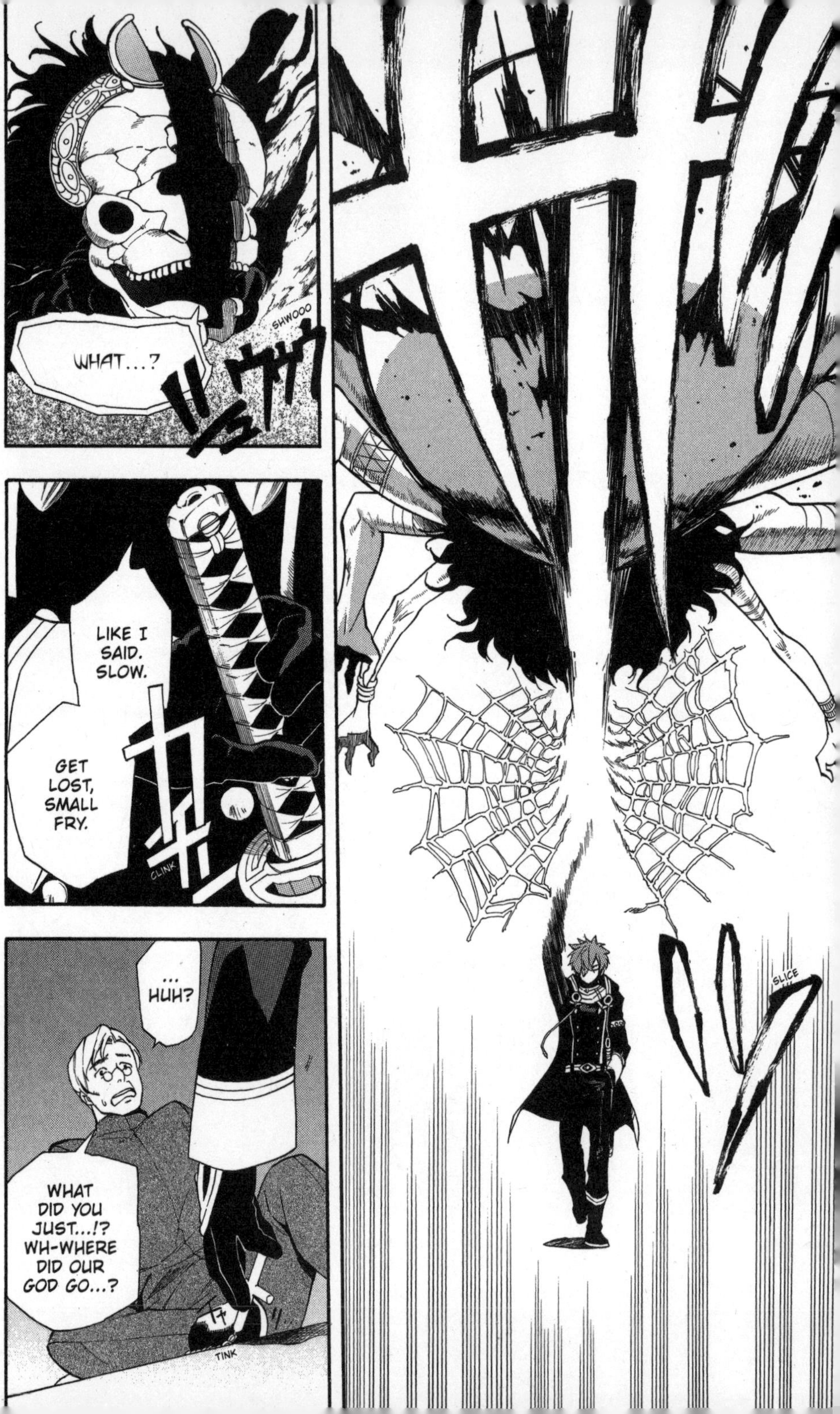
SLICE
WHAT...?
SHWOOO
LIKE I SAID. SLOW.
GET LOST, SMALL FRY.
CLINK
... HUH?
WHAT DID YOU JUST...!? WH-WHERE DID OUR GOD GO...?
TINK

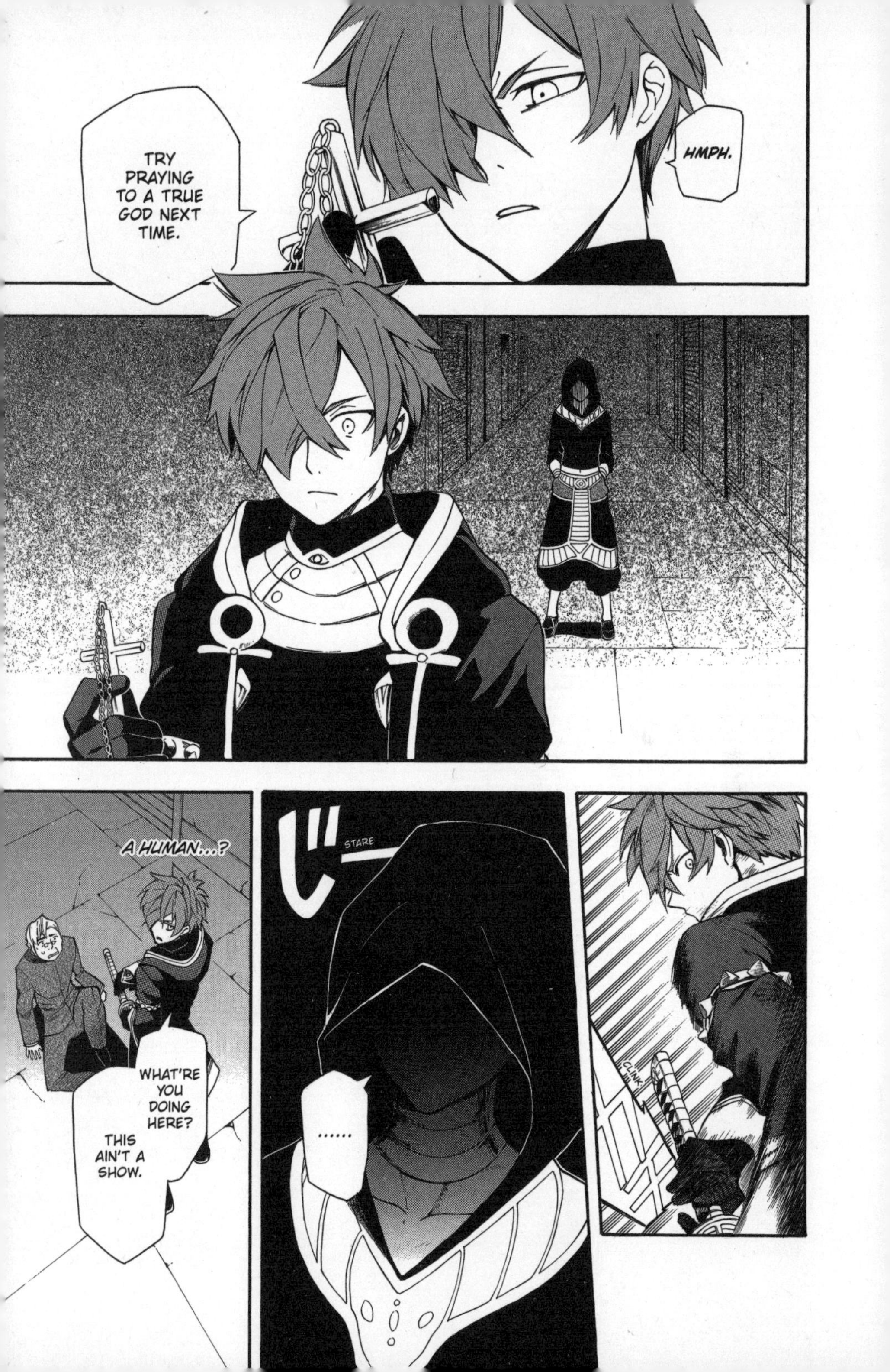
HMPH.
TRY PRAYING TO A TRUE GOD NEXT TIME.
CLINK
STARE
......
A HUMAN...?
WHAT'RE YOU DOING HERE? THIS AIN'T A SHOW.

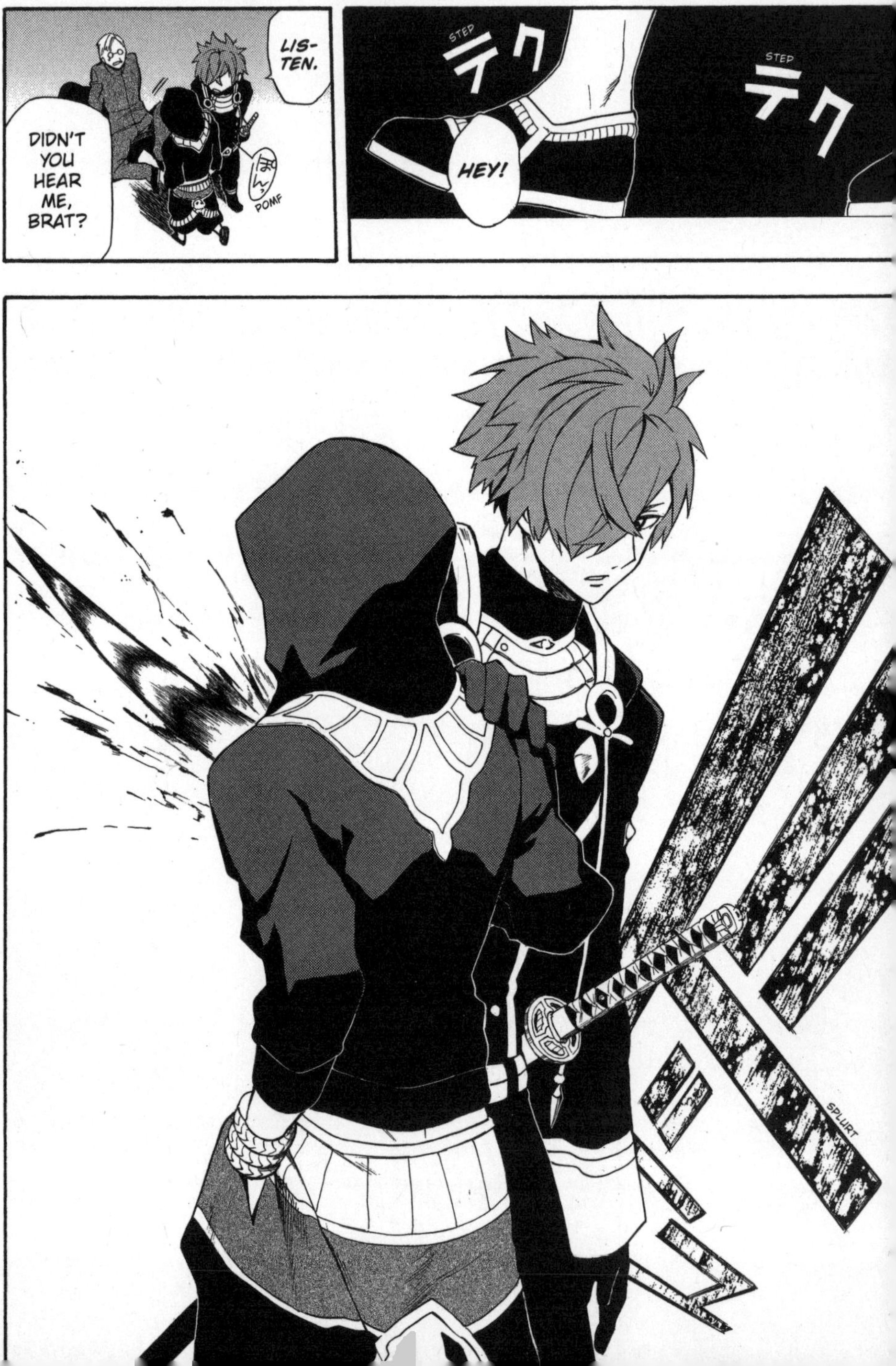
STEP
テク
STEP
テク
HEY!
LIS-TEN.
DIDN'T YOU HEAR ME, BRAT?
ぽん
POMF
SPLURT

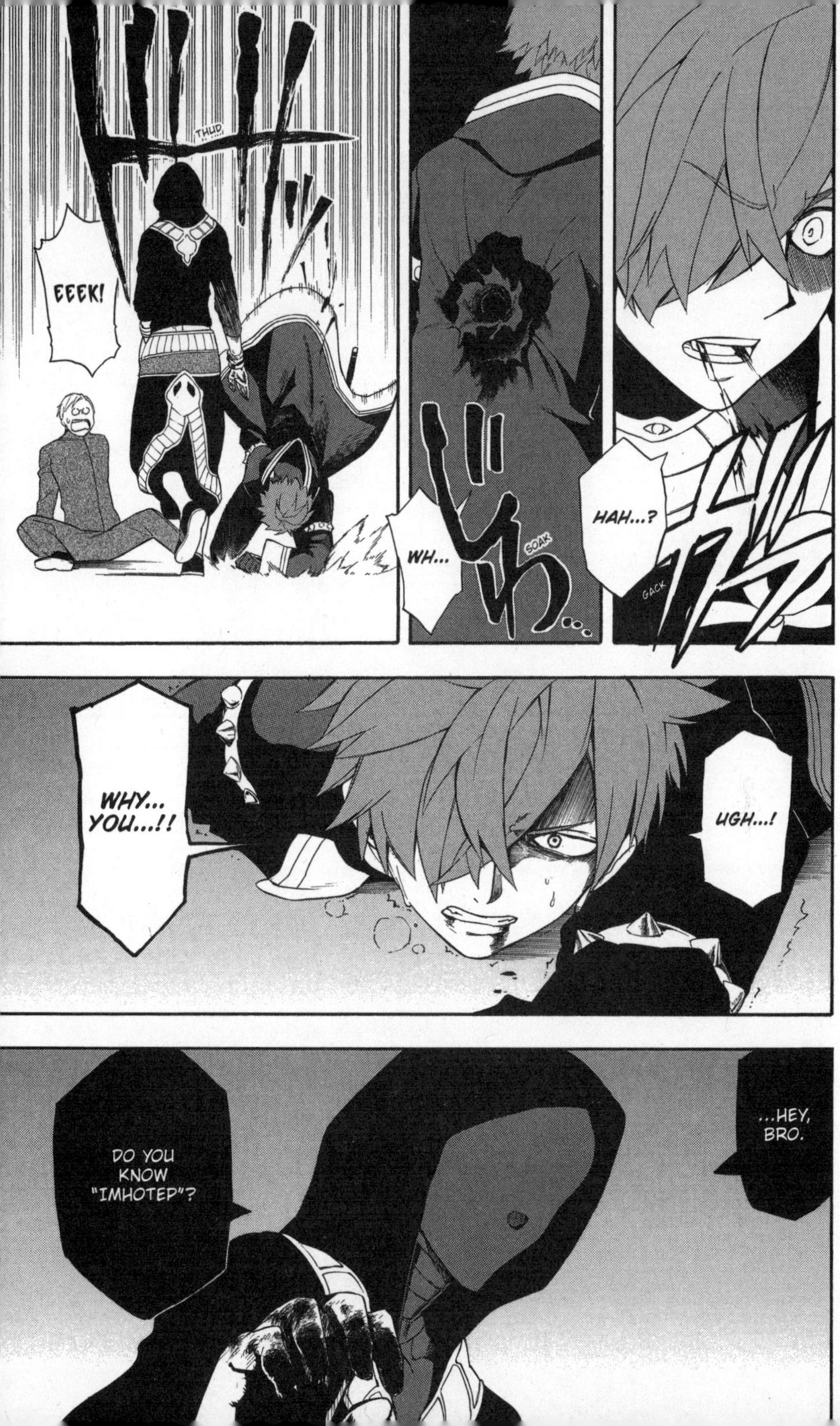

HAH...?
GACK
WH...
じわ…
SOAK
THUD
EEEK!
UGH...!
WHY... YOU...!!
...HEY, BRO.
DO YOU KNOW "IMHOTEP"?

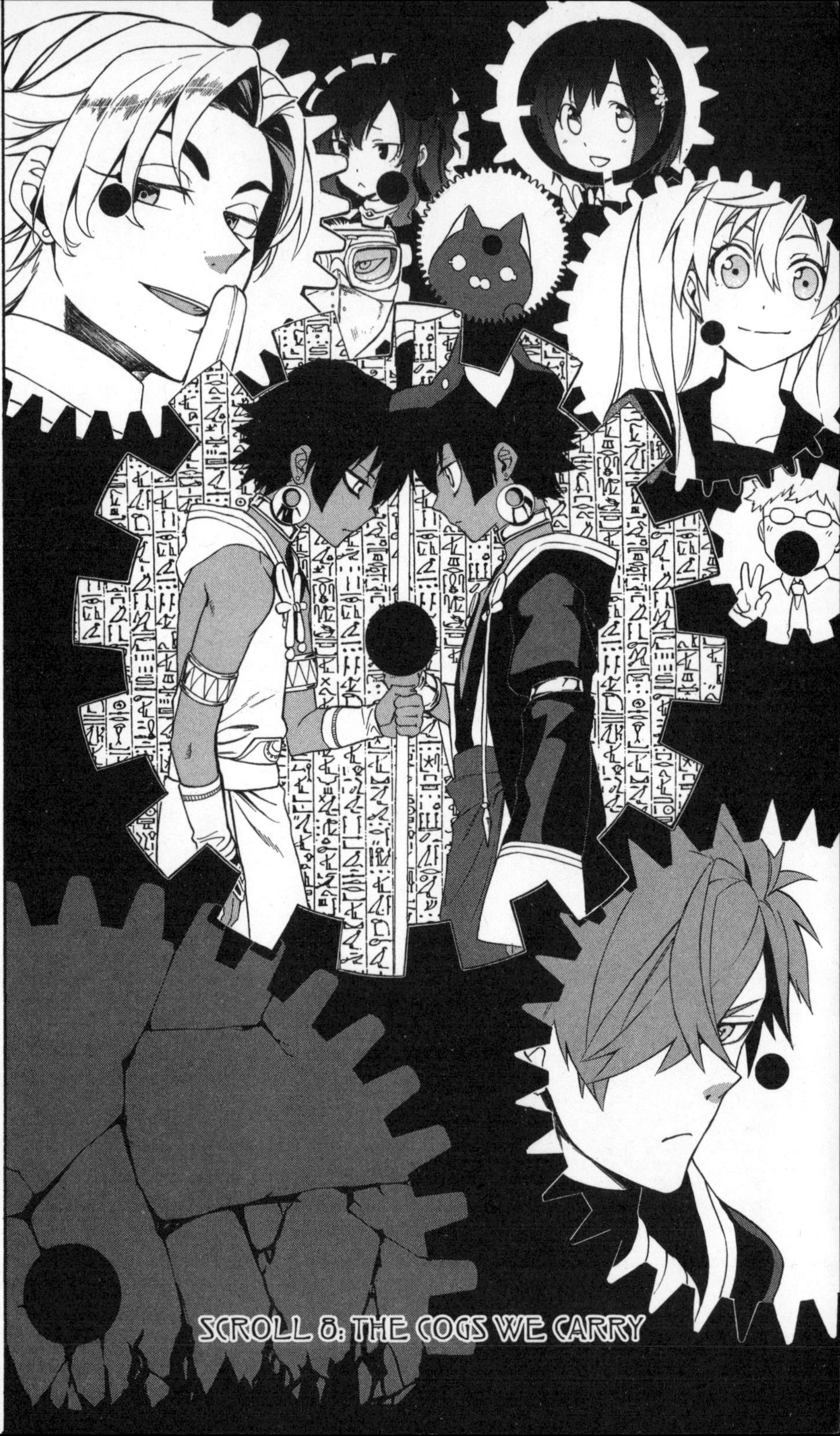
SCROLL 8: THE COGS WE CARRY

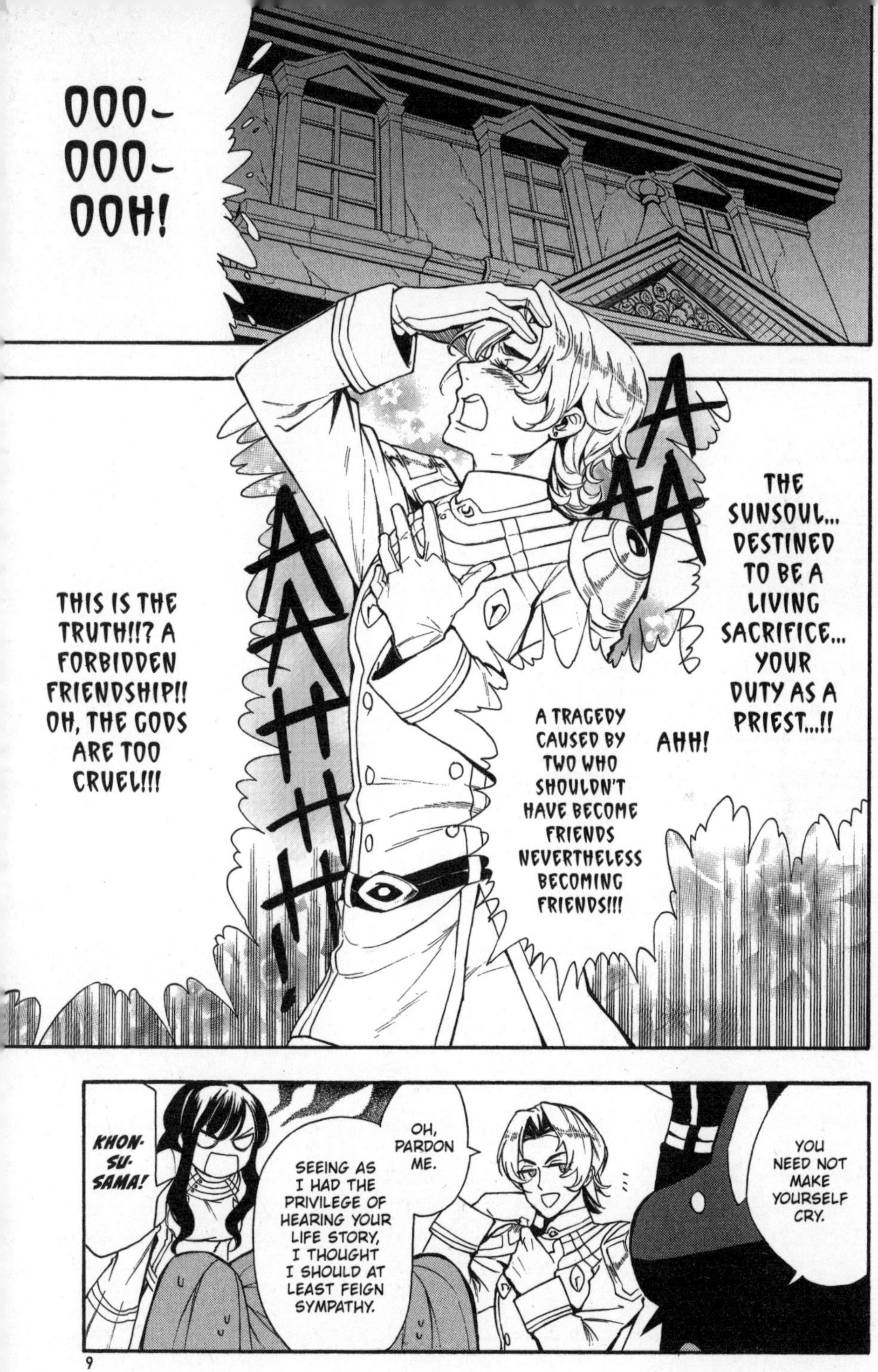

OOO-OOO-OOH!
THE SUNSOUL... DESTINED TO BE A LIVING SACRIFICE... YOUR DUTY AS A PRIEST...!!
AHH!
A TRAGEDY CAUSED BY TWO WHO SHOULDN'T HAVE BECOME FRIENDS NEVERTHELESS BECOMING FRIENDS!!!
AAA
THIS IS THE TRUTH!!? A FORBIDDEN FRIENDSHIP!! OH, THE GODS ARE TOO CRUEL!!!
AAHHHH!
YOU NEED NOT MAKE YOURSELF CRY.
OH, PARDON ME.
SEEING AS I HAD THE PRIVILEGE OF HEARING YOUR LIFE STORY, I THOUGHT I SHOULD AT LEAST FEIGN SYMPATHY.
KHON-SU-SAMA!

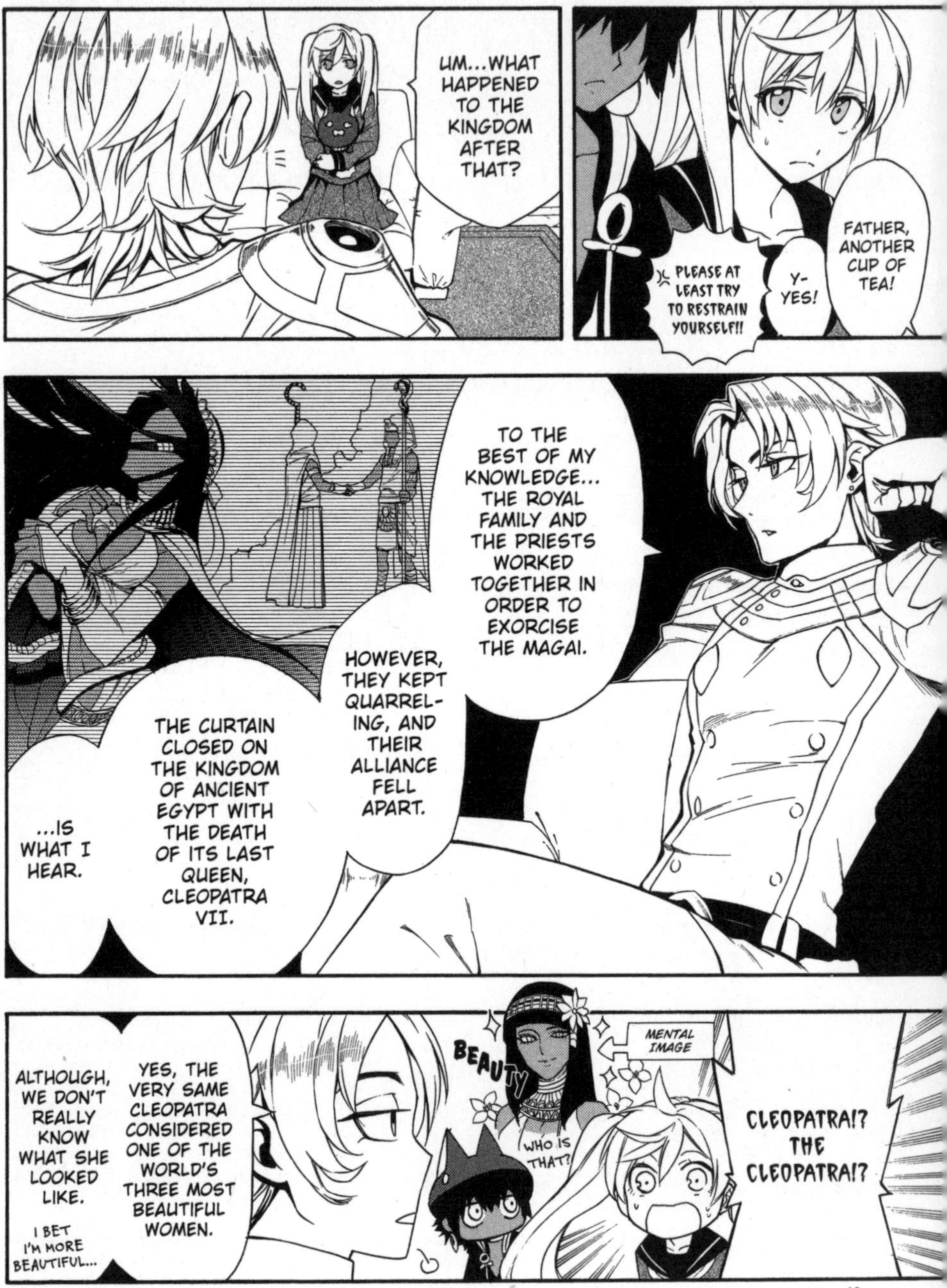

FATHER, ANOTHER CUP OF TEA!
Y-YES!
PLEASE AT LEAST TRY TO RESTRAIN YOURSELF!!
UM...WHAT HAPPENED TO THE KINGDOM AFTER THAT?
TO THE BEST OF MY KNOWLEDGE... THE ROYAL FAMILY AND THE PRIESTS WORKED TOGETHER IN ORDER TO EXORCISE THE MAGAI.
HOWEVER, THEY KEPT QUARREL-ING, AND THEIR ALLIANCE FELL APART.
THE CURTAIN CLOSED ON THE KINGDOM OF ANCIENT EGYPT WITH THE DEATH OF ITS LAST QUEEN, CLEOPATRA VII.
...IS WHAT I HEAR.
CLEOPATRA!? THE CLEOPATRA!?
MENTAL IMAGE
BEAUTY
WHO IS THAT?
YES, THE VERY SAME CLEOPATRA CONSIDERED ONE OF THE WORLD'S THREE MOST BEAUTIFUL WOMEN.
ALTHOUGH, WE DON'T REALLY KNOW WHAT SHE LOOKED LIKE.
I BET I'M MORE BEAUTIFUL...

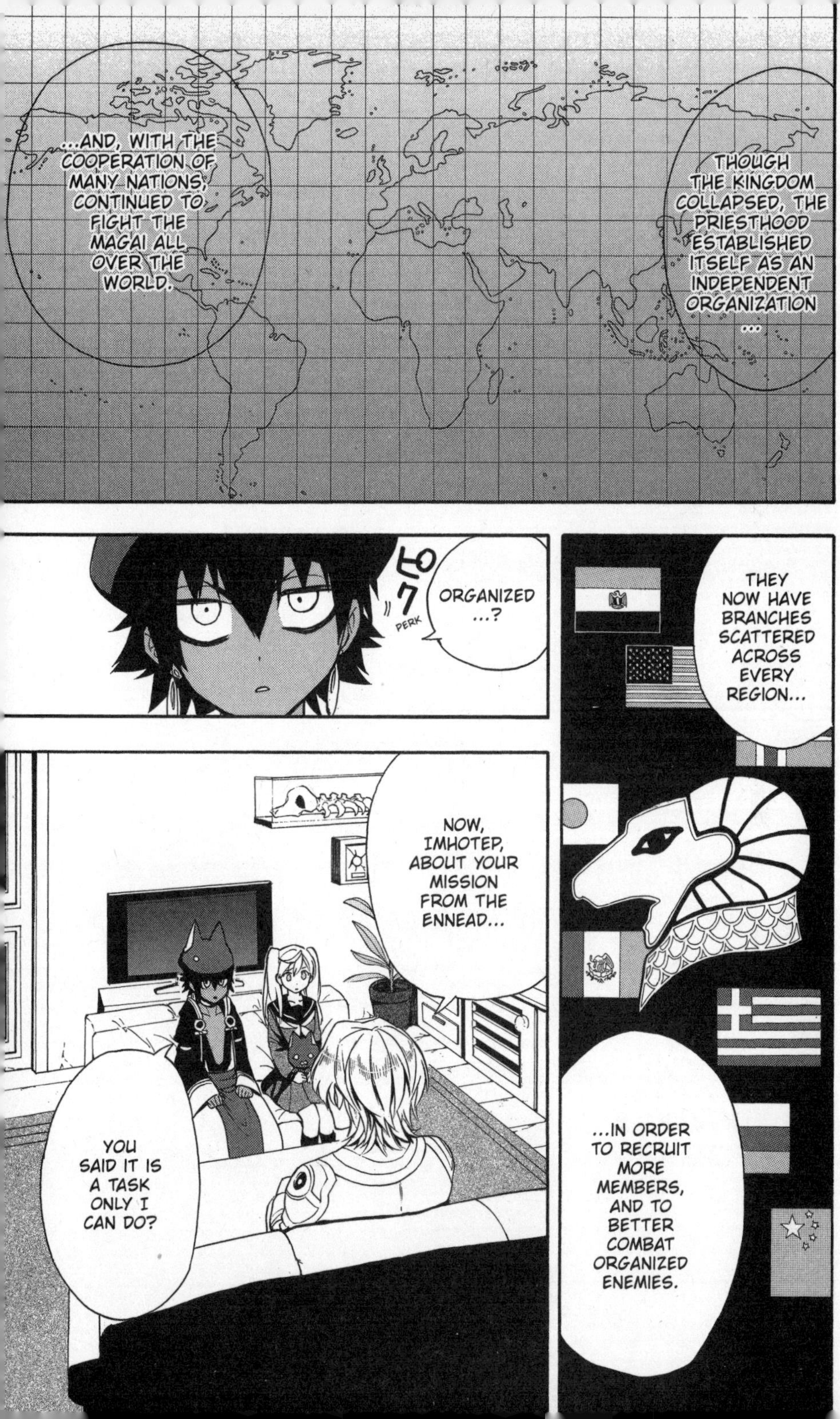
THOUGH THE KINGDOM COLLAPSED, THE PRIESTHOOD ESTABLISHED ITSELF AS AN INDEPENDENT ORGANIZATION...
...AND, WITH THE COOPERATION OF MANY NATIONS, CONTINUED TO FIGHT THE MAGAI ALL OVER THE WORLD.
THEY NOW HAVE BRANCHES SCATTERED ACROSS EVERY REGION...
...IN ORDER TO RECRUIT MORE MEMBERS, AND TO BETTER COMBAT ORGANIZED ENEMIES.
ピク
PERK
ORGANIZED...?
NOW, IMHOTEP, ABOUT YOUR MISSION FROM THE ENNEAD...
YOU SAID IT IS A TASK ONLY I CAN DO?

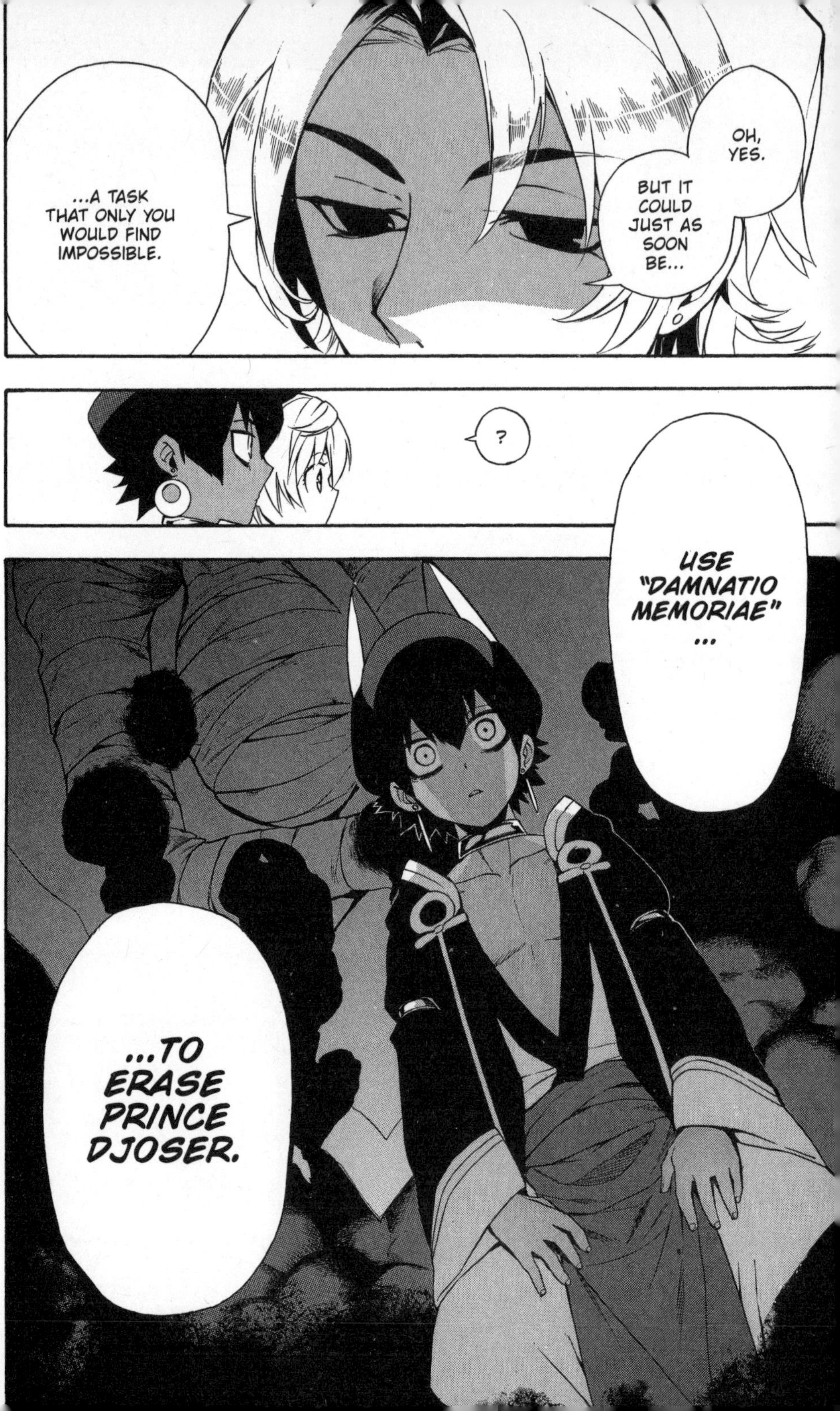
OH, YES.
BUT IT COULD JUST AS SOON BE...
...A TASK THAT ONLY YOU WOULD FIND IMPOSSIBLE.
?
USE "DAMNATIO MEMORIAE"...
...TO ERASE PRINCE DJOSER.

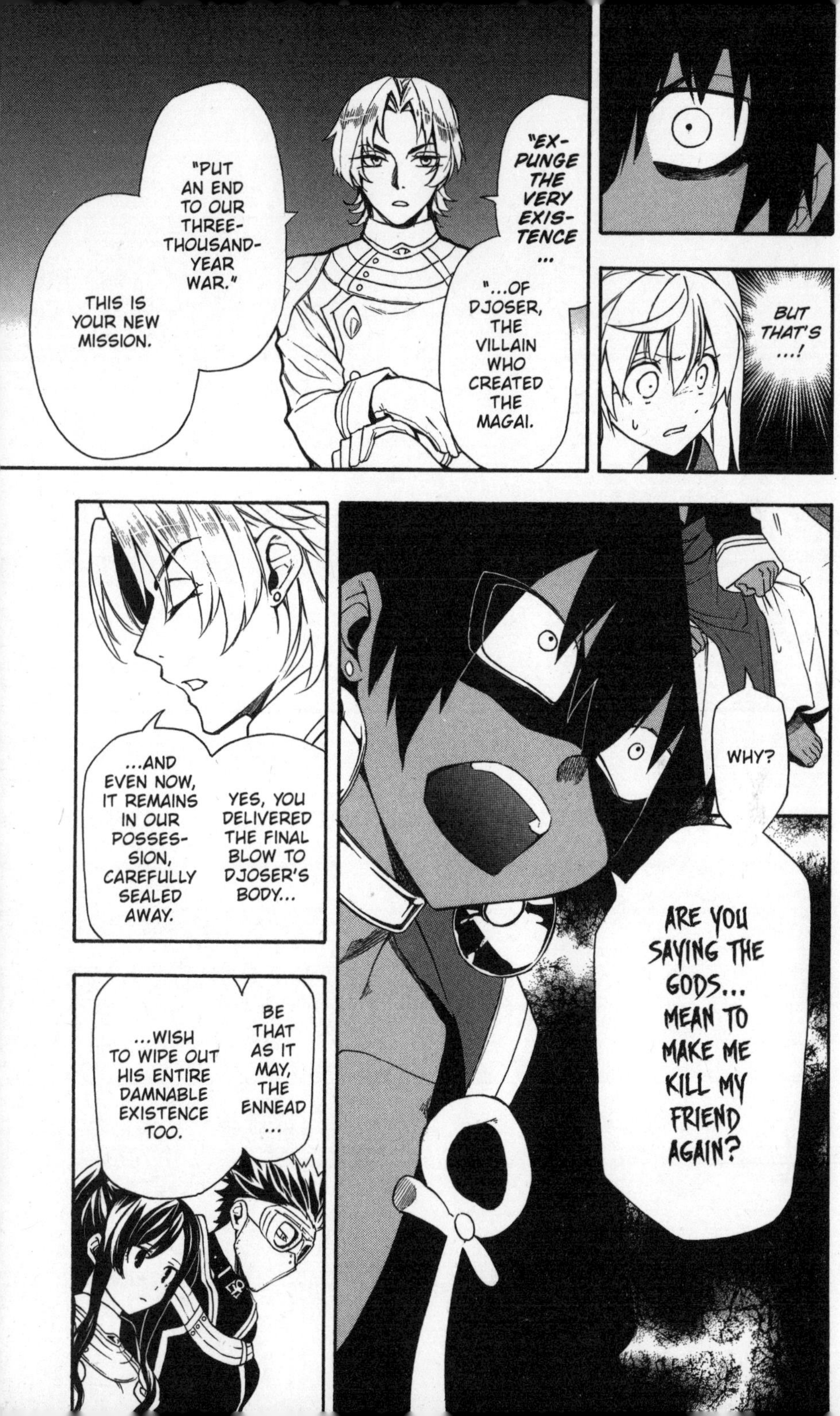
BUT THAT'S ...!
"EX-PUNGE THE VERY EXISTENCE ...
"...OF DJOSER, THE VILLAIN WHO CREATED THE MAGAI.
"PUT AN END TO OUR THREE-THOUSAND-YEAR WAR."
THIS IS YOUR NEW MISSION.
WHY?
ARE YOU SAYING THE GODS... MEAN TO MAKE ME KILL MY FRIEND AGAIN?
YES, YOU DELIVERED THE FINAL BLOW TO DJOSER'S BODY...
...AND EVEN NOW, IT REMAINS IN OUR POSSES-SION, CAREFULLY SEALED AWAY.
BE THAT AS IT MAY, THE ENNEAD ...
...WISH TO WIPE OUT HIS ENTIRE DAMNABLE EXISTENCE TOO.

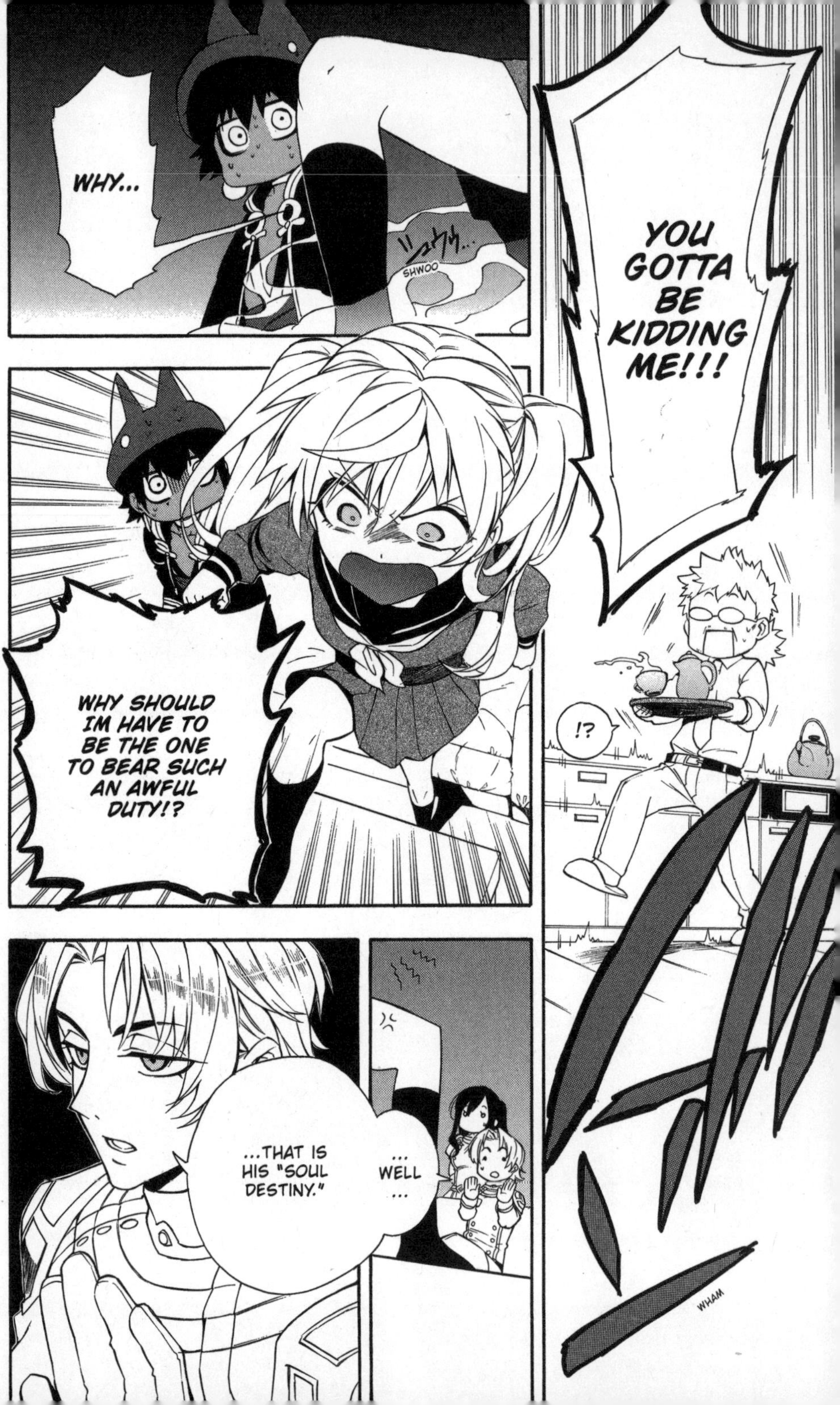
YOU GOTTA BE KIDDING ME!!!
!?
WHAM
WHY...
SHWOO
WHY SHOULD IM HAVE TO BE THE ONE TO BEAR SUCH AN AWFUL DUTY!?
... WELL ...
...THAT IS HIS "SOUL DESTINY."

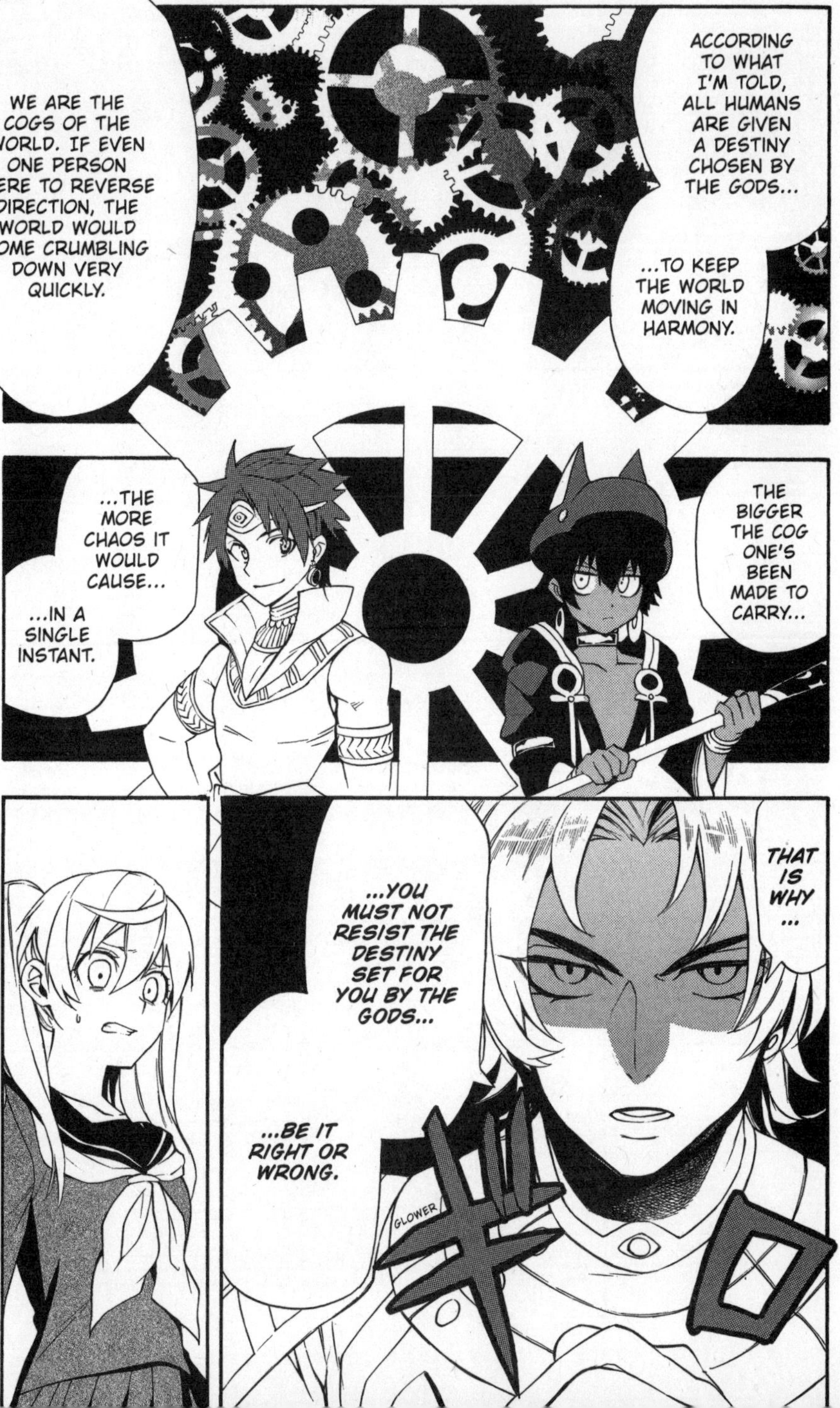
ACCORDING TO WHAT I'M TOLD, ALL HUMANS ARE GIVEN A DESTINY CHOSEN BY THE GODS...
...TO KEEP THE WORLD MOVING IN HARMONY.
WE ARE THE COGS OF THE WORLD. IF EVEN ONE PERSON WERE TO REVERSE DIRECTION, THE WORLD WOULD COME CRUMBLING DOWN VERY QUICKLY.
THE BIGGER THE COG ONE'S BEEN MADE TO CARRY...
...THE MORE CHAOS IT WOULD CAUSE...
...IN A SINGLE INSTANT.
THAT IS WHY...
...YOU MUST NOT RESIST THE DESTINY SET FOR YOU BY THE GODS...
...BE IT RIGHT OR WRONG.
GLOWER

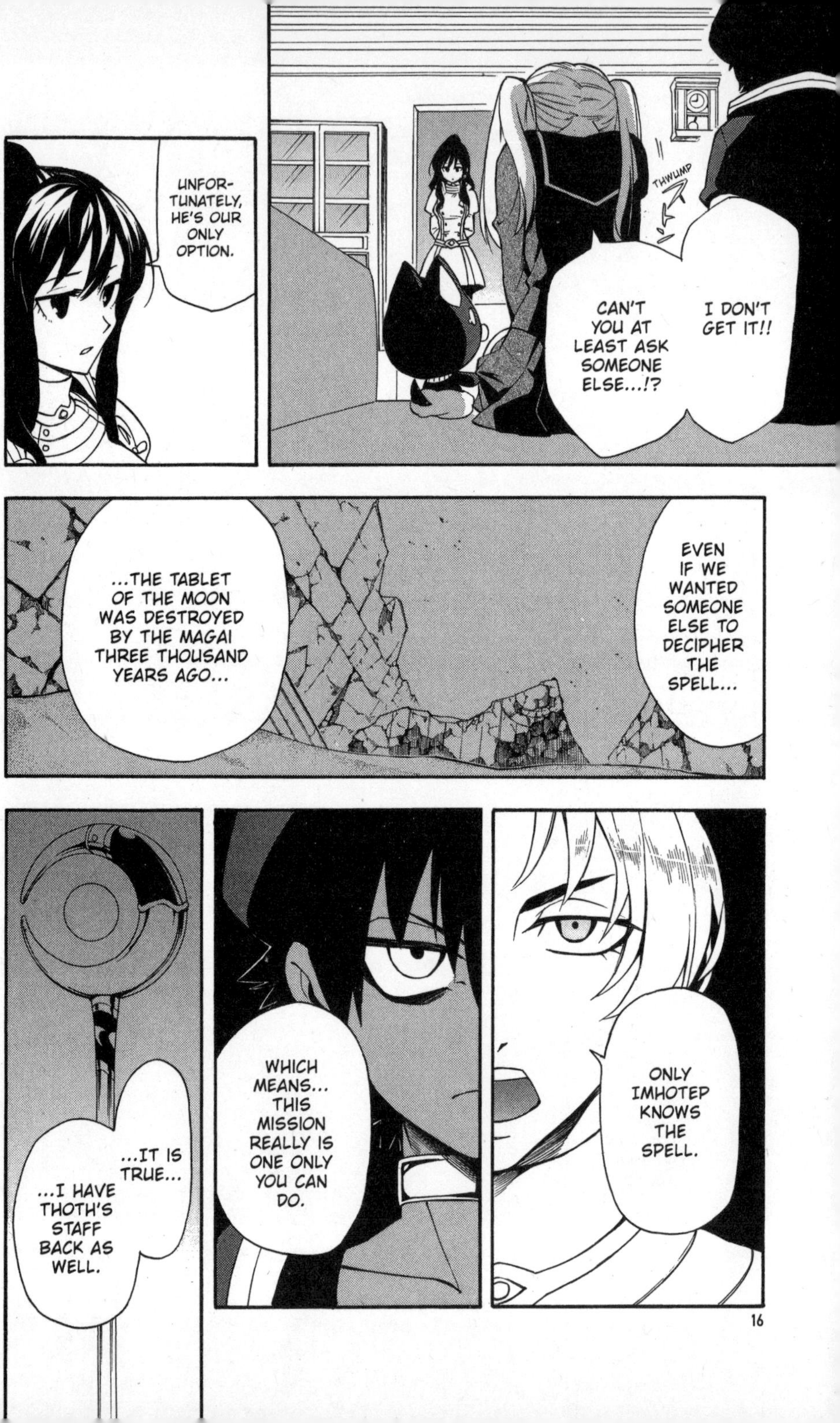
THWUMP
I DON'T GET IT!!
CAN'T YOU AT LEAST ASK SOMEONE ELSE...!?
UNFOR-TUNATELY, HE'S OUR ONLY OPTION.
EVEN IF WE WANTED SOMEONE ELSE TO DECIPHER THE SPELL...
...THE TABLET OF THE MOON WAS DESTROYED BY THE MAGAI THREE THOUSAND YEARS AGO...
ONLY IMHOTEP KNOWS THE SPELL.
WHICH MEANS... THIS MISSION REALLY IS ONE ONLY YOU CAN DO.
...IT IS TRUE...
...I HAVE THOTH'S STAFF BACK AS WELL.

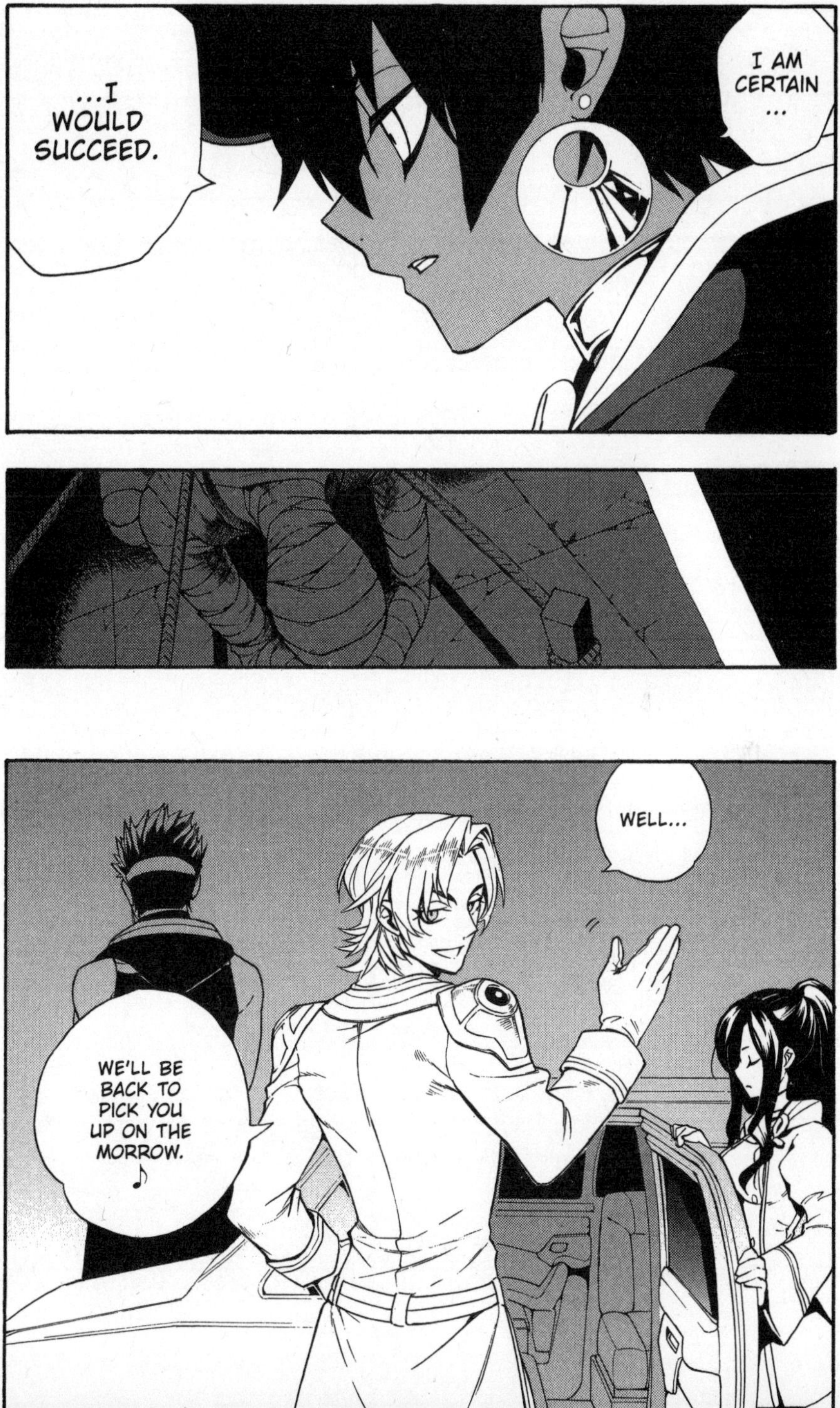
I AM CERTAIN ...
...I WOULD SUCCEED.
WELL...
WE'LL BE BACK TO PICK YOU UP ON THE MORROW. ♪

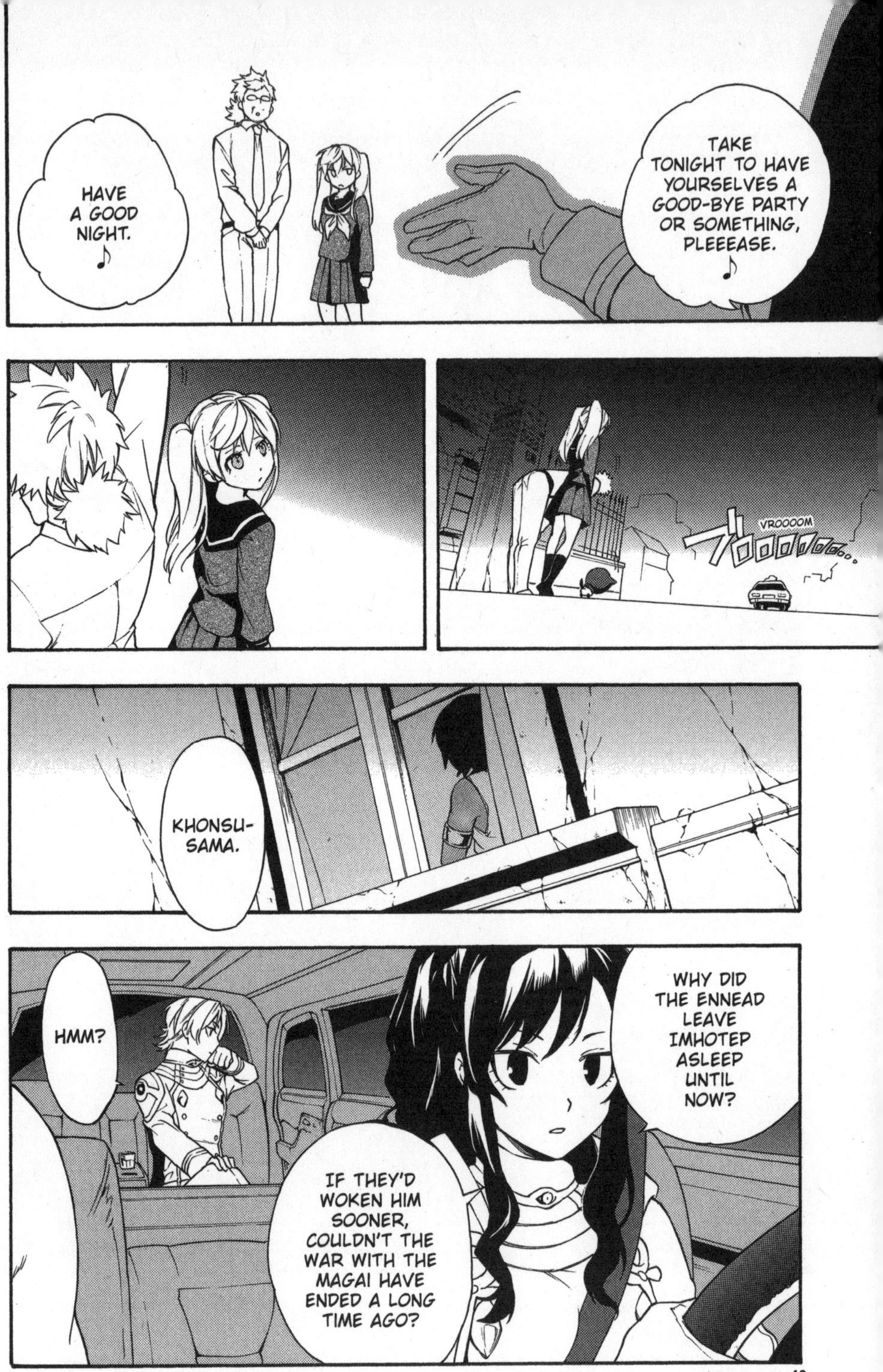
TAKE TONIGHT TO HAVE YOURSELVES A GOOD-BYE PARTY OR SOMETHING, PLEEEASE. ♪
HAVE A GOOD NIGHT. ♪
VROOOOM
KHONSU-SAMA.
HMM?
WHY DID THE ENNEAD LEAVE IMHOTEP ASLEEP UNTIL NOW?
IF THEY'D WOKEN HIM SOONER, COULDN'T THE WAR WITH THE MAGAI HAVE ENDED A LONG TIME AGO?

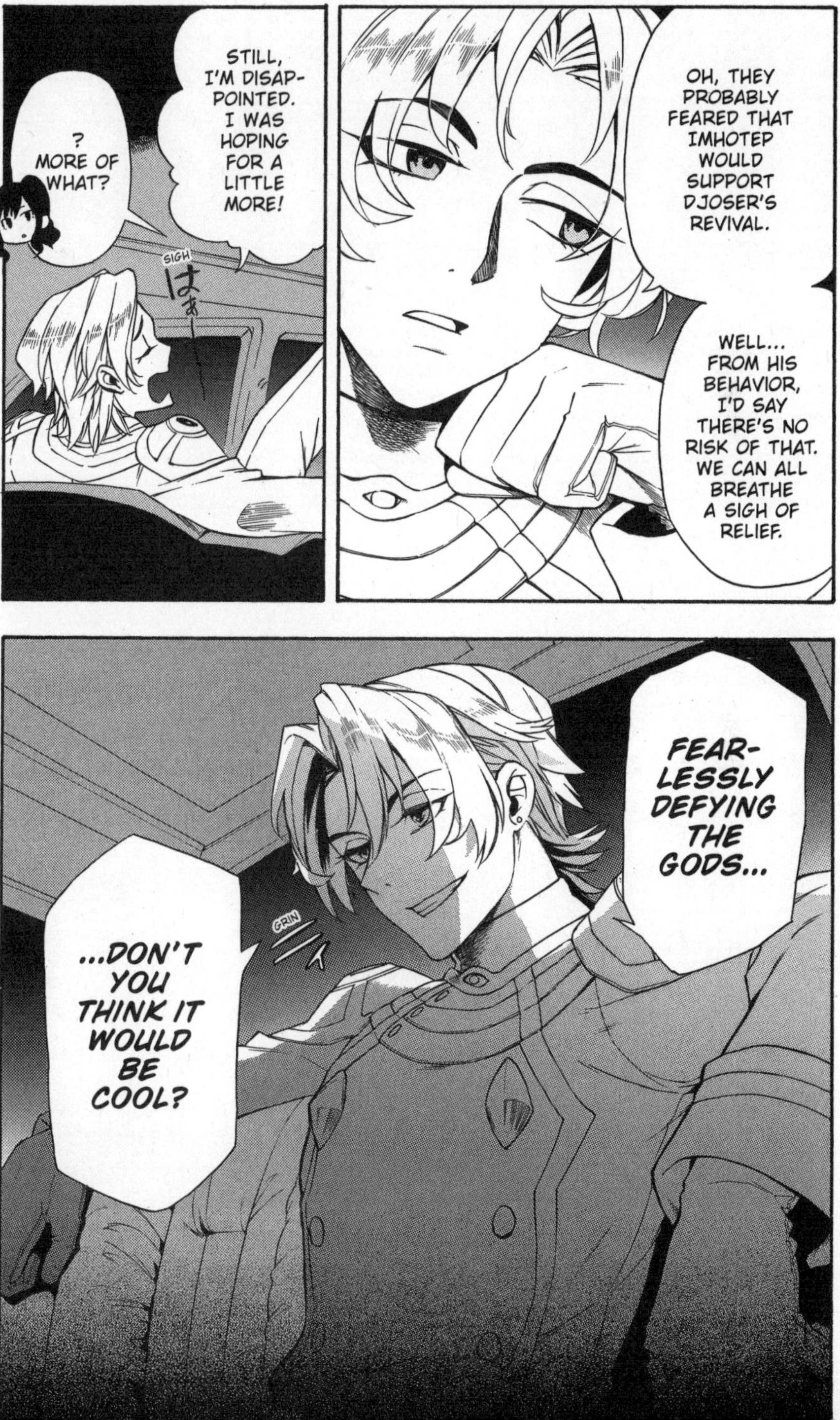
OH, THEY PROBABLY FEARED THAT IMHOTEP WOULD SUPPORT DJOSER'S REVIVAL.
WELL... FROM HIS BEHAVIOR, I'D SAY THERE'S NO RISK OF THAT. WE CAN ALL BREATHE A SIGH OF RELIEF.
STILL, I'M DISAP-POINTED. I WAS HOPING FOR A LITTLE MORE!
? MORE OF WHAT?
SIGH
はぁ
FEAR-LESSLY DEFYING THE GODS...
GRIN
...DON'T YOU THINK IT WOULD BE COOL?

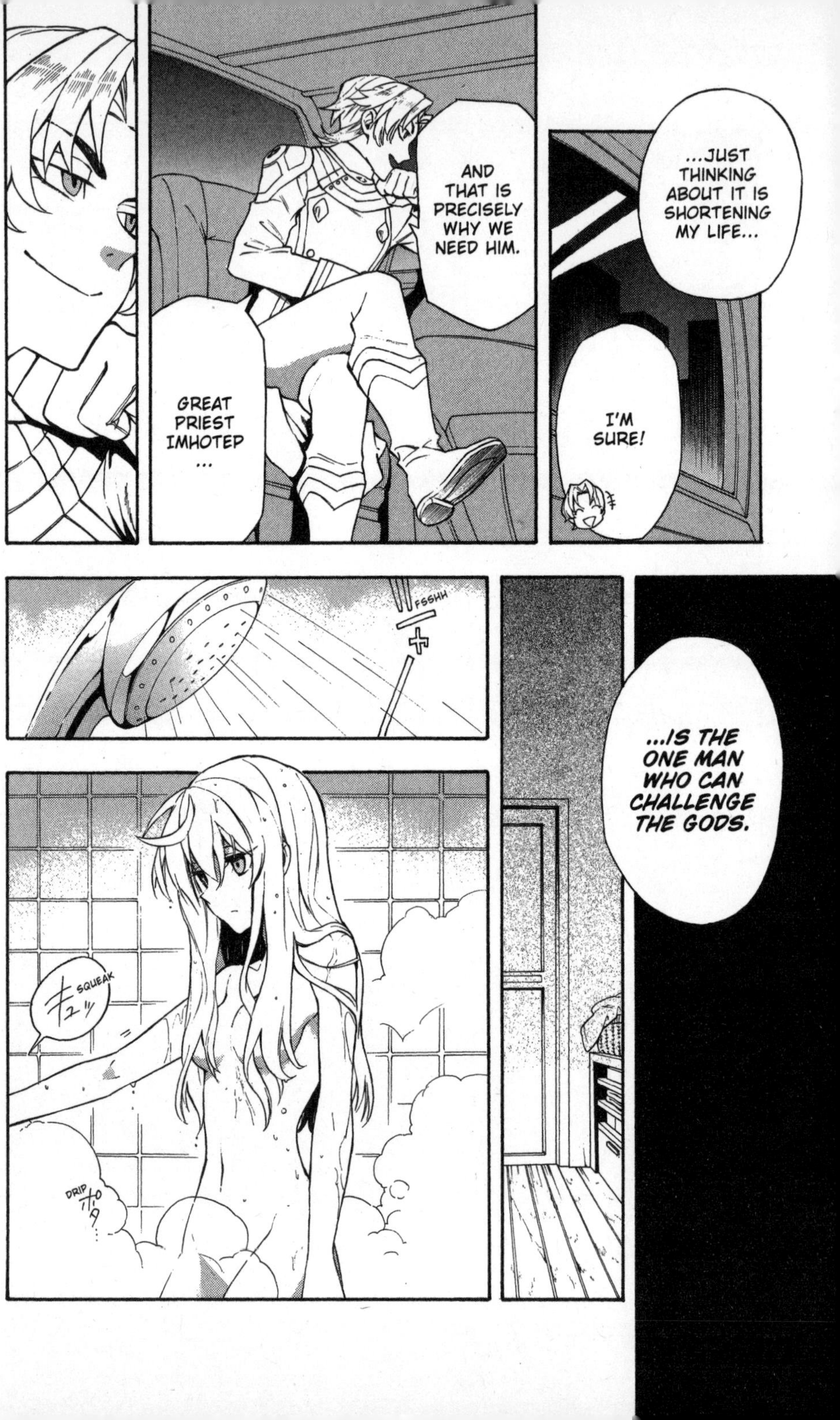
...JUST THINKING ABOUT IT IS SHORTENING MY LIFE...
I'M SURE!
AND THAT IS PRECISELY WHY WE NEED HIM.
GREAT PRIEST IMHOTEP ...
...IS THE ONE MAN WHO CAN CHALLENGE THE GODS.
FSSHH
SQUEAK
DRIP

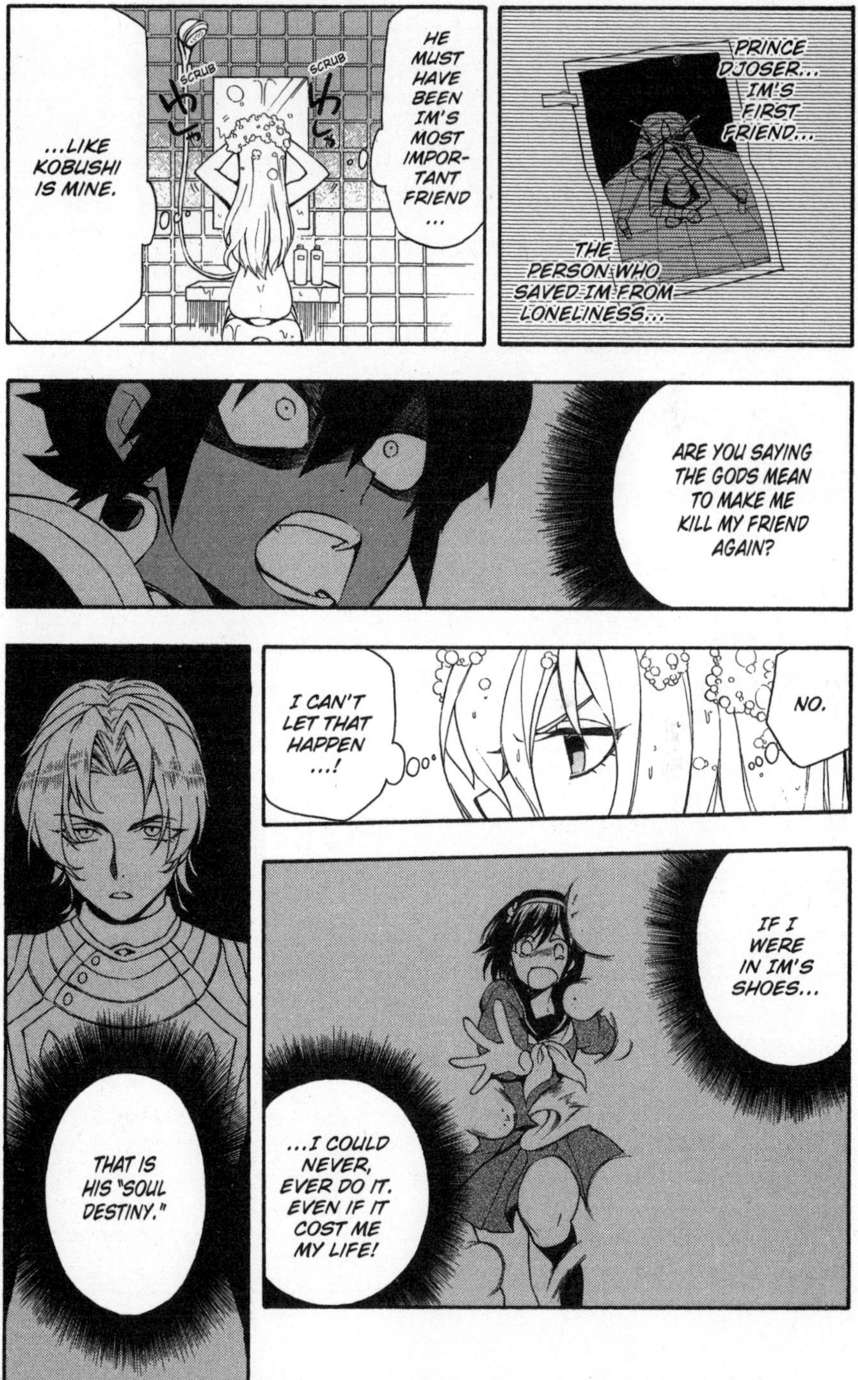
PRINCE DJOSER... IM'S FIRST FRIEND...
THE PERSON WHO SAVED IM FROM LONELINESS...
HE MUST HAVE BEEN IM'S MOST IMPORTANT FRIEND...
SCRUB
SCRUB
...LIKE KOBUSHI IS MINE.
ARE YOU SAYING THE GODS MEAN TO MAKE ME KILL MY FRIEND AGAIN?
NO.
I CAN'T LET THAT HAPPEN...!
IF I WERE IN IM'S SHOES...
...I COULD NEVER, EVER DO IT. EVEN IF IT COST ME MY LIFE!
THAT IS HIS "SOUL DESTINY."

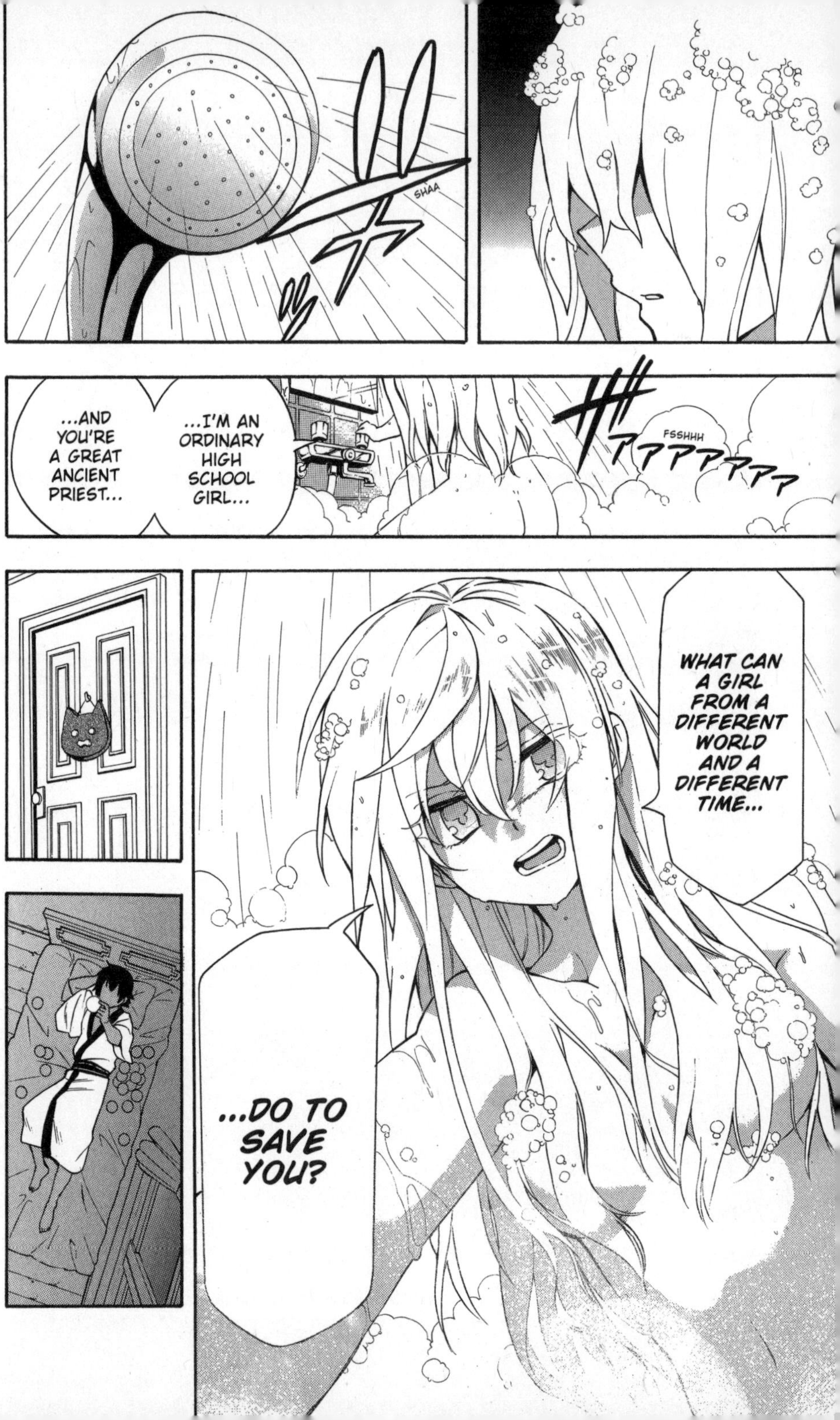
SHAA
FSSHHH
...I'M AN ORDINARY HIGH SCHOOL GIRL...
...AND YOU'RE A GREAT ANCIENT PRIEST...
WHAT CAN A GIRL FROM A DIFFERENT WORLD AND A DIFFERENT TIME...
...DO TO SAVE YOU?

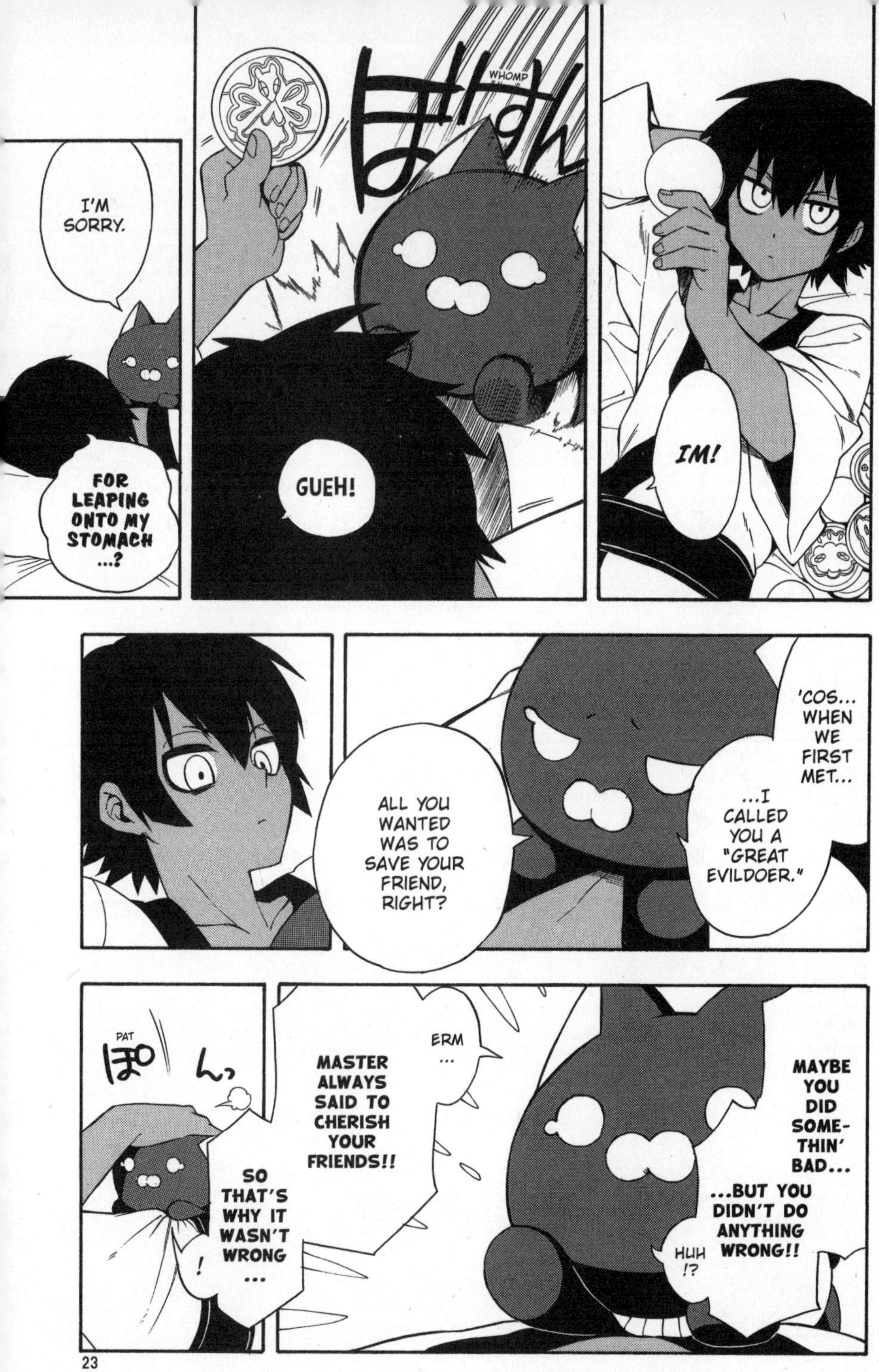
IM!
WHOMP
ぼすん
GUEH!
I'M SORRY.
FOR LEAPING ONTO MY STOMACH ...?
'COS... WHEN WE FIRST MET...
...I CALLED YOU A "GREAT EVILDOER."
ALL YOU WANTED WAS TO SAVE YOUR FRIEND, RIGHT?
MAYBE YOU DID SOME-THIN' BAD...
...BUT YOU DIDN'T DO ANYTHING WRONG!!
HUH !?
ERM ...
MASTER ALWAYS SAID TO CHERISH YOUR FRIENDS!!
SO THAT'S WHY IT WASN'T WRONG ...
PAT
ぽんっ
!

...... THANK YOU... ... ANUBIS.
BEEEAM
TIK
TOK
TIK
TOK
TIK
TOK
IM-SAMA... DON'T GOOO SNIFFLE...
MNYA...
WHISTLE

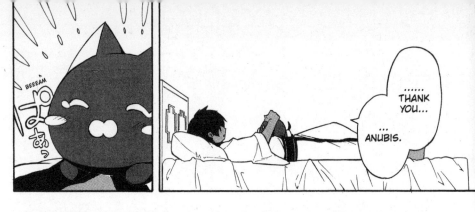

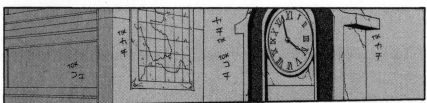

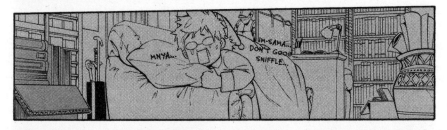

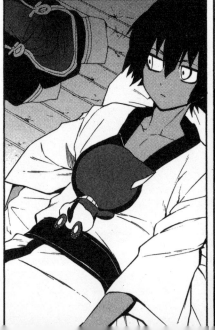

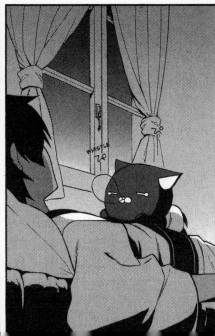

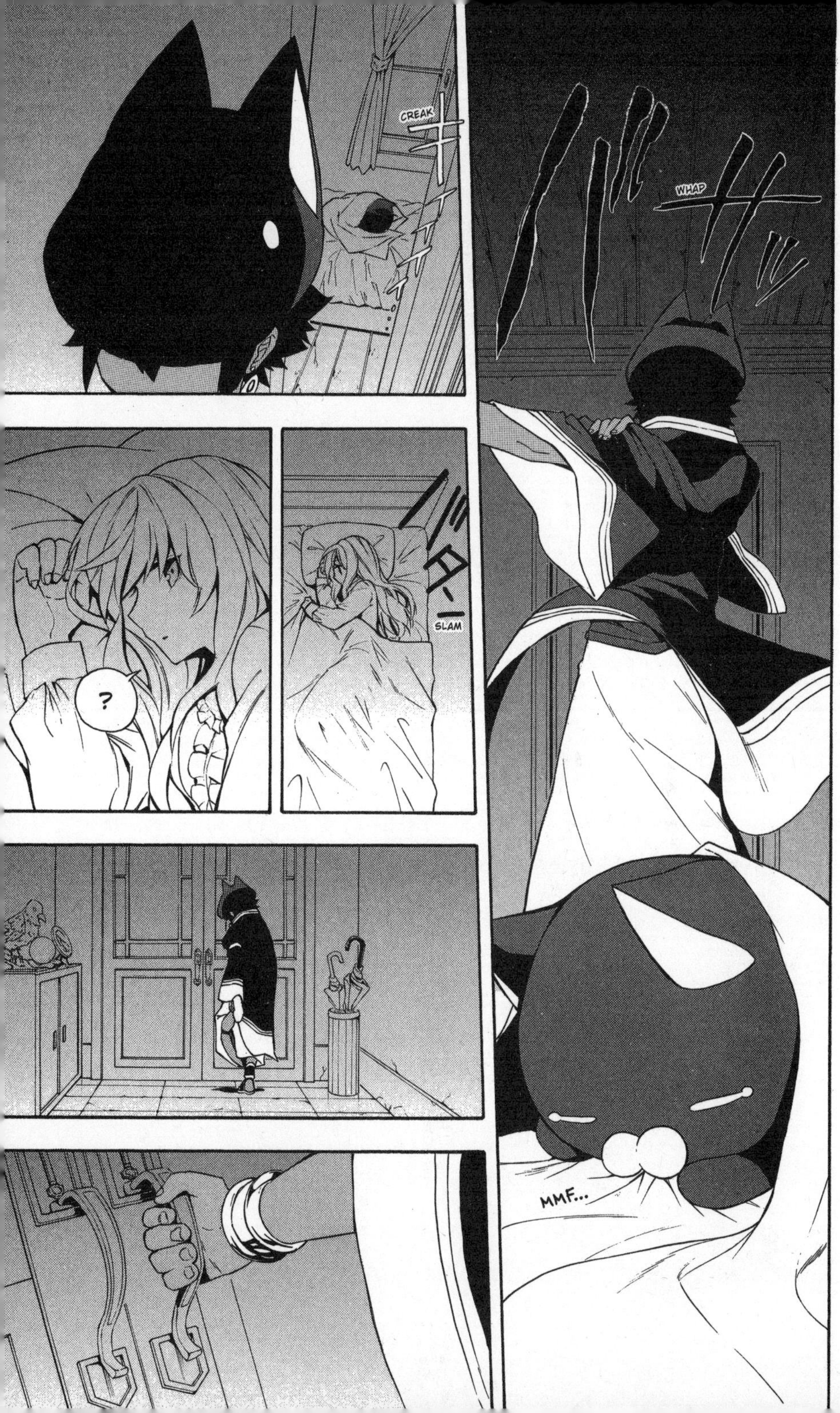
WHAP
MMF...
CREAK
SLAM
?

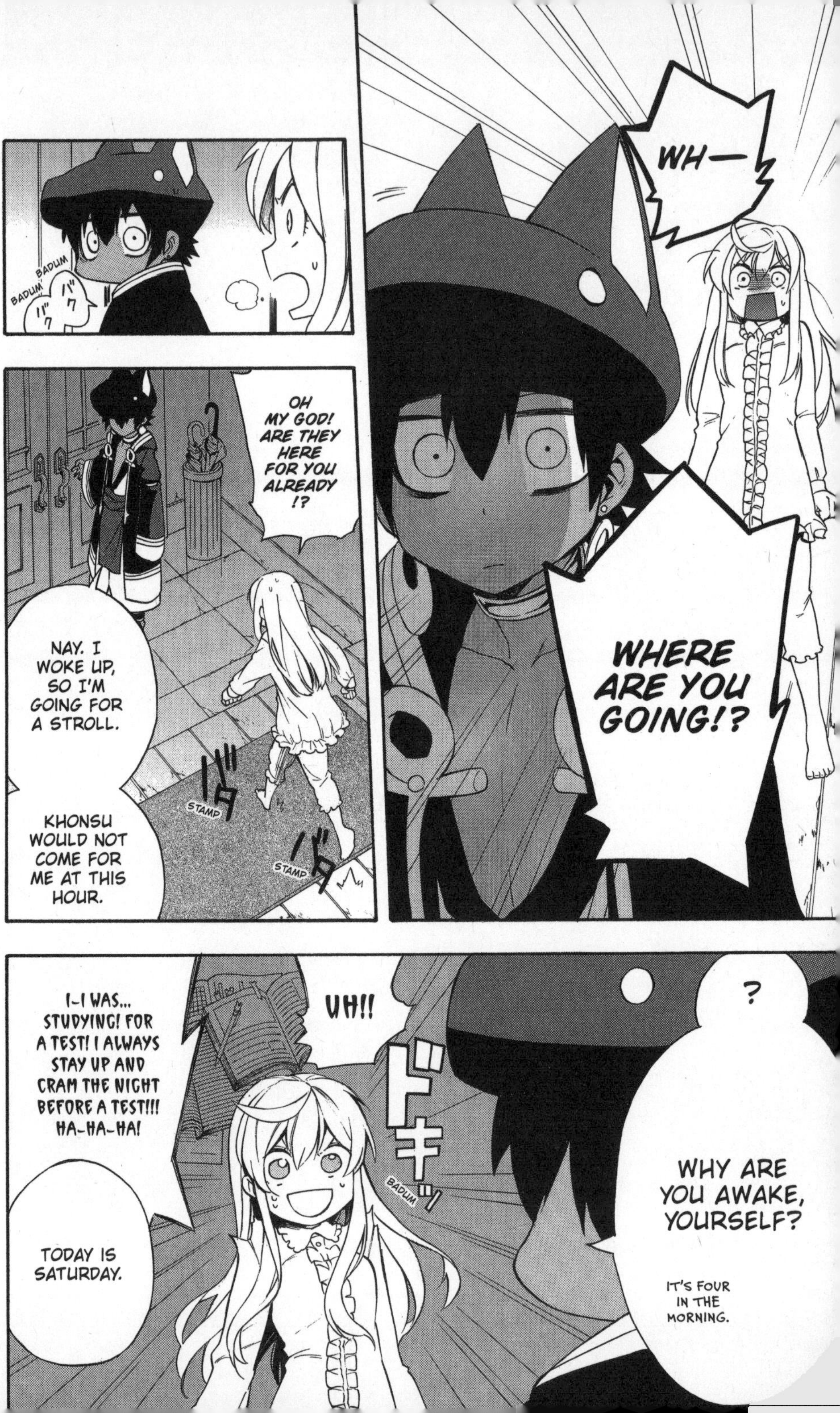
WH—
WHERE ARE YOU GOING!?
BADUM
BADUM
バク
バク
OH MY GOD! ARE THEY HERE FOR YOU ALREADY!?
NAY. I WOKE UP, SO I'M GOING FOR A STROLL.
STAMP
STAMP
KHONSU WOULD NOT COME FOR ME AT THIS HOUR.
?
WHY ARE YOU AWAKE, YOURSELF?
IT'S FOUR IN THE MORNING.
UH!!
ドキッ
BADUM
I-I WAS... STUDYING! FOR A TEST! I ALWAYS STAY UP AND CRAM THE NIGHT BEFORE A TEST!!! HA-HA-HA!
TODAY IS SATURDAY.

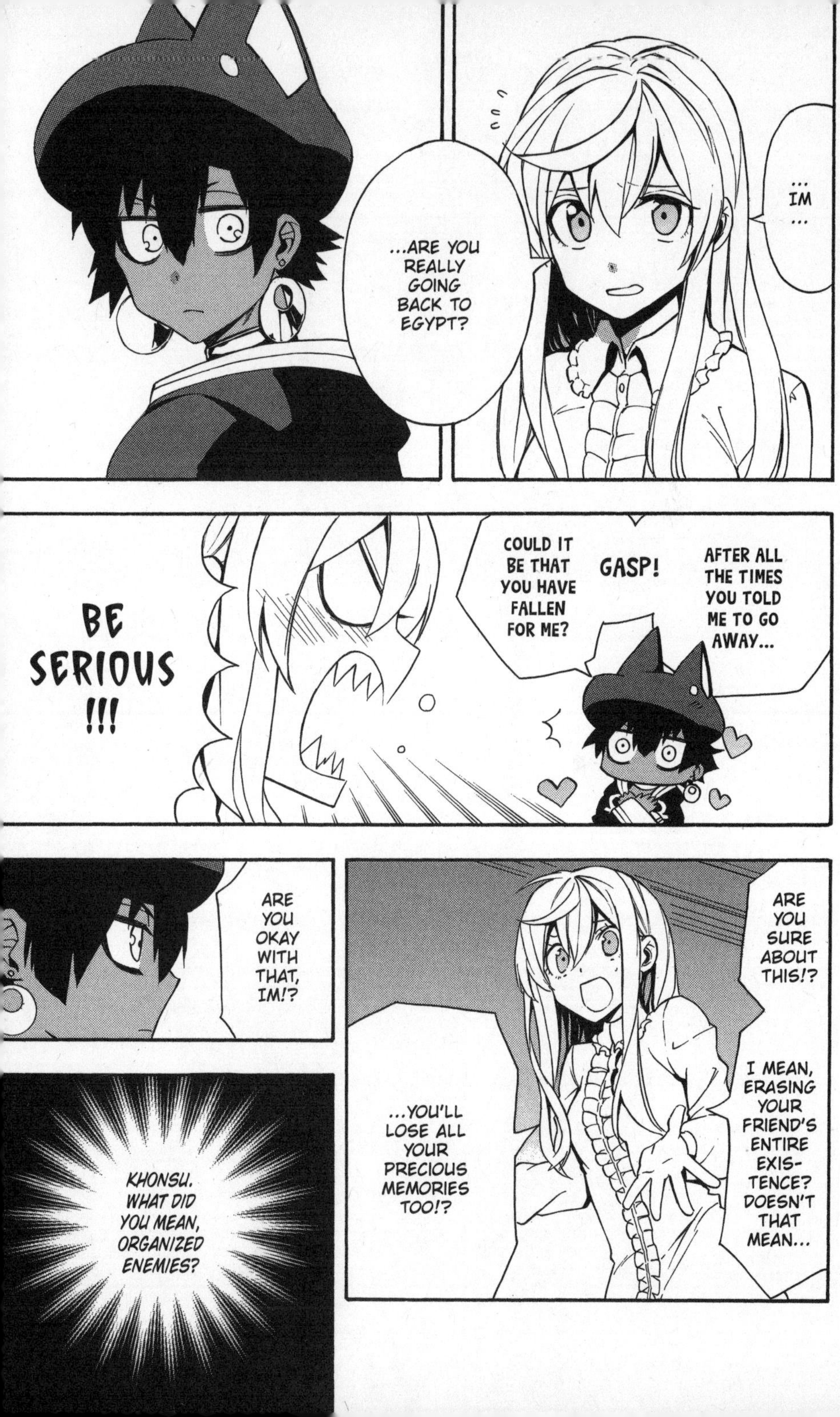
...IM...
...ARE YOU REALLY GOING BACK TO EGYPT?
AFTER ALL THE TIMES YOU TOLD ME TO GO AWAY...
GASP!
COULD IT BE THAT YOU HAVE FALLEN FOR ME?
BE SERIOUS!!!
ARE YOU SURE ABOUT THIS!?
I MEAN, ERASING YOUR FRIEND'S ENTIRE EXIS-TENCE? DOESN'T THAT MEAN...
...YOU'LL LOSE ALL YOUR PRECIOUS MEMORIES TOO!?
ARE YOU OKAY WITH THAT, IM!?
KHONSU. WHAT DID YOU MEAN, ORGANIZED ENEMIES?

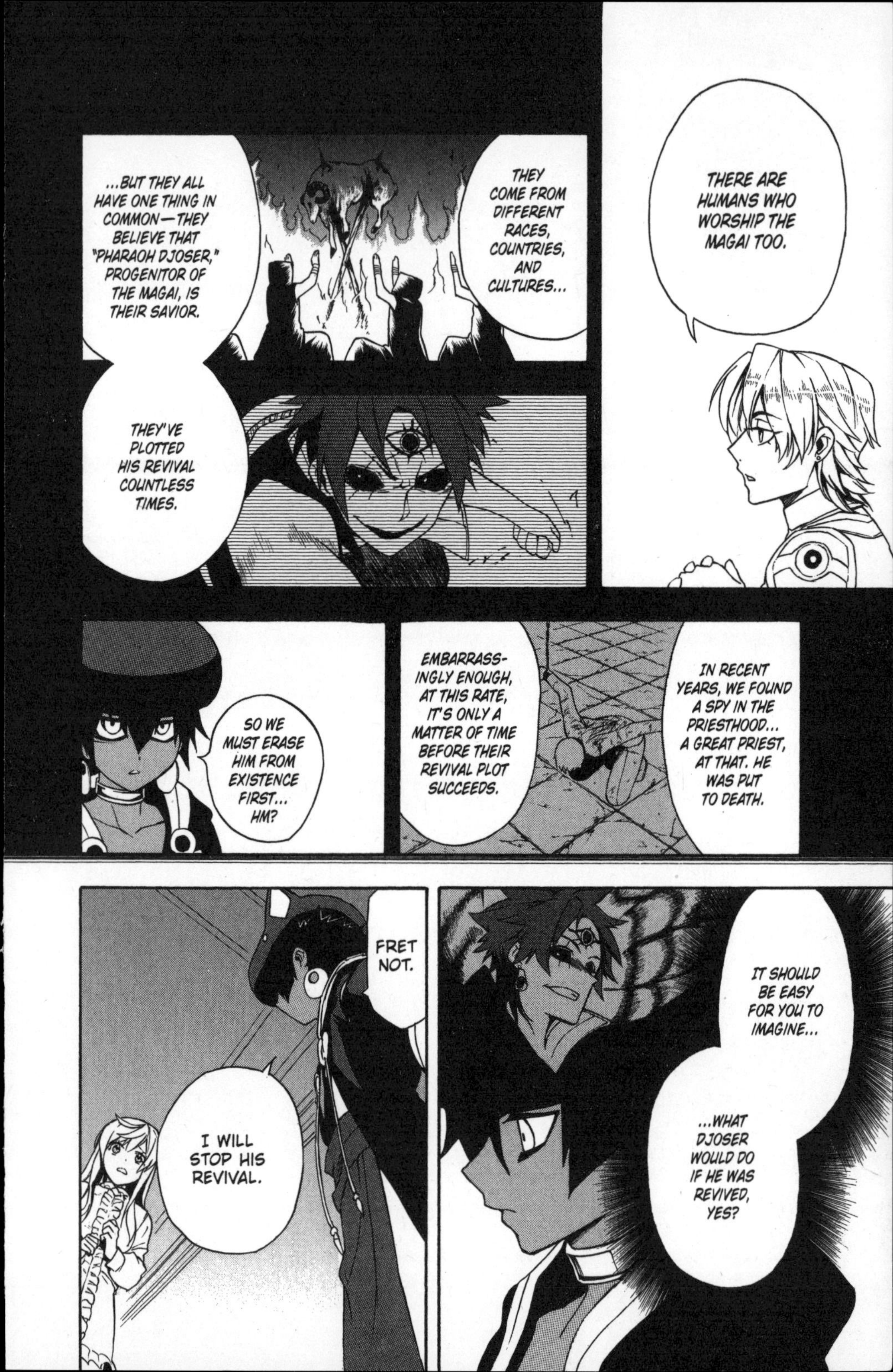
THERE ARE HUMANS WHO WORSHIP THE MAGAI TOO.
THEY COME FROM DIFFERENT RACES, COUNTRIES, AND CULTURES...
...BUT THEY ALL HAVE ONE THING IN COMMON—THEY BELIEVE THAT "PHARAOH DJOSER," PROGENITOR OF THE MAGAI, IS THEIR SAVIOR.
THEY'VE PLOTTED HIS REVIVAL COUNTLESS TIMES.
IN RECENT YEARS, WE FOUND A SPY IN THE PRIESTHOOD... A GREAT PRIEST, AT THAT. HE WAS PUT TO DEATH.
EMBARRASS-INGLY ENOUGH, AT THIS RATE, IT'S ONLY A MATTER OF TIME BEFORE THEIR REVIVAL PLOT SUCCEEDS.
SO WE MUST ERASE HIM FROM EXISTENCE FIRST... HM?
IT SHOULD BE EASY FOR YOU TO IMAGINE...
...WHAT DJOSER WOULD DO IF HE WAS REVIVED, YES?
FRET NOT.
I WILL STOP HIS REVIVAL.

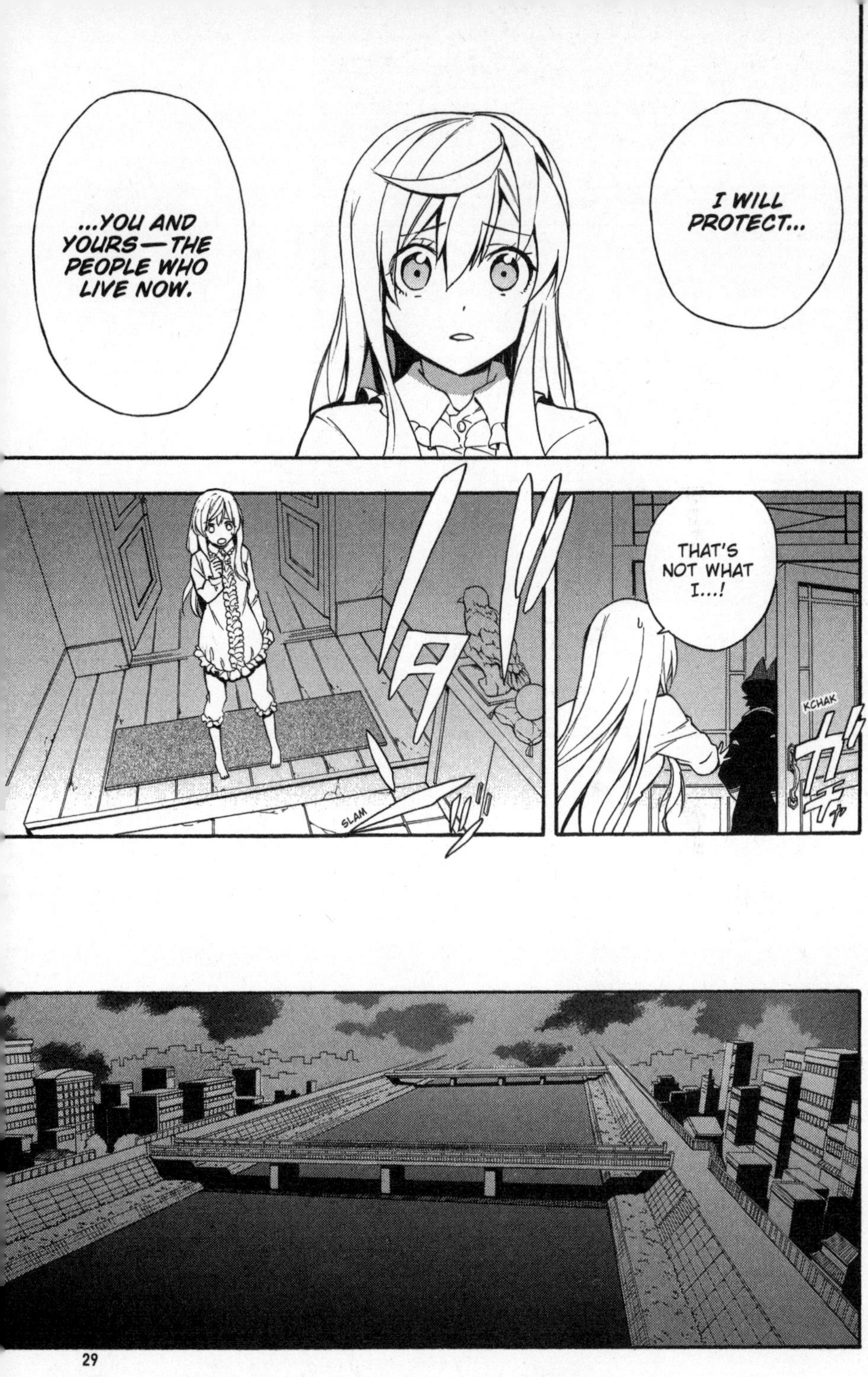
I WILL PROTECT...
...YOU AND YOURS—THE PEOPLE WHO LIVE NOW.
THAT'S NOT WHAT I...!
KCHAK
SLAM

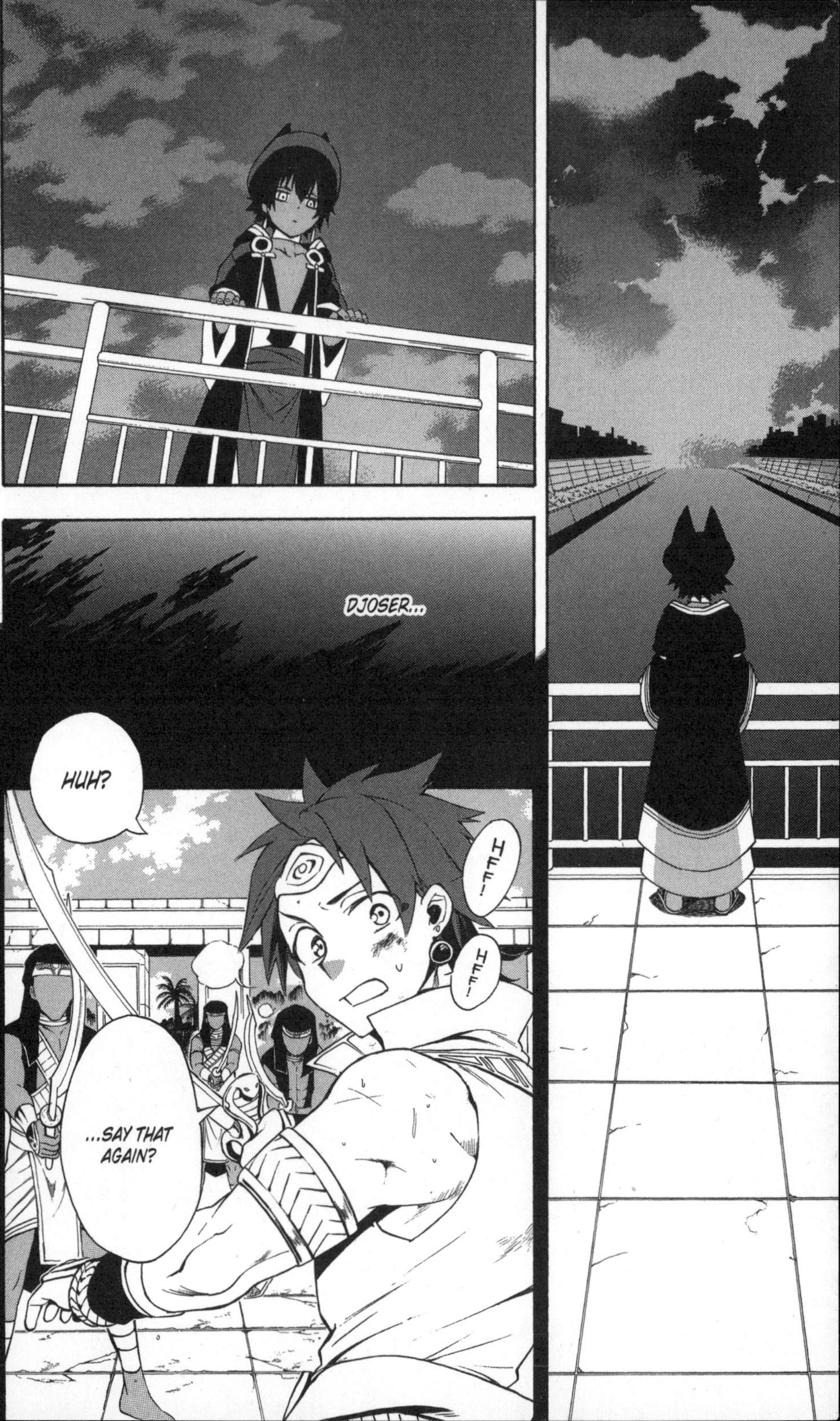
DJOSER...
HFF!
HFF!
HUH?
...SAY THAT AGAIN?

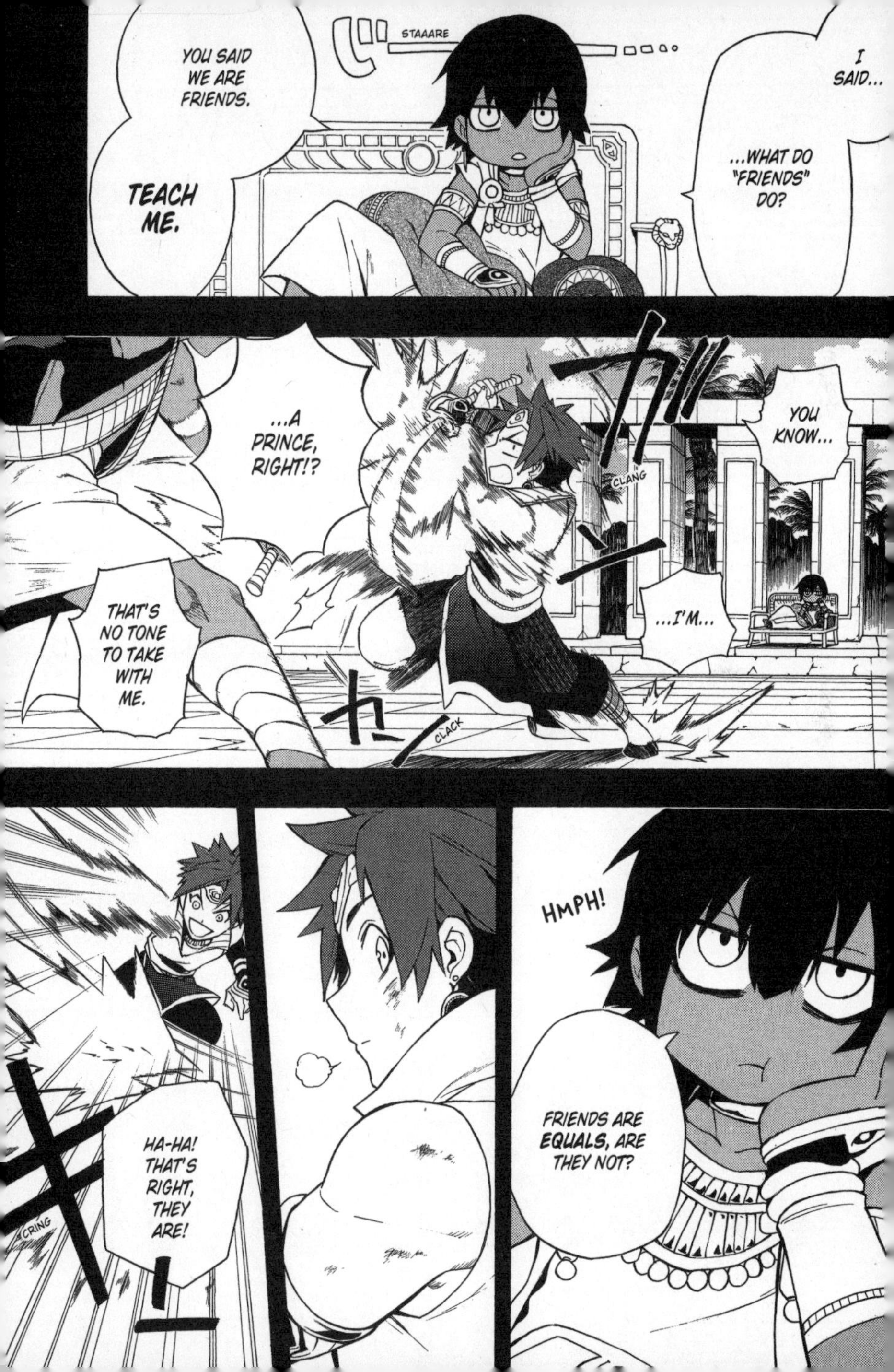
I SAID...
...WHAT DO "FRIENDS" DO?
STAAARE
YOU SAID WE ARE FRIENDS.
TEACH ME.
YOU KNOW...
...I'M...
CLANG
...A PRINCE, RIGHT!?
THAT'S NO TONE TO TAKE WITH ME.
CLACK
HMPH!
FRIENDS ARE EQUALS, ARE THEY NOT?
HA-HA! THAT'S RIGHT, THEY ARE!
CRING

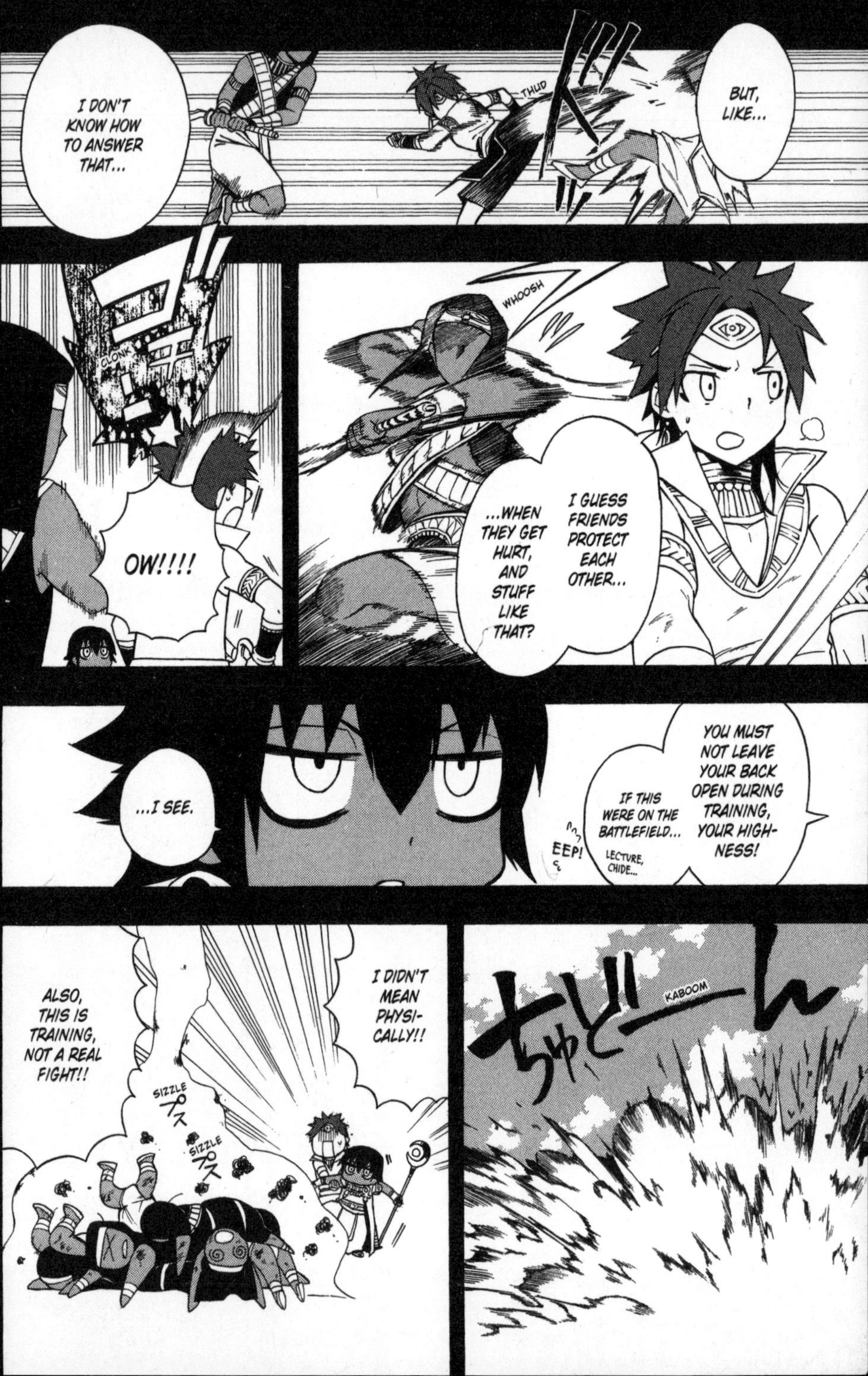
BUT, LIKE...
THUD
I DON'T KNOW HOW TO ANSWER THAT...
WHOOSH
I GUESS FRIENDS PROTECT EACH OTHER...
...WHEN THEY GET HURT, AND STUFF LIKE THAT?
CLONK
OW!!!!
YOU MUST NOT LEAVE YOUR BACK OPEN DURING TRAINING, YOUR HIGHNESS!
IF THIS WERE ON THE BATTLEFIELD...
LECTURE, CHIDE...
EEP!
...I SEE.
ちゅどーん
KABOOM
I DIDN'T MEAN PHYSI-CALLY!!
ALSO, THIS IS TRAINING, NOT A REAL FIGHT!!
SIZZLE
プス
SIZZLE
プス

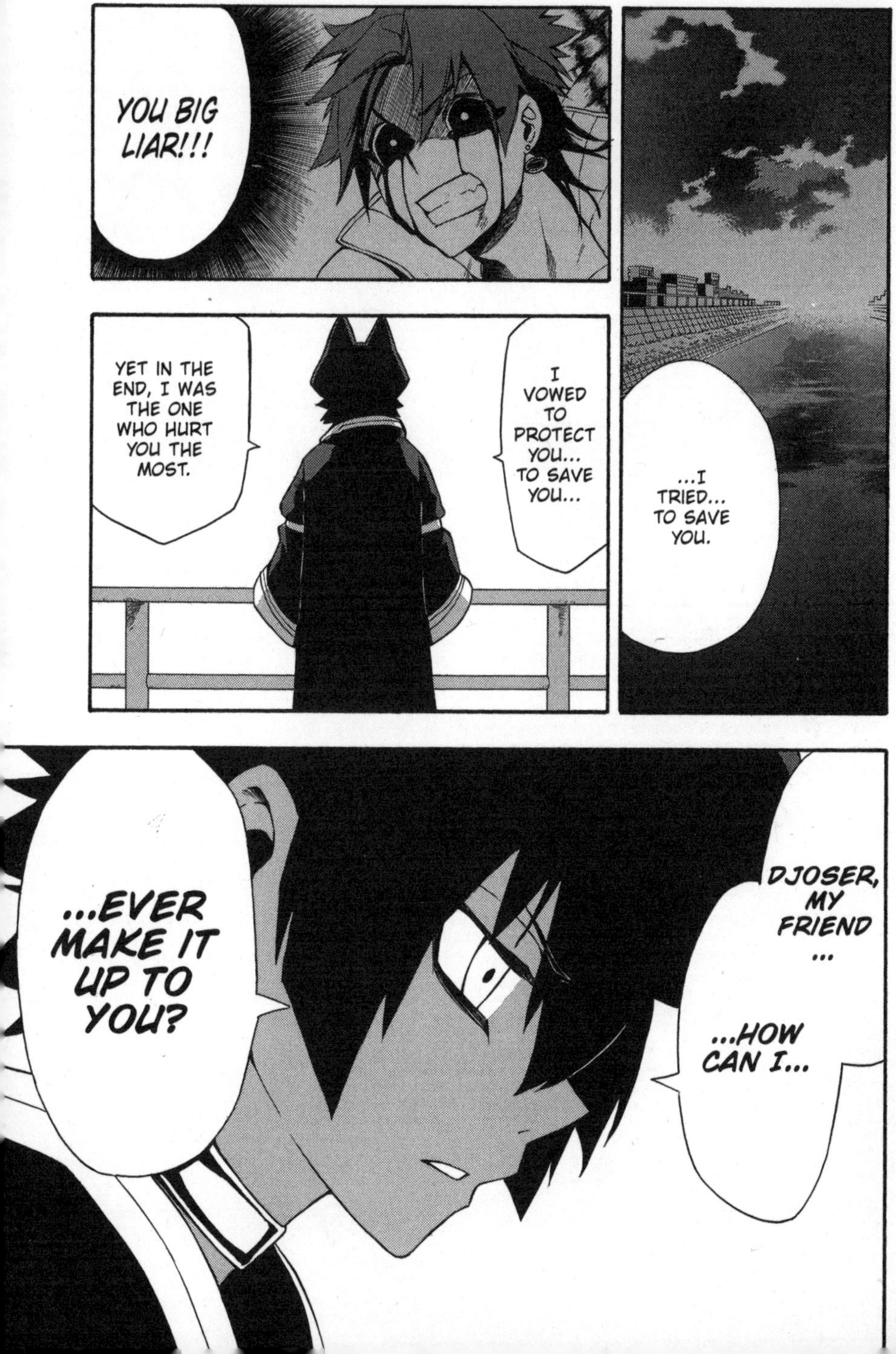
...I TRIED... TO SAVE YOU.
YOU BIG LIAR!!!
I VOWED TO PROTECT YOU... TO SAVE YOU...
YET IN THE END, I WAS THE ONE WHO HURT YOU THE MOST.
DJOSER, MY FRIEND ...
...HOW CAN I...
...EVER MAKE IT UP TO YOU?

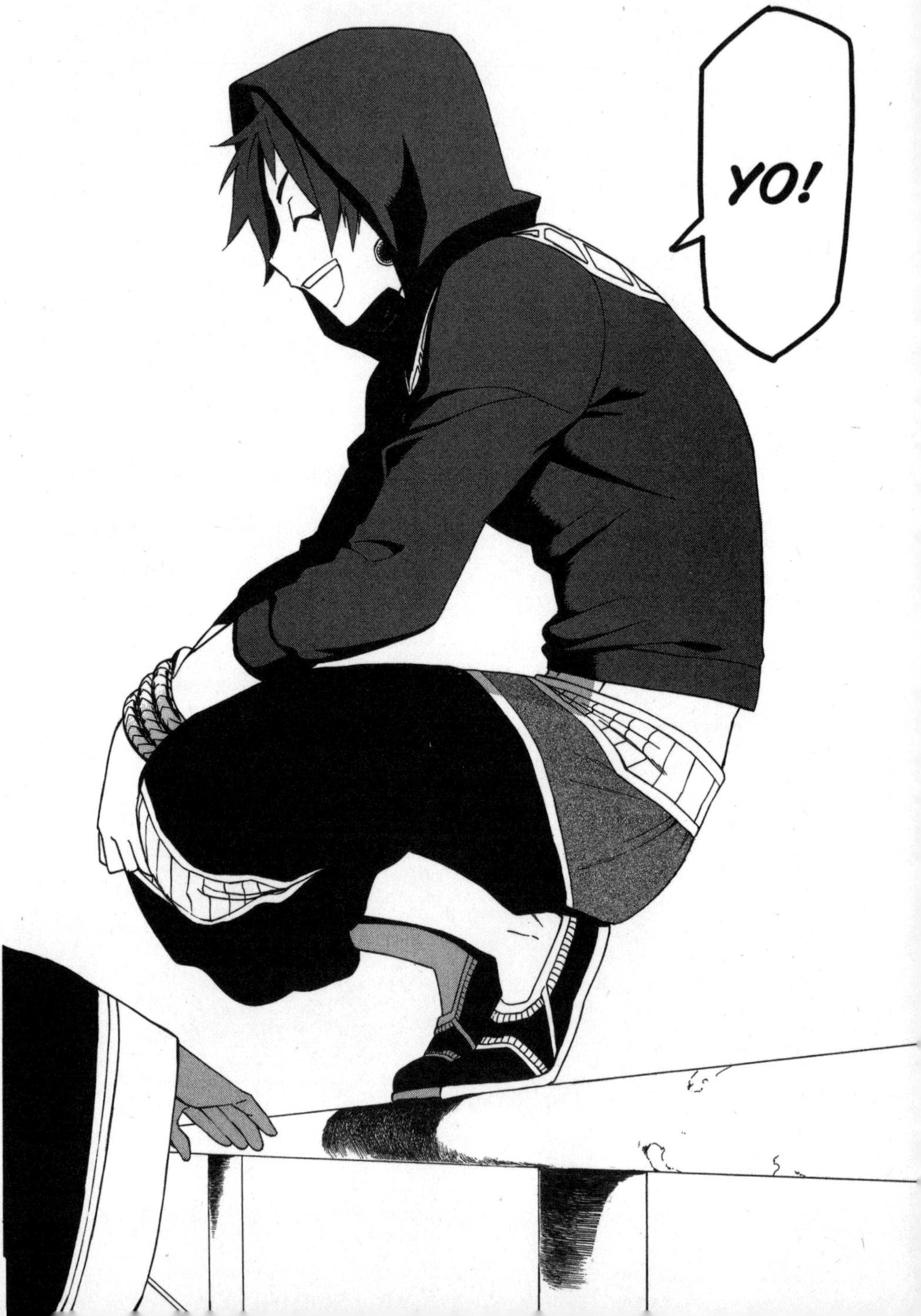
YO!

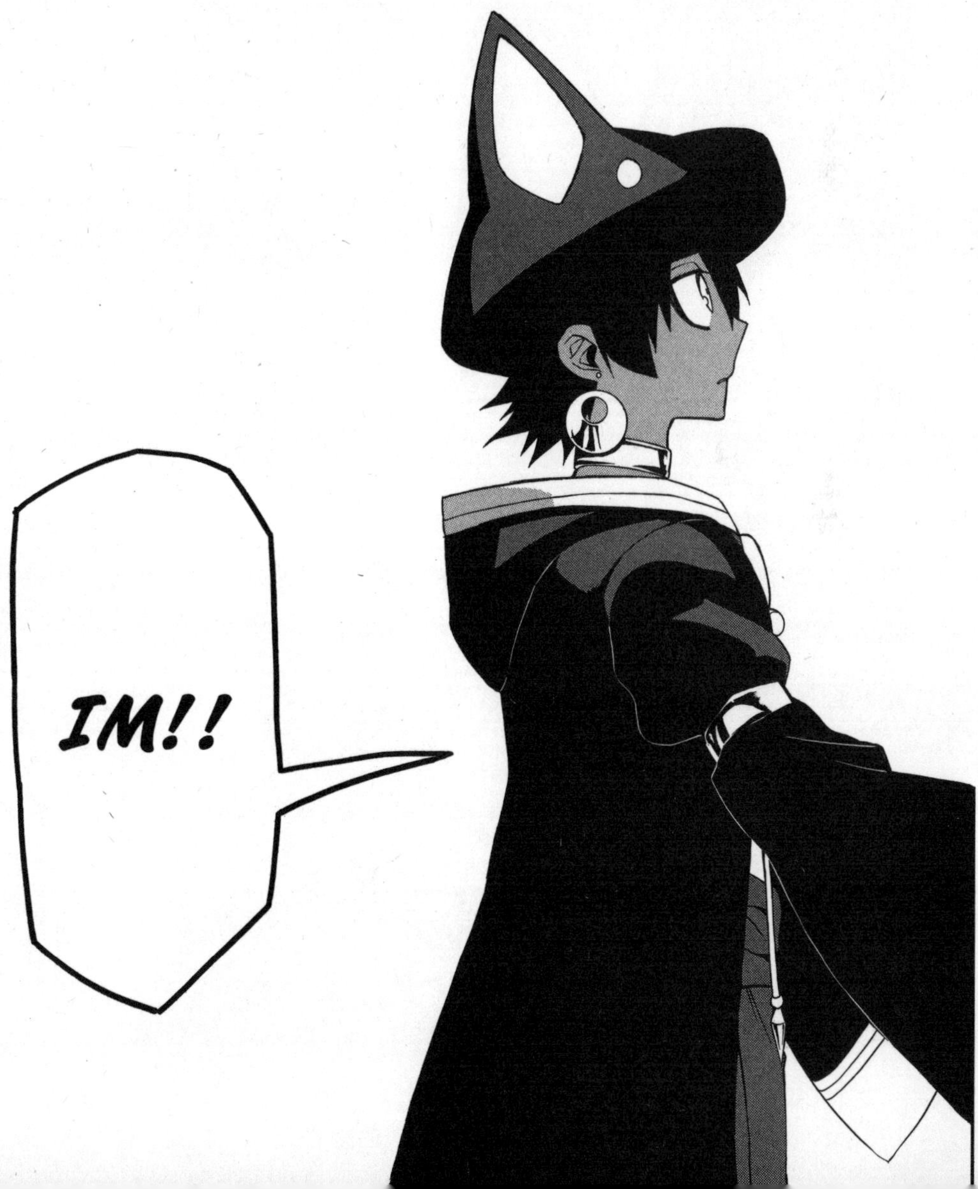
IM!!

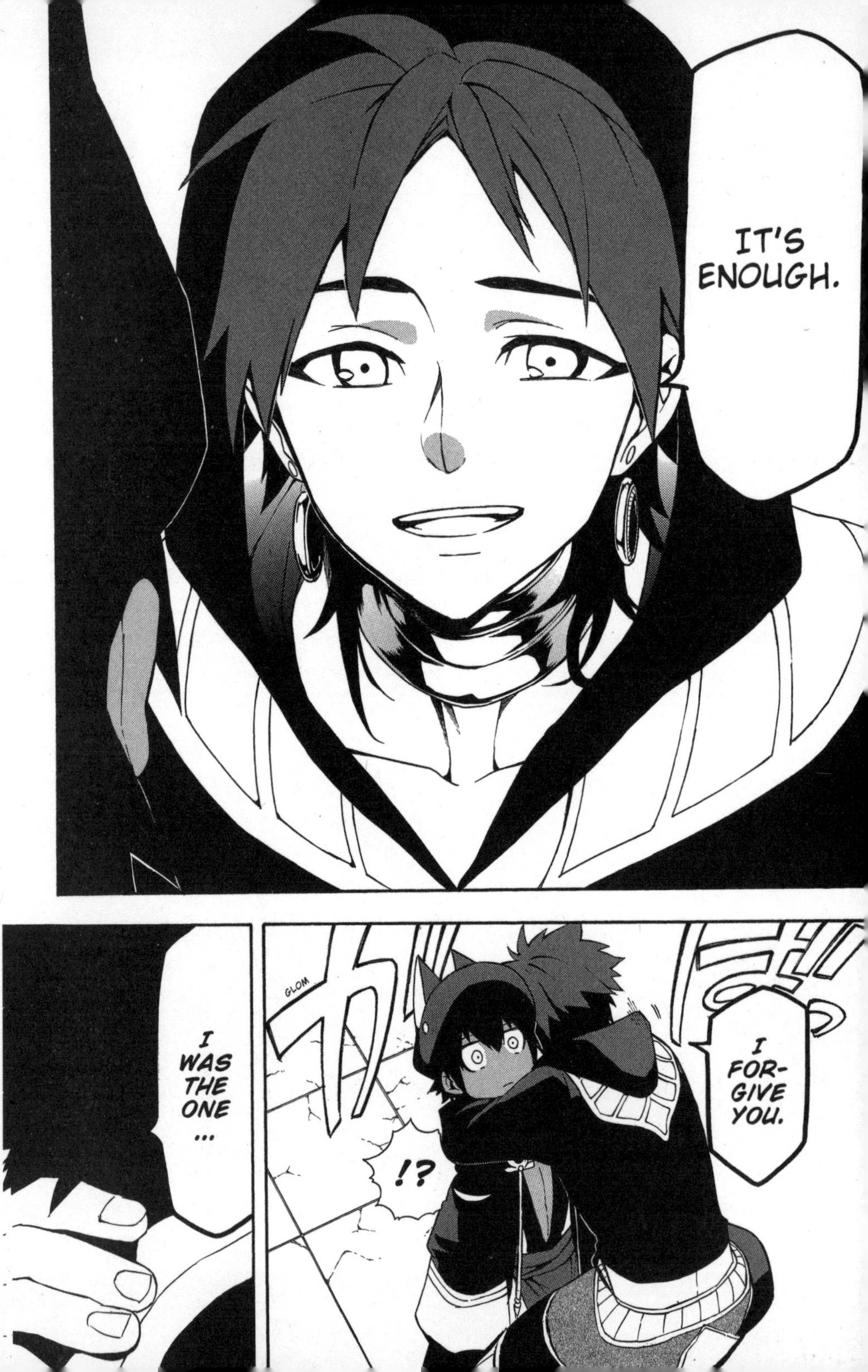
IT'S ENOUGH.
GLOM
I FOR-GIVE YOU.
!?
I WAS THE ONE ...

I'M SORRY, BUD.

YOU WERE THE ONLY PERSON...

...WHO HAD MY BACK FROM THE START, AND I DIDN'T KNOW IT...!

...WHO WAS WRONG...!

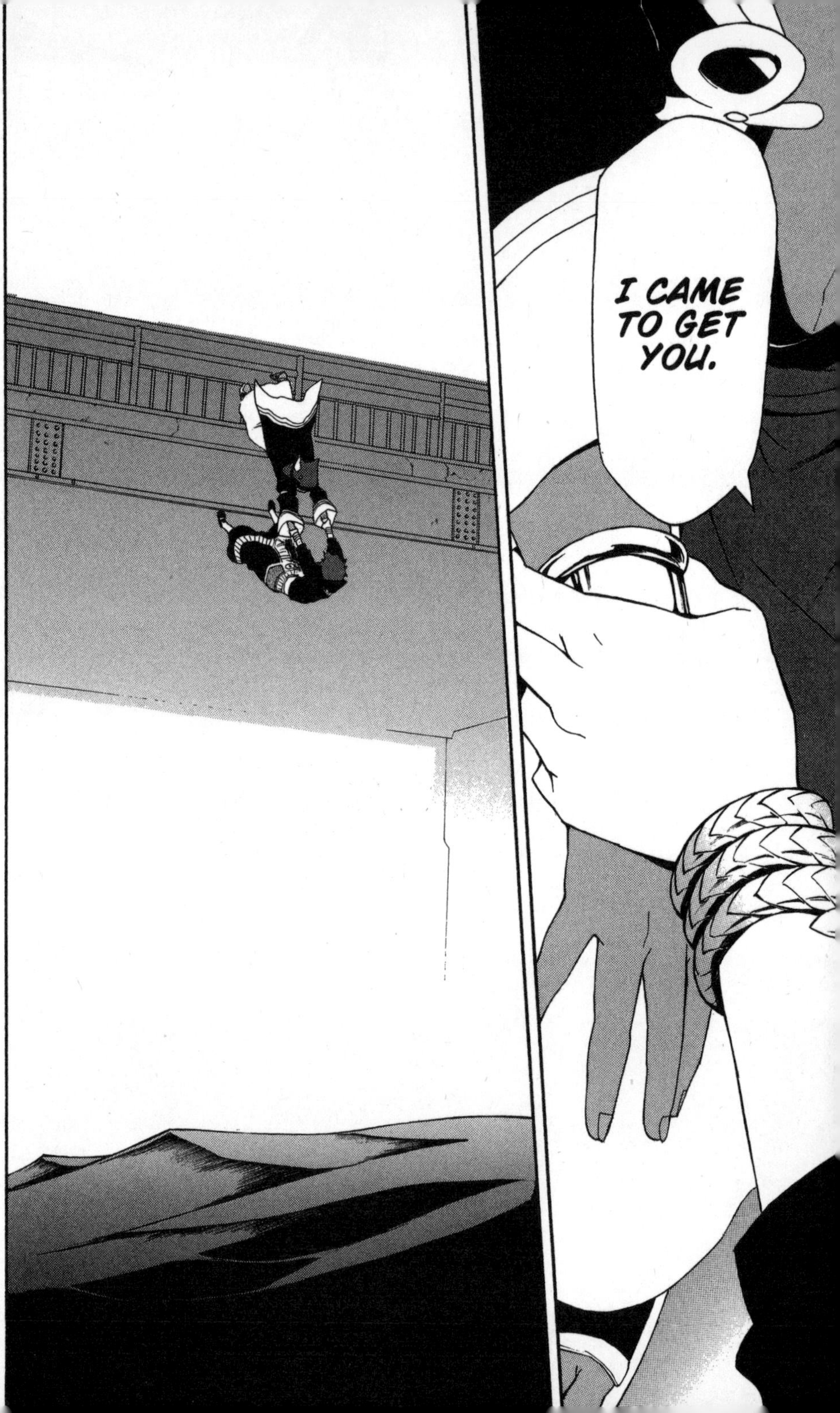
I CAME TO GET YOU.

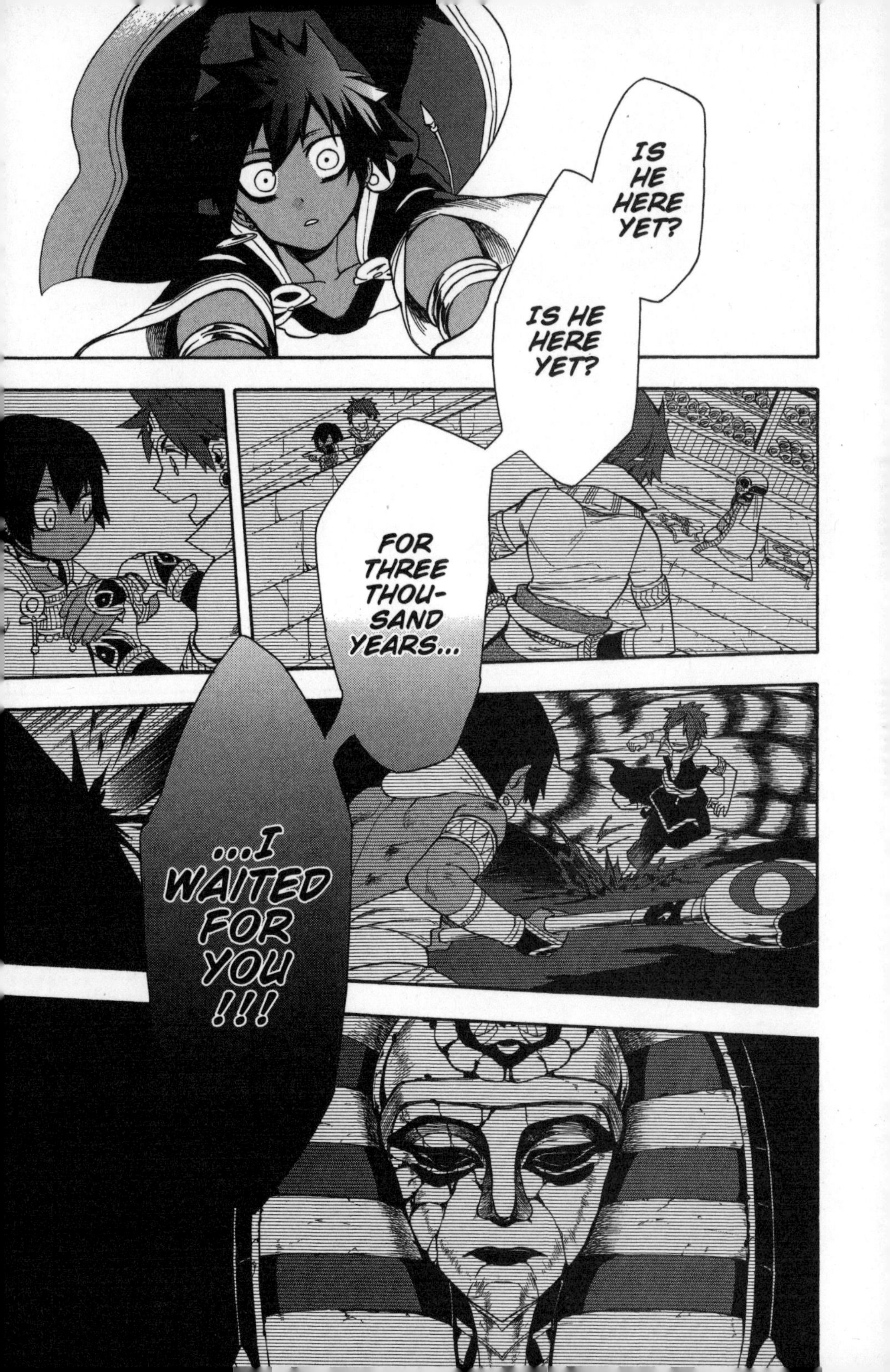
IS HE HERE YET?
IS HE HERE YET?
FOR THREE THOU-SAND YEARS...
...I WAITED FOR YOU!!!

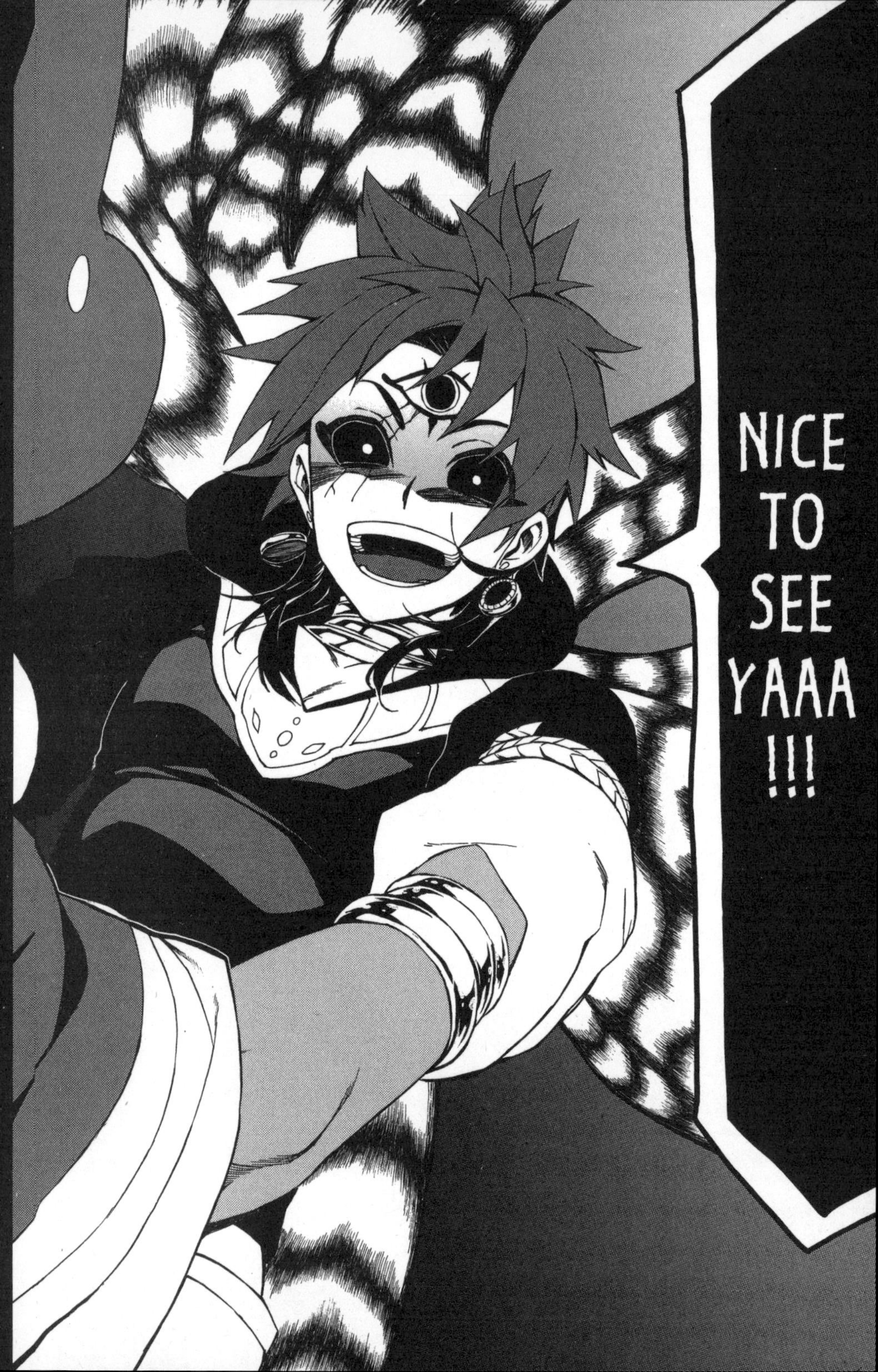
NICE TO SEE YAAA !!!

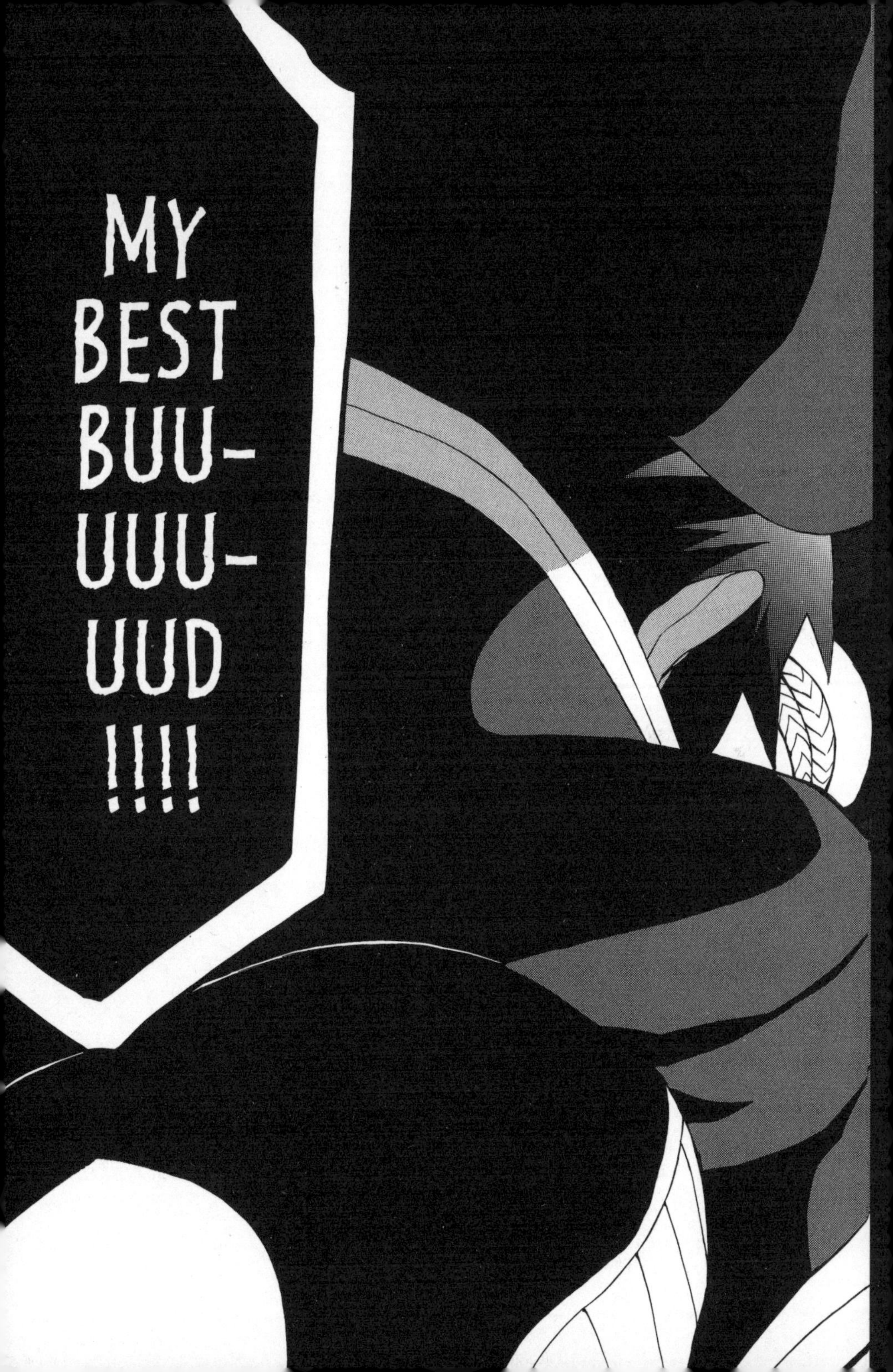
MY BEST BUU-UUU-UUD!!!!

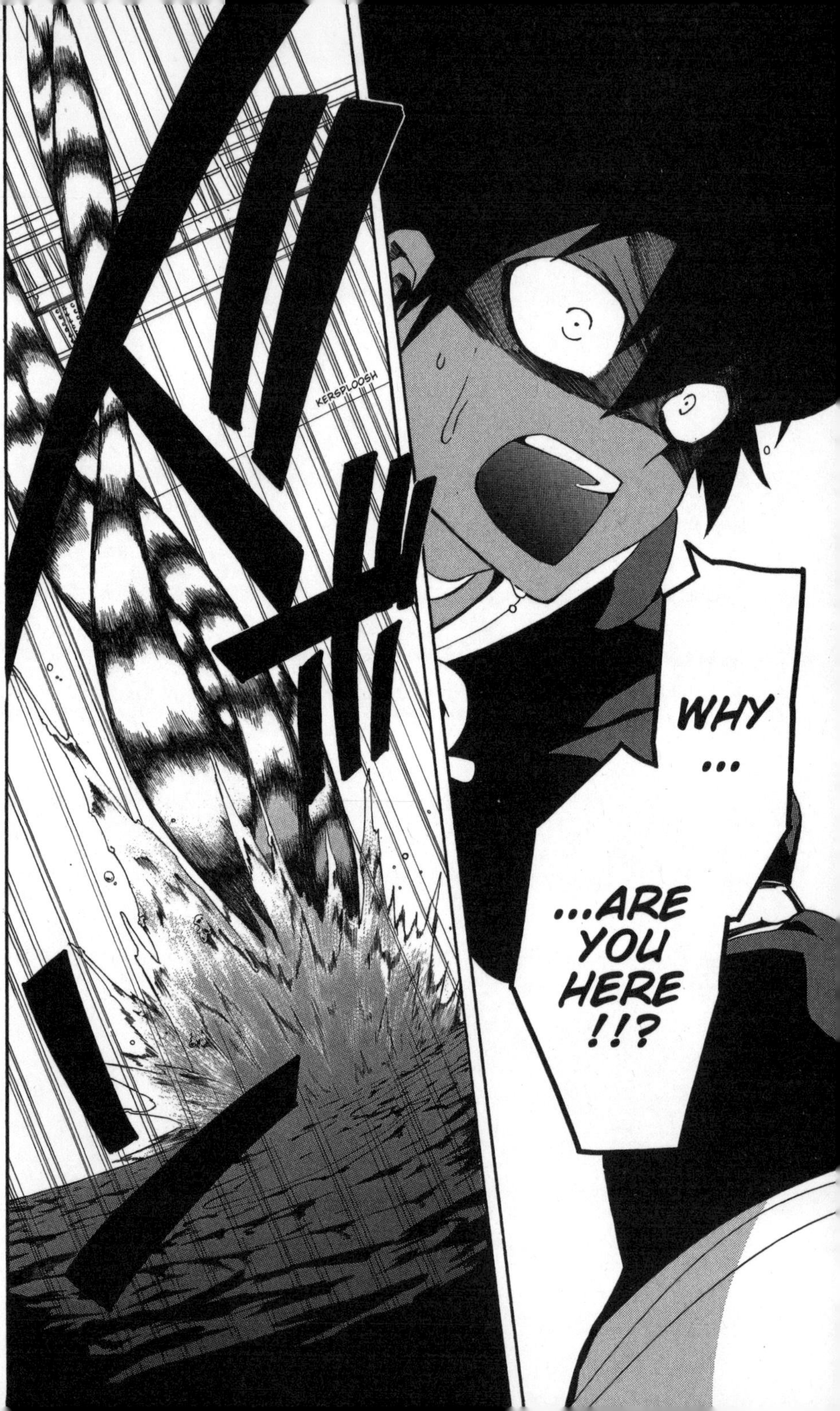
WHY ...
...ARE YOU HERE!!?
KERSPLOOSH

Im
Great Priest Imhotep

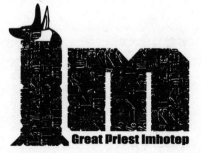

Great Priest Imhotep

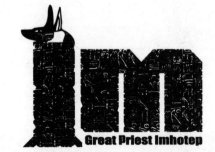

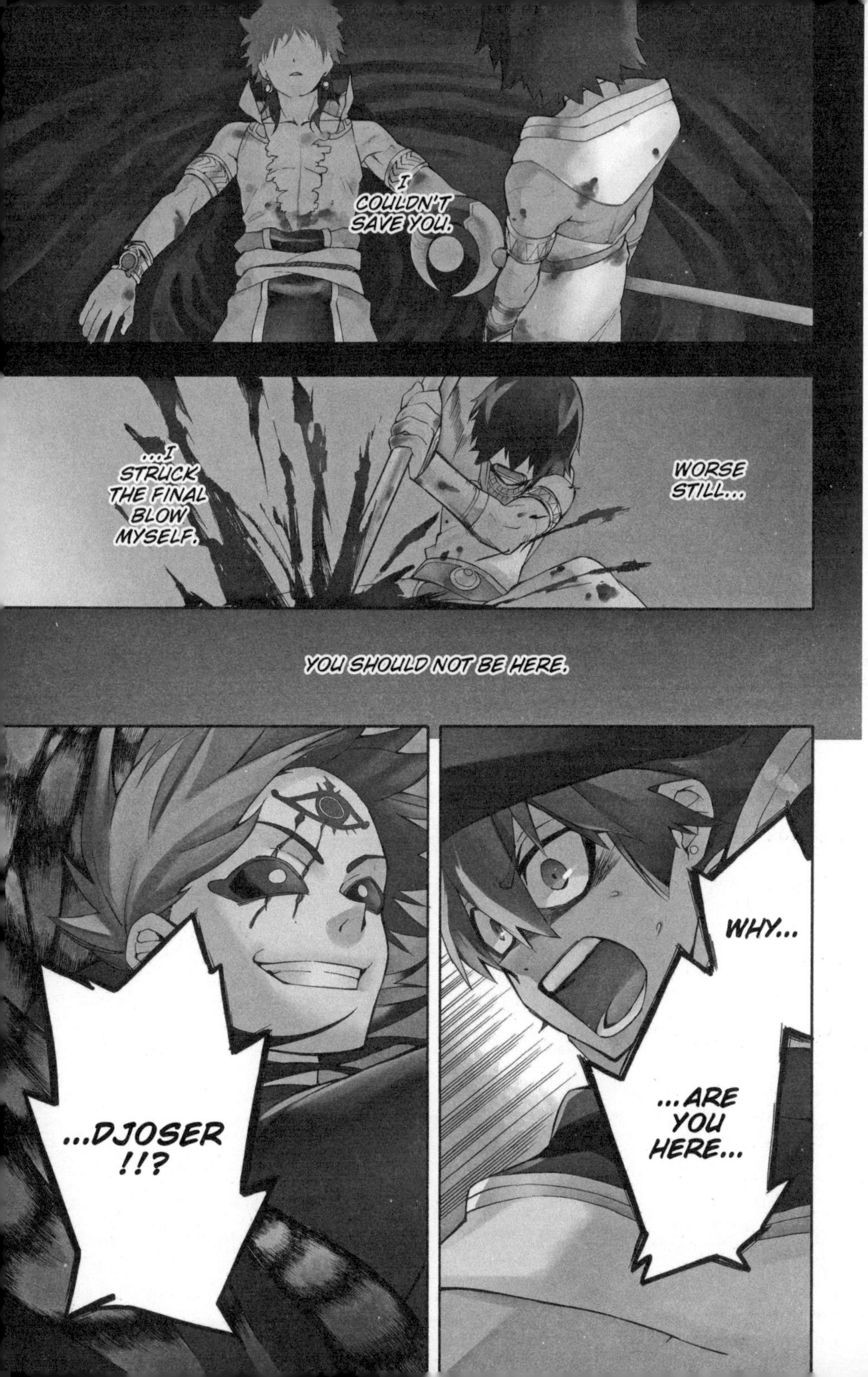
I COULDN'T SAVE YOU.
WORSE STILL...
...I STRUCK THE FINAL BLOW MYSELF.
YOU SHOULD NOT BE HERE.
WHY...
...ARE YOU HERE...
...DJOSER !!?

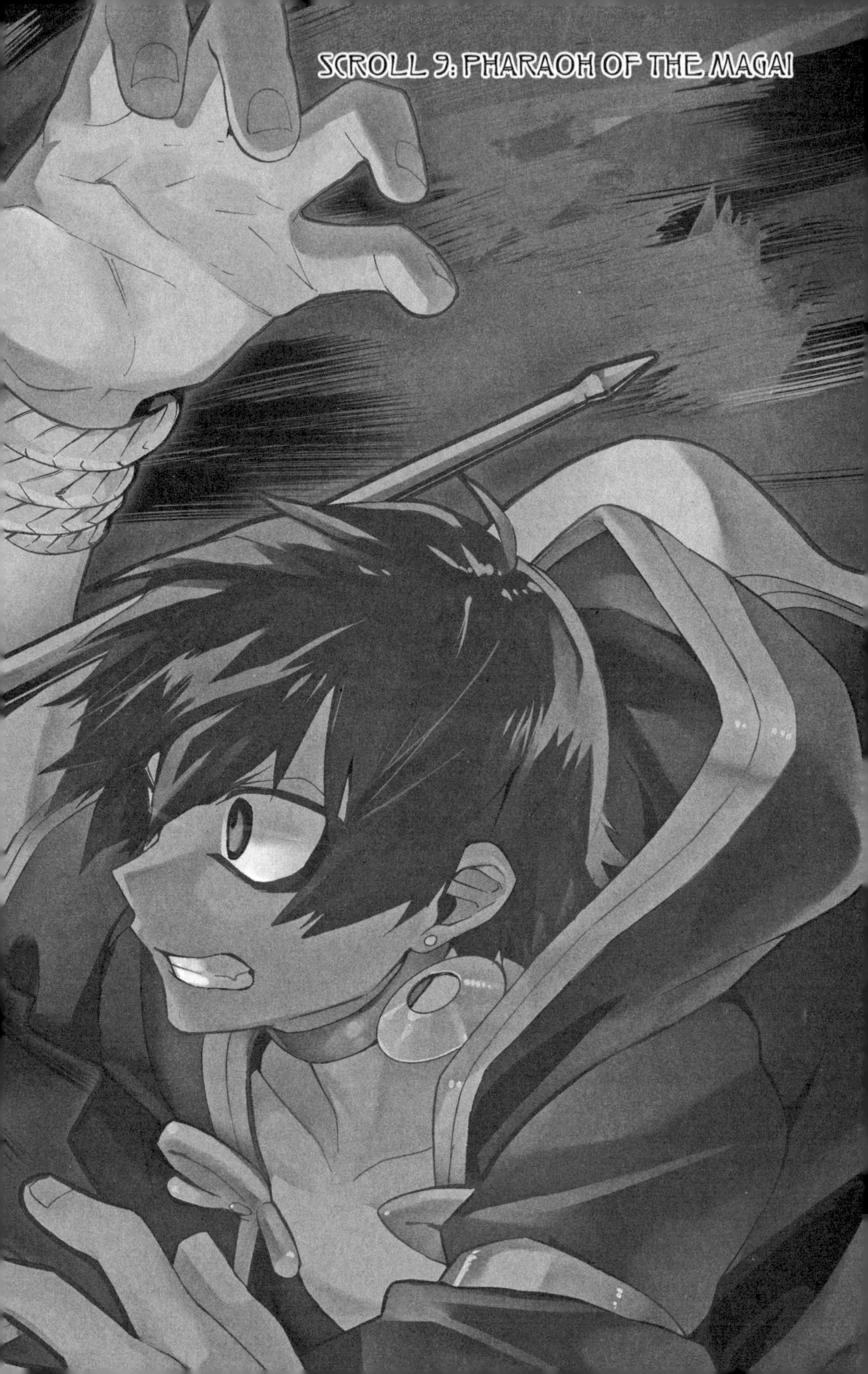
SCROLL 9: PHARAOH OF THE MAGAI

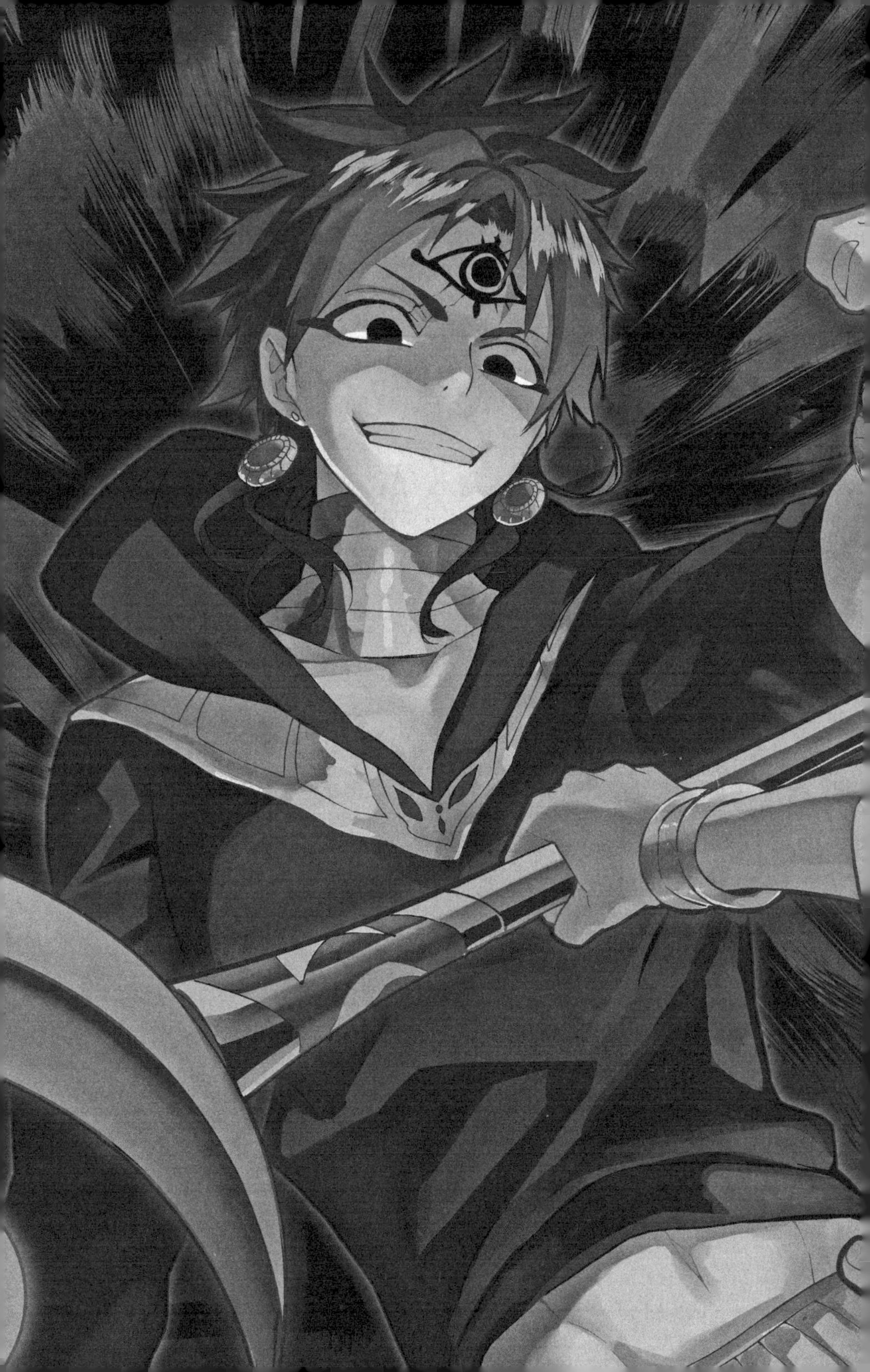

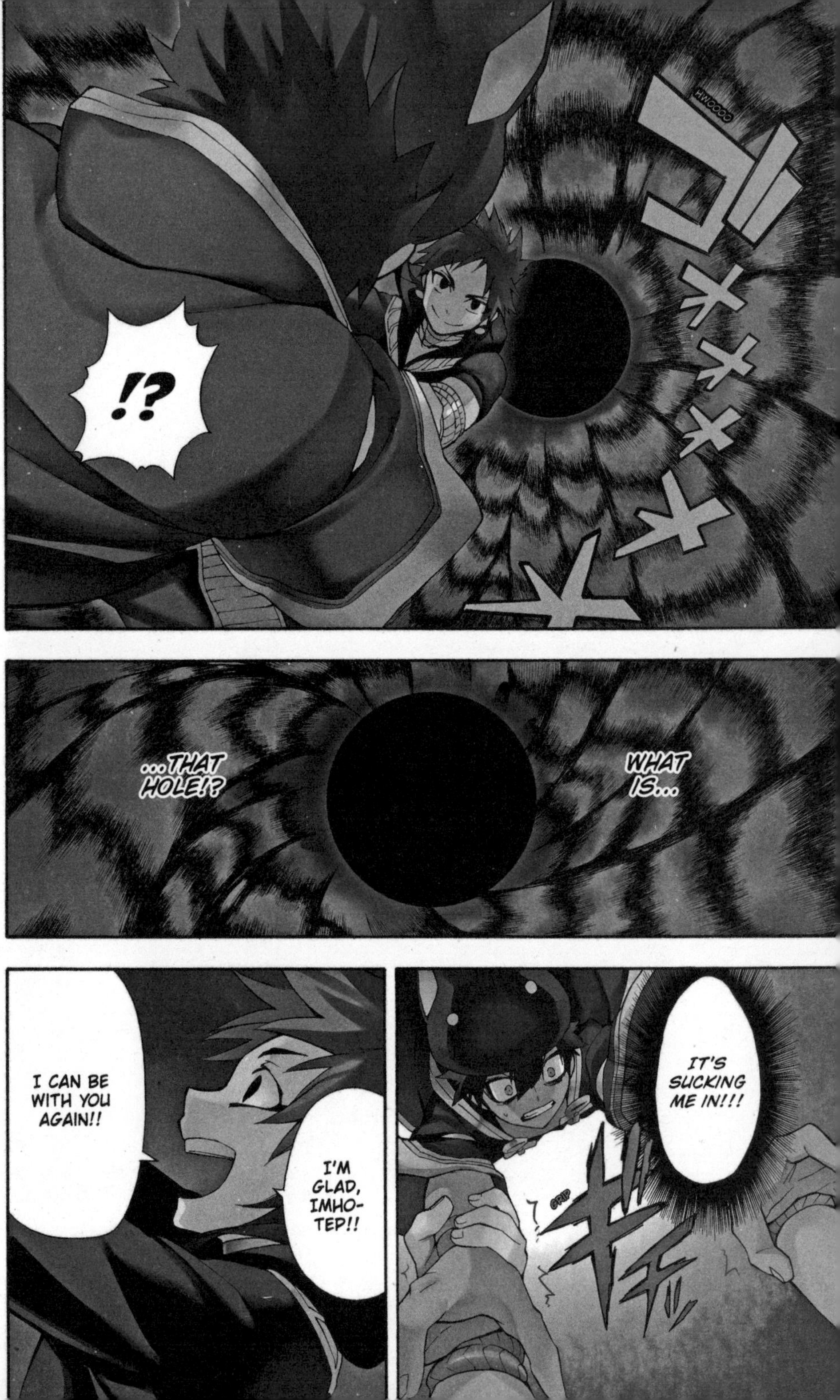
HWOOOO
!?
WHAT IS...
...THAT HOLE!?
IT'S SUCKING ME IN!!!
GRIP
I'M GLAD, IMHOTEP!!
I CAN BE WITH YOU AGAIN!!

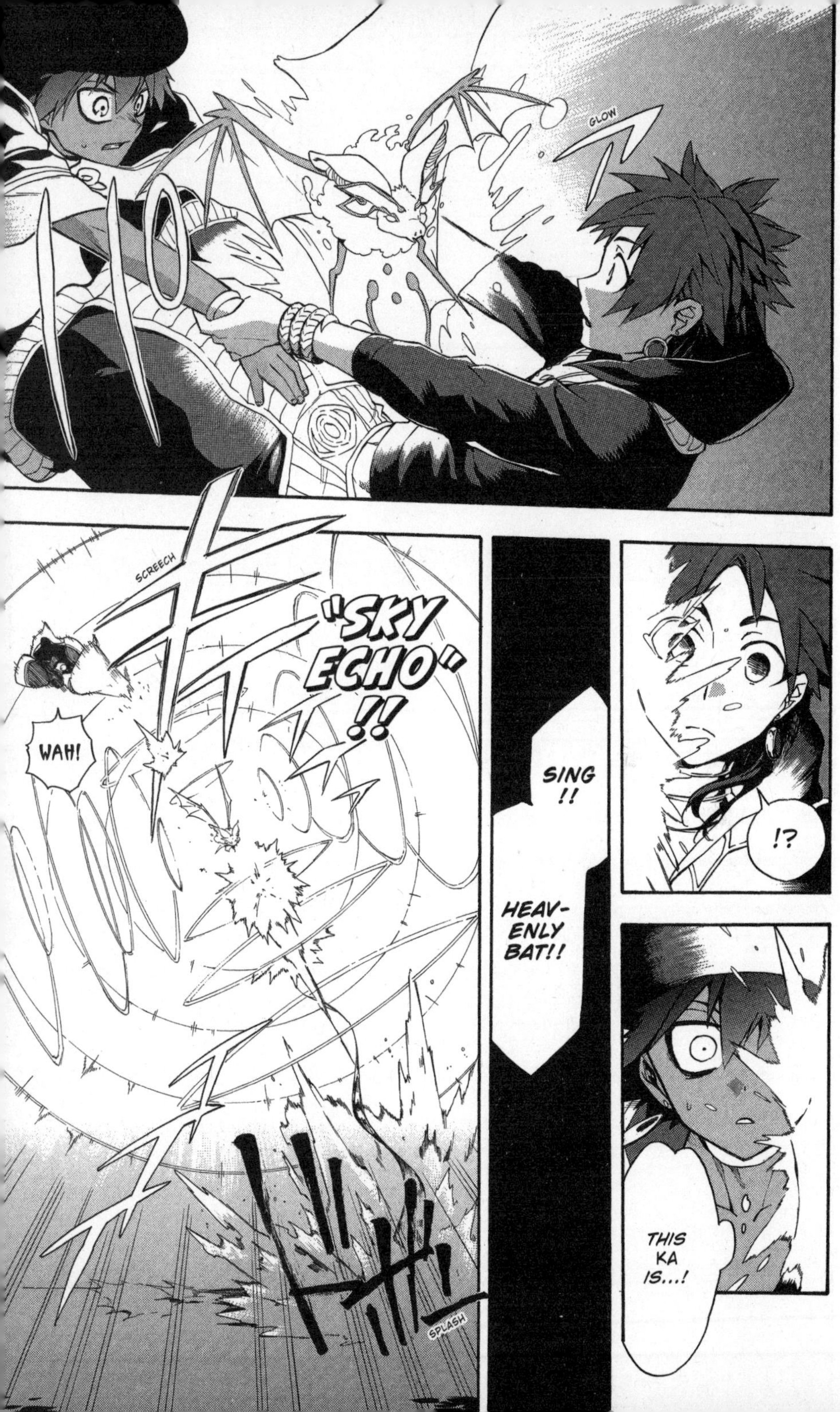
GLOW
!?
THIS KA IS...!
SING!!
HEAV-ENLY BAT!!
SCREECH
"SKY ECHO"!!
WAH!
SPLASH

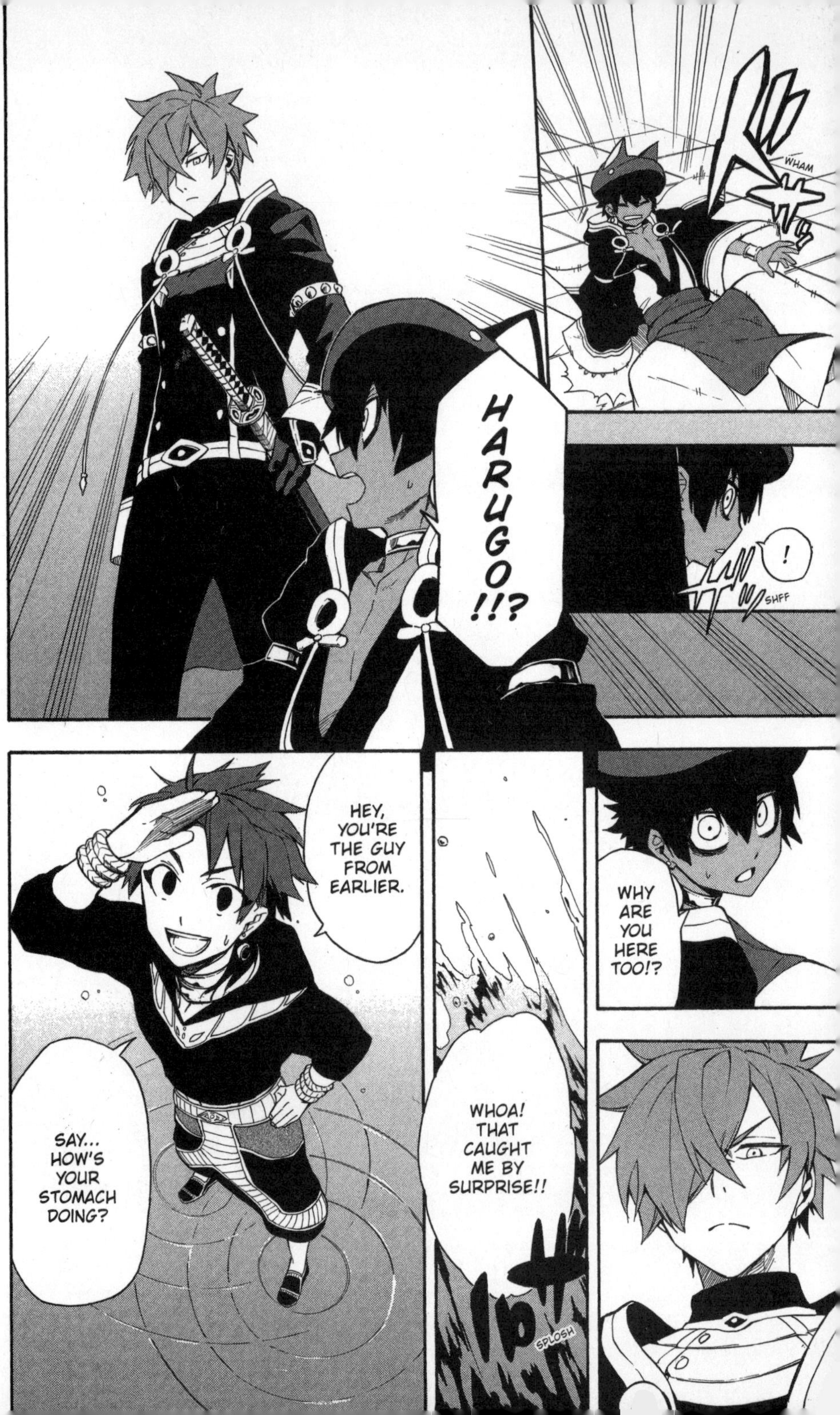
WHAM
!
SHFF
HARUGO!!?
WHY ARE YOU HERE TOO!?
WHOA! THAT CAUGHT ME BY SURPRISE!!
SPLOSH
HEY, YOU'RE THE GUY FROM EARLIER.
SAY... HOW'S YOUR STOMACH DOING?

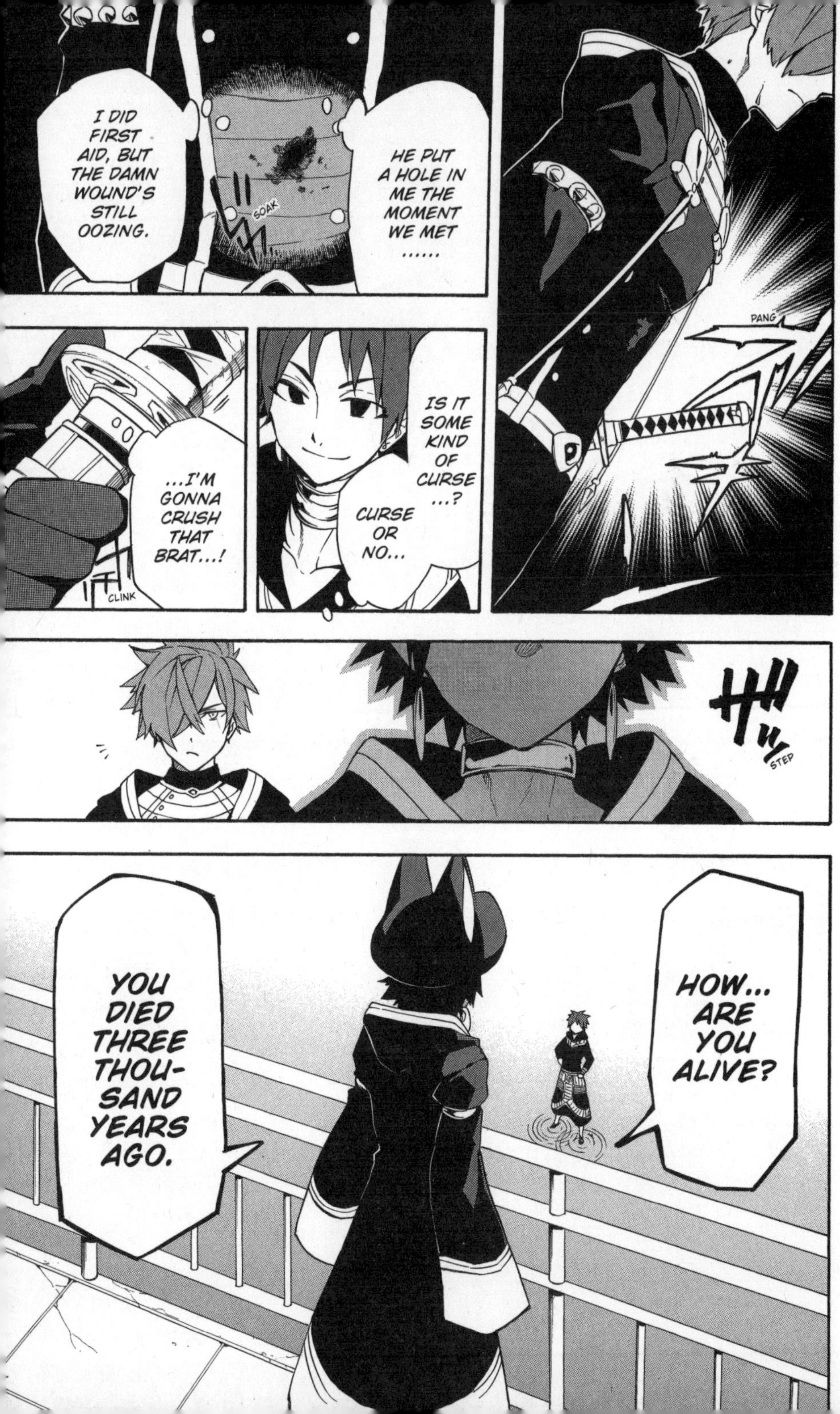
PANG
HE PUT A HOLE IN ME THE MOMENT WE MET ......
I DID FIRST AID, BUT THE DAMN WOUND'S STILL OOZING.
SOAK
IS IT SOME KIND OF CURSE ...?
CURSE OR NO...
...I'M GONNA CRUSH THAT BRAT...!
CLINK
STEP
HOW... ARE YOU ALIVE?
YOU DIED THREE THOU-SAND YEARS AGO.

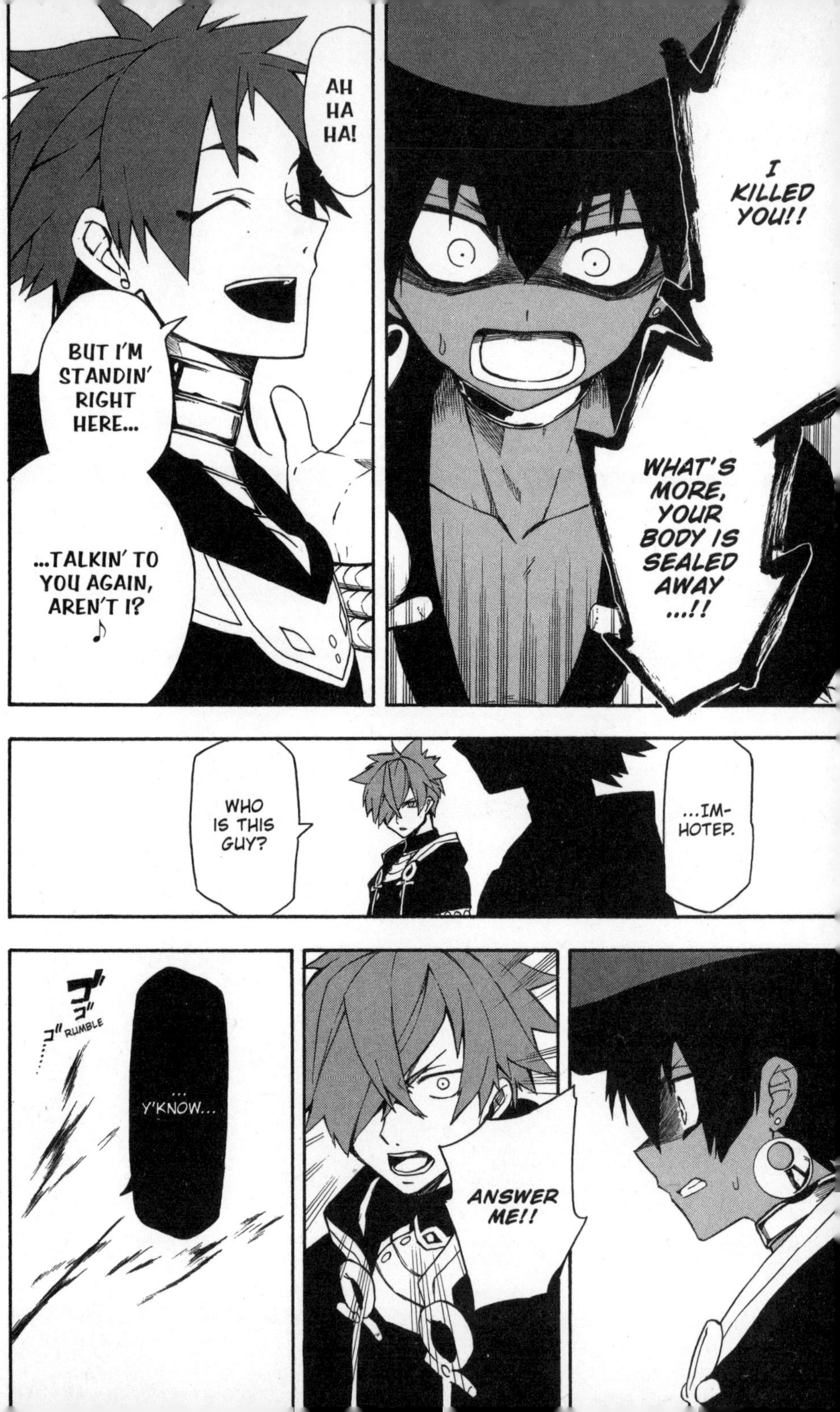
I KILLED YOU!!
WHAT'S MORE, YOUR BODY IS SEALED AWAY ...!!
AH HA HA!
BUT I'M STANDIN' RIGHT HERE...
...TALKIN' TO YOU AGAIN, AREN'T I? ♪
...IM-HOTEP.
WHO IS THIS GUY?
ANSWER ME!!
ゴゴゴ RUMBLE
... Y'KNOW...

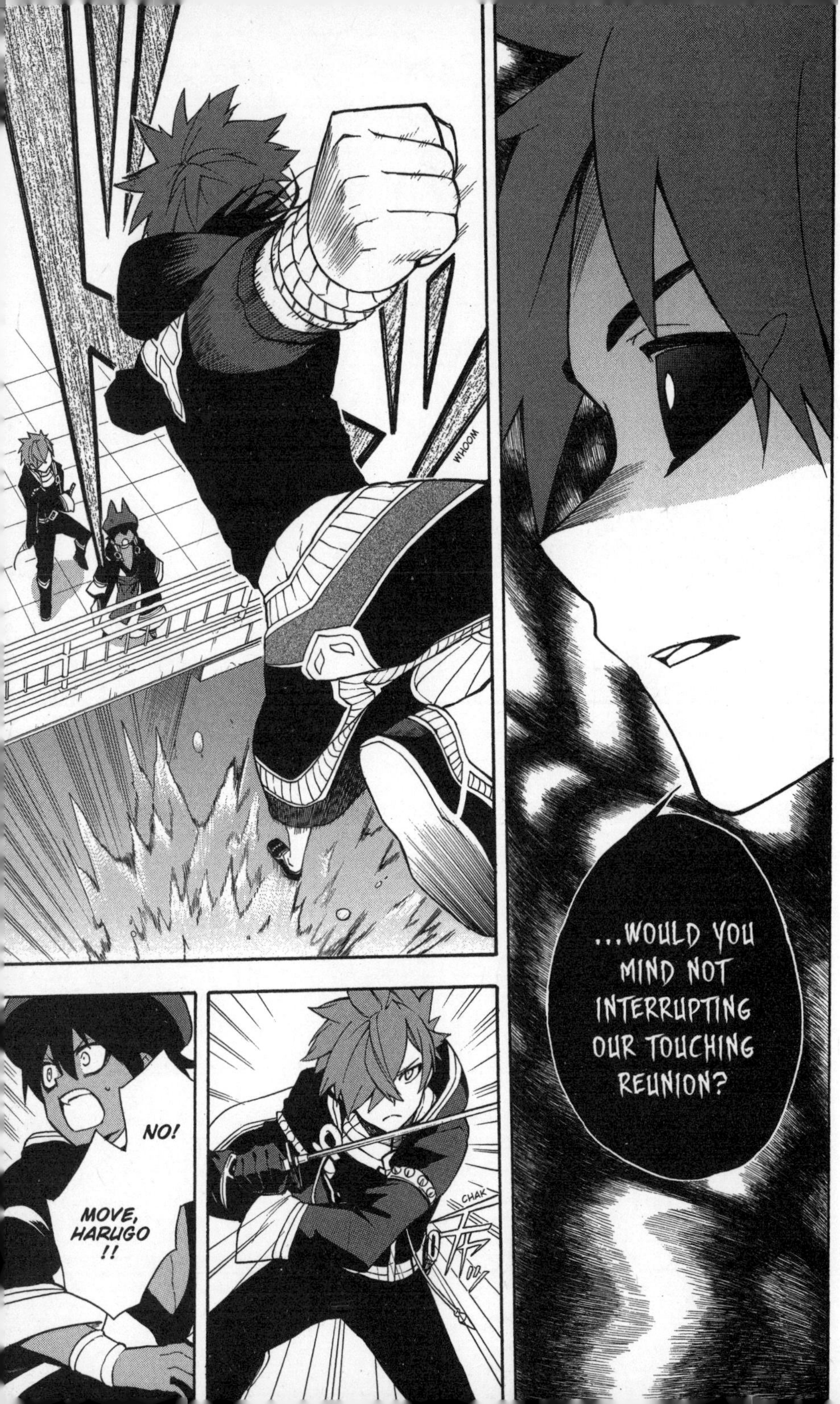
...WOULD YOU MIND NOT INTERRUPTING OUR TOUCHING REUNION?
WHOOM
CHAK
NO!
MOVE, HARUGO!!

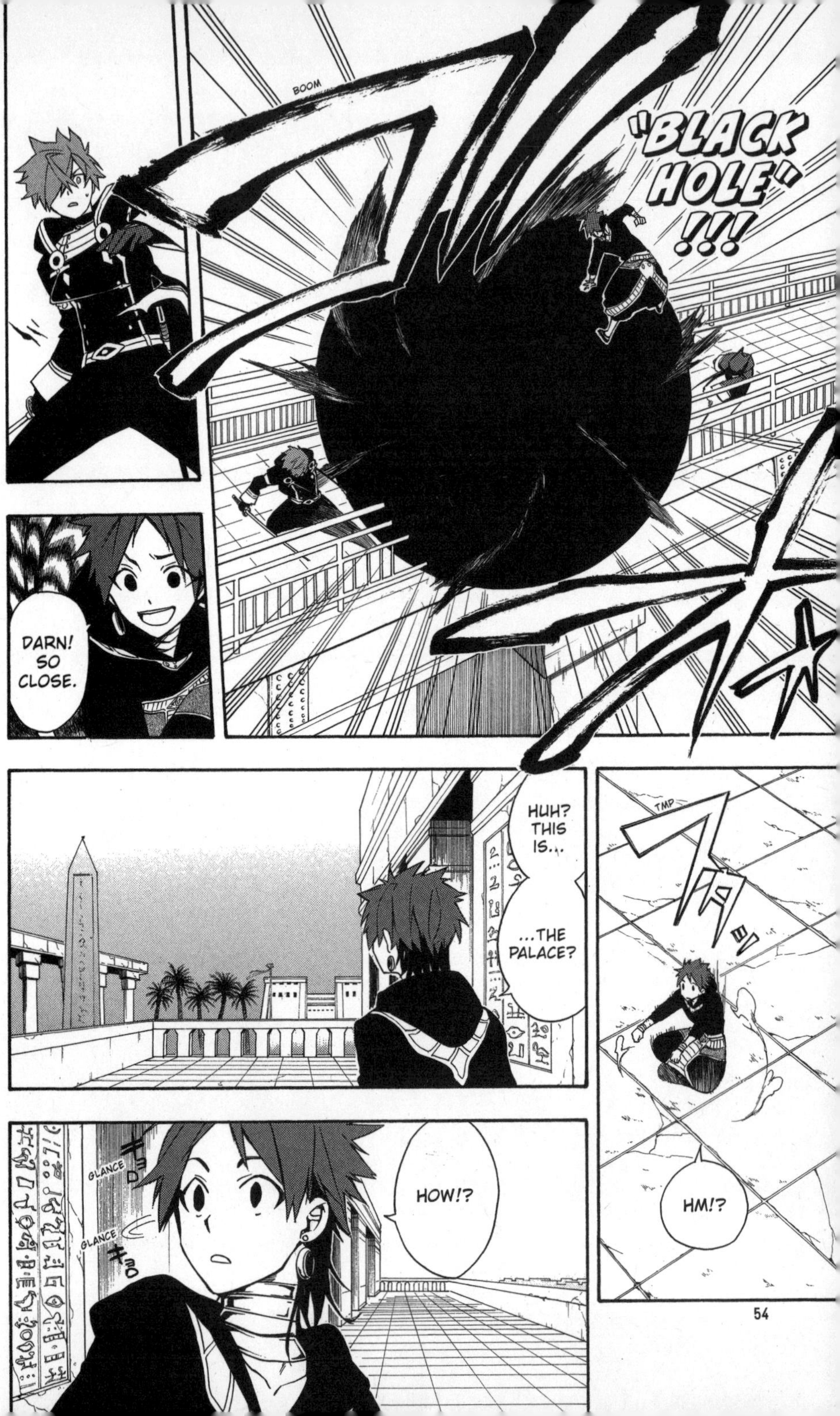
BOOM
"BLACK HOLE"!!!
DARN! SO CLOSE.
TMP
HM!?
HUH? THIS IS...
...THE PALACE?
GLANCE
GLANCE
HOW!?

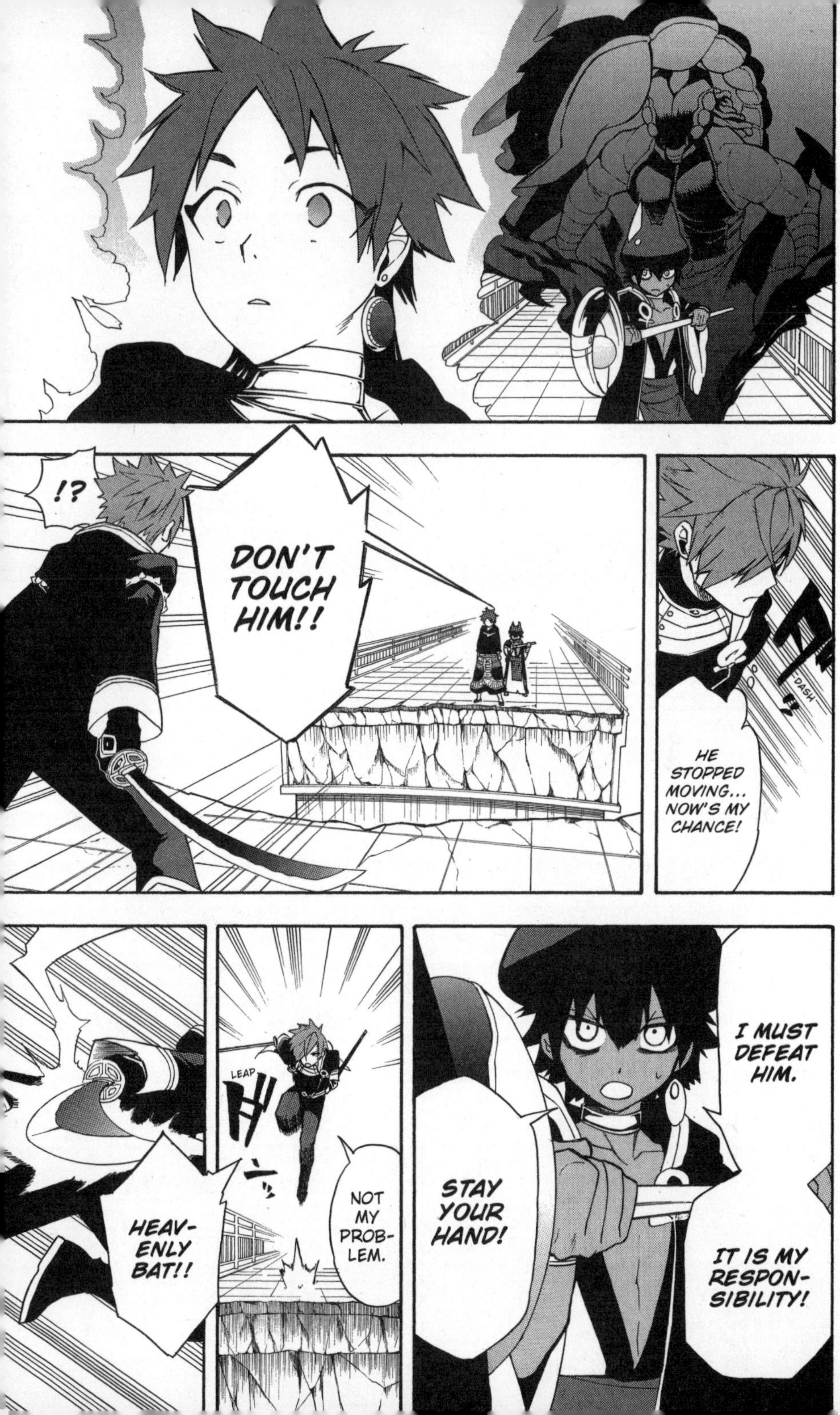

DASH
HE STOPPED MOVING... NOW'S MY CHANCE!
DON'T TOUCH HIM!!
!?
I MUST DEFEAT HIM.
STAY YOUR HAND!
IT IS MY RESPON-SIBILITY!
NOT MY PROB-LEM.
LEAP
HEAV-ENLY BAT!!

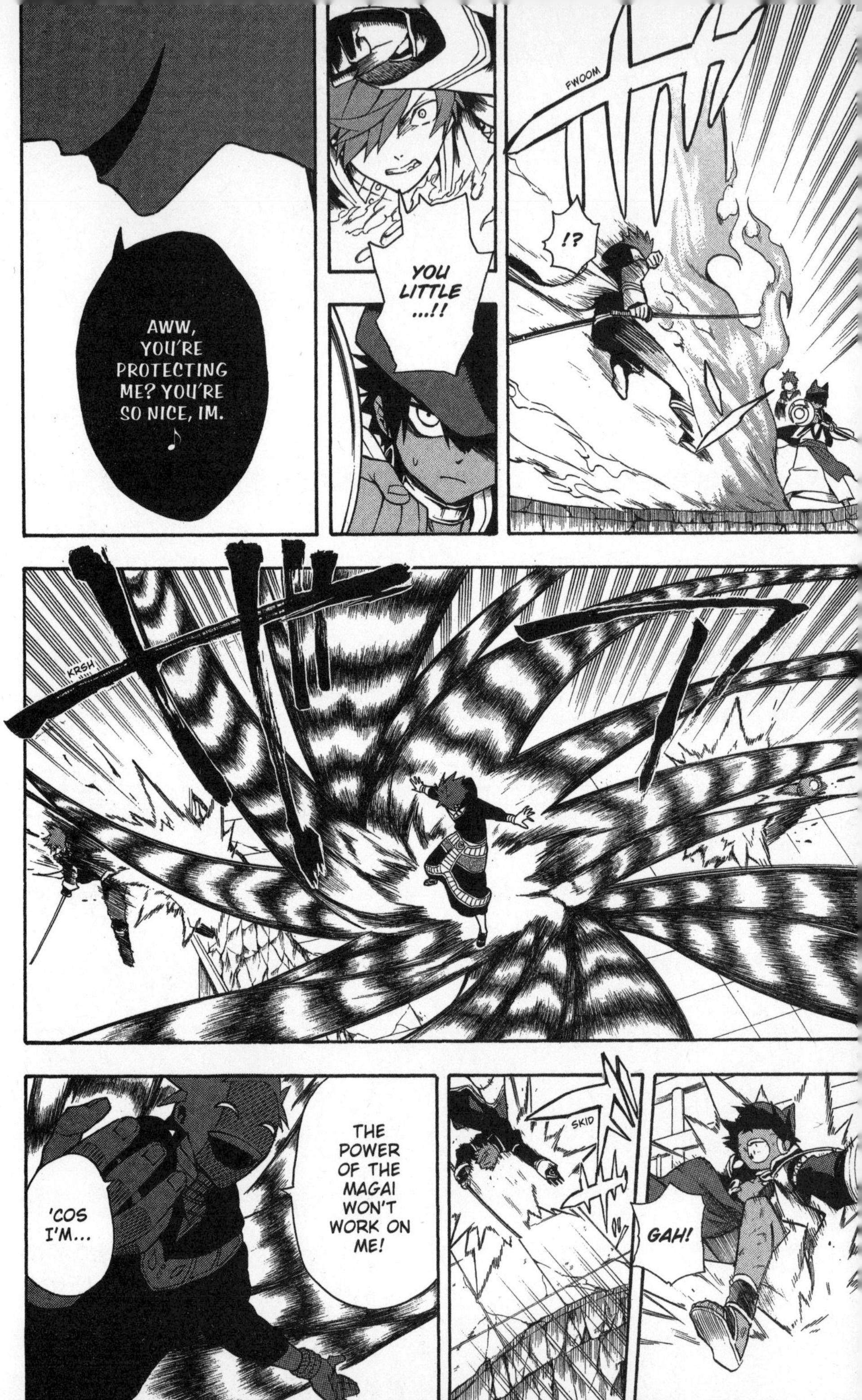
FWOOM
!?
YOU LITTLE ...!!
AWW, YOU'RE PROTECTING ME? YOU'RE SO NICE, IM. ♪
KRSH
GAH!
SKID
THE POWER OF THE MAGAI WON'T WORK ON ME!
'COS I'M...

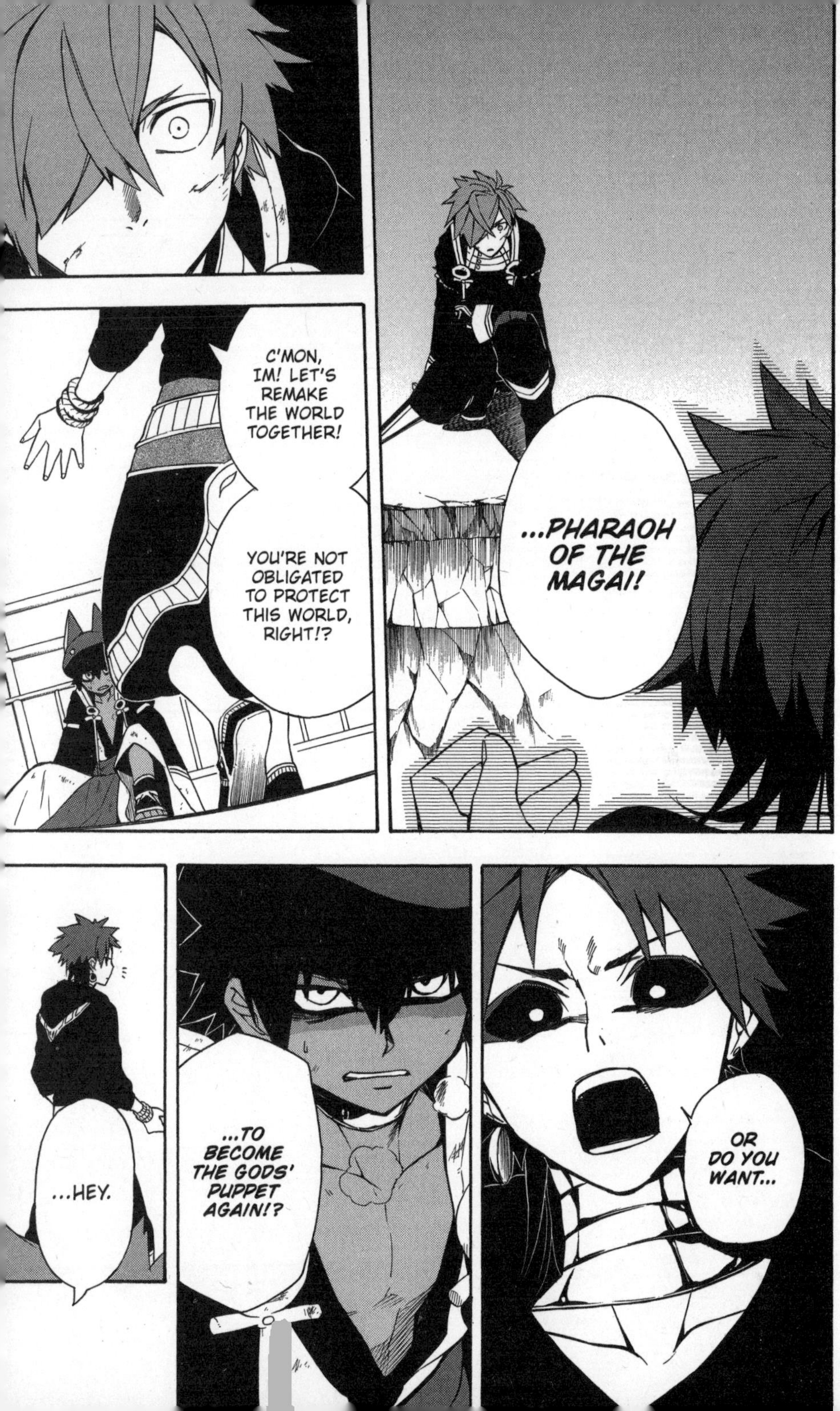
...PHARAOH OF THE MAGAI!
C'MON, IM! LET'S REMAKE THE WORLD TOGETHER!
YOU'RE NOT OBLIGATED TO PROTECT THIS WORLD, RIGHT!?
OR DO YOU WANT...
...TO BECOME THE GODS' PUPPET AGAIN!?
...HEY.

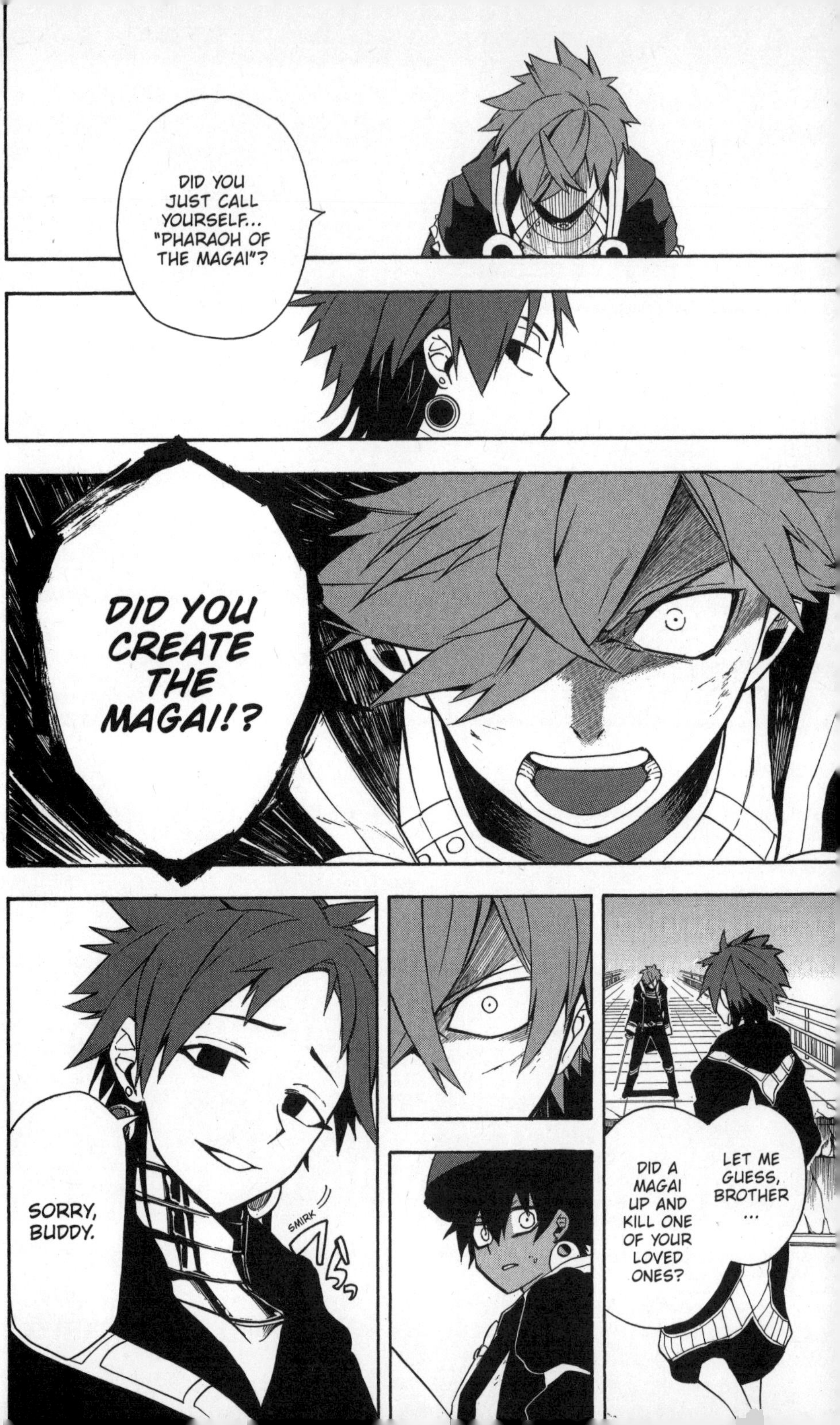

DID YOU JUST CALL YOURSELF... "PHARAOH OF THE MAGAI"?
DID YOU CREATE THE MAGAI!?
LET ME GUESS, BROTHER...
DID A MAGAI UP AND KILL ONE OF YOUR LOVED ONES?
SMIRK
SORRY, BUDDY.

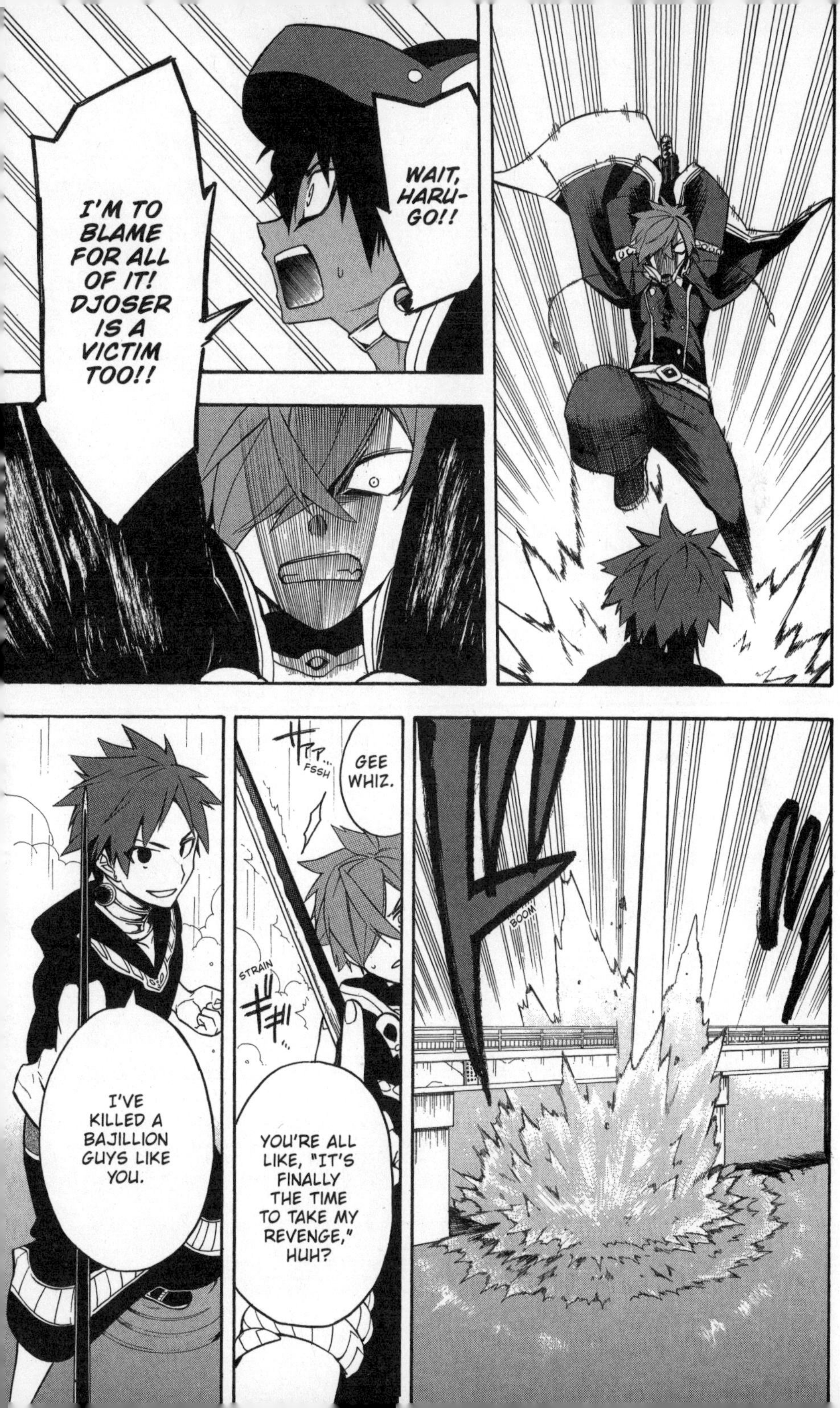
WAIT, HARU-GO!!
I'M TO BLAME FOR ALL OF IT! DJOSER IS A VICTIM TOO!!
BOOM
GEE WHIZ.
FSSH
STRAIN
YOU'RE ALL LIKE, "IT'S FINALLY THE TIME TO TAKE MY REVENGE," HUH?
I'VE KILLED A BAJILLION GUYS LIKE YOU.

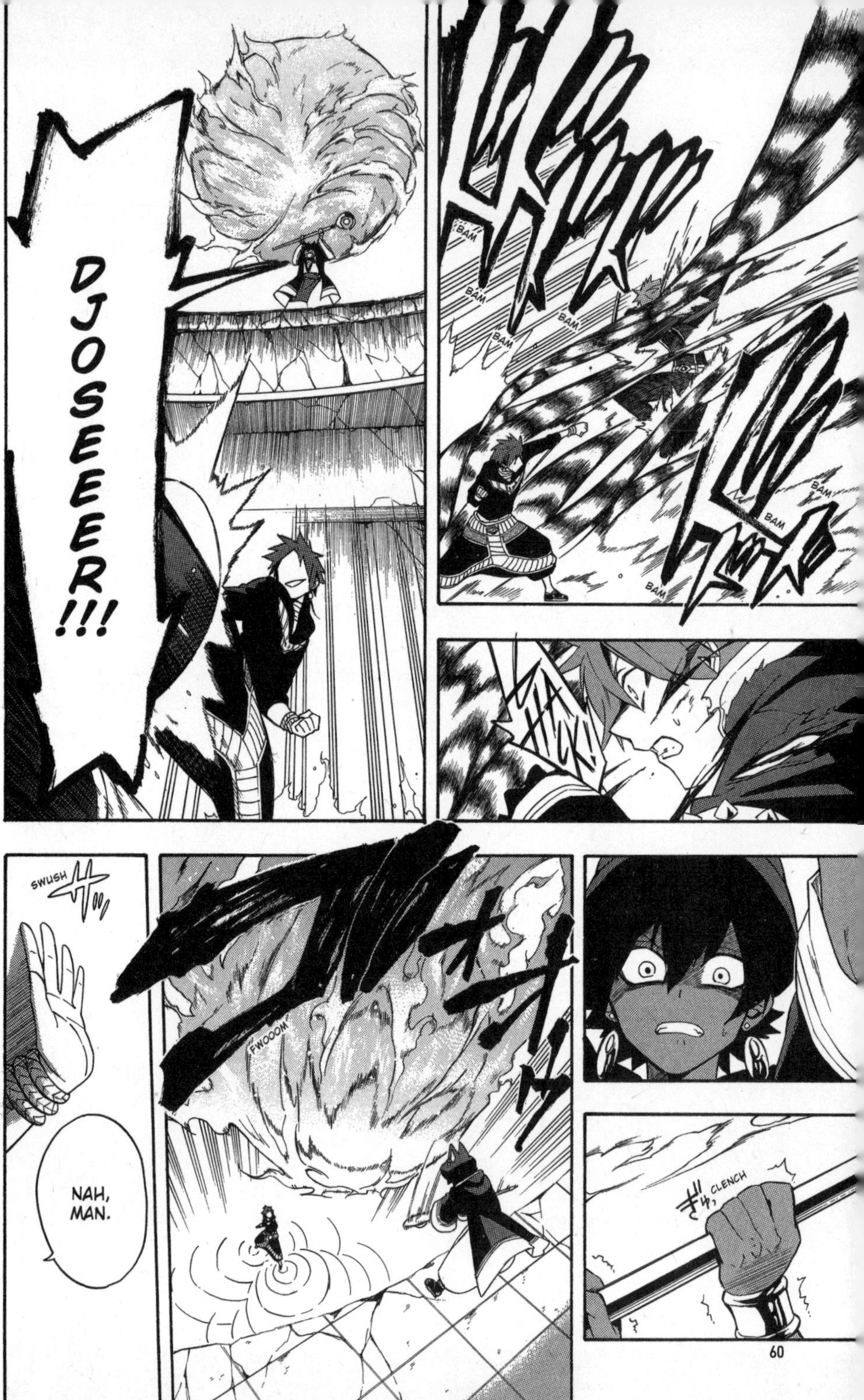
BAM
BAM
BAM
BAM
BAM
BAM
BAM
HACK!
DJOSEEEER!!!
CLENCH
FWOOOM
SWUSH
NAH, MAN.

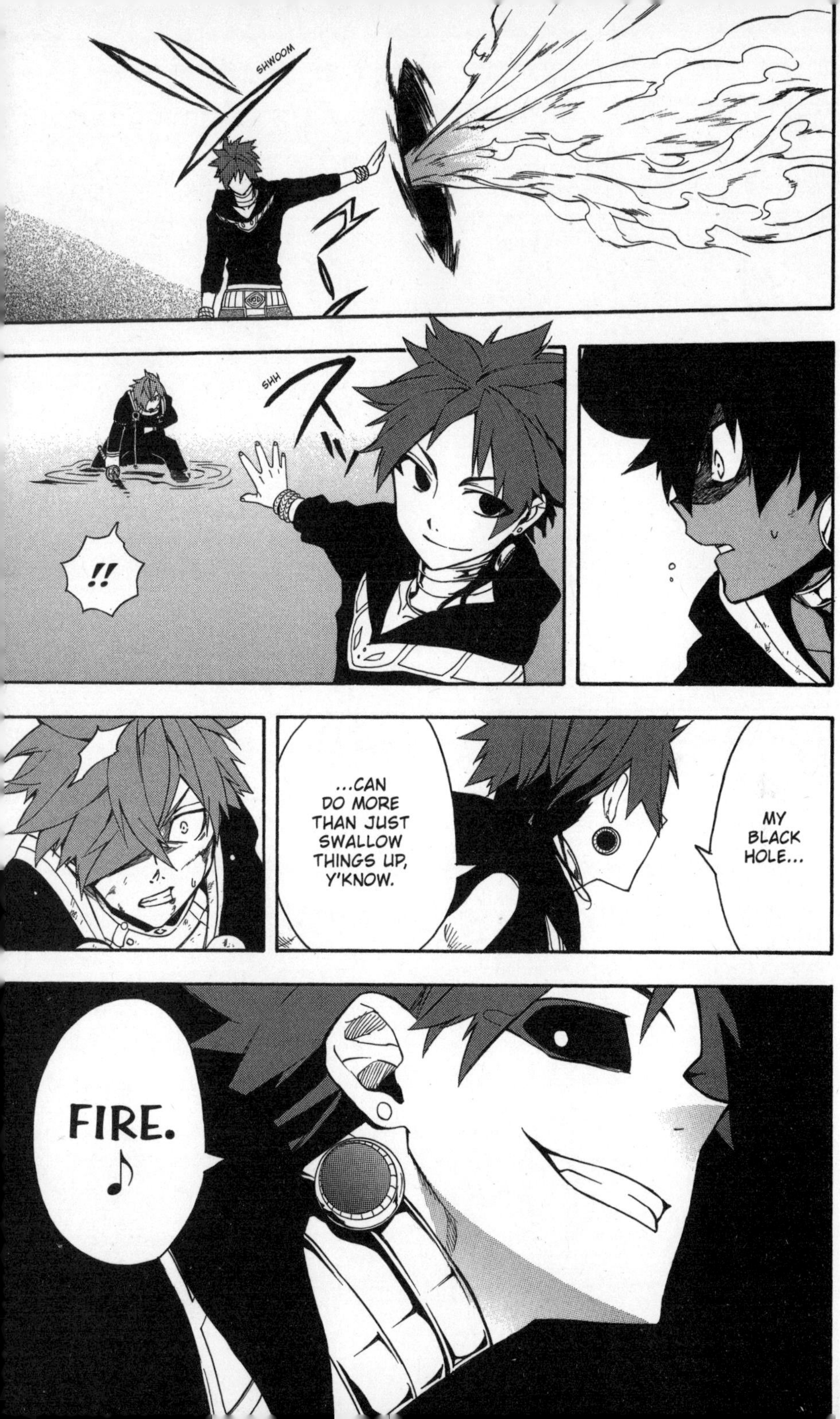
SHWOOM
SHH
!!
MY BLACK HOLE...
...CAN DO MORE THAN JUST SWALLOW THINGS UP, Y'KNOW.
FIRE. ♪

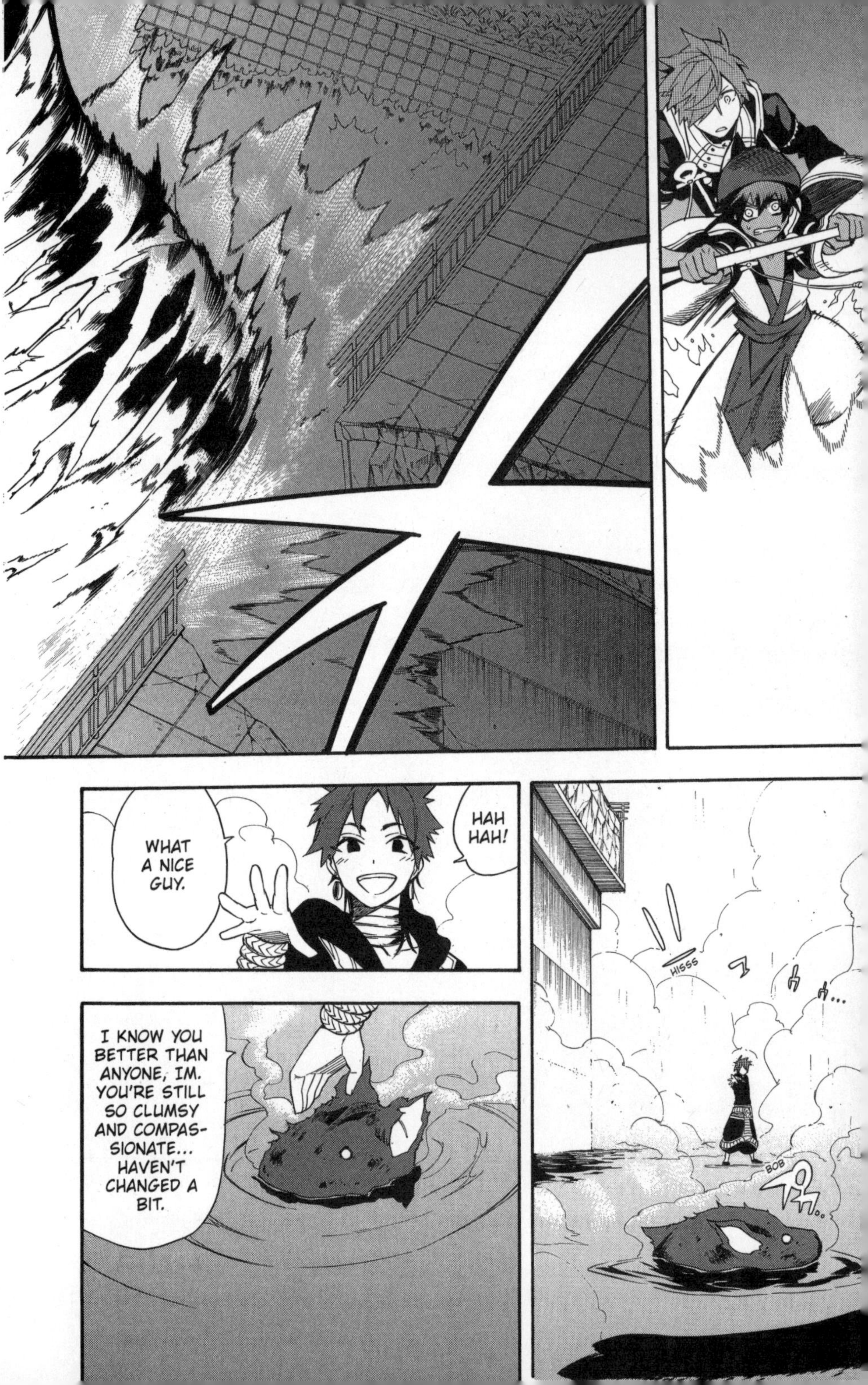
HISSS
BOB
HAH HAH!
WHAT A NICE GUY.
I KNOW YOU BETTER THAN ANYONE, IM. YOU'RE STILL SO CLUMSY AND COMPASSIONATE... HAVEN'T CHANGED A BIT.

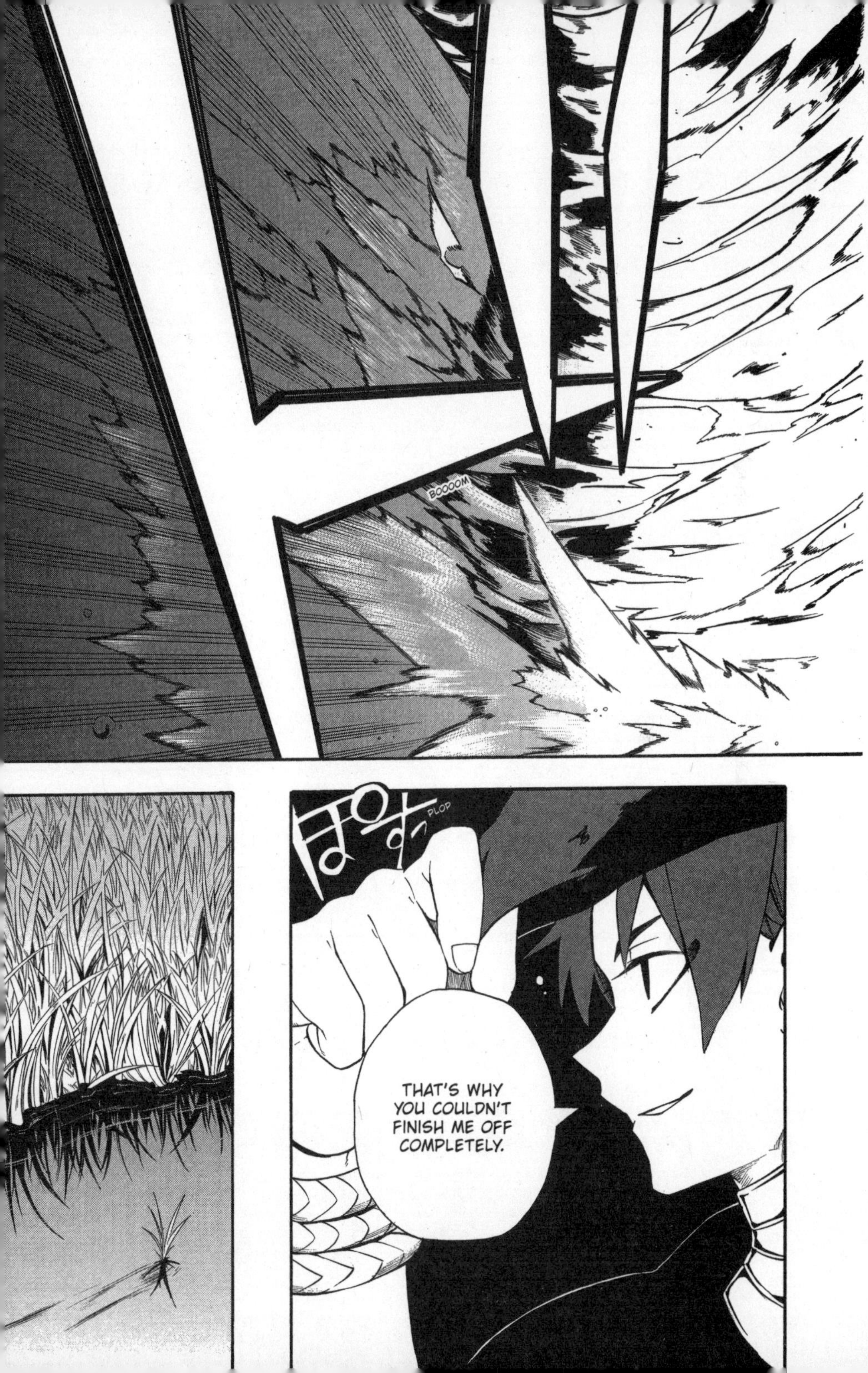
BOOOOM
ぽすっ
PLOP
THAT'S WHY YOU COULDN'T FINISH ME OFF COMPLETELY.

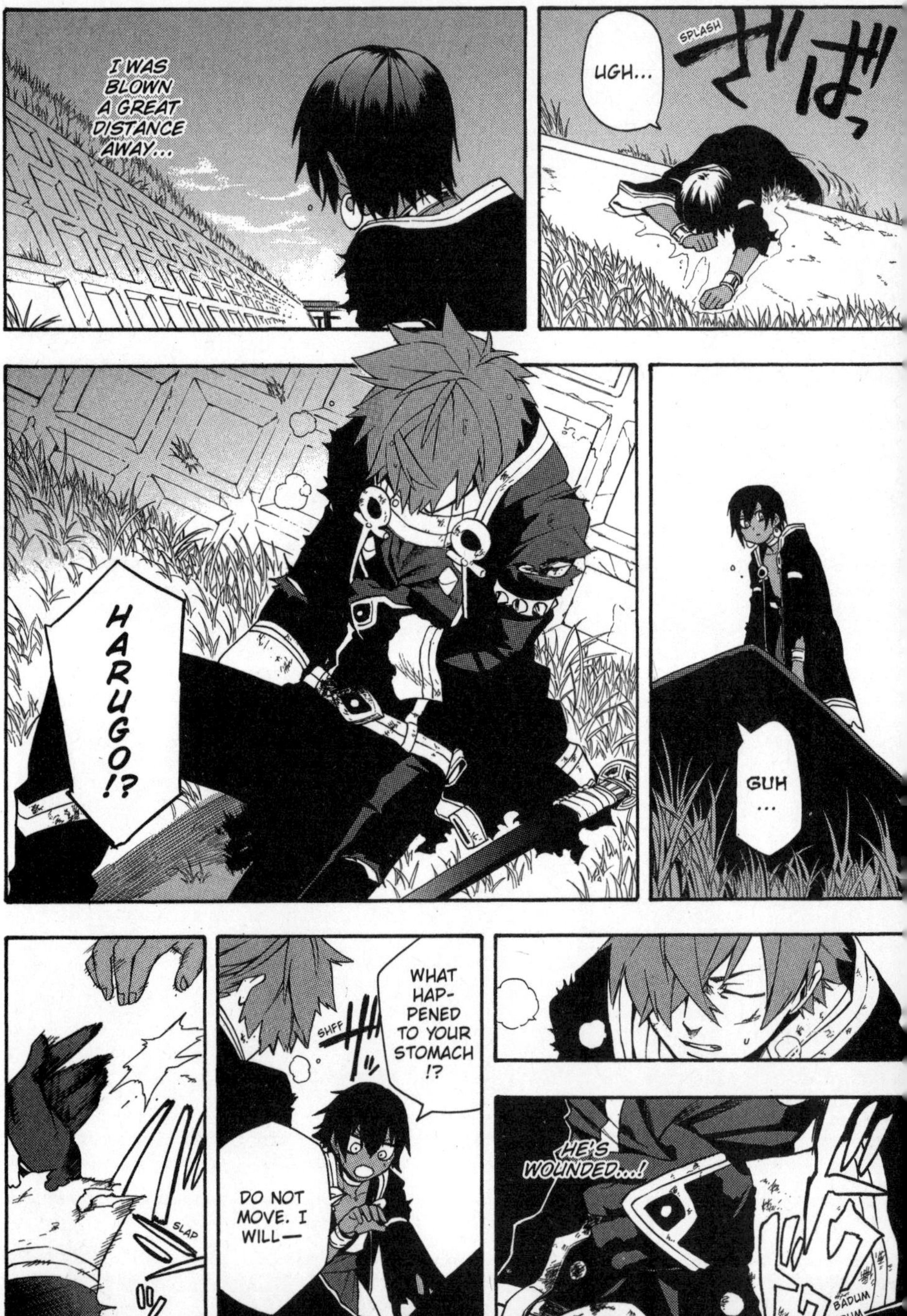
SPLASH
ざばっ
UGH...
I WAS BLOWN A GREAT DISTANCE AWAY...
GUH ...
HARUGO!?
HE'S WOUNDED...!
BADUM
BADUM
SHFF
WHAT HAP-PENED TO YOUR STOMACH!?
DO NOT MOVE. I WILL—
SLAP

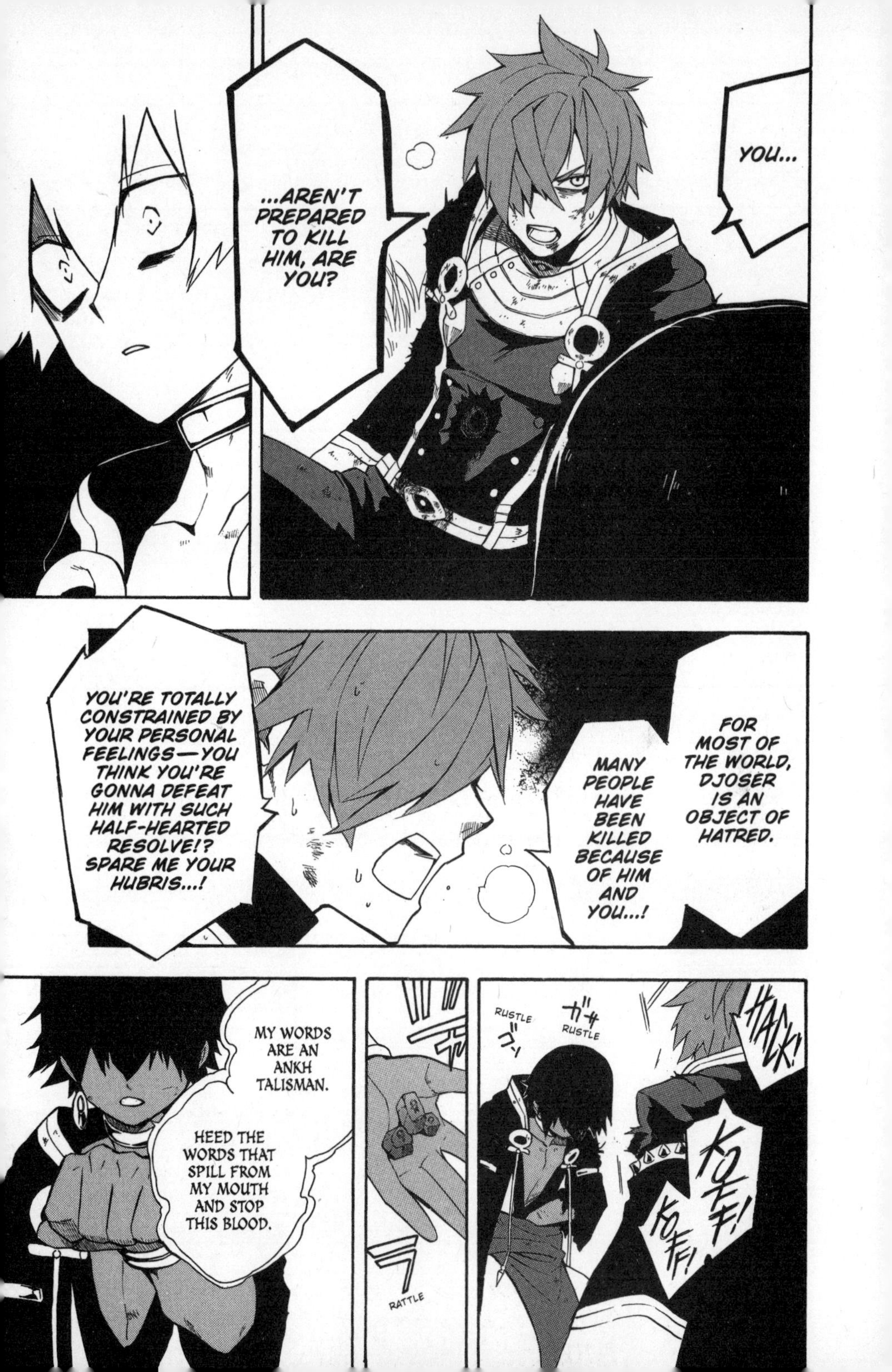
YOU...
...AREN'T PREPARED TO KILL HIM, ARE YOU?
FOR MOST OF THE WORLD, DJOSER IS AN OBJECT OF HATRED.
MANY PEOPLE HAVE BEEN KILLED BECAUSE OF HIM AND YOU...!
YOU'RE TOTALLY CONSTRAINED BY YOUR PERSONAL FEELINGS—YOU THINK YOU'RE GONNA DEFEAT HIM WITH SUCH HALF-HEARTED RESOLVE!? SPARE ME YOUR HUBRIS...!
HACK!
KOFF!
KOFF!
RUSTLE
RUSTLE
RATTLE
MY WORDS ARE AN ANKH TALISMAN.
HEED THE WORDS THAT SPILL FROM MY MOUTH AND STOP THIS BLOOD.

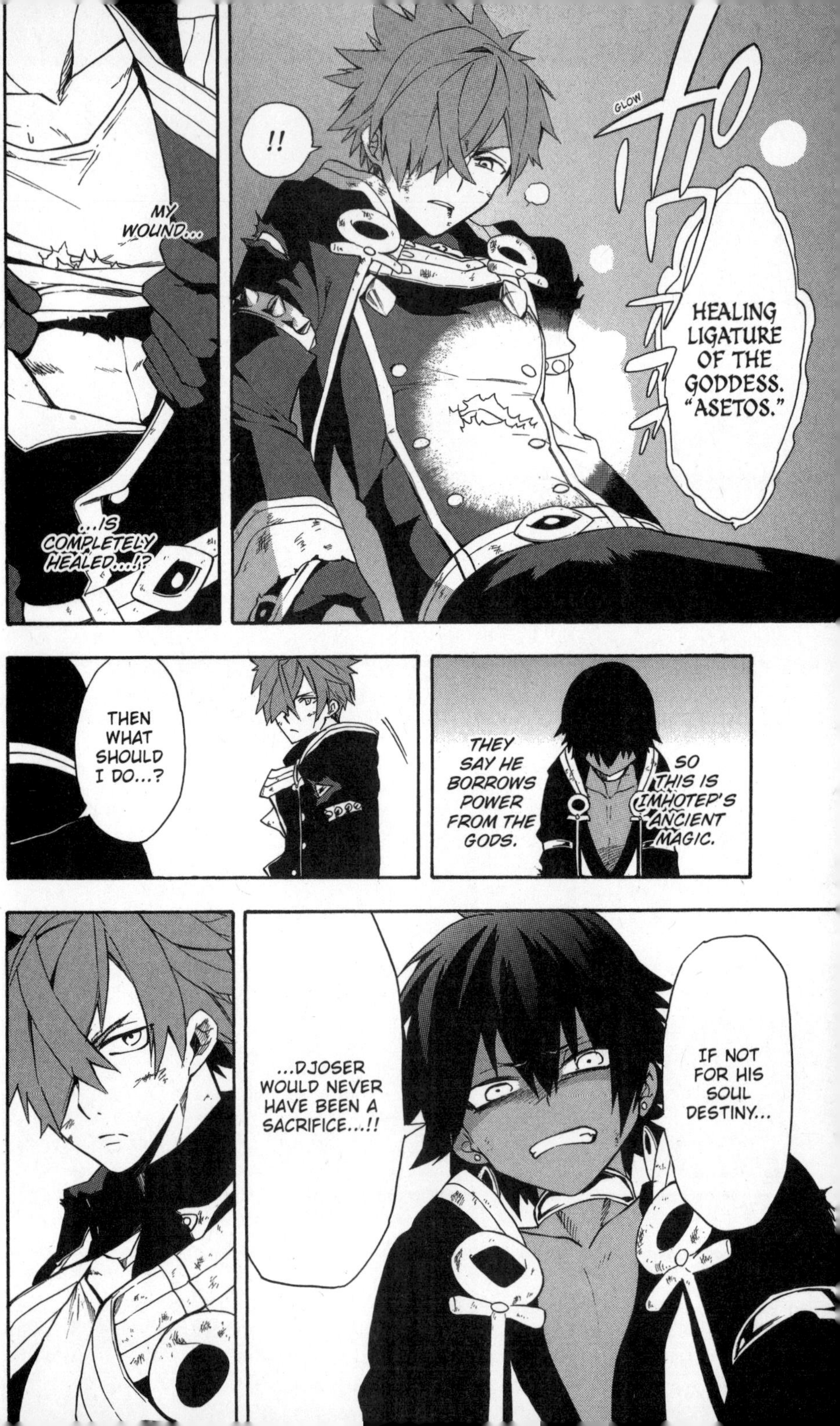
GLOW
HEALING LIGATURE OF THE GODDESS. "ASETOS."
!!
MY WOUND...
...IS COMPLETELY HEALED...!?
SO THIS IS IMHOTEP'S ANCIENT MAGIC.
THEY SAY HE BORROWS POWER FROM THE GODS.
THEN WHAT SHOULD I DO...?
IF NOT FOR HIS SOUL DESTINY...
...DJOSER WOULD NEVER HAVE BEEN A SACRIFICE...!!

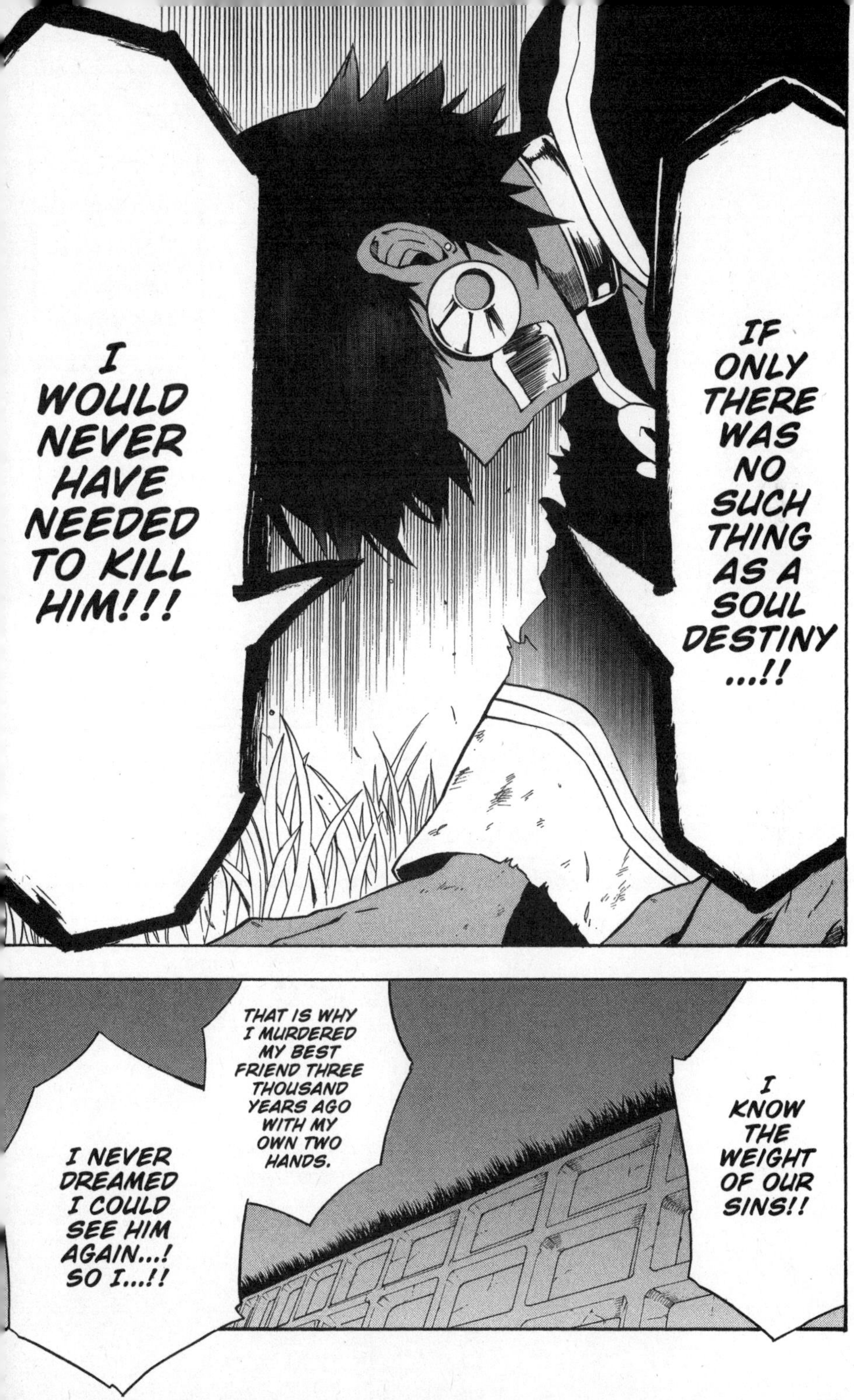
IF ONLY THERE WAS NO SUCH THING AS A SOUL DESTINY ...!!
I WOULD NEVER HAVE NEEDED TO KILL HIM!!!
I KNOW THE WEIGHT OF OUR SINS!!
THAT IS WHY I MURDERED MY BEST FRIEND THREE THOUSAND YEARS AGO WITH MY OWN TWO HANDS.
I NEVER DREAMED I COULD SEE HIM AGAIN...! SO I...!!

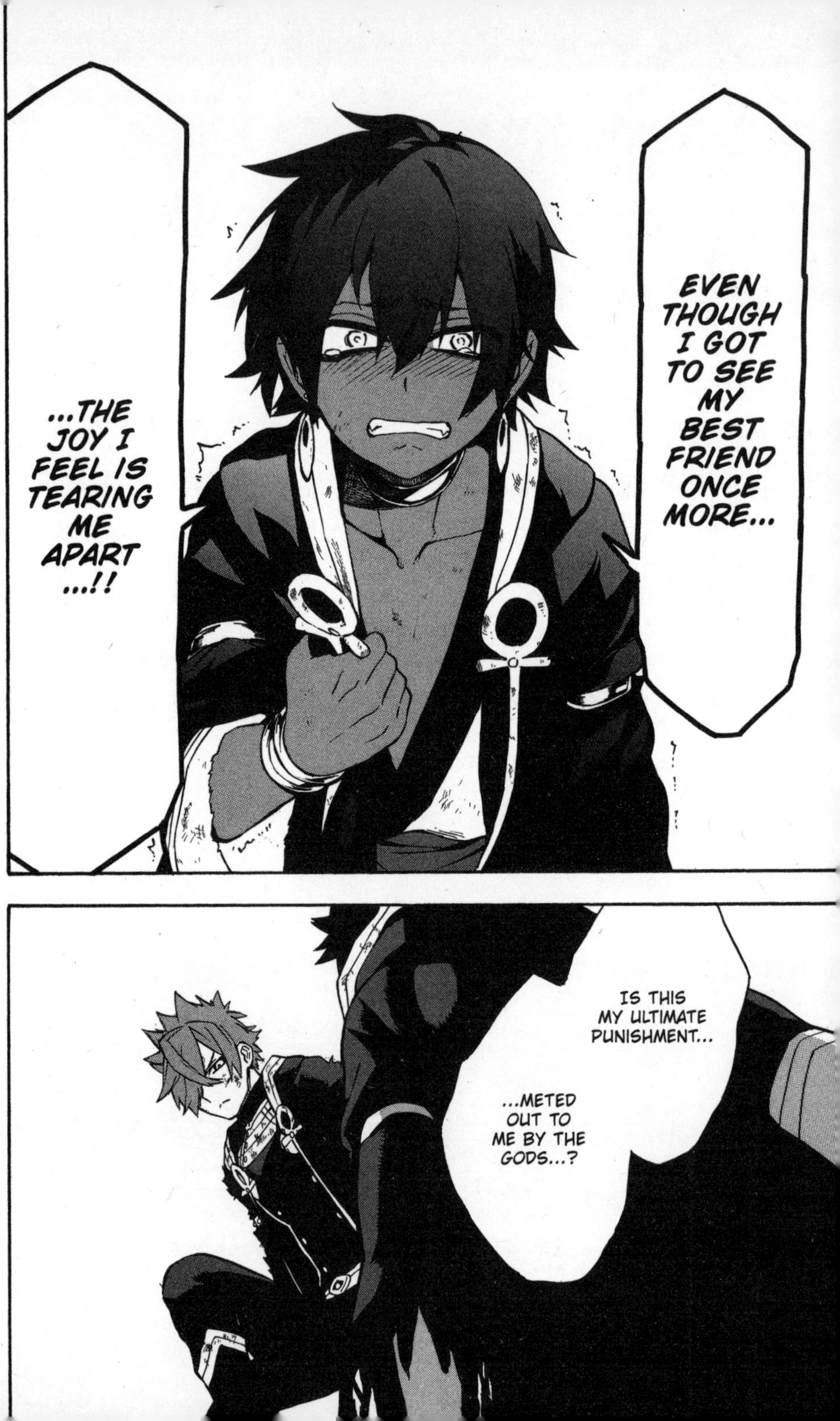
EVEN THOUGH I GOT TO SEE MY BEST FRIEND ONCE MORE...
...THE JOY I FEEL IS TEARING ME APART ...!!
IS THIS MY ULTIMATE PUNISHMENT...
...METED OUT TO ME BY THE GODS...?

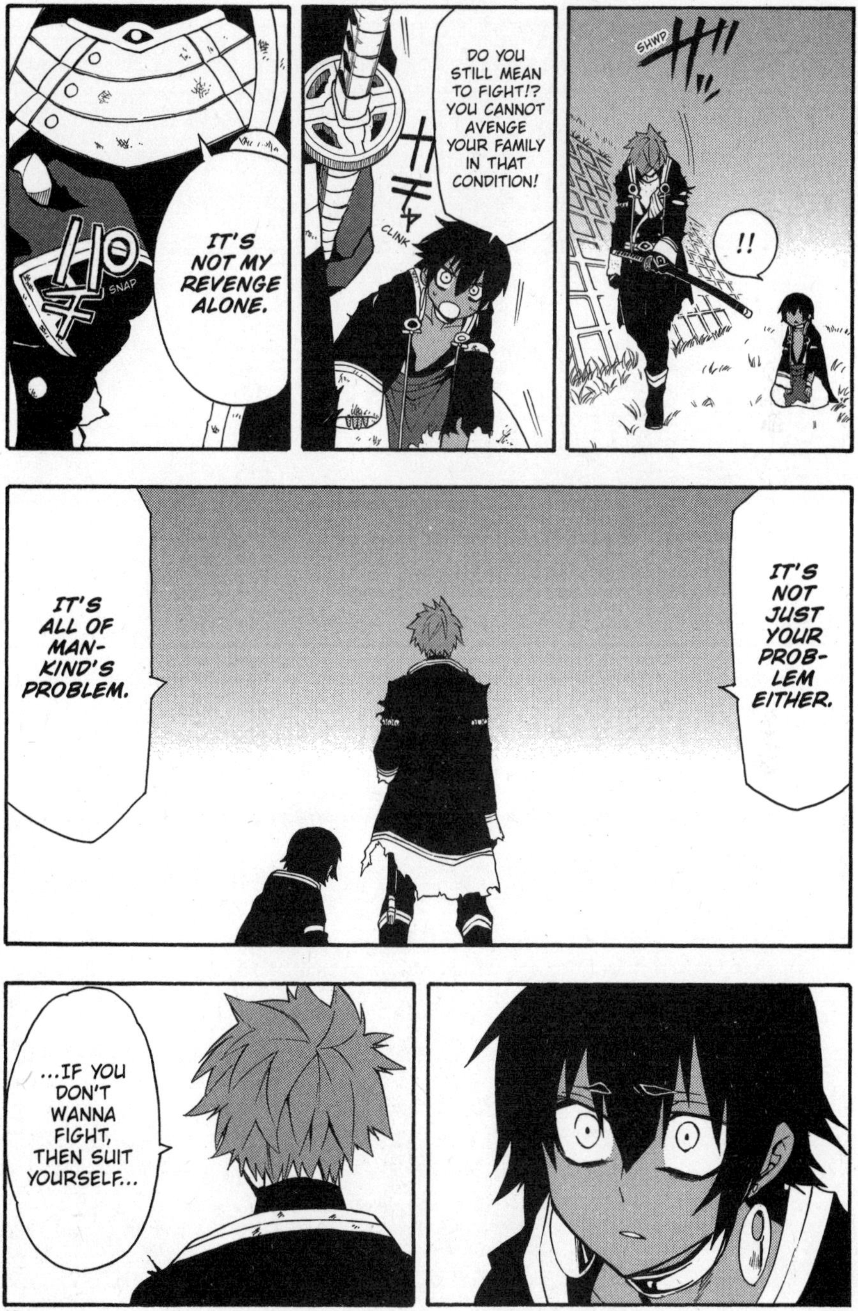
SHWP
!!
DO YOU STILL MEAN TO FIGHT!? YOU CANNOT AVENGE YOUR FAMILY IN THAT CONDITION!
CLINK
IT'S NOT MY REVENGE ALONE.
SNAP
IT'S NOT JUST YOUR PROB-LEM EITHER.
IT'S ALL OF MAN-KIND'S PROBLEM.
...IF YOU DON'T WANNA FIGHT, THEN SUIT YOURSELF...

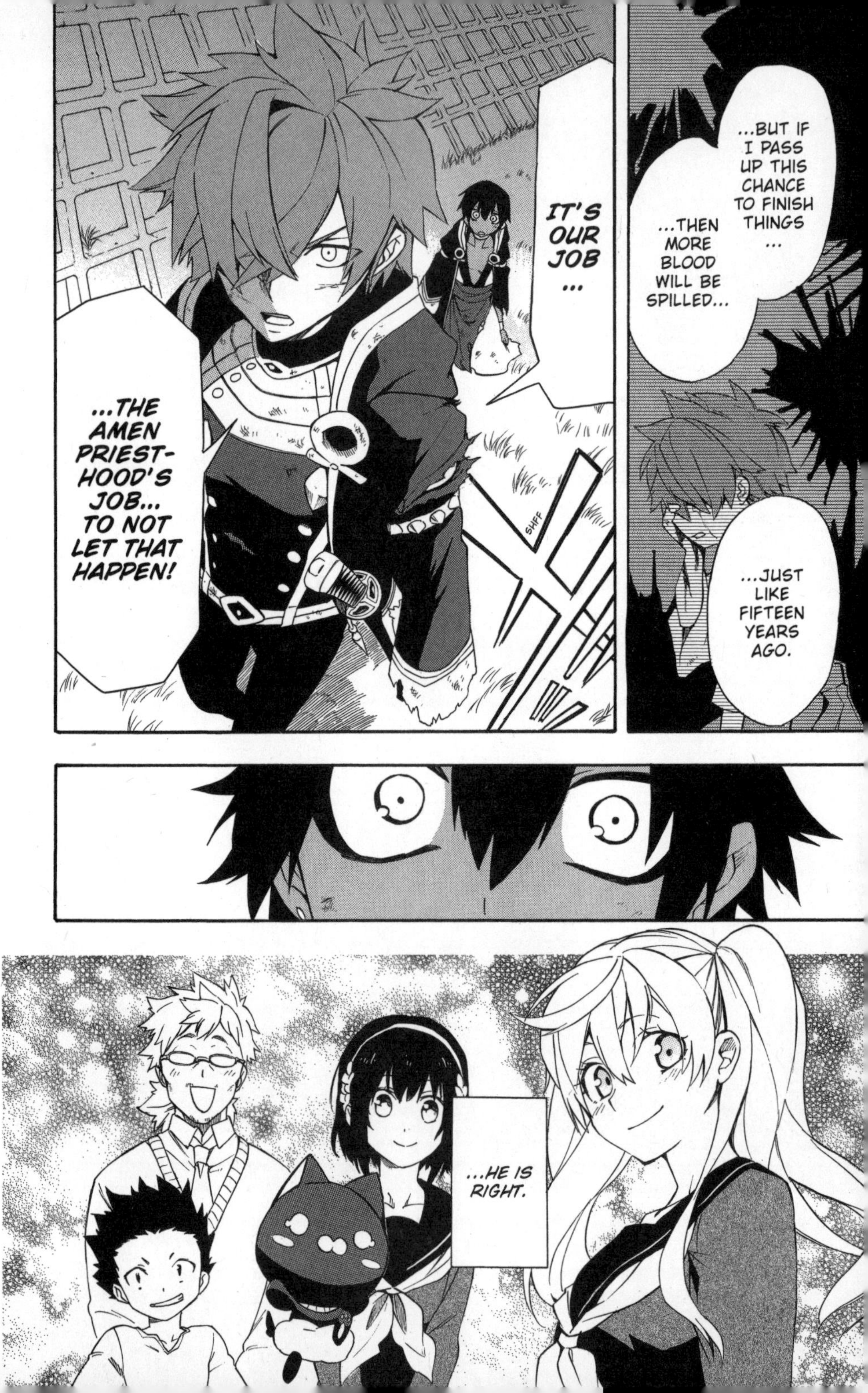
...BUT IF I PASS UP THIS CHANCE TO FINISH THINGS ...
...THEN MORE BLOOD WILL BE SPILLED...
...JUST LIKE FIFTEEN YEARS AGO.
IT'S OUR JOB ...
...THE AMEN PRIEST-HOOD'S JOB... TO NOT LET THAT HAPPEN!
SHFF
...HE IS RIGHT.

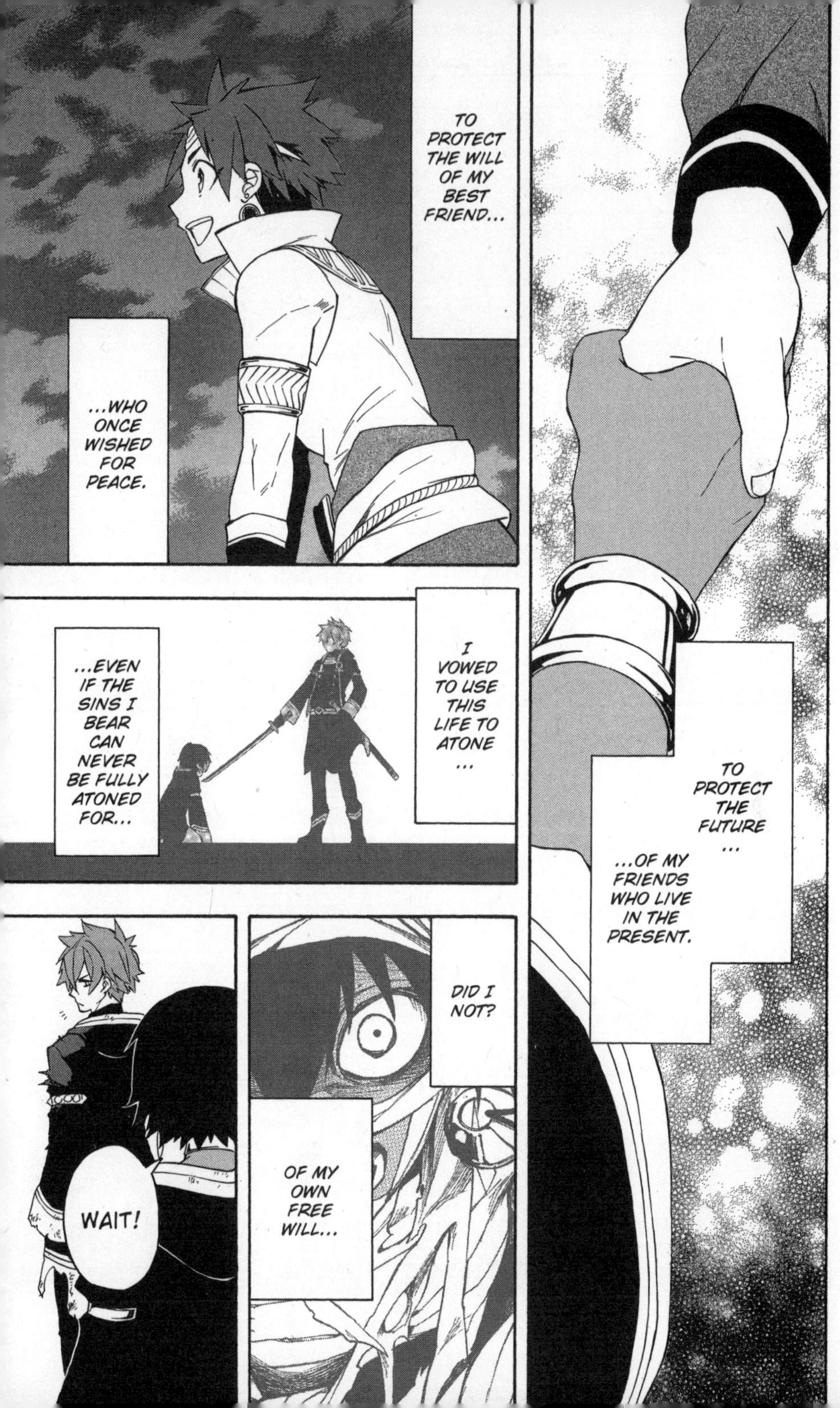
TO PROTECT THE FUTURE...
...OF MY FRIENDS WHO LIVE IN THE PRESENT.
TO PROTECT THE WILL OF MY BEST FRIEND...
...WHO ONCE WISHED FOR PEACE.
I VOWED TO USE THIS LIFE TO ATONE...
...EVEN IF THE SINS I BEAR CAN NEVER BE FULLY ATONED FOR...
DID I NOT?
OF MY OWN FREE WILL...
WAIT!

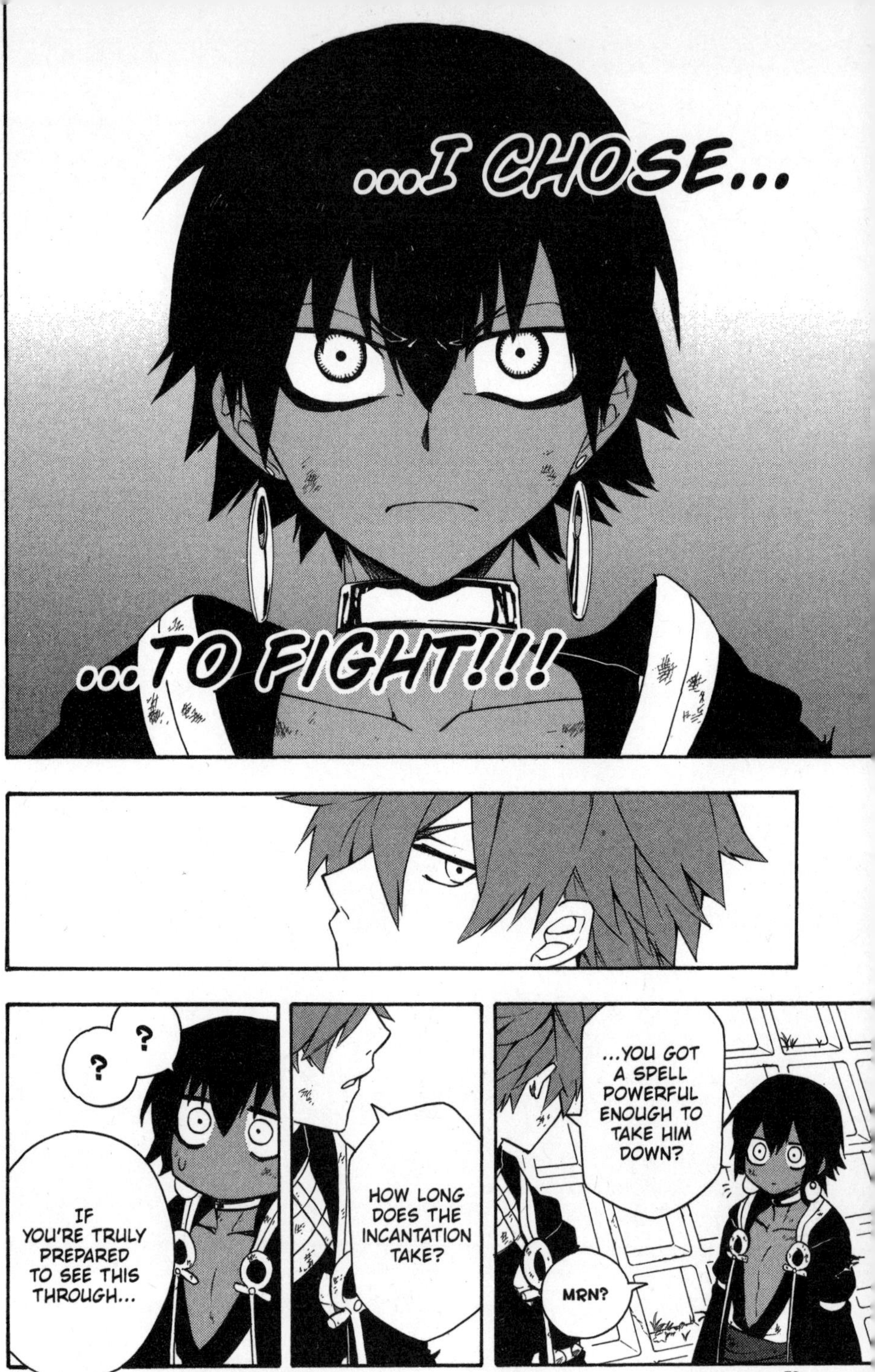
...I CHOSE...
...TO FIGHT!!!
...YOU GOT A SPELL POWERFUL ENOUGH TO TAKE HIM DOWN?
MRN?
HOW LONG DOES THE INCANTATION TAKE?
? ?
IF YOU'RE TRULY PREPARED TO SEE THIS THROUGH...

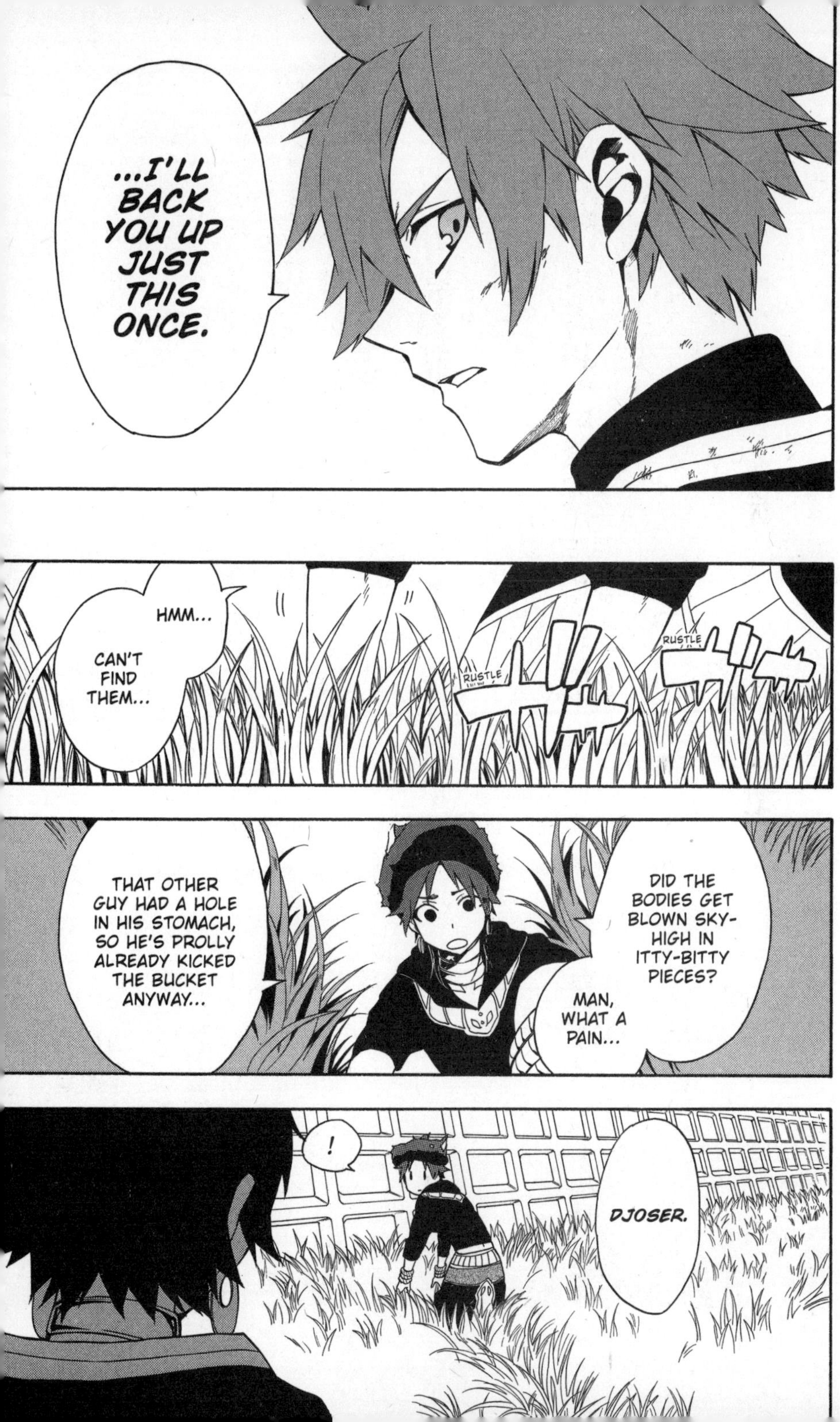
...I'LL BACK YOU UP JUST THIS ONCE.
RUSTLE
RUSTLE
HMM...
CAN'T FIND THEM...
DID THE BODIES GET BLOWN SKY-HIGH IN ITTY-BITTY PIECES?
MAN, WHAT A PAIN...
THAT OTHER GUY HAD A HOLE IN HIS STOMACH, SO HE'S PROLLY ALREADY KICKED THE BUCKET ANYWAY...
DJOSER.
!

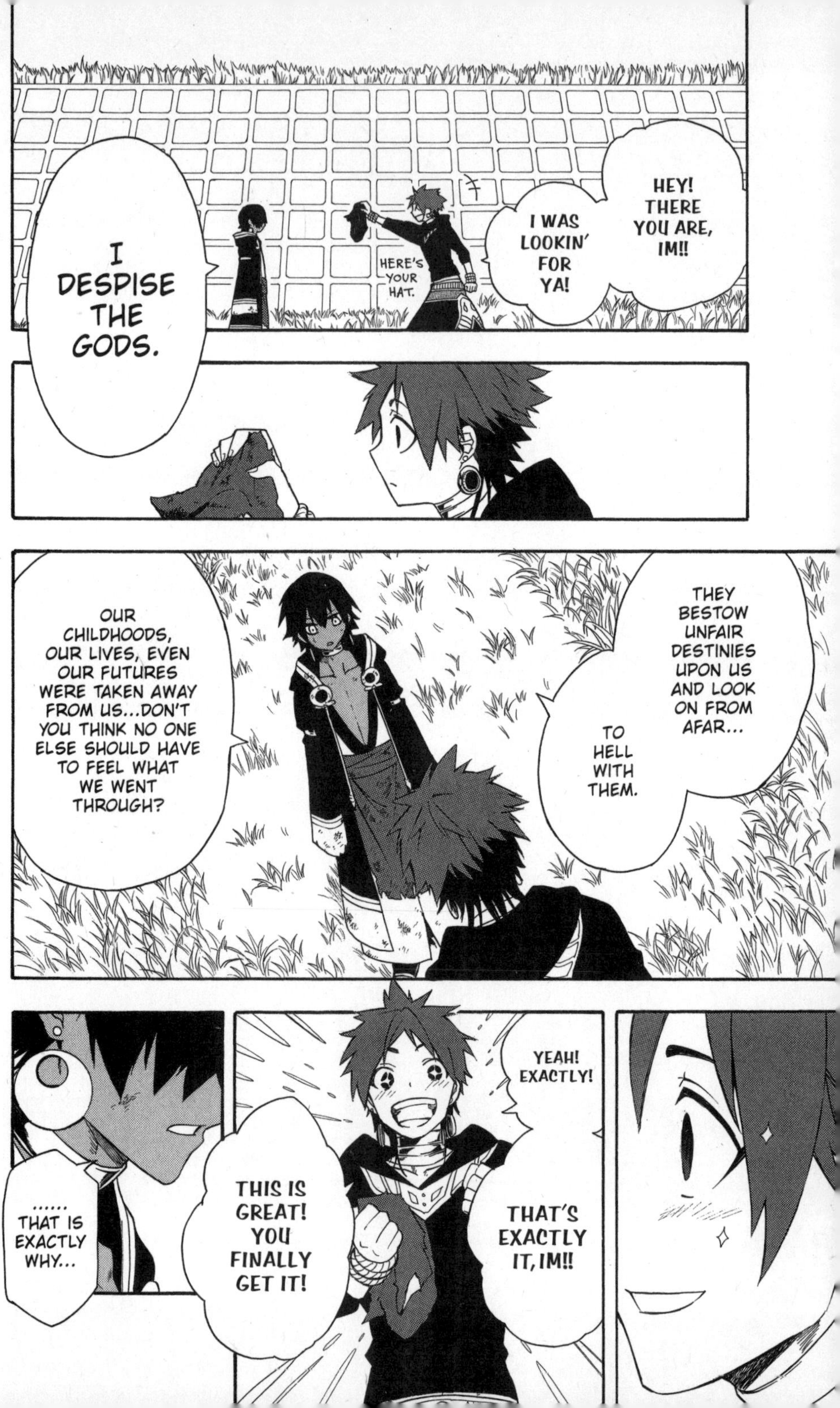
HEY! THERE YOU ARE, IM!!
I WAS LOOKIN' FOR YA!
HERE'S YOUR HAT.
I DESPISE THE GODS.
THEY BESTOW UNFAIR DESTINIES UPON US AND LOOK ON FROM AFAR...
TO HELL WITH THEM.
OUR CHILDHOODS, OUR LIVES, EVEN OUR FUTURES WERE TAKEN AWAY FROM US...DON'T YOU THINK NO ONE ELSE SHOULD HAVE TO FEEL WHAT WE WENT THROUGH?
YEAH! EXACTLY!
THAT'S EXACTLY IT, IM!!
THIS IS GREAT! YOU FINALLY GET IT!
......
THAT IS EXACTLY WHY...

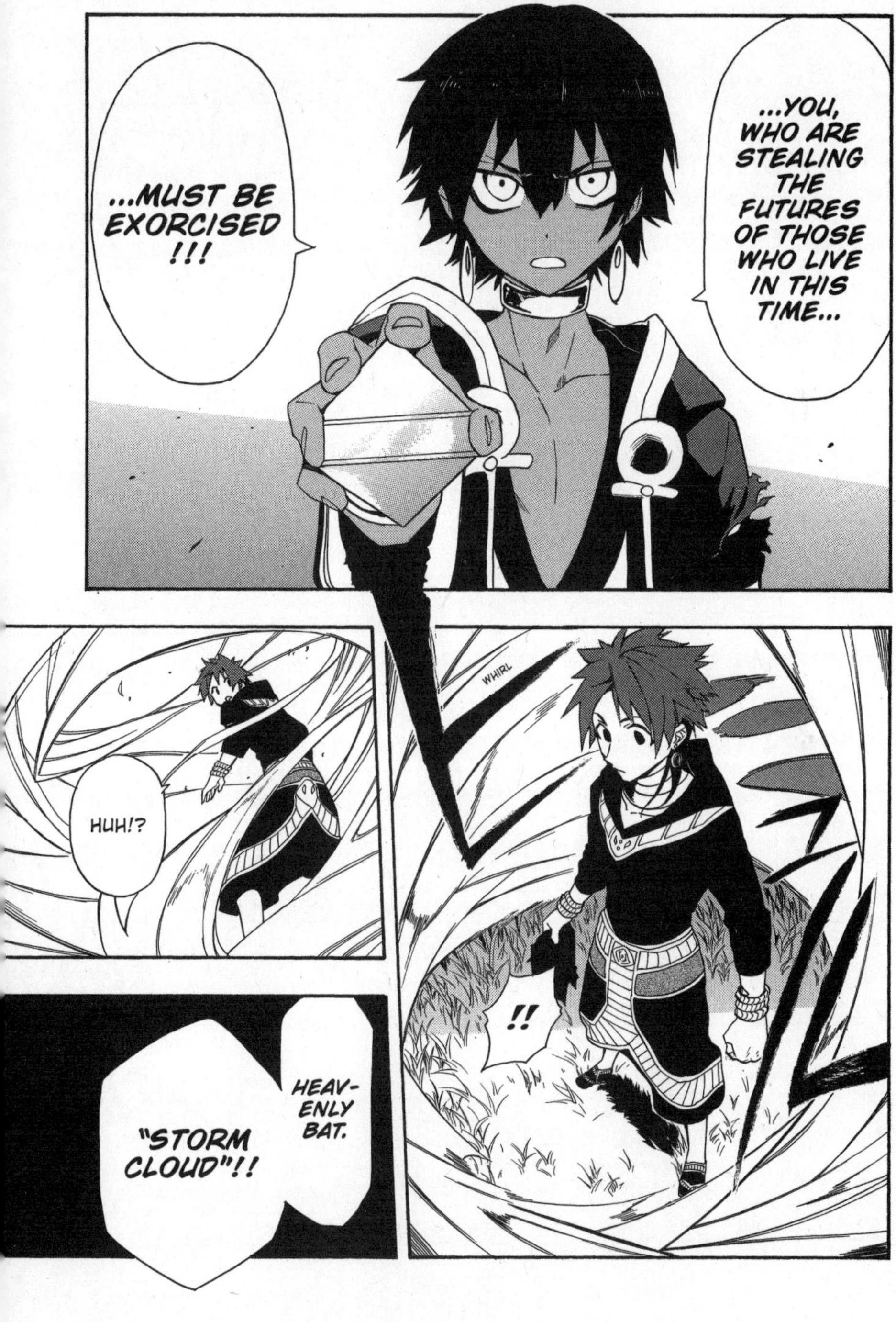
...YOU, WHO ARE STEALING THE FUTURES OF THOSE WHO LIVE IN THIS TIME...
...MUST BE EXORCISED!!!
WHIRL
!!
HUH!?
HEAV-ENLY BAT.
"STORM CLOUD"!!

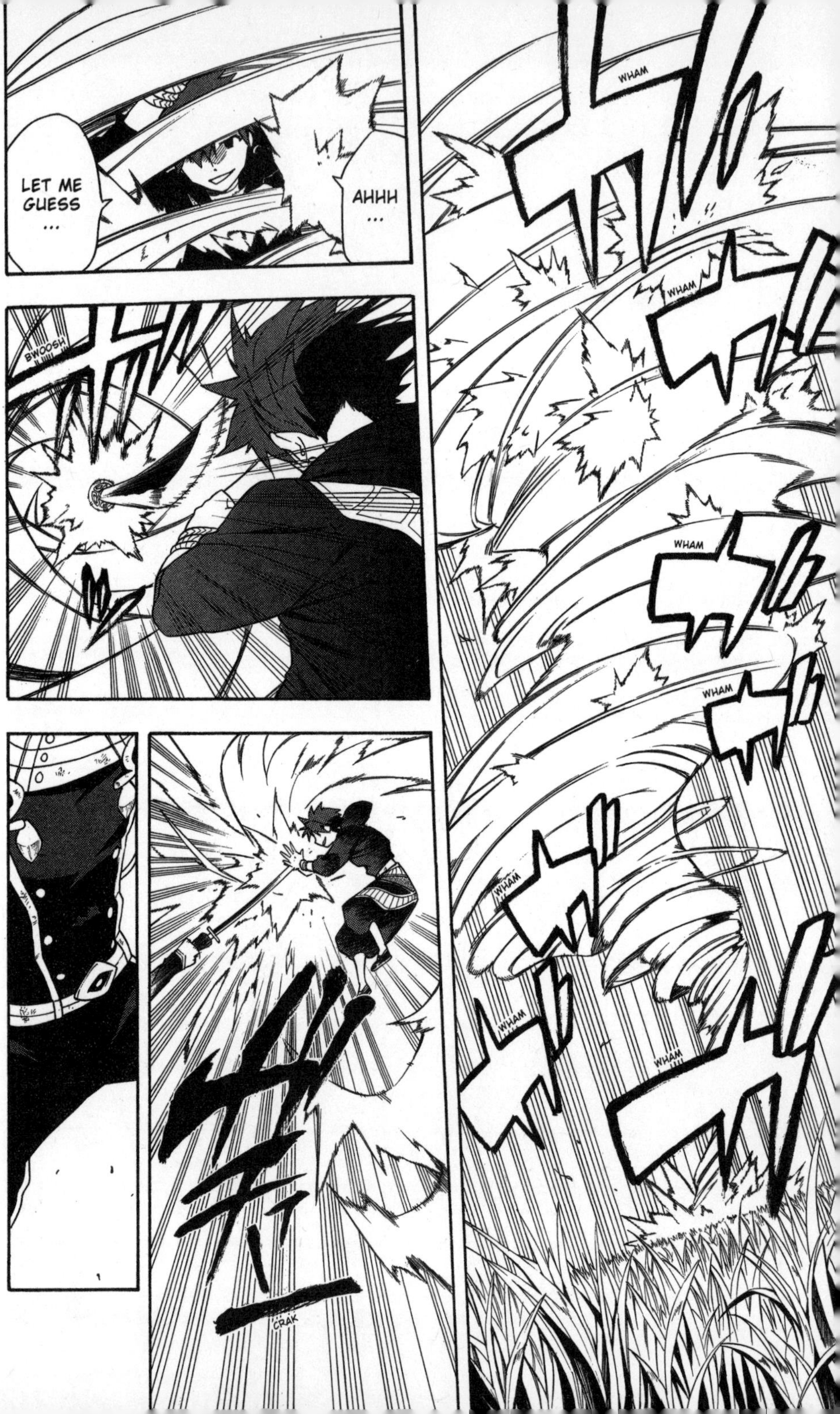
WHAM
WHAM
WHAM
WHAM
WHAM
WHAM
WHAM
AHHH ...
LET ME GUESS ...
BWOOSH
CRAK

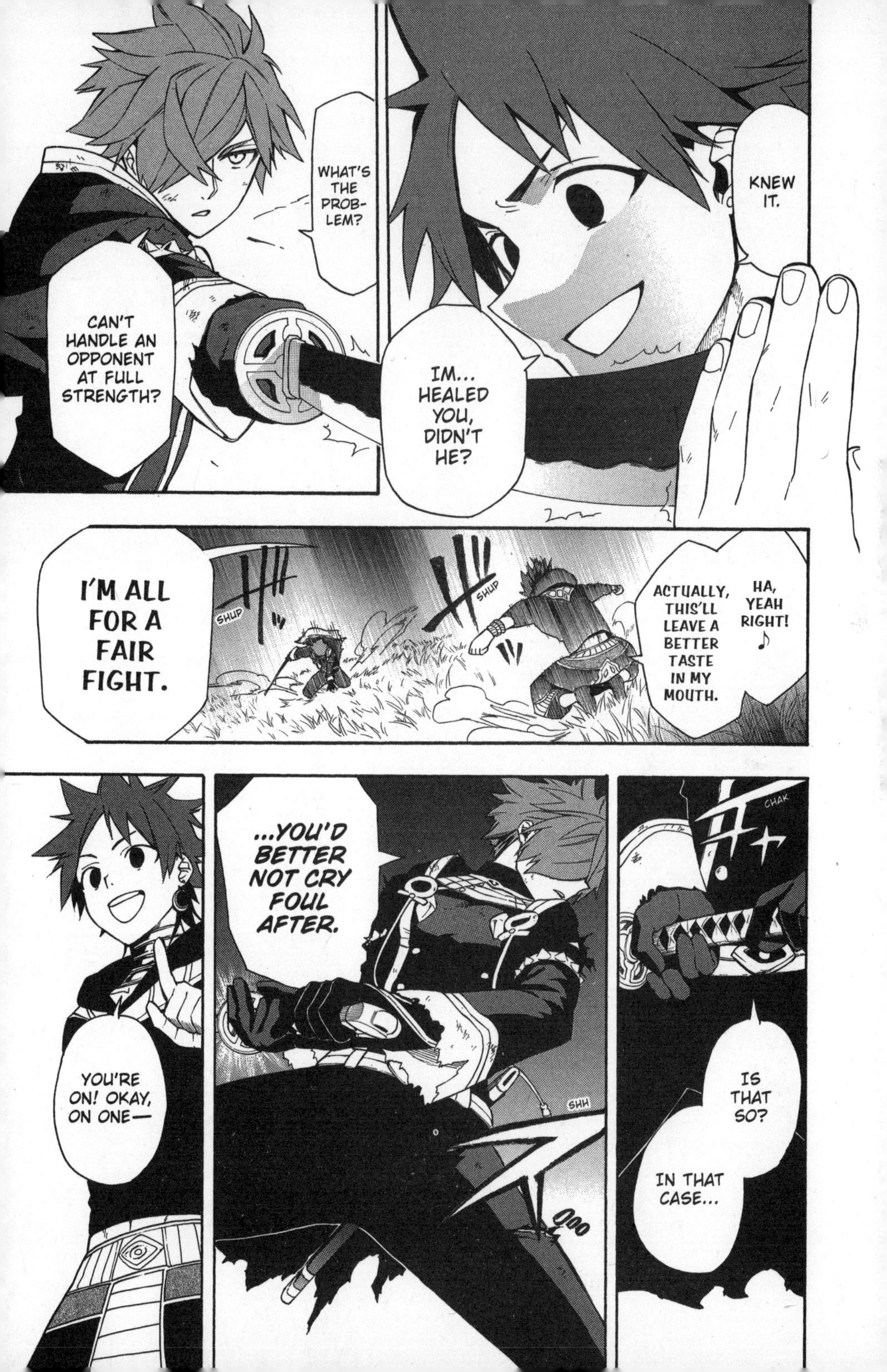
KNEW IT.
IM... HEALED YOU, DIDN'T HE?
WHAT'S THE PROB-LEM?
CAN'T HANDLE AN OPPONENT AT FULL STRENGTH?
HA, YEAH RIGHT! ♪
ACTUALLY, THIS'LL LEAVE A BETTER TASTE IN MY MOUTH.
SHUP
SHUP
I'M ALL FOR A FAIR FIGHT.
CHAK
IS THAT SO?
IN THAT CASE...
...YOU'D BETTER NOT CRY FOUL AFTER.
SHH
YOU'RE ON! OKAY, ON ONE—

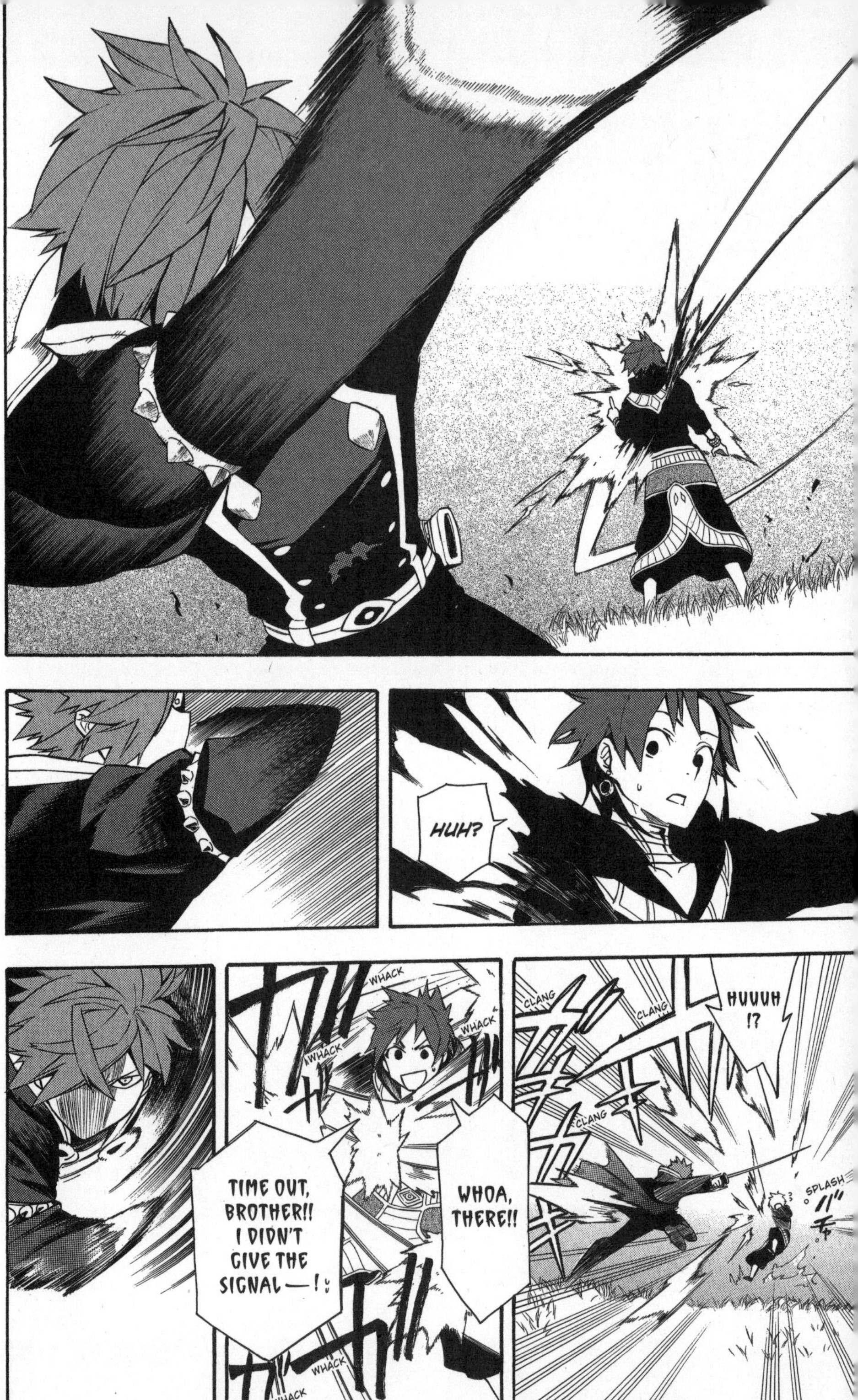
HUH?
HUUUH !?
CLANG
CLANG
CLANG
SPLASH
WHACK
WHACK
WHACK
WHOA, THERE!!
TIME OUT, BROTHER!! I DIDN'T GIVE THE SIGNAL—!
WHACK
WHACK

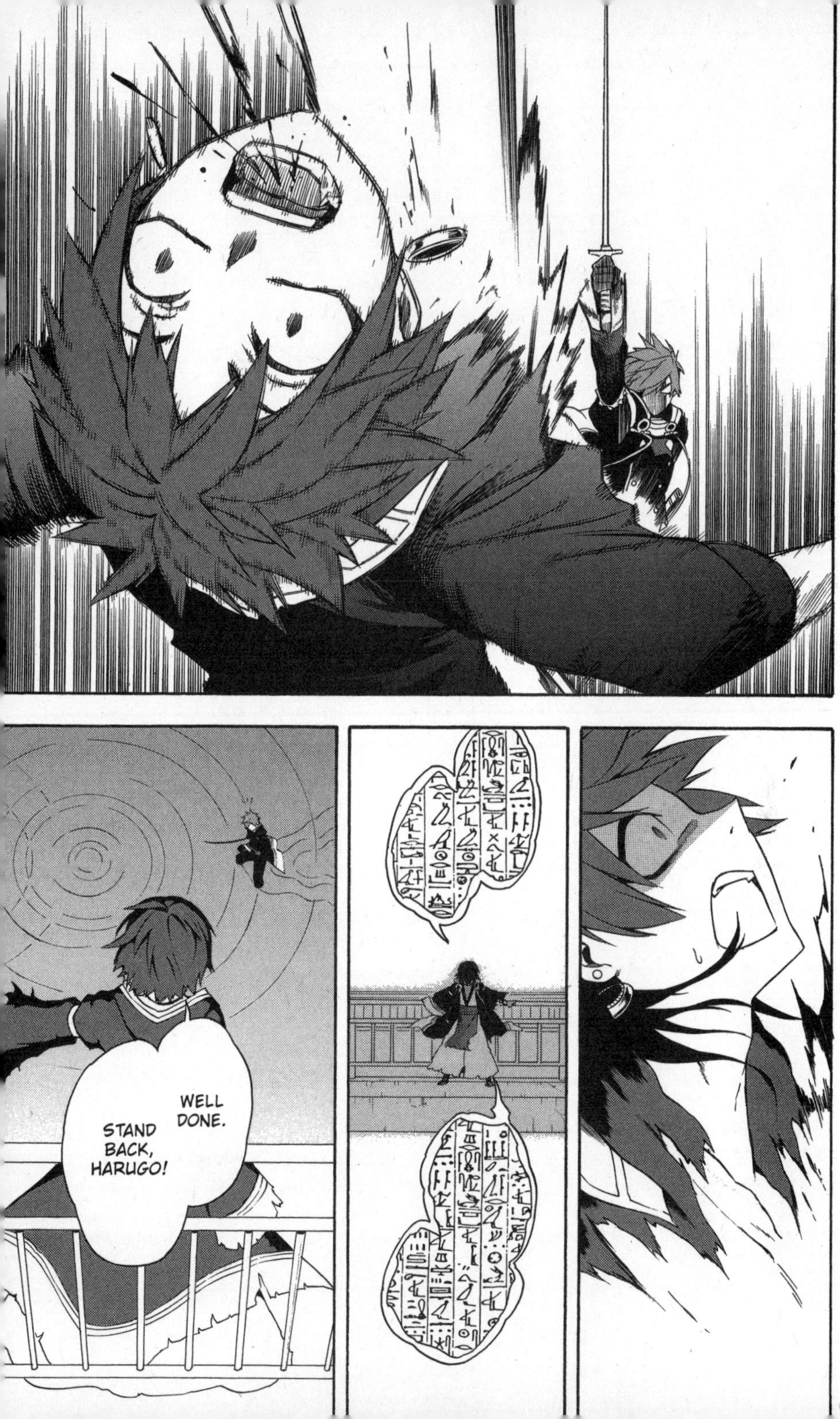
WELL DONE.
STAND BACK, HARUGO!

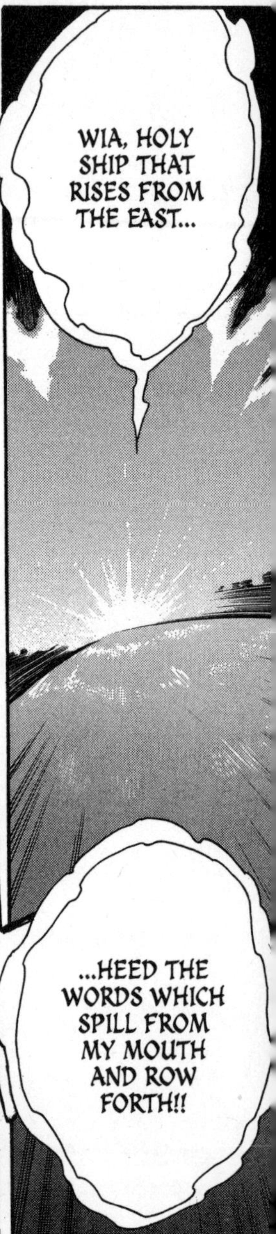
WIA, HOLY SHIP THAT RISES FROM THE EAST...
...HEED THE WORDS WHICH SPILL FROM MY MOUTH AND ROW FORTH!!
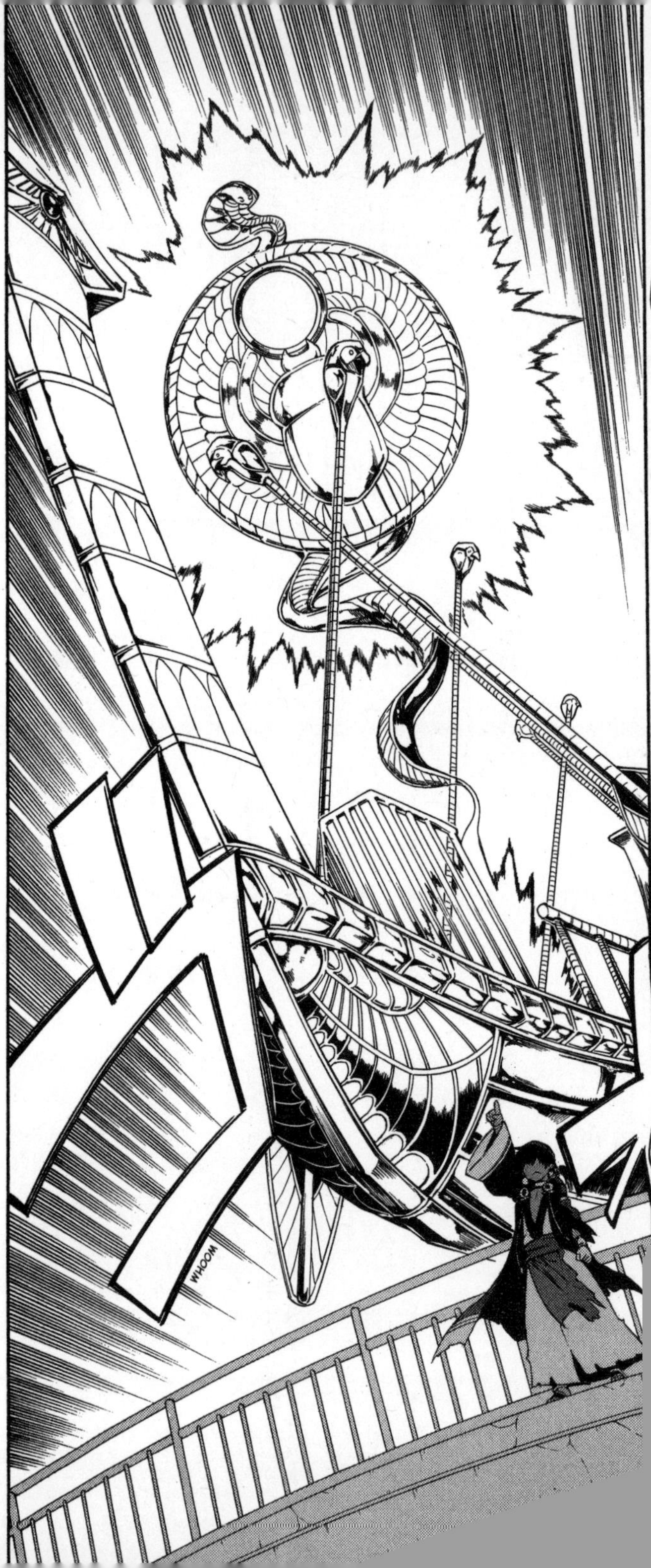
WHOOM

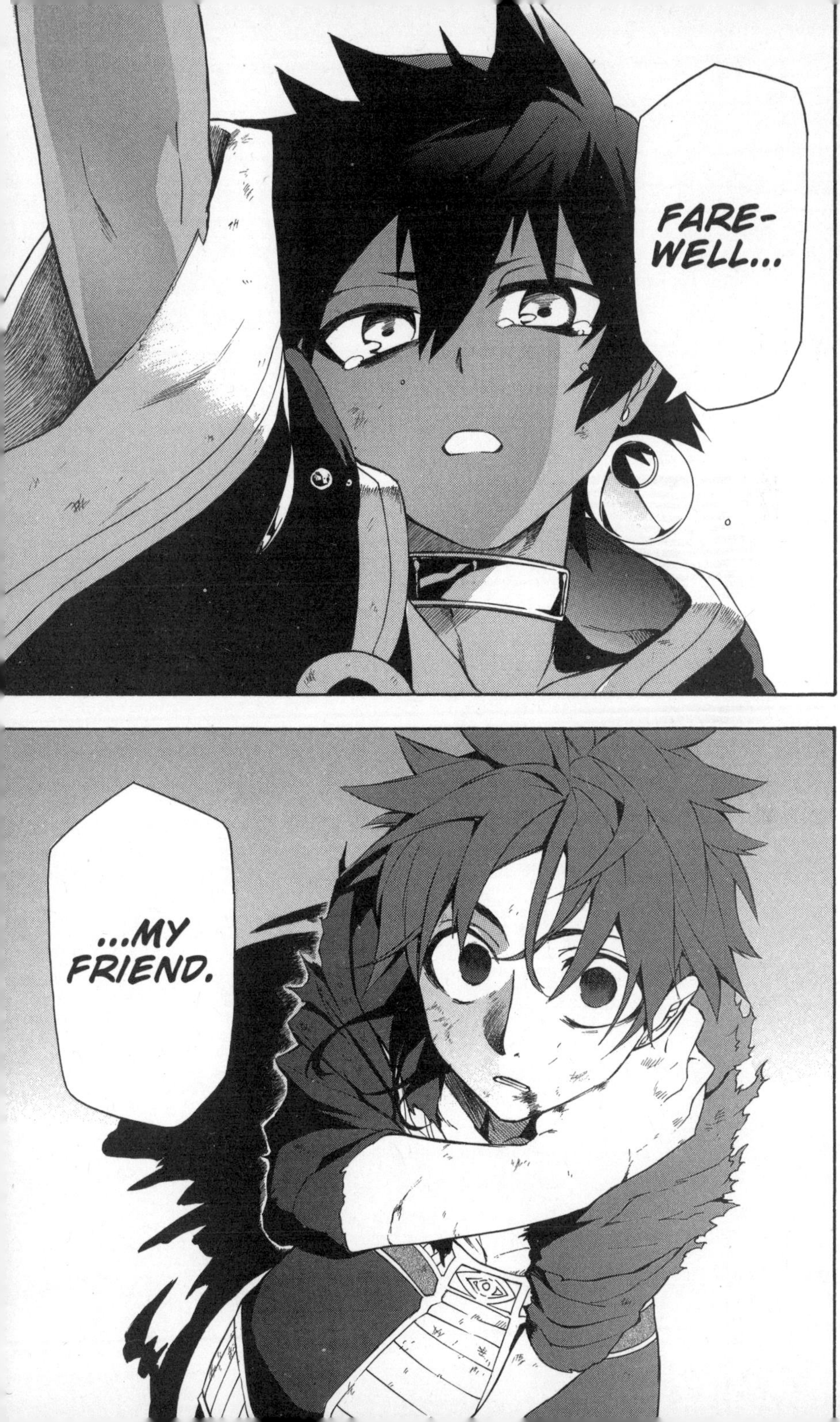
FARE-WELL...
...MY FRIEND.

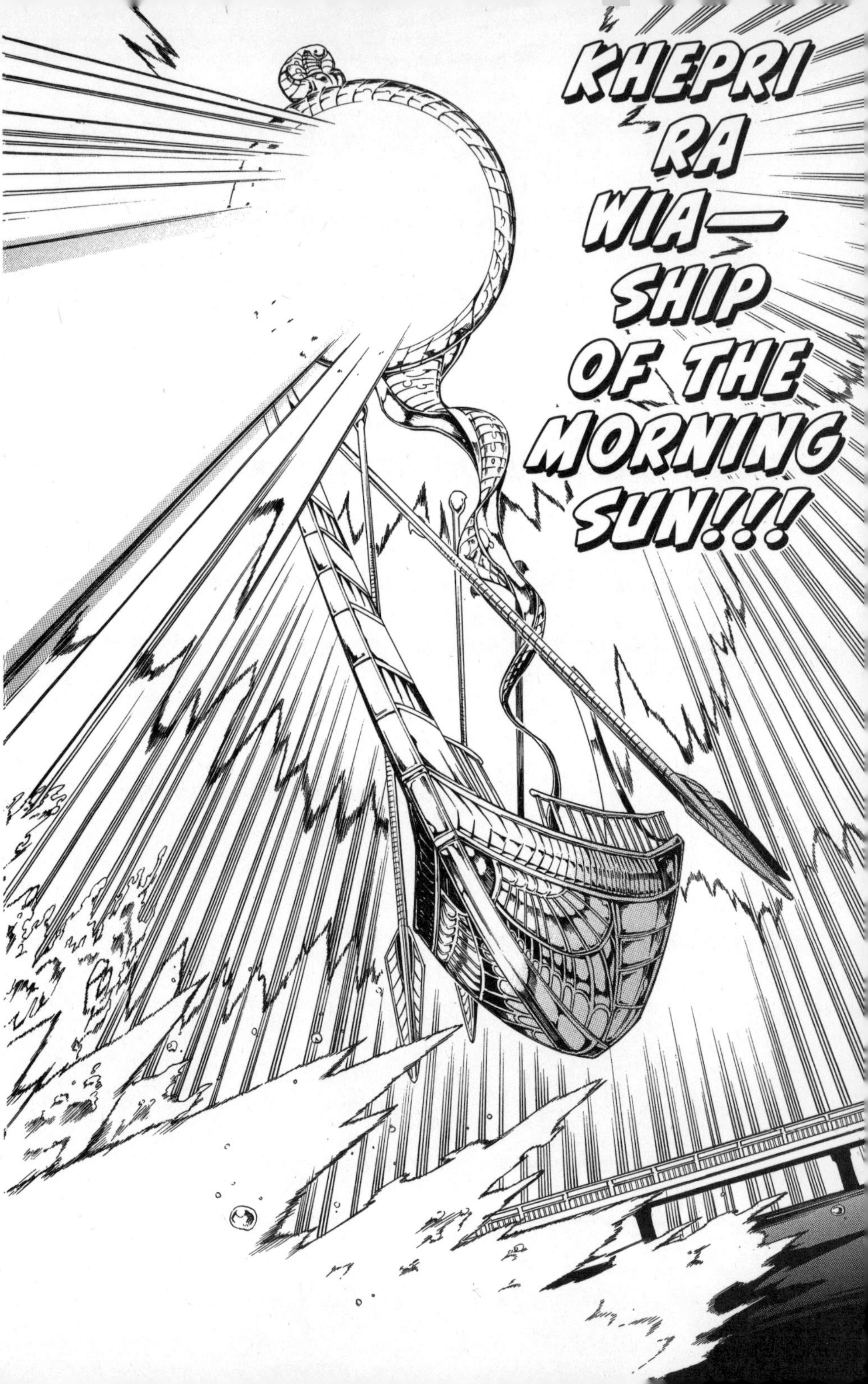
KHEPRI RA WIA—SHIP OF THE MORNING SUN!!!

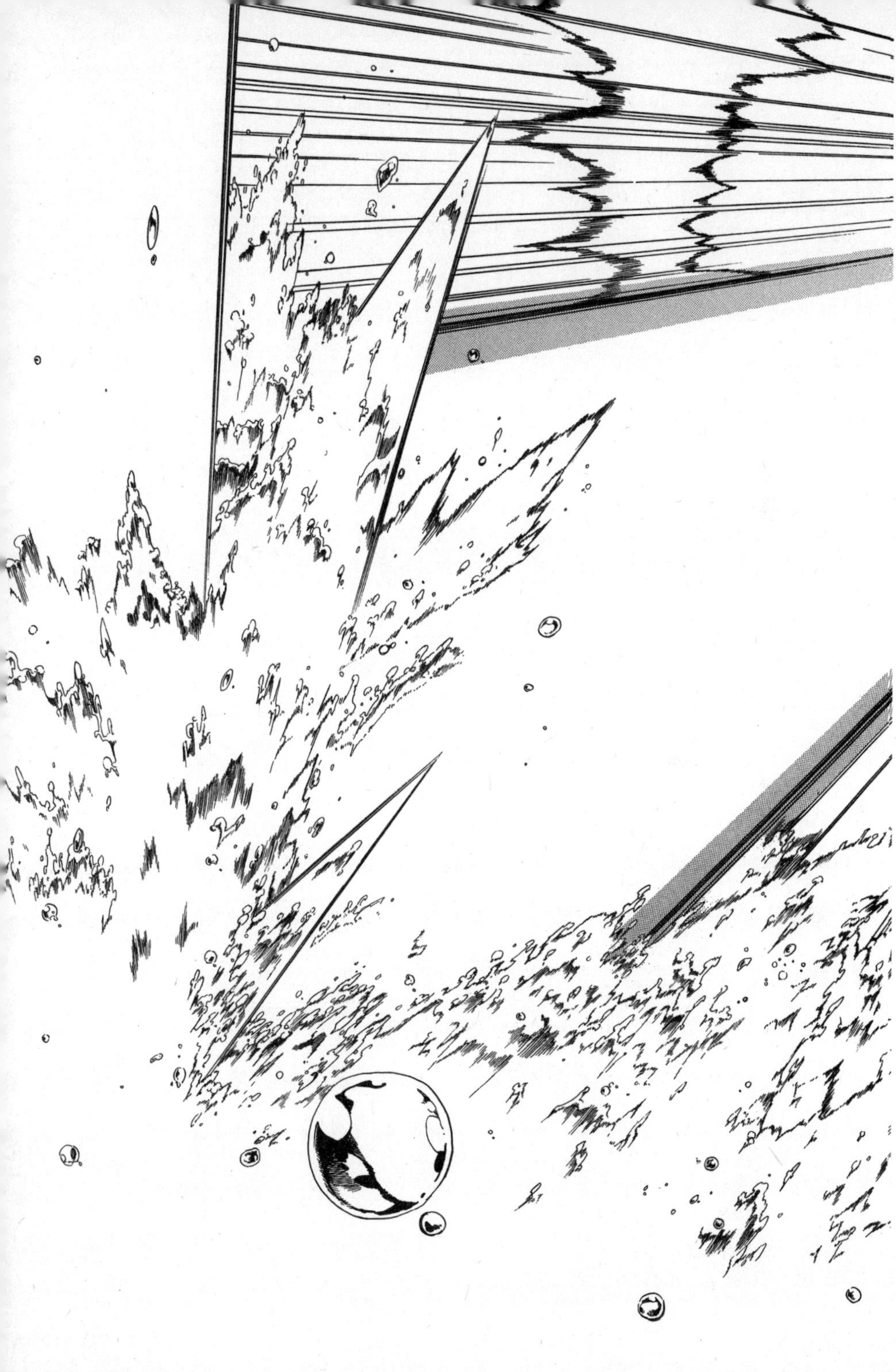

PSHOOM

I...

...M...

DID WE DO IT...!?

HFF!

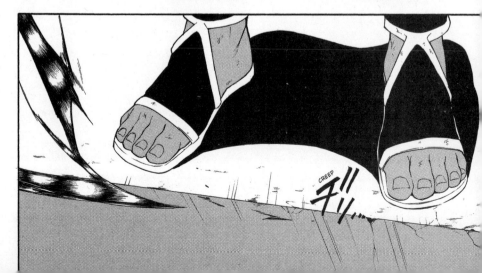

CREEP

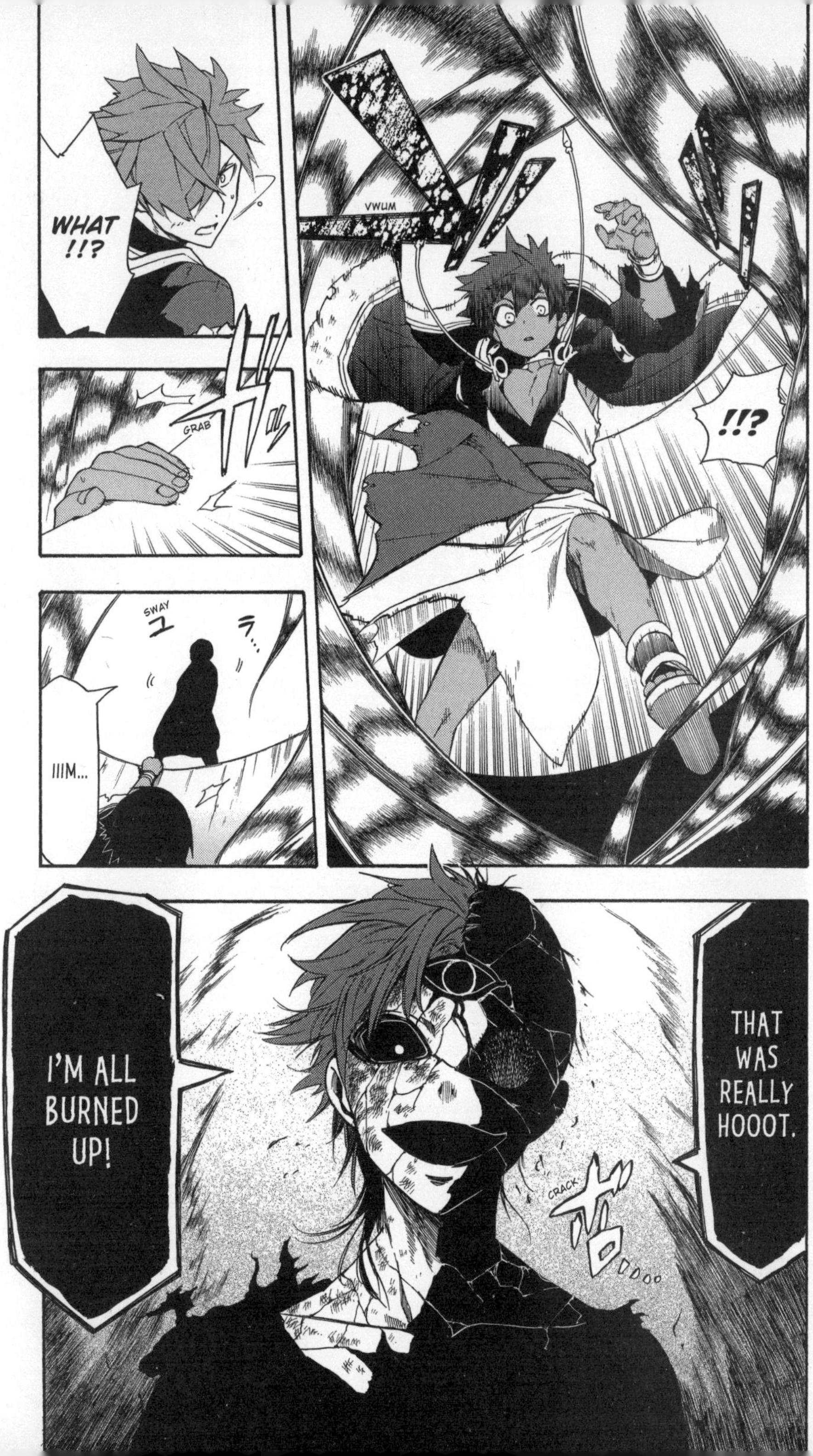
VWUM
!!?
WHAT !!?
GRAB
SWAY
IIIM...
THAT WAS REALLY HOOOT.
I'M ALL BURNED UP!
CRACK

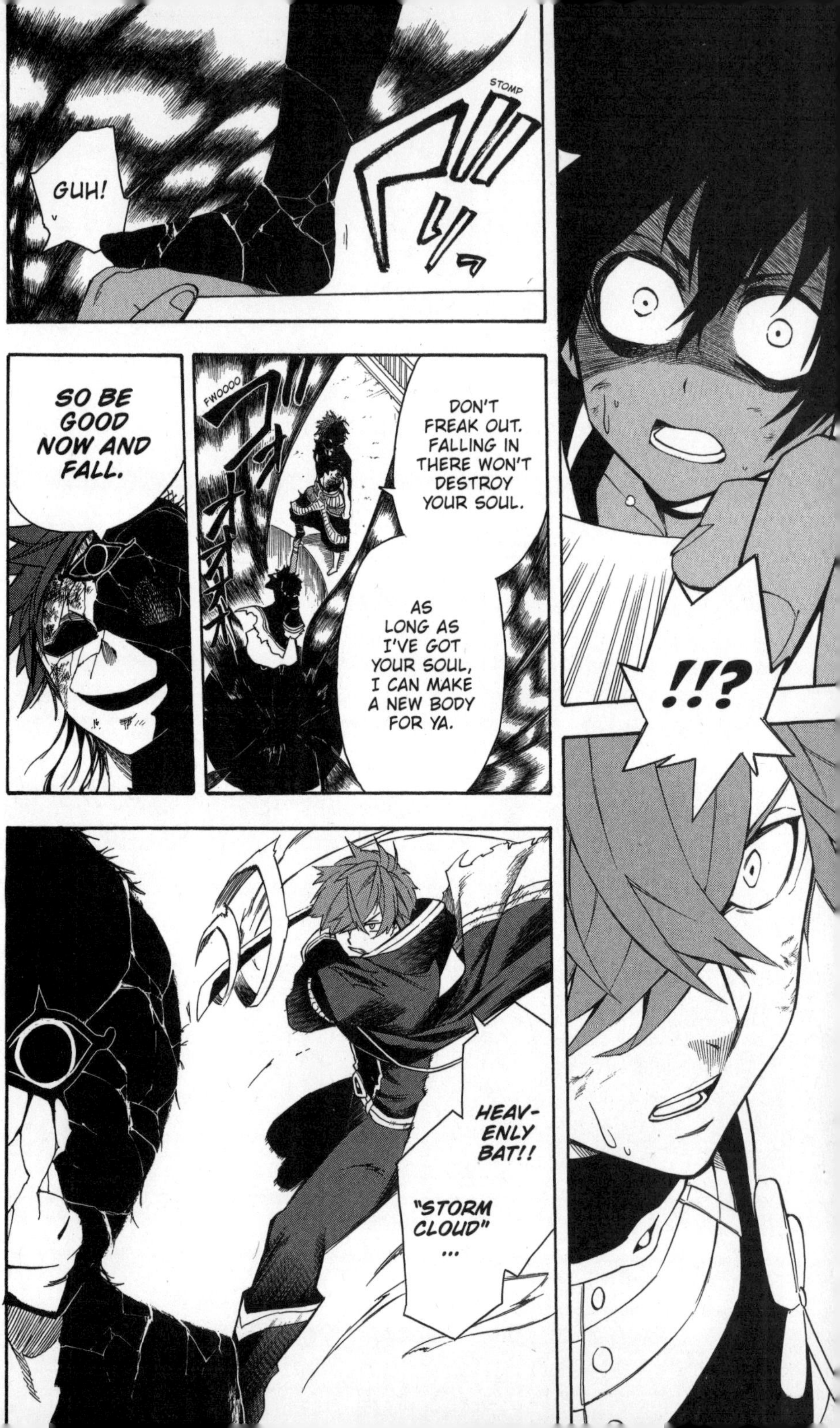
!!?
STOMP
GUH!
FWOOOO
DON'T FREAK OUT. FALLING IN THERE WON'T DESTROY YOUR SOUL.
AS LONG AS I'VE GOT YOUR SOUL, I CAN MAKE A NEW BODY FOR YA.
SO BE GOOD NOW AND FALL.
HEAV-ENLY BAT!!
"STORM CLOUD"
...

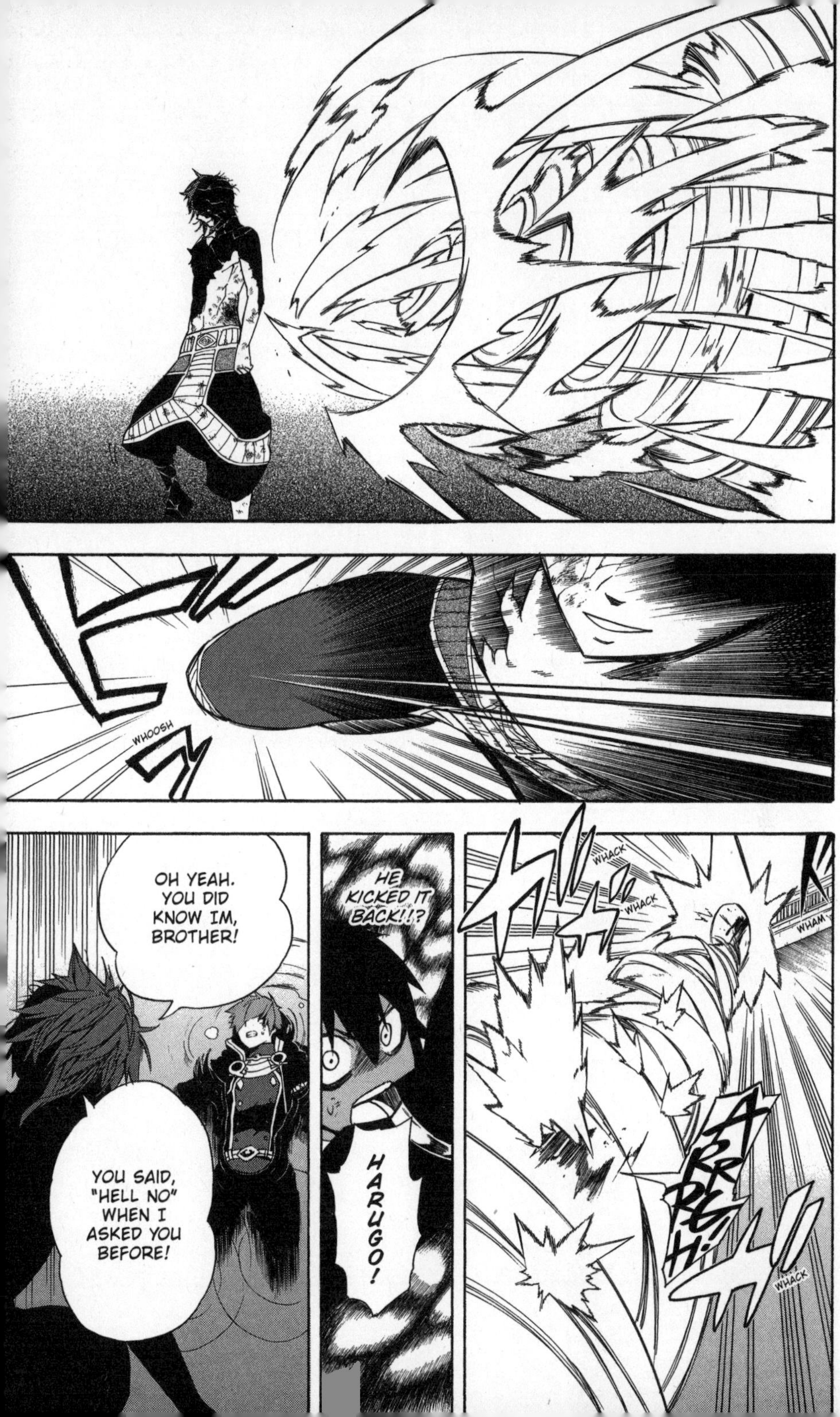
WHOOSH
WHACK
WHACK
WHAM
ARRGH!!
WHACK
HE KICKED IT BACK!!?
HARUGO!
OH YEAH. YOU DID KNOW IM, BROTHER!
YOU SAID, "HELL NO" WHEN I ASKED YOU BEFORE!

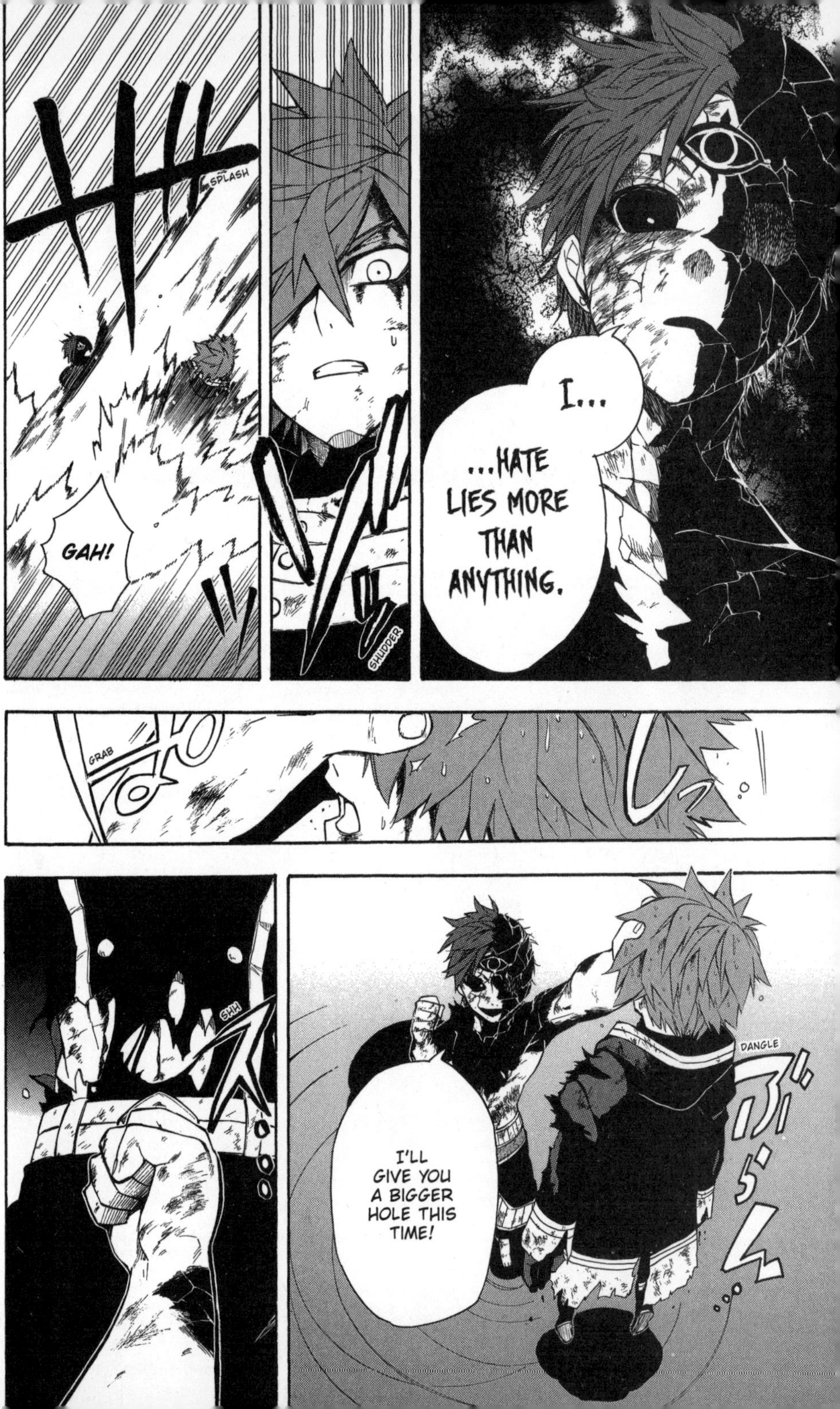
I...
...HATE LIES MORE THAN ANYTHING.
SHUDDER
SPLASH
GAH!
GRAB
DANGLE
I'LL GIVE YOU A BIGGER HOLE THIS TIME!
SHH

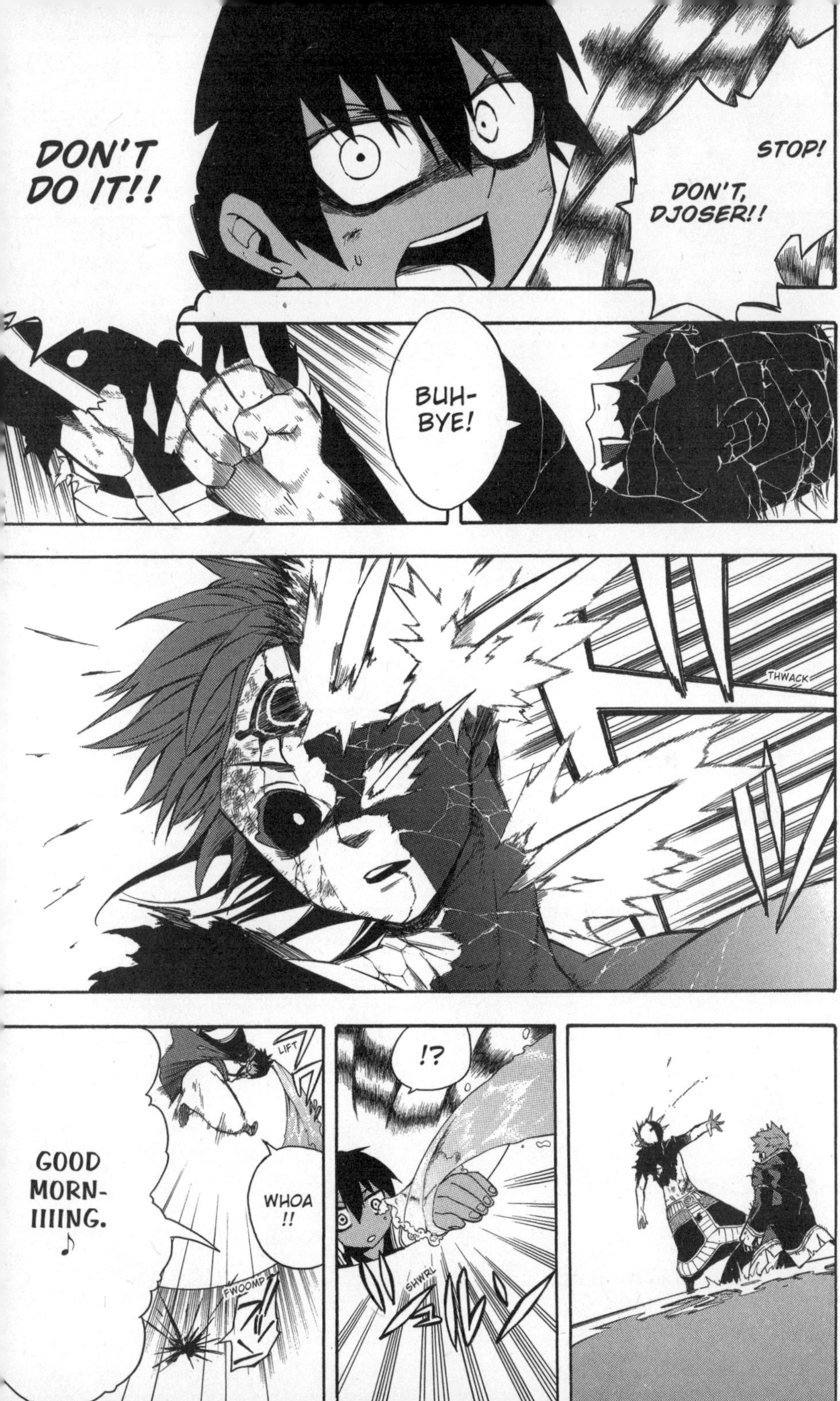
STOP!
DON'T, DJOSER!!
DON'T DO IT!!
BUH-BYE!
THWACK
!?
WHOA !!
SHWRL
LIFT
GOOD MORN-IIIING. ♪
FWOOMP

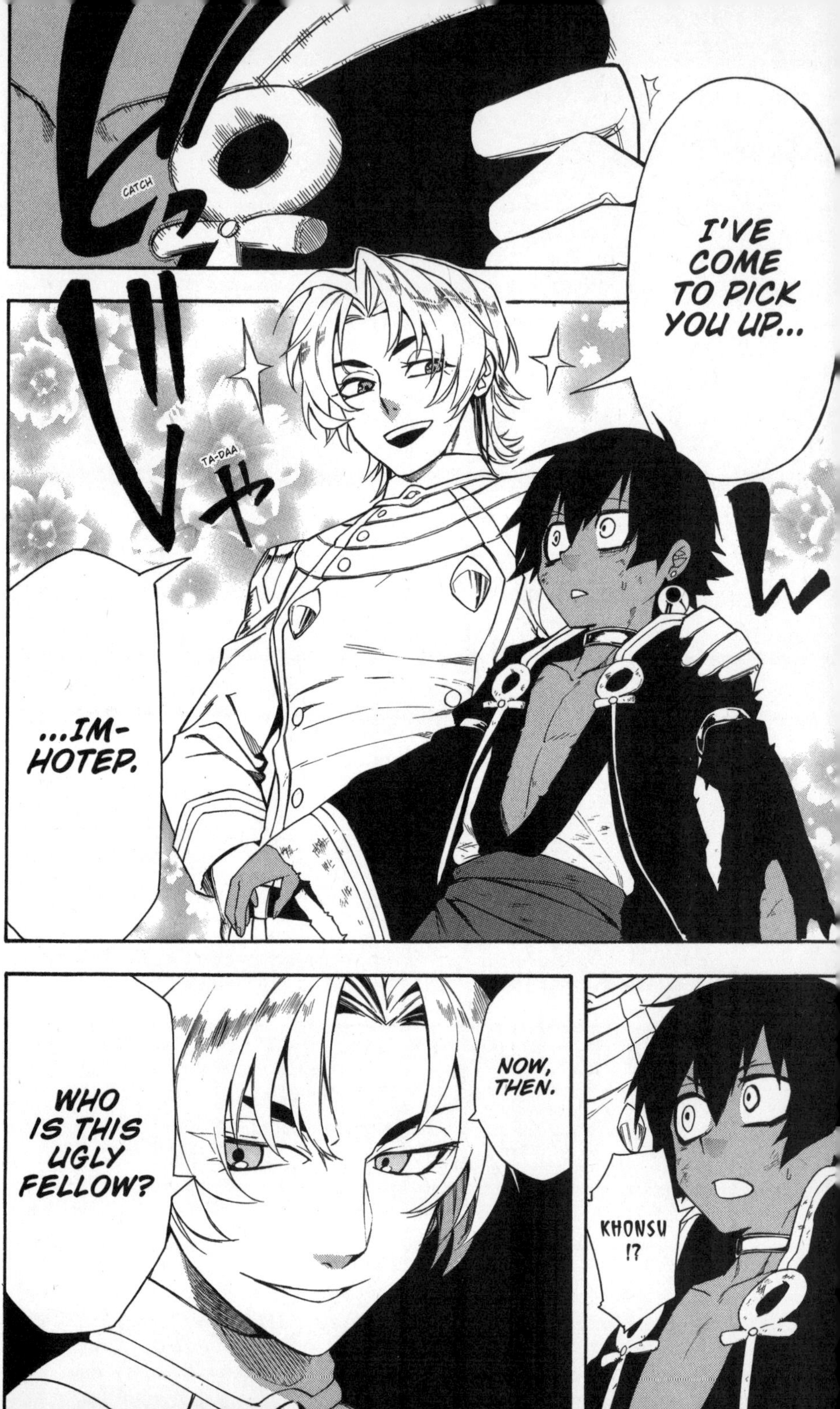
CATCH
I'VE COME TO PICK YOU UP...
TA-DAA
...IM-HOTEP.
KHONSU !?
NOW, THEN.
WHO IS THIS UGLY FELLOW?

Great Priest Imhotep

Great Priest Imhotep

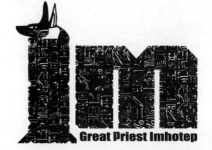

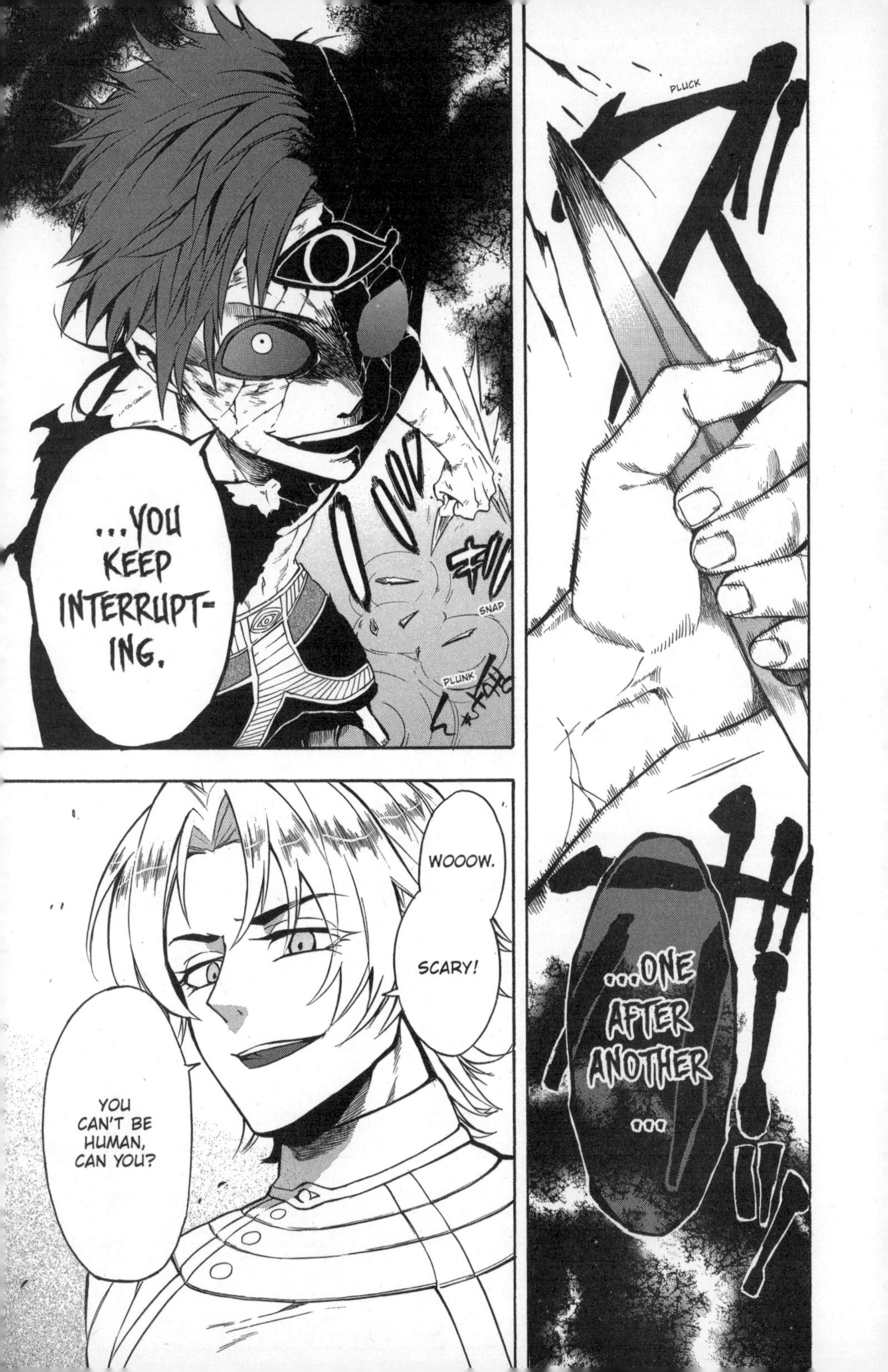
PLUCK
...ONE AFTER ANOTHER ...
SNAP
PLUNK
...YOU KEEP INTERRUPTING.
WOOOW.
SCARY!
YOU CAN'T BE HUMAN, CAN YOU?

SCROLL 10: WARRIORS OF AMEN

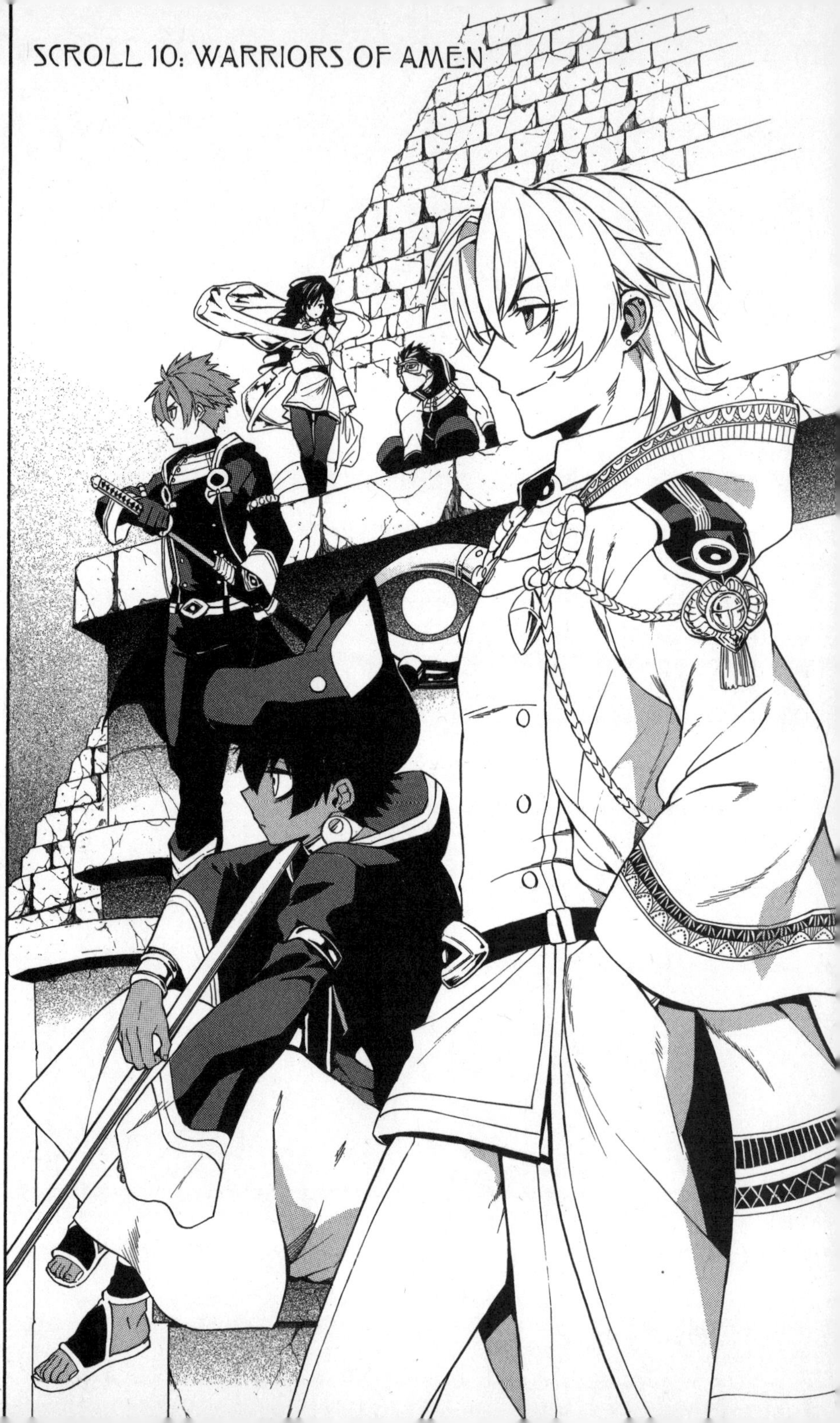

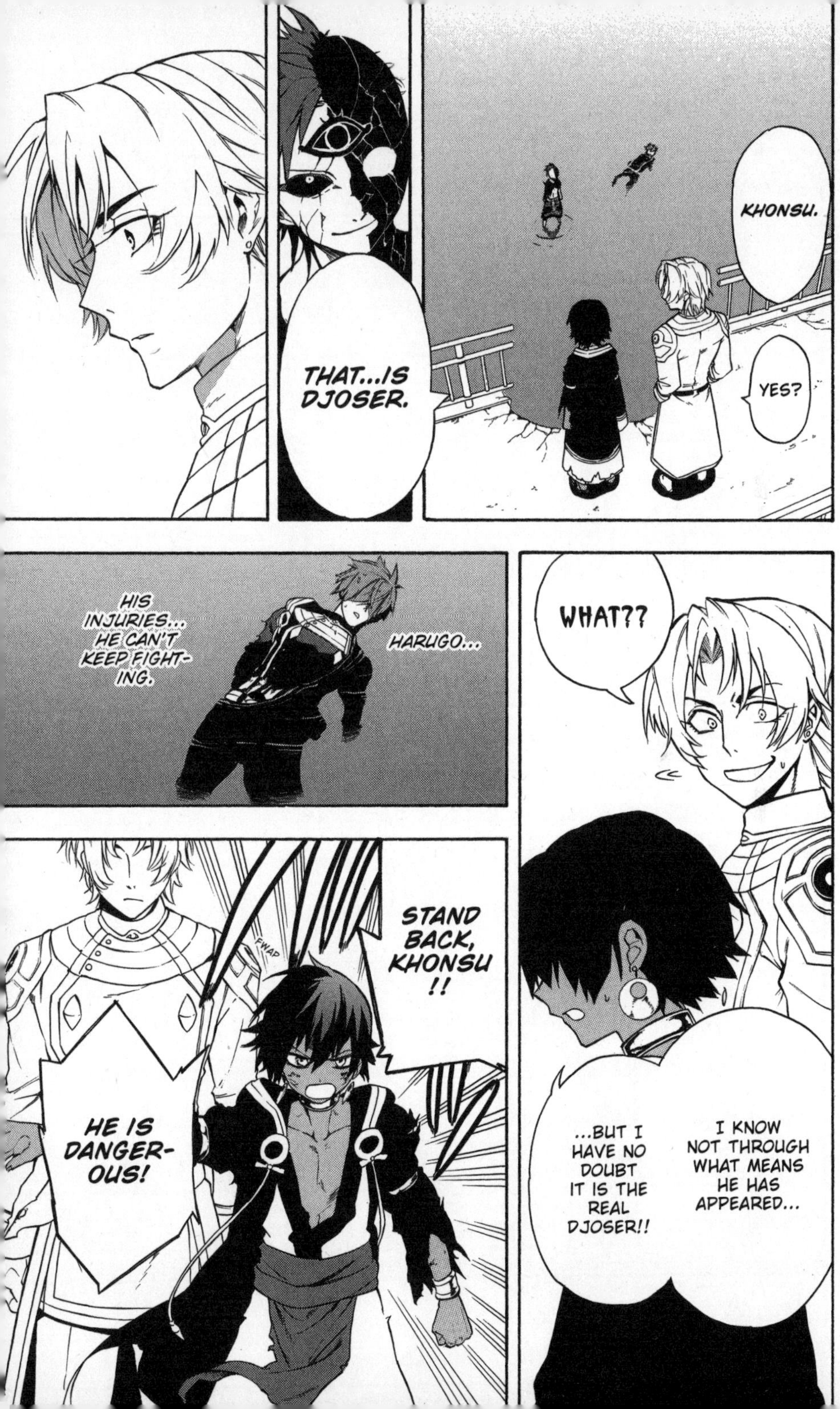
KHONSU.
YES?
THAT...IS DJOSER.
WHAT??
I KNOW NOT THROUGH WHAT MEANS HE HAS APPEARED...
...BUT I HAVE NO DOUBT IT IS THE REAL DJOSER!!
HARUGO...
HIS INJURIES... HE CAN'T KEEP FIGHT-ING.
STAND BACK, KHONSU!!
FWAP
HE IS DANGER-OUS!

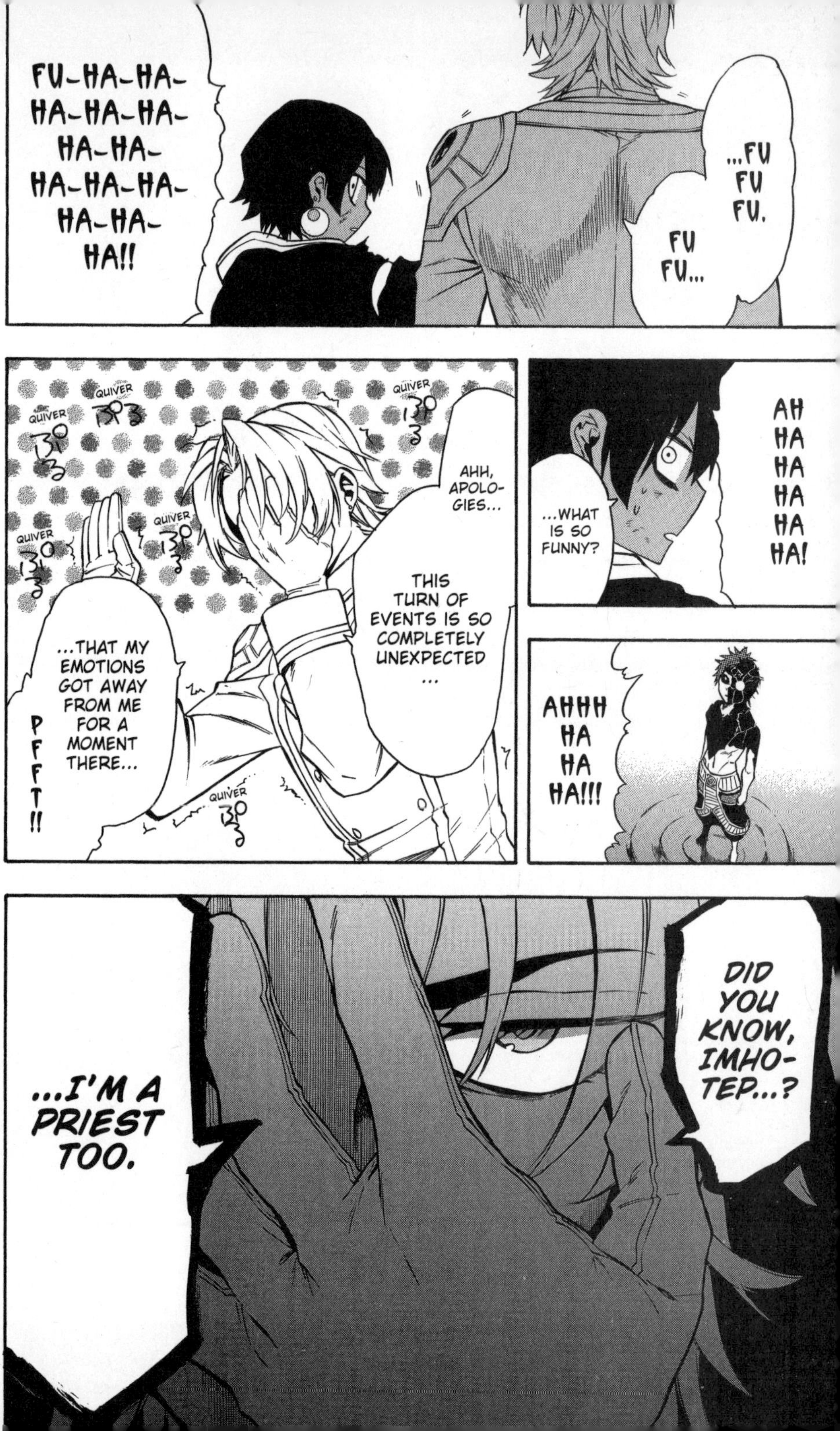
...FU FU FU.
FU FU...
FU-HA-HA-HA-HA-HA-HA-HA-HA-HA-HA-HA-HA-HA!!
AH HA HA HA HA HA!
...WHAT IS SO FUNNY?
AHHH HA HA HA!!!
QUIVER
QUIVER
QUIVER
AHH, APOLOGIES...
THIS TURN OF EVENTS IS SO COMPLETELY UNEXPECTED...
QUIVER
QUIVER
...THAT MY EMOTIONS GOT AWAY FROM ME FOR A MOMENT THERE...
PFFT!!
QUIVER
DID YOU KNOW, IMHOTEP...?
...I'M A PRIEST TOO.

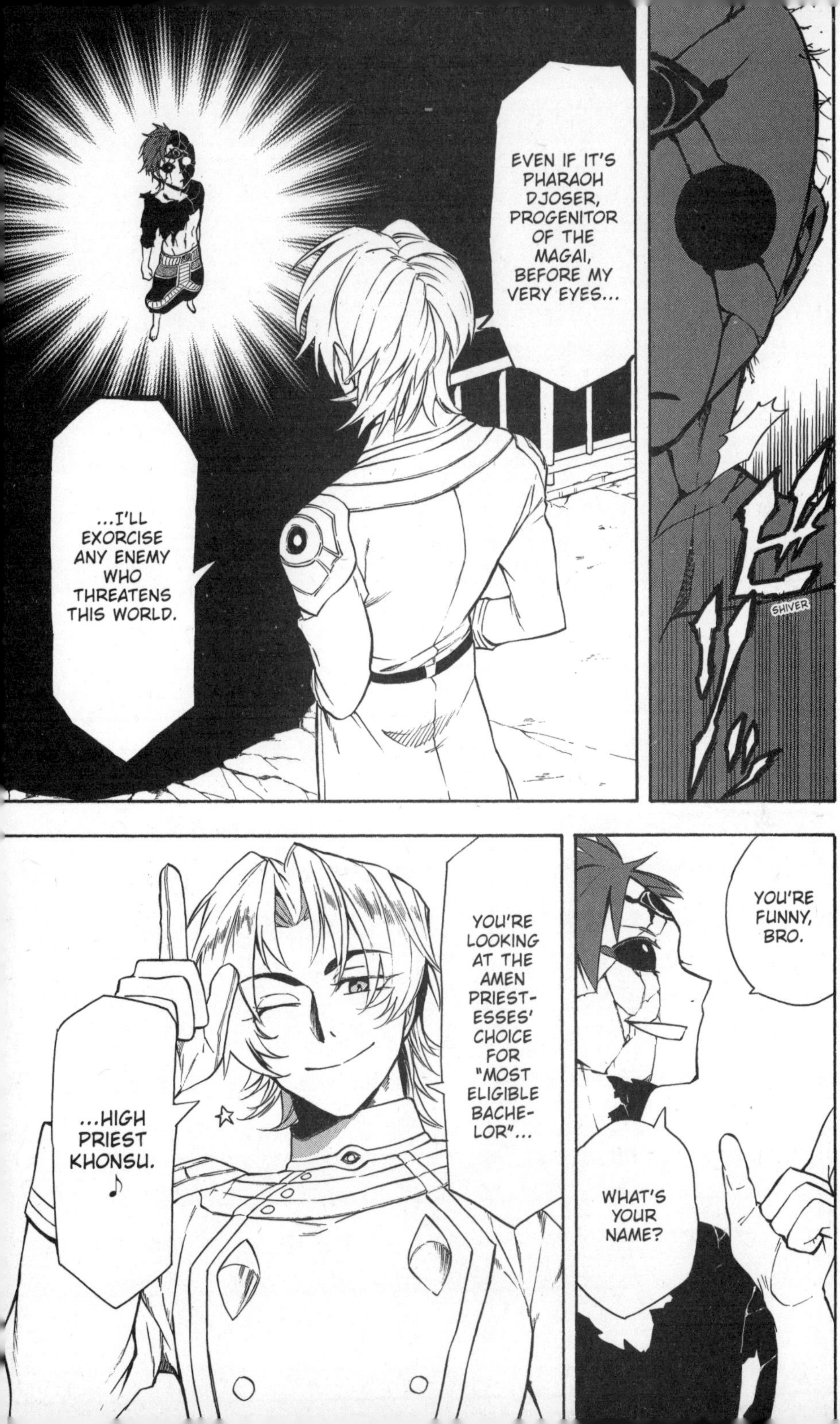
SHIVER
EVEN IF IT'S PHARAOH DJOSER, PROGENITOR OF THE MAGAI, BEFORE MY VERY EYES...
...I'LL EXORCISE ANY ENEMY WHO THREATENS THIS WORLD.
YOU'RE FUNNY, BRO.
WHAT'S YOUR NAME?
YOU'RE LOOKING AT THE AMEN PRIEST-ESSES' CHOICE FOR "MOST ELIGIBLE BACHE-LOR"...
...HIGH PRIEST KHONSU. ♪

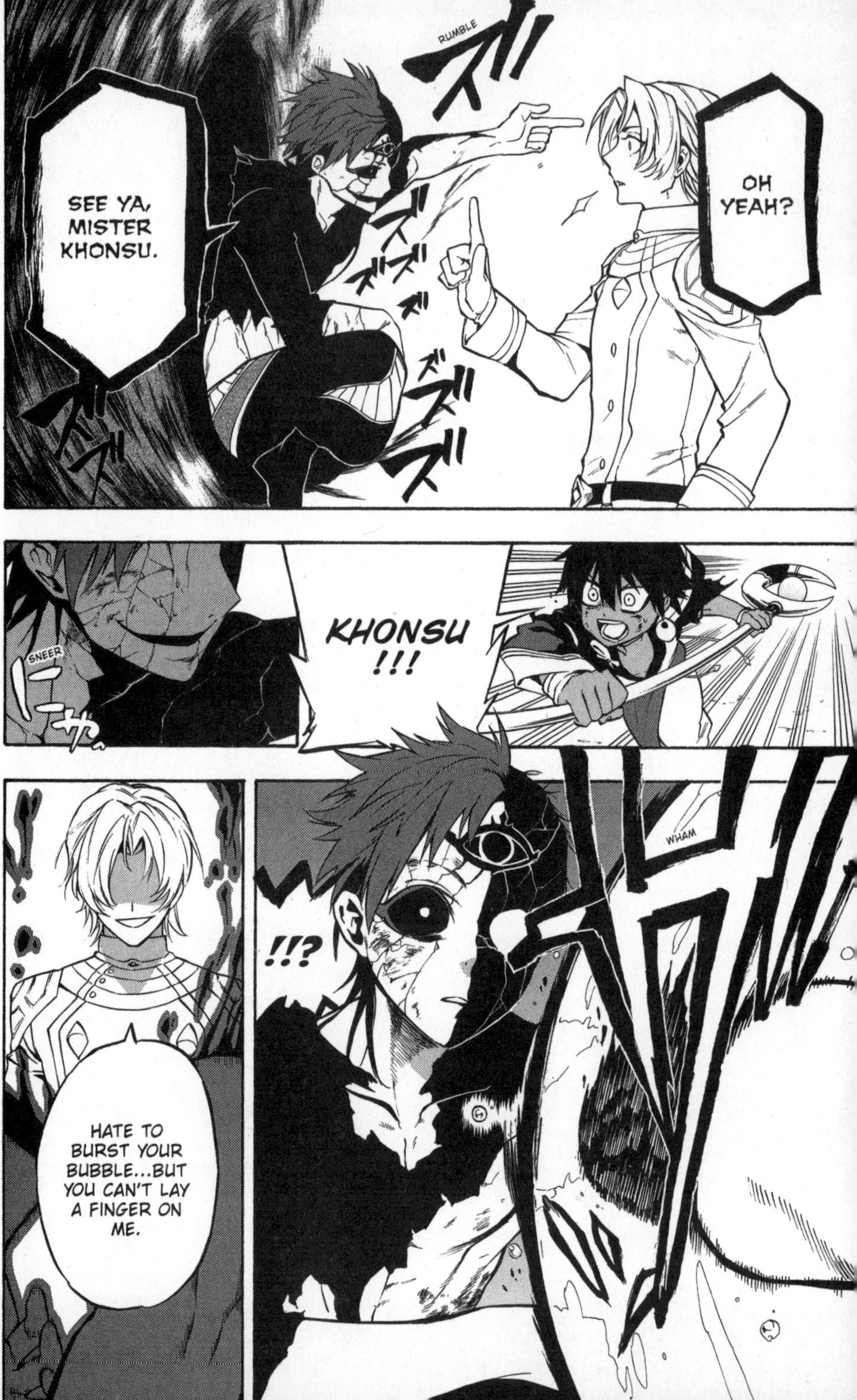
RUMBLE
OH YEAH?
SEE YA, MISTER KHONSU.
KHONSU!!!
SNEER
WHAM
!!?
HATE TO BURST YOUR BUBBLE...BUT YOU CAN'T LAY A FINGER ON ME.

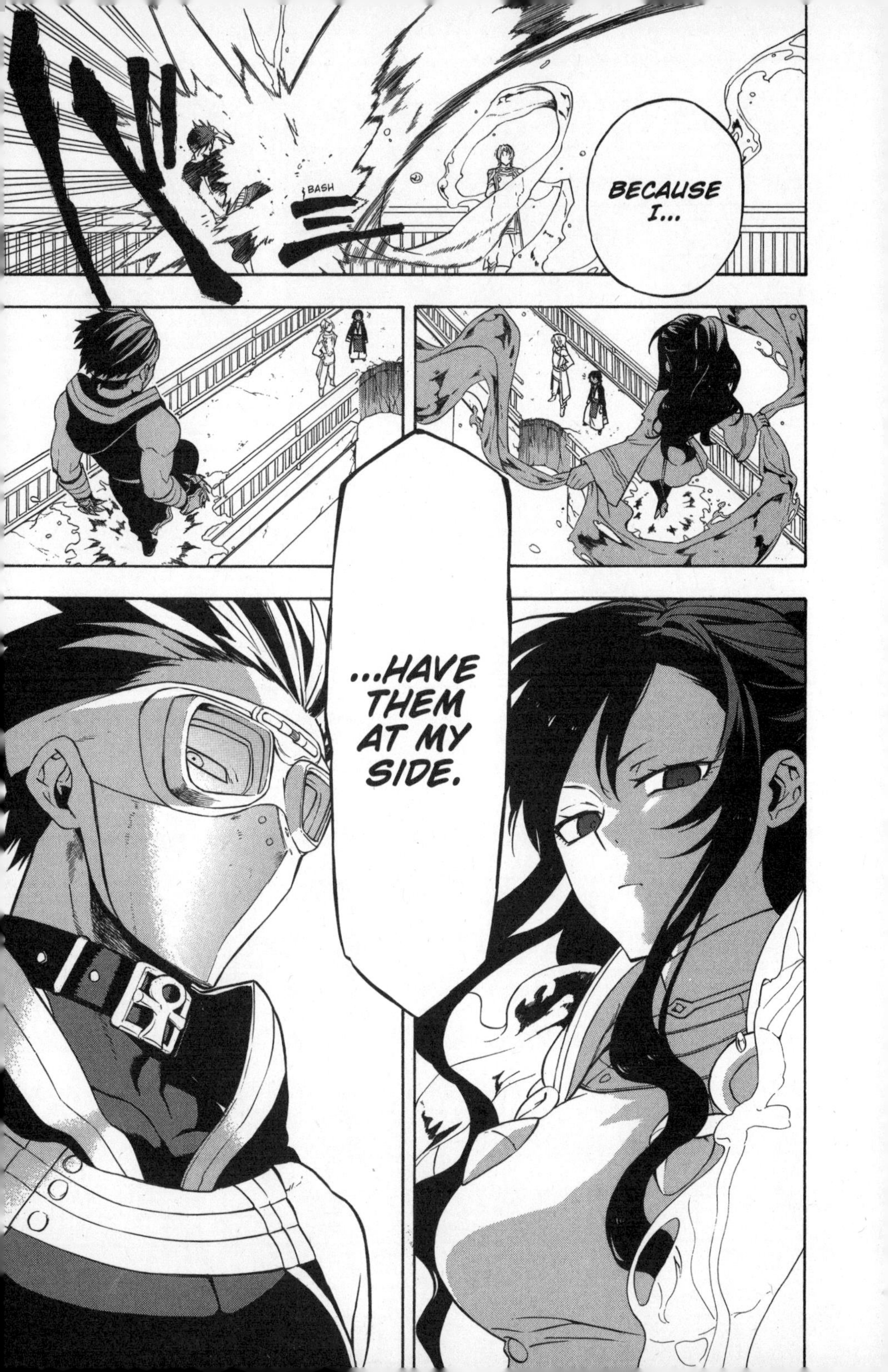
BASH
BECAUSE I...
...HAVE THEM AT MY SIDE.

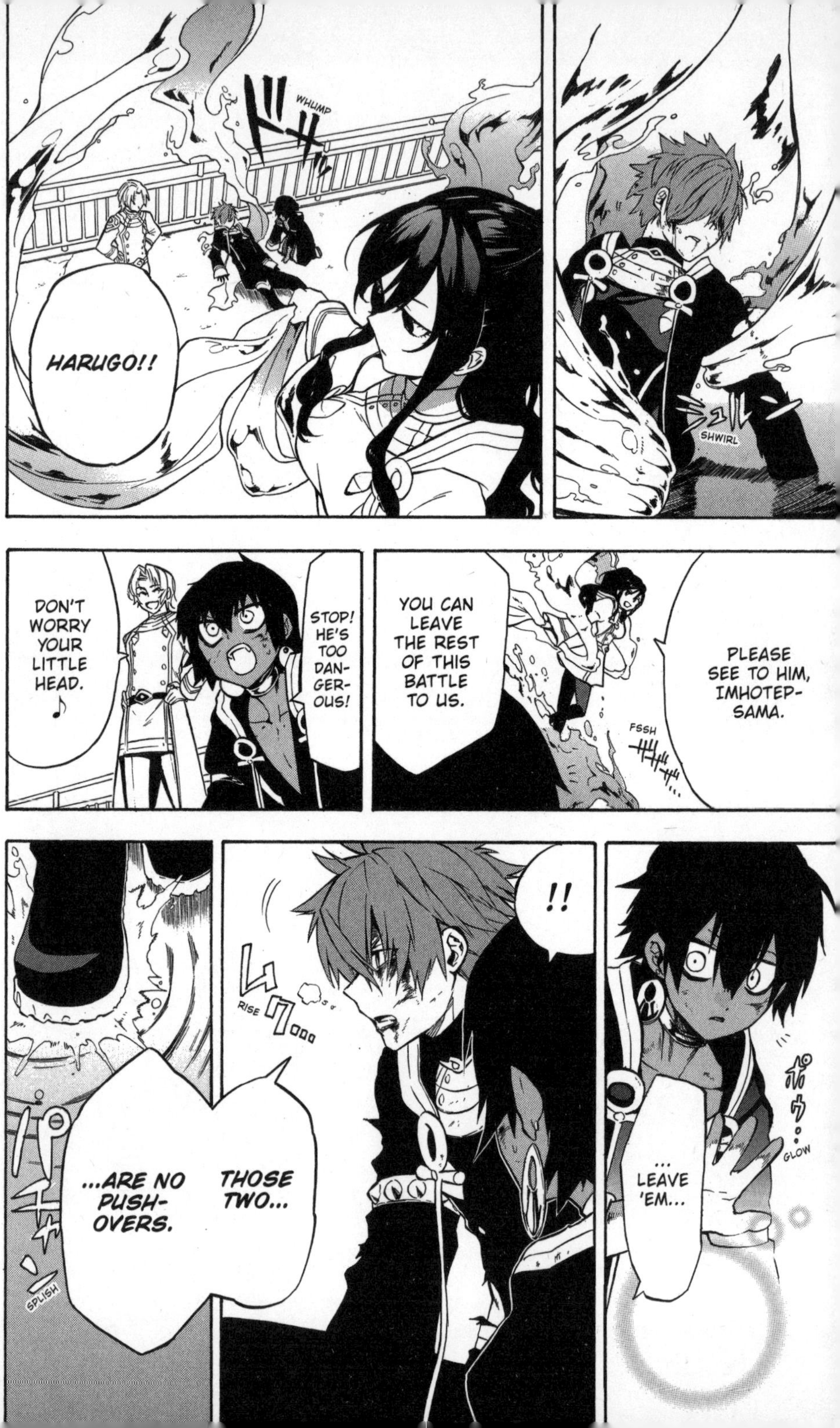
SHWIRL
WHUMP
HARUGO!!
PLEASE SEE TO HIM, IMHOTEP-SAMA.
FSSH
YOU CAN LEAVE THE REST OF THIS BATTLE TO US.
STOP! HE'S TOO DAN-GER-OUS!
DON'T WORRY YOUR LITTLE HEAD. ♪
GLOW
... LEAVE 'EM...
!!
RISE
THOSE TWO...
...ARE NO PUSH-OVERS.
SPLISH

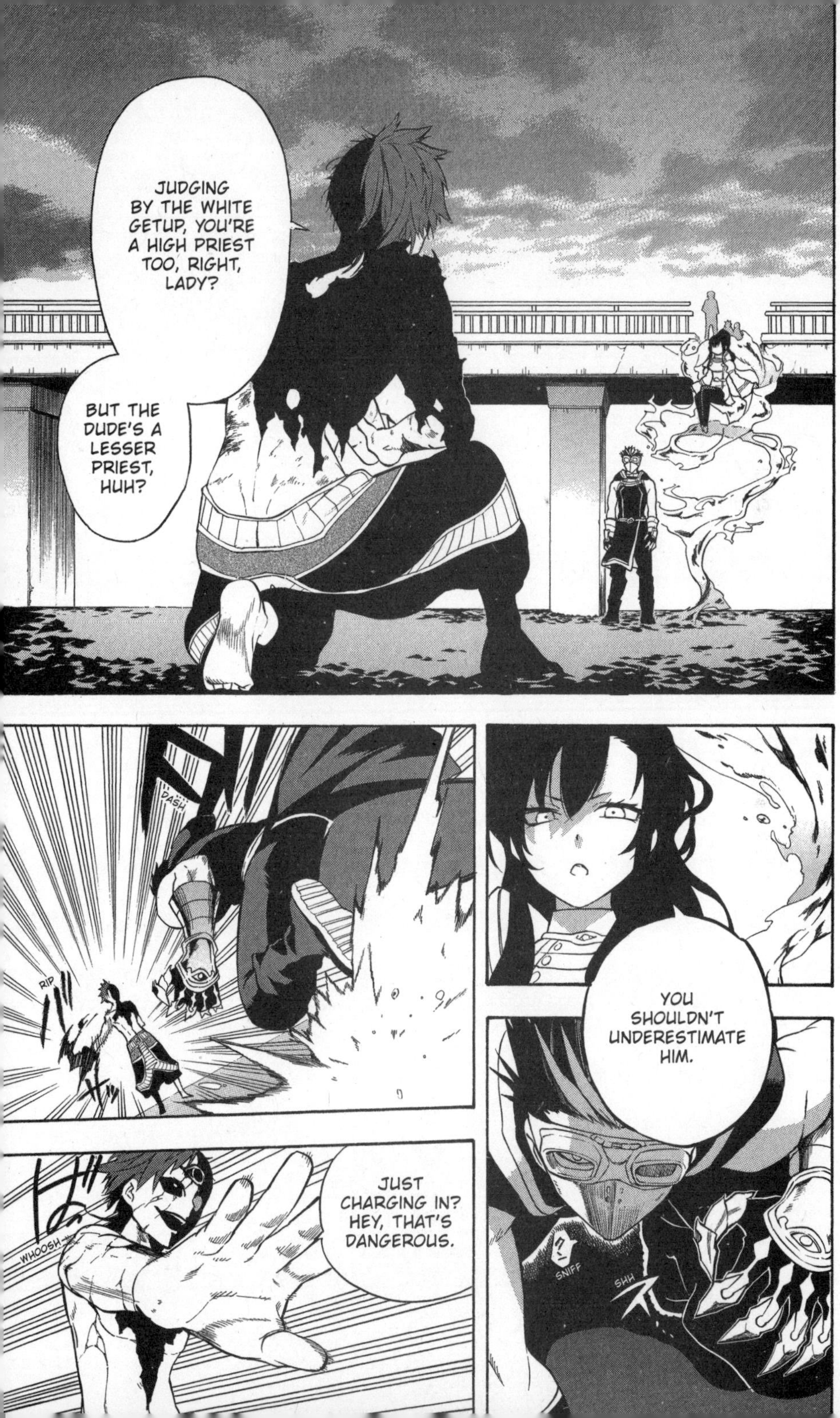
JUDGING BY THE WHITE GETUP, YOU'RE A HIGH PRIEST TOO, RIGHT, LADY?
BUT THE DUDE'S A LESSER PRIEST, HUH?
YOU SHOULDN'T UNDERESTIMATE HIM.
DASH
RIP
SNIFF
SHH
JUST CHARGING IN? HEY, THAT'S DANGEROUS.
WHOOSH

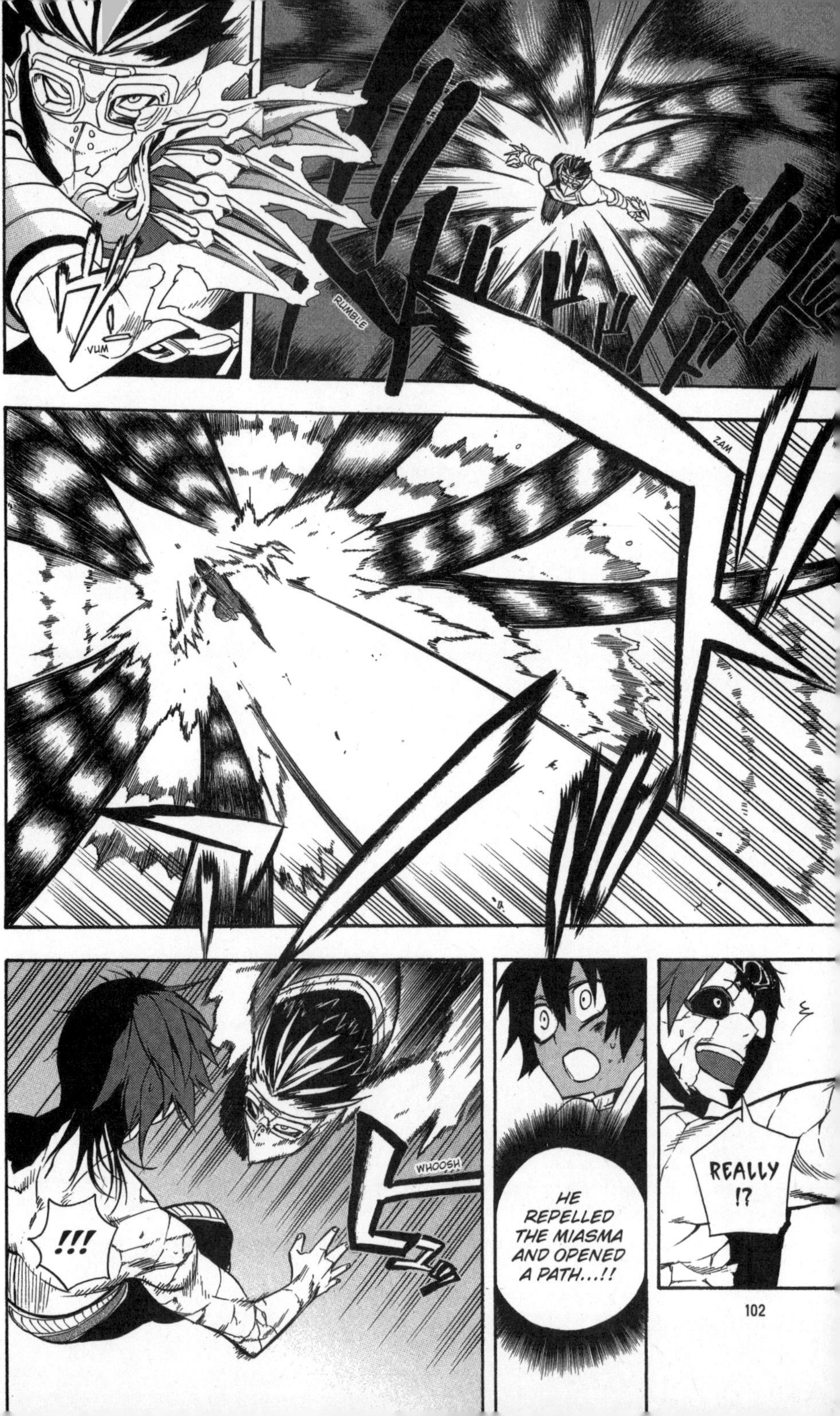
RUMBLE
VUM
ZAM
REALLY !?
HE REPELLED THE MIASMA AND OPENED A PATH...!!
WHOOSH
!!!

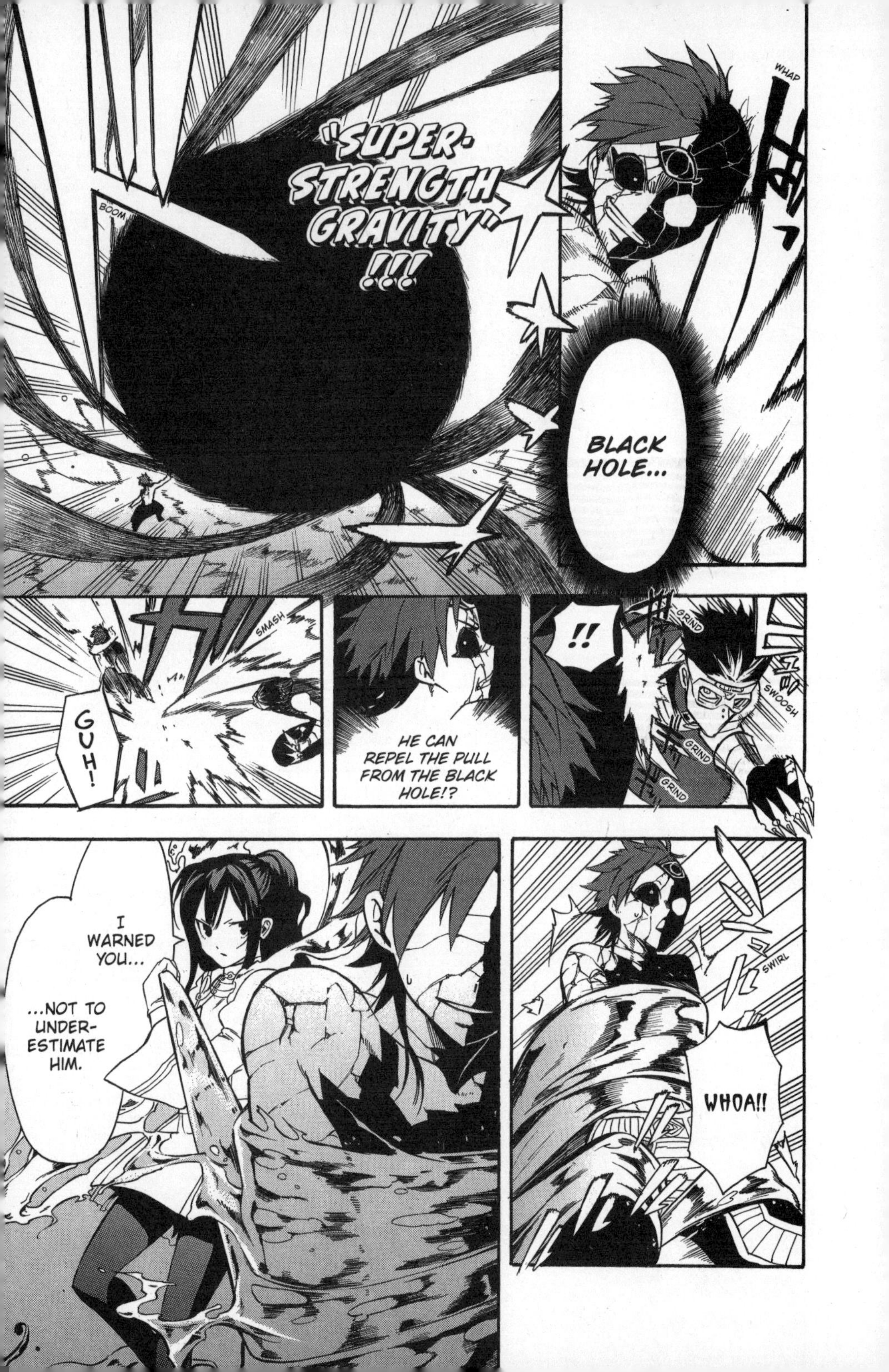
WHAP
BLACK HOLE...
"SUPER-STRENGTH GRAVITY"!!!
BOOM
!!
GRIND
SWOOSH
GRIND
GRIND
HE CAN REPEL THE PULL FROM THE BLACK HOLE!?
SMASH
GUH!
SWIRL
WHOA!!
I WARNED YOU...
...NOT TO UNDER-ESTIMATE HIM.

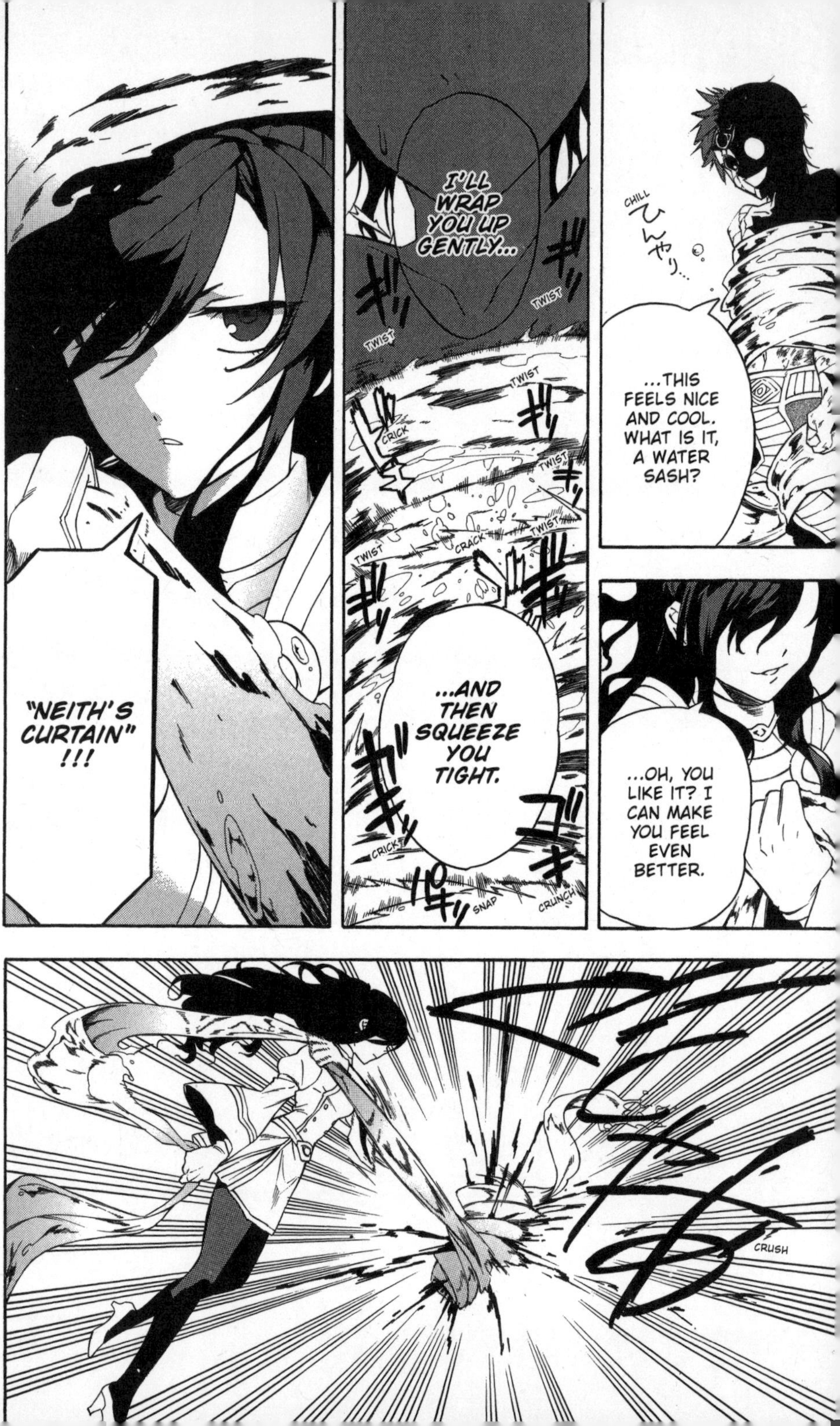
CHILL
ひんやり…
...THIS FEELS NICE AND COOL. WHAT IS IT, A WATER SASH?
...OH, YOU LIKE IT? I CAN MAKE YOU FEEL EVEN BETTER.
I'LL WRAP YOU UP GENTLY...
TWIST
TWIST
TWIST
CRICK
TWIST
TWIST
CRACK
TWIST
...AND THEN SQUEEZE YOU TIGHT.
CRICK
SNAP
CRUNCH
"NEITH'S CURTAIN"!!!
CRUSH

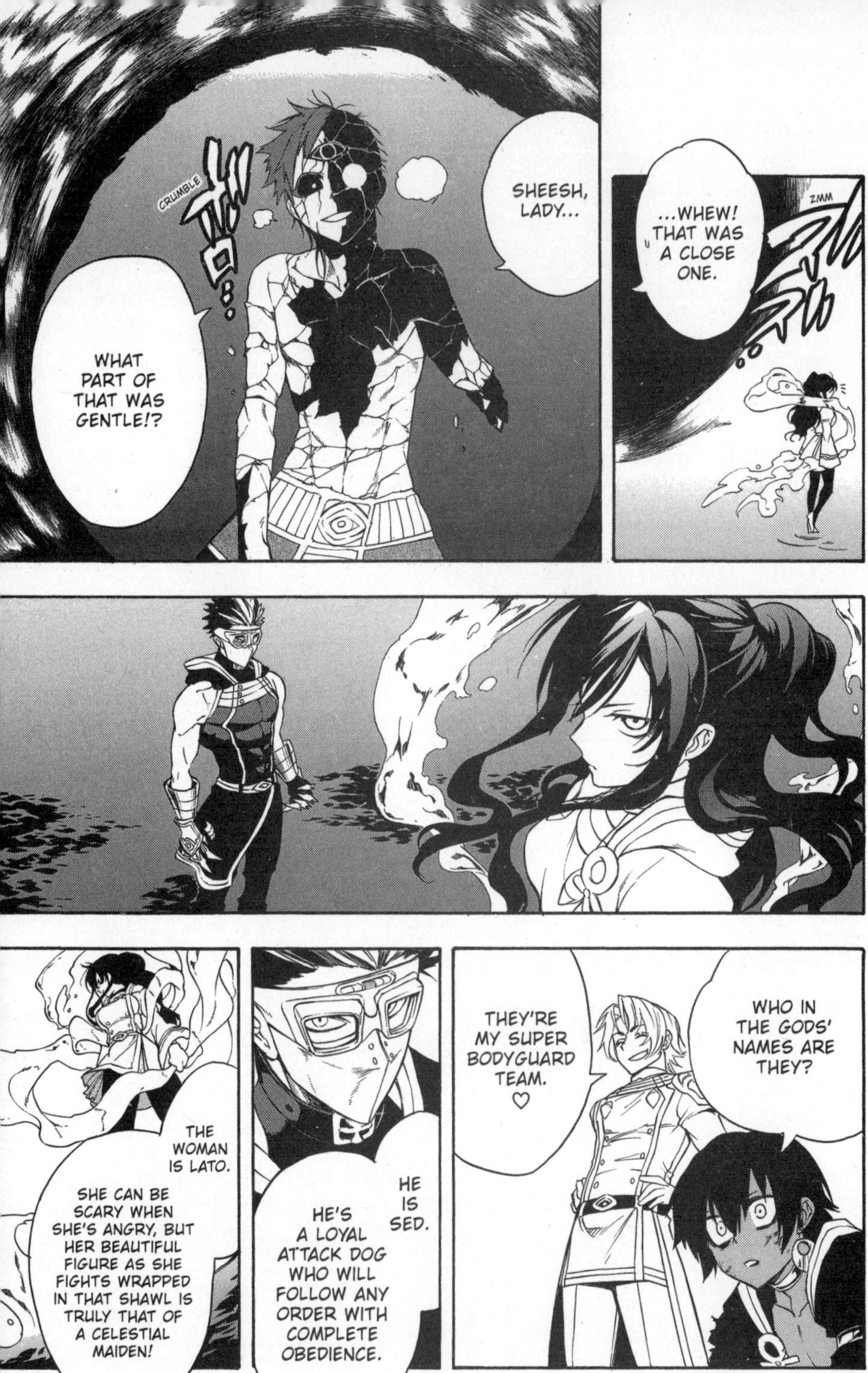
...WHEW! THAT WAS A CLOSE ONE.
ZMM
SHEESH, LADY...
CRUMBLE
WHAT PART OF THAT WAS GENTLE!?
WHO IN THE GODS' NAMES ARE THEY?
THEY'RE MY SUPER BODYGUARD TEAM. ♡
HE IS SED.
HE'S A LOYAL ATTACK DOG WHO WILL FOLLOW ANY ORDER WITH COMPLETE OBEDIENCE.
THE WOMAN IS LATO.
SHE CAN BE SCARY WHEN SHE'S ANGRY, BUT HER BEAUTIFUL FIGURE AS SHE FIGHTS WRAPPED IN THAT SHAWL IS TRULY THAT OF A CELESTIAL MAIDEN!

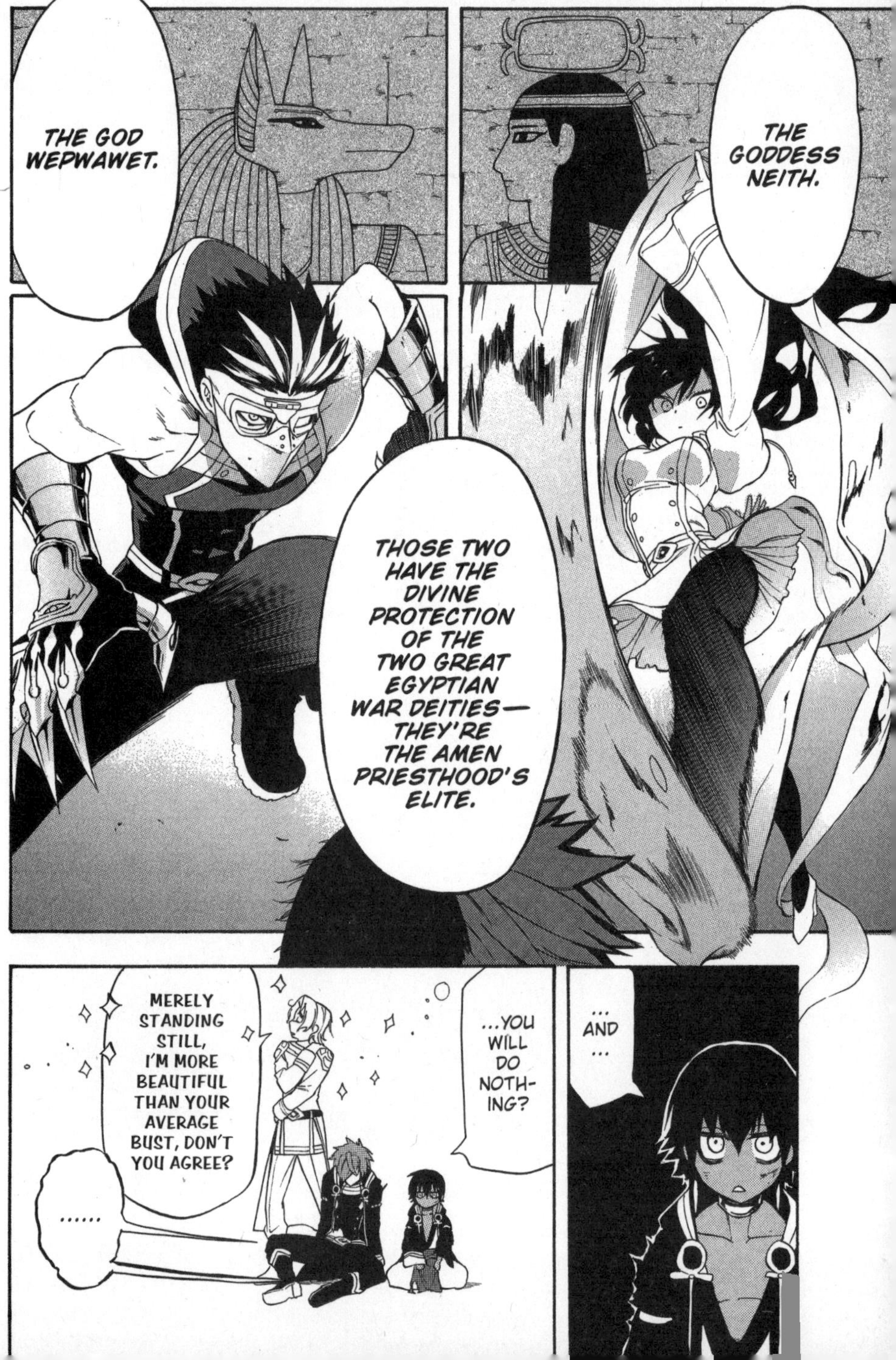
THE GODDESS NEITH.
THE GOD WEPWAWET.
THOSE TWO HAVE THE DIVINE PROTECTION OF THE TWO GREAT EGYPTIAN WAR DEITIES—THEY'RE THE AMEN PRIESTHOOD'S ELITE.
...AND...
...YOU WILL DO NOTH-ING?
MERELY STANDING STILL, I'M MORE BEAUTIFUL THAN YOUR AVERAGE BUST, DON'T YOU AGREE?
......

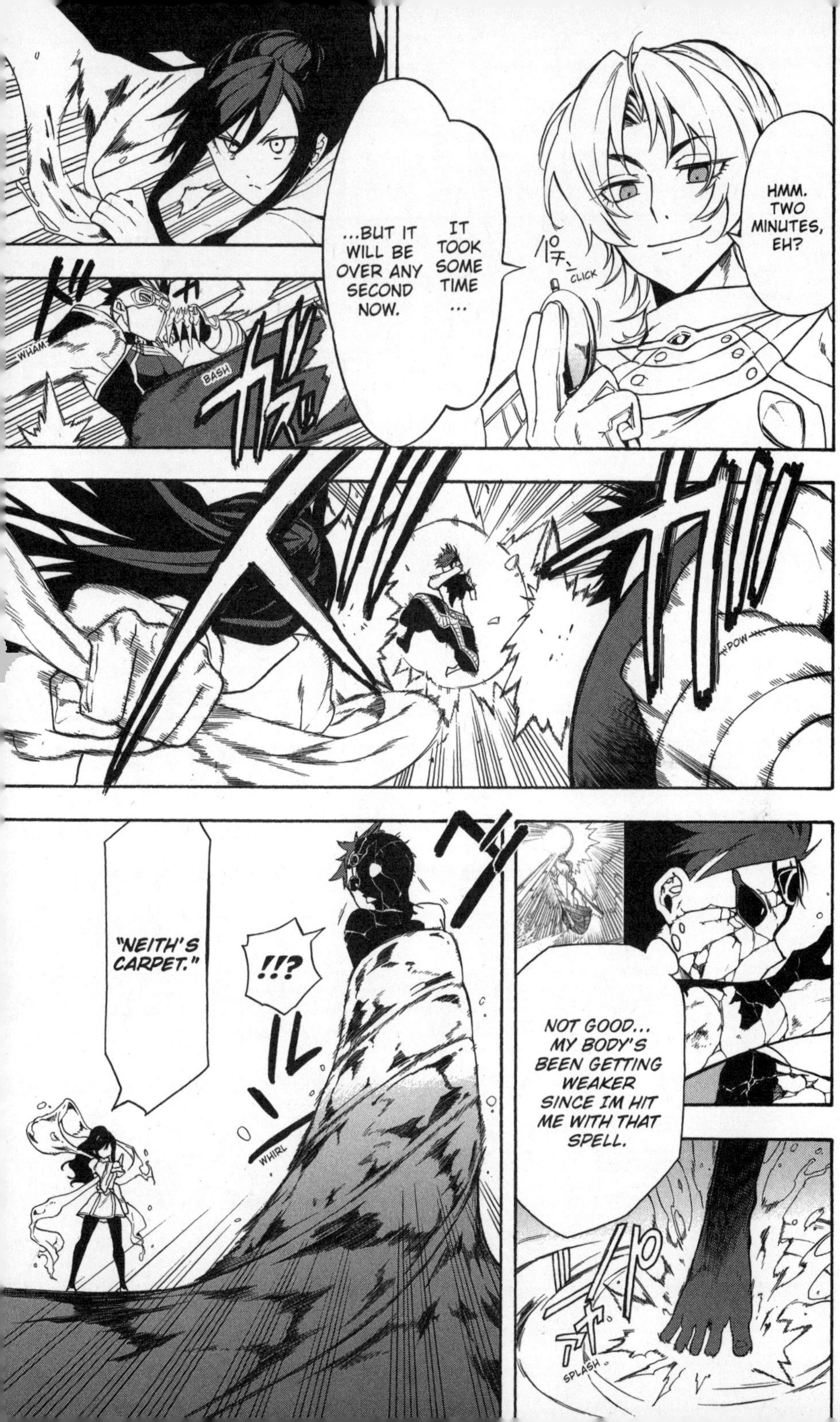
HMM. TWO MINUTES, EH?
IT TOOK SOME TIME ...
...BUT IT WILL BE OVER ANY SECOND NOW.
CLICK
WHAM
BASH
POW
NOT GOOD... MY BODY'S BEEN GETTING WEAKER SINCE IM HIT ME WITH THAT SPELL.
SPLASH
"NEITH'S CARPET."
!!?
WHIRL

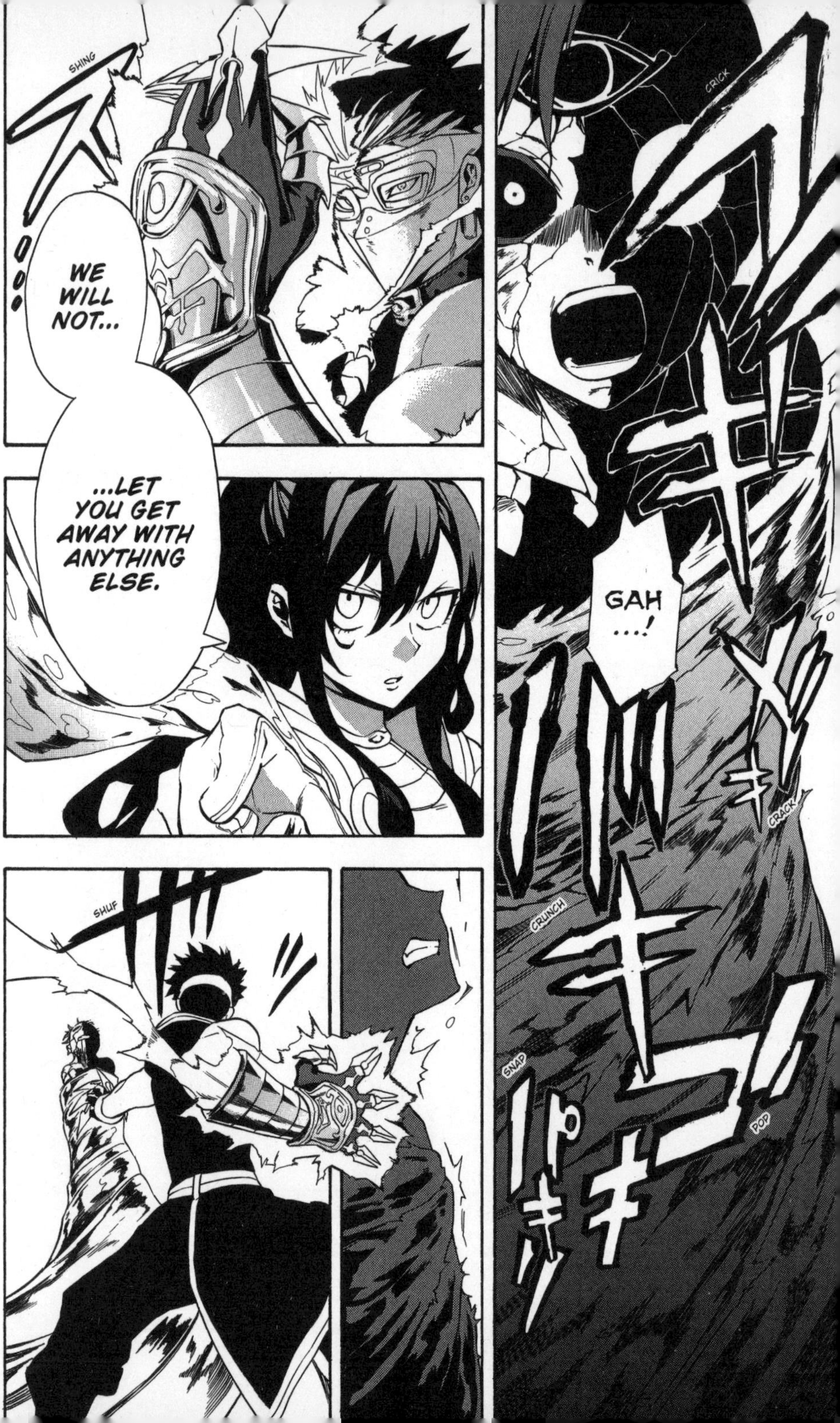
CRICK
GAH ...!
CRACK
CRUNCH
SNAP
POP
SHING
WE WILL NOT...
...LET YOU GET AWAY WITH ANYTHING ELSE.
SHUF

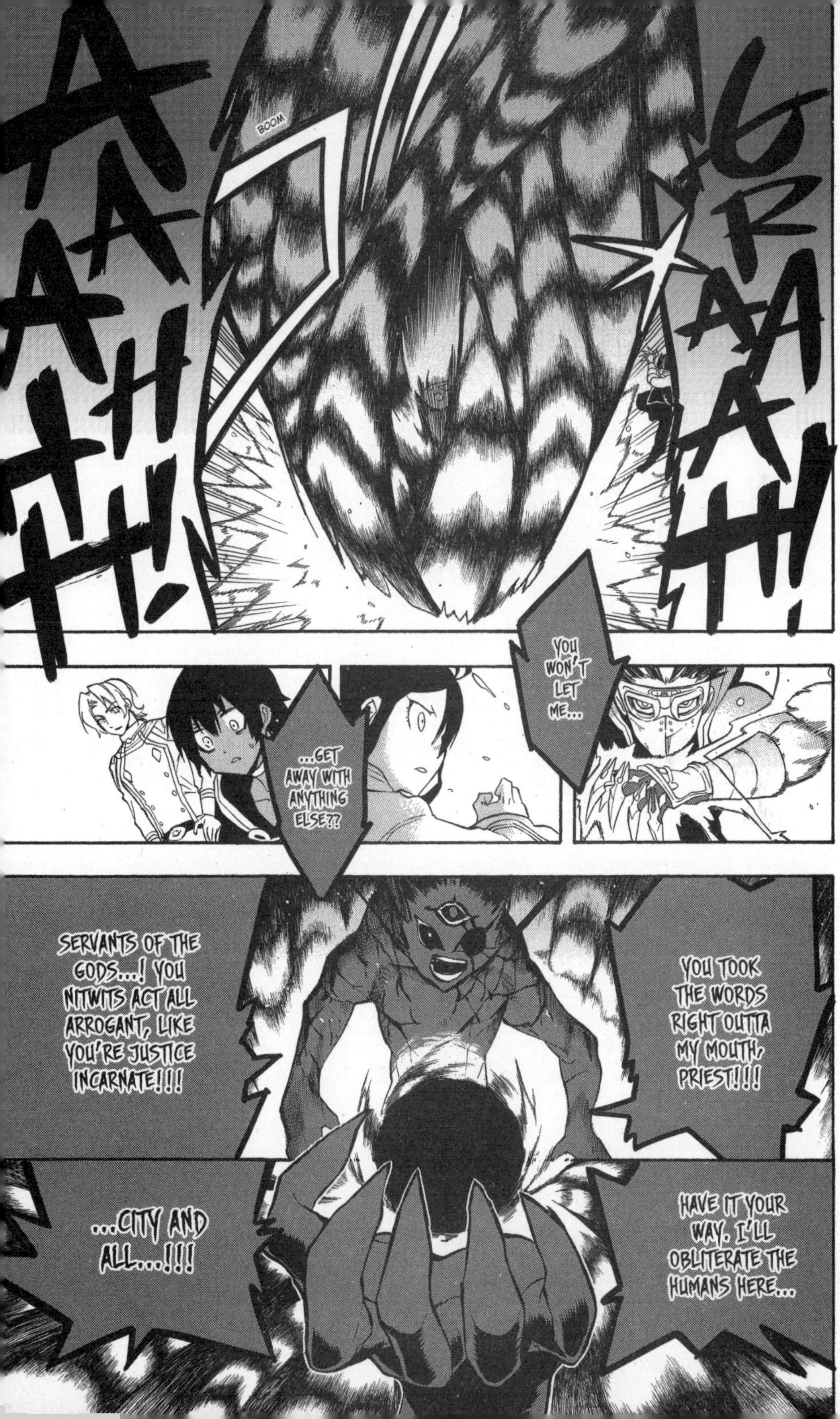
GRAAAH!!
BOOM
AAAHHH!!
YOU WON'T LET ME...
...GET AWAY WITH ANYTHING ELSE??
YOU TOOK THE WORDS RIGHT OUTTA MY MOUTH, PRIEST!!!
SERVANTS OF THE GODS...! YOU NITWITS ACT ALL ARROGANT, LIKE YOU'RE JUSTICE INCARNATE!!!
HAVE IT YOUR WAY. I'LL OBLITERATE THE HUMANS HERE...
...CITY AND ALL...!!!

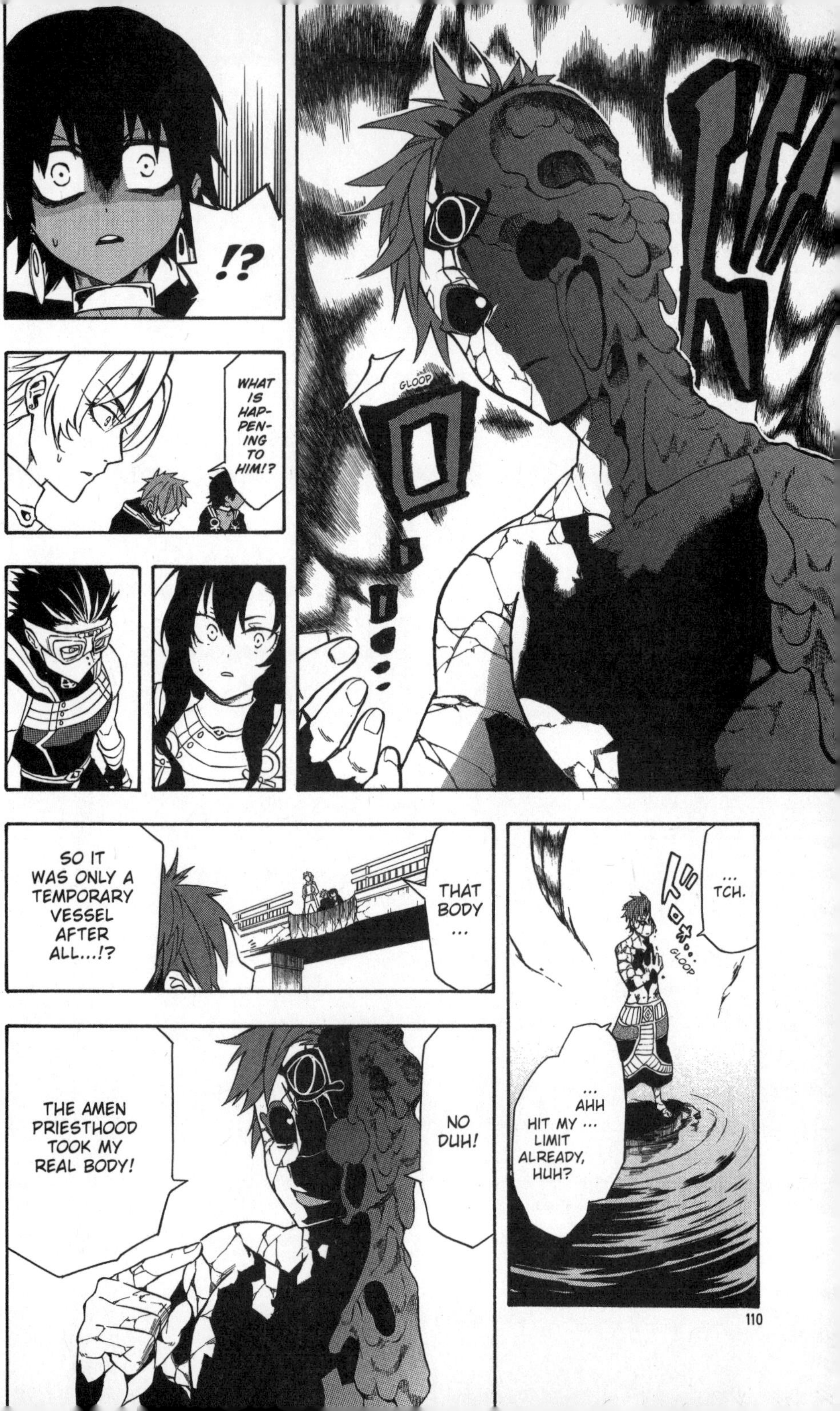
GLOOP
!?
WHAT IS HAPPENING TO HIM!?
... TCH.
GLOOP
... AHH HIT MY ... LIMIT ALREADY, HUH?
THAT BODY ...
SO IT WAS ONLY A TEMPORARY VESSEL AFTER ALL...!?
NO DUH!
THE AMEN PRIESTHOOD TOOK MY REAL BODY!

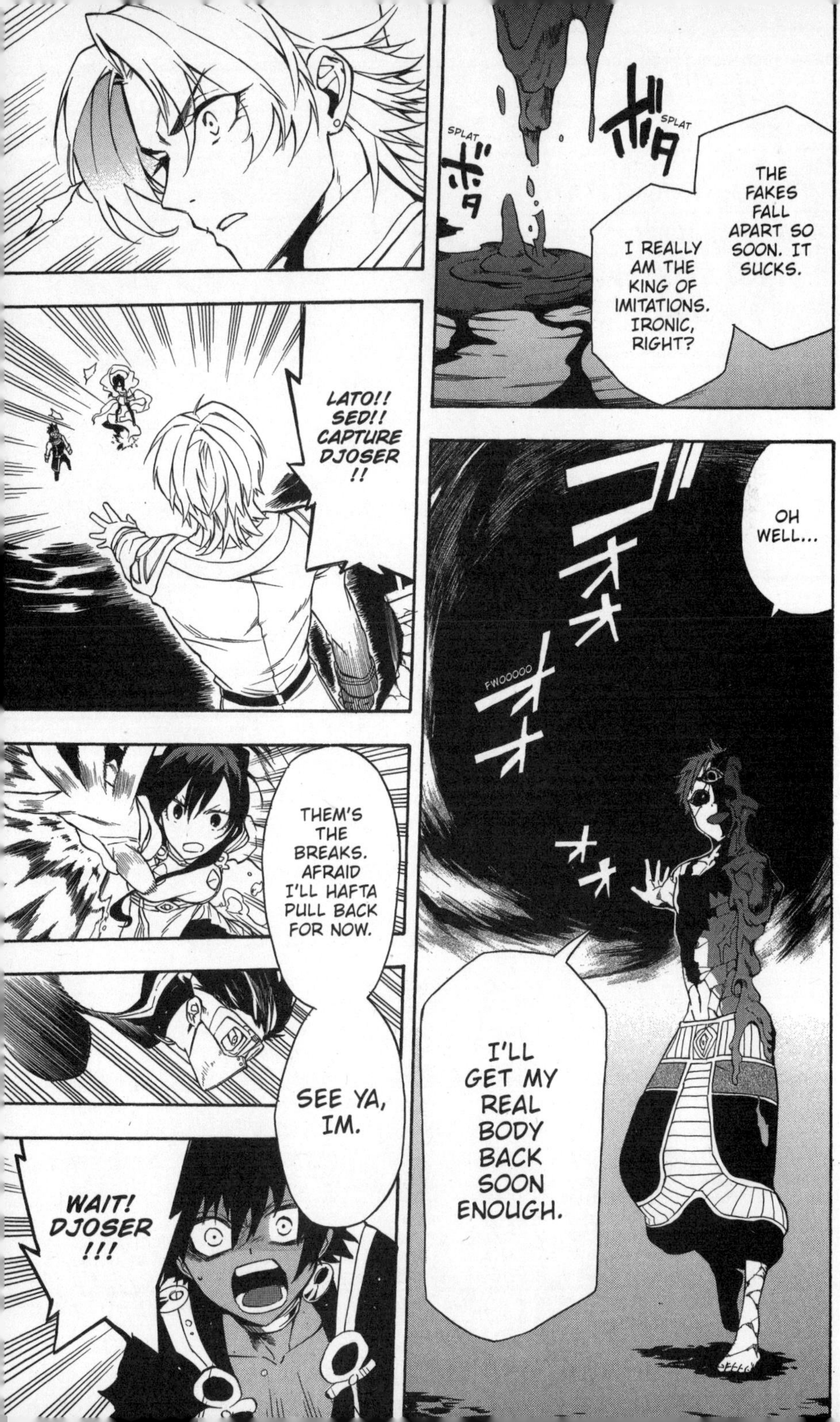
SPLAT
SPLAT
THE FAKES FALL APART SO SOON. IT SUCKS.
I REALLY AM THE KING OF IMITATIONS. IRONIC, RIGHT?
OH WELL...
FWOOOOO
I'LL GET MY REAL BODY BACK SOON ENOUGH.
LATO!! SED!! CAPTURE DJOSER!!
THEM'S THE BREAKS. AFRAID I'LL HAFTA PULL BACK FOR NOW.
SEE YA, IM.
WAIT! DJOSER!!!

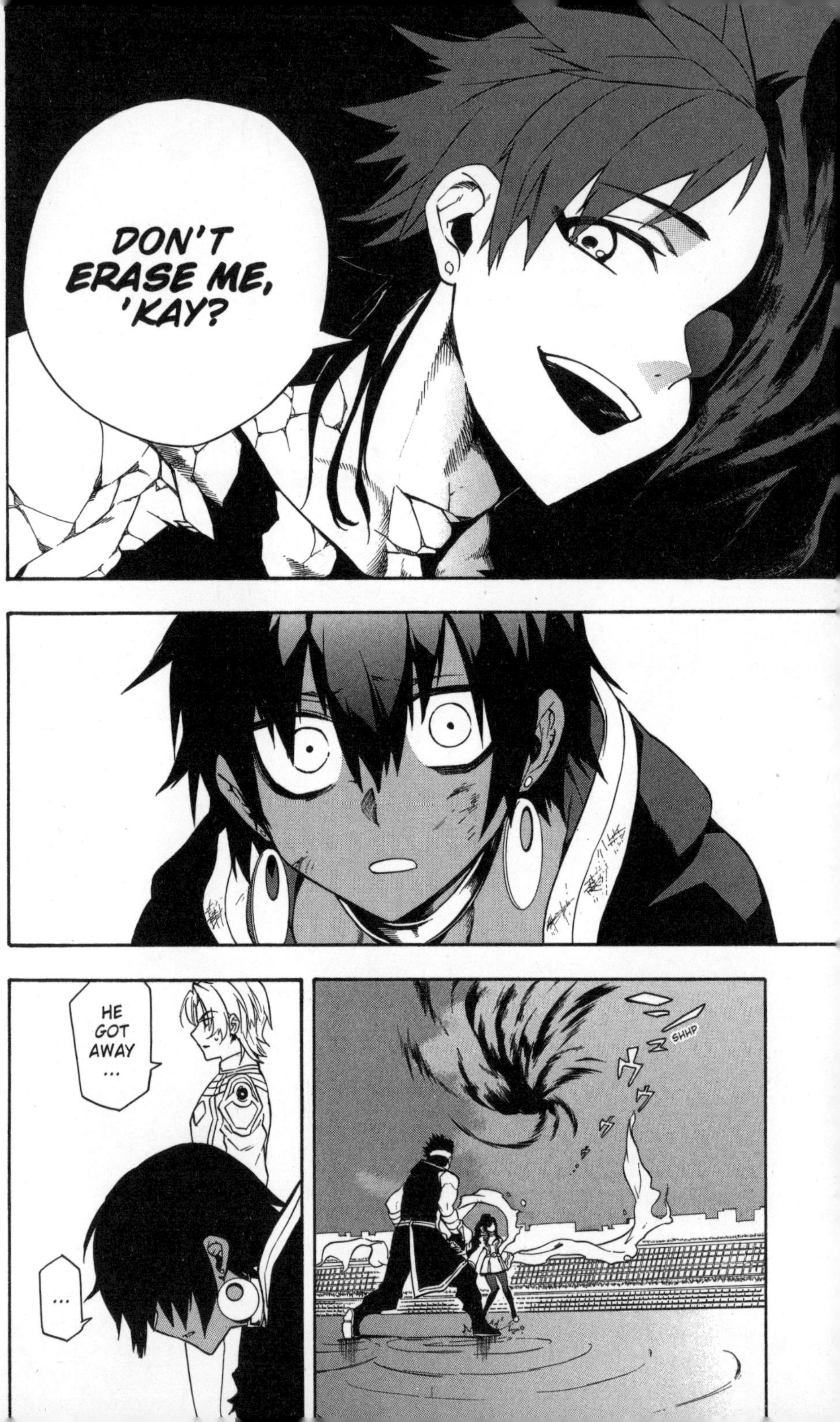
DON'T ERASE ME, 'KAY?
SHHP
HE GOT AWAY ...
...

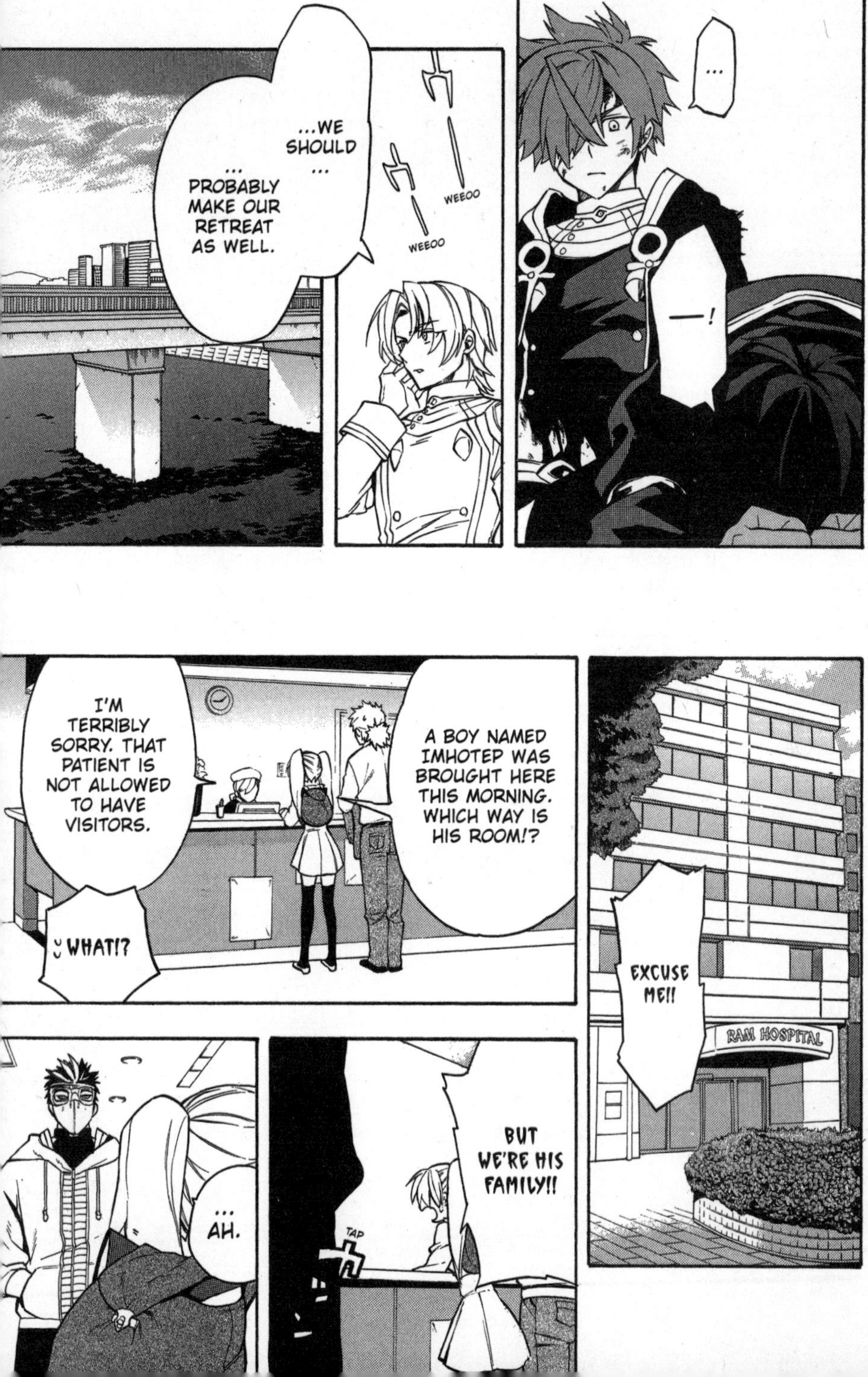
...
—!
WEEOO
WEEOO
...WE SHOULD ... ... PROBABLY MAKE OUR RETREAT AS WELL.
EXCUSE ME!!
A BOY NAMED IMHOTEP WAS BROUGHT HERE THIS MORNING. WHICH WAY IS HIS ROOM!?
I'M TERRIBLY SORRY. THAT PATIENT IS NOT ALLOWED TO HAVE VISITORS.
WHAT!?
RAM HOSPITAL
BUT WE'RE HIS FAMILY!!
TAP
... AH.

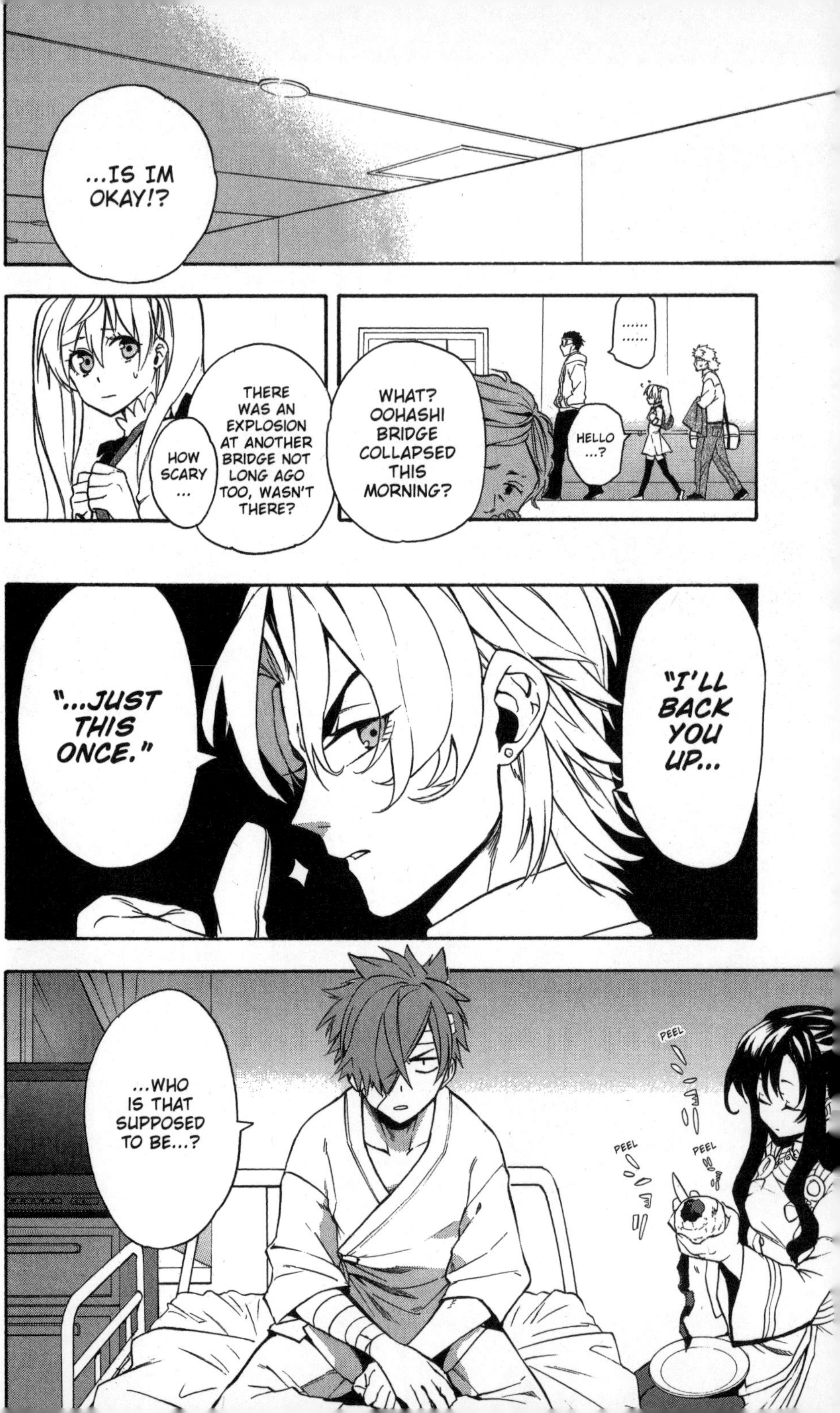
...IS IM OKAY!?
......
......
HELLO ...?
WHAT? OOHASHI BRIDGE COLLAPSED THIS MORNING?
THERE WAS AN EXPLOSION AT ANOTHER BRIDGE NOT LONG AGO TOO, WASN'T THERE?
HOW SCARY ...
"I'LL BACK YOU UP...
"...JUST THIS ONCE."
PEEL
PEEL
PEEL
...WHO IS THAT SUPPOSED TO BE...?

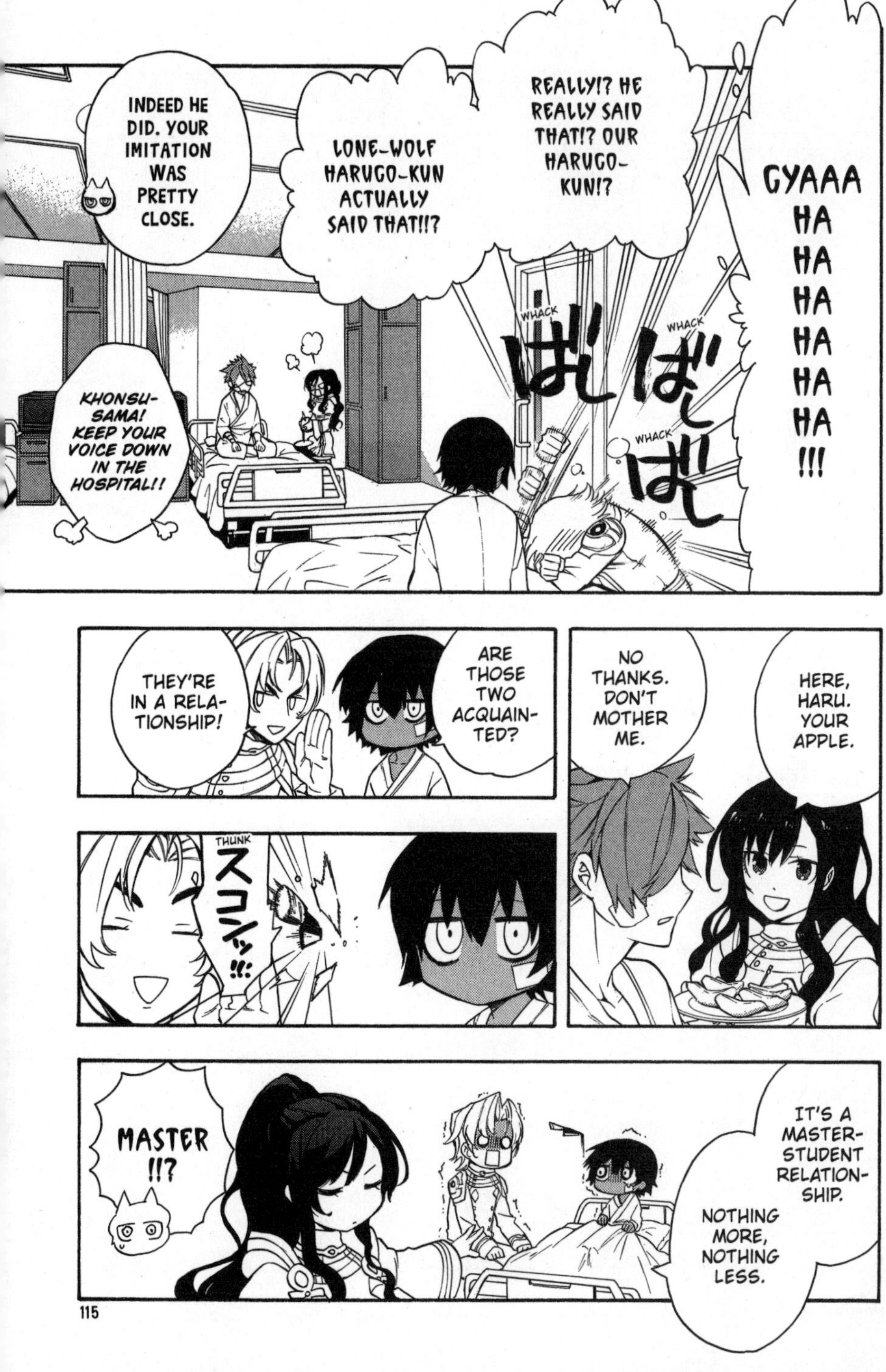

GYAAA HA HA HA HA HA HA!!!
REALLY!? HE REALLY SAID THAT!? OUR HARUGO-KUN!?
LONE-WOLF HARUGO-KUN ACTUALLY SAID THAT!!?
WHACK
ばし
WHACK
ばし
WHACK
ばし
INDEED HE DID. YOUR IMITATION WAS PRETTY CLOSE.
KHONSU-SAMA! KEEP YOUR VOICE DOWN IN THE HOSPITAL!!
HERE, HARU. YOUR APPLE.
NO THANKS. DON'T MOTHER ME.
ARE THOSE TWO ACQUAINTED?
THEY'RE IN A RELATIONSHIP!
THUNK
スコンッ!!
IT'S A MASTER-STUDENT RELATIONSHIP.
NOTHING MORE, NOTHING LESS.
MASTER!!?

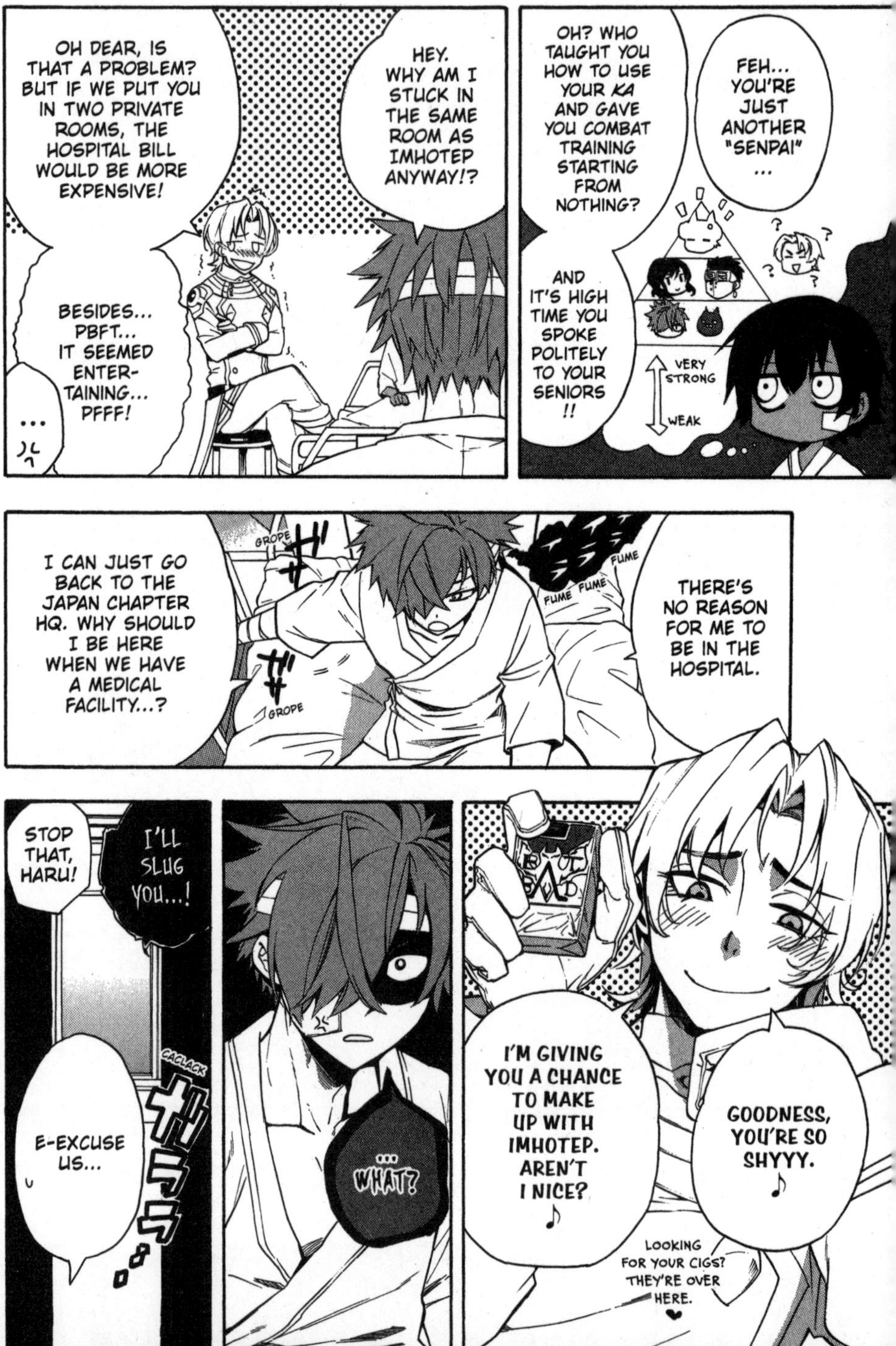
FEH... YOU'RE JUST ANOTHER "SENPAI" ...
OH? WHO TAUGHT YOU HOW TO USE YOUR *KA* AND GAVE YOU COMBAT TRAINING STARTING FROM NOTHING?
AND IT'S HIGH TIME YOU SPOKE POLITELY TO YOUR SENIORS !!
VERY STRONG
WEAK
HEY. WHY AM I STUCK IN THE SAME ROOM AS IMHOTEP ANYWAY!?
OH DEAR, IS THAT A PROBLEM? BUT IF WE PUT YOU IN TWO PRIVATE ROOMS, THE HOSPITAL BILL WOULD BE MORE EXPENSIVE!
BESIDES... PBFT... IT SEEMED ENTER-TAINING... PFFF!
...
THERE'S NO REASON FOR ME TO BE IN THE HOSPITAL.
FUME FUME FUME
GROPE
I CAN JUST GO BACK TO THE JAPAN CHAPTER HQ. WHY SHOULD I BE HERE WHEN WE HAVE A MEDICAL FACILITY...?
GROPE
GOODNESS, YOU'RE SO SHYYY. ♪
I'M GIVING YOU A CHANCE TO MAKE UP WITH IMHOTEP. AREN'T I NICE? ♪
LOOKING FOR YOUR CIGS? THEY'RE OVER HERE. ♥
...WHAT?
I'LL SLUG YOU...!
STOP THAT, HARU!
CACLACK
E-EXCUSE US...

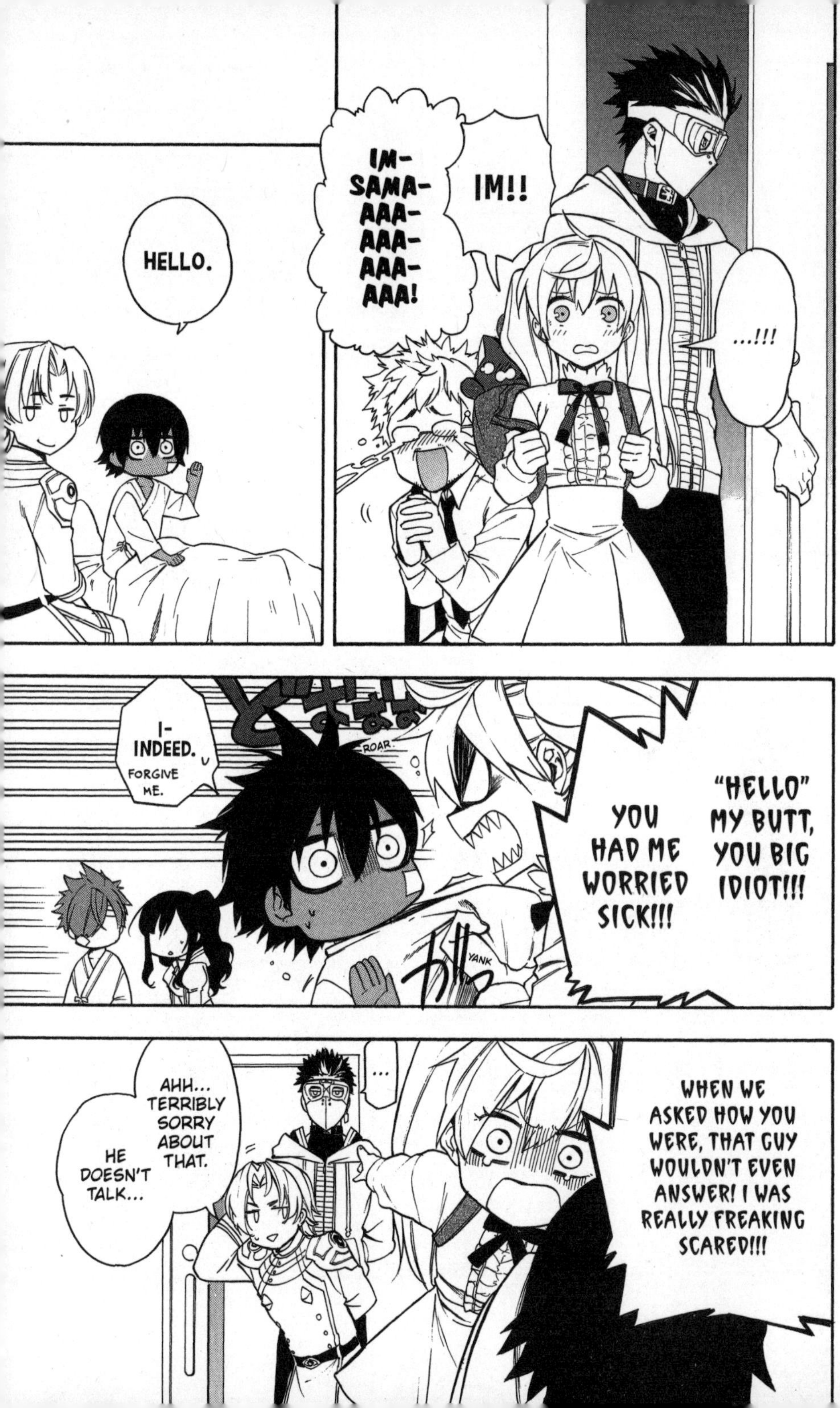
IM!!
IM-SAMA-AAA-AAA-AAA-AAA!
...!!!
HELLO.
"HELLO" MY BUTT, YOU BIG IDIOT!!!
YOU HAD ME WORRIED SICK!!!
ROAR
YANK
I-INDEED. FORGIVE ME.
WHEN WE ASKED HOW YOU WERE, THAT GUY WOULDN'T EVEN ANSWER! I WAS REALLY FREAKING SCARED!!!
...
AHH... TERRIBLY SORRY ABOUT THAT.
HE DOESN'T TALK...

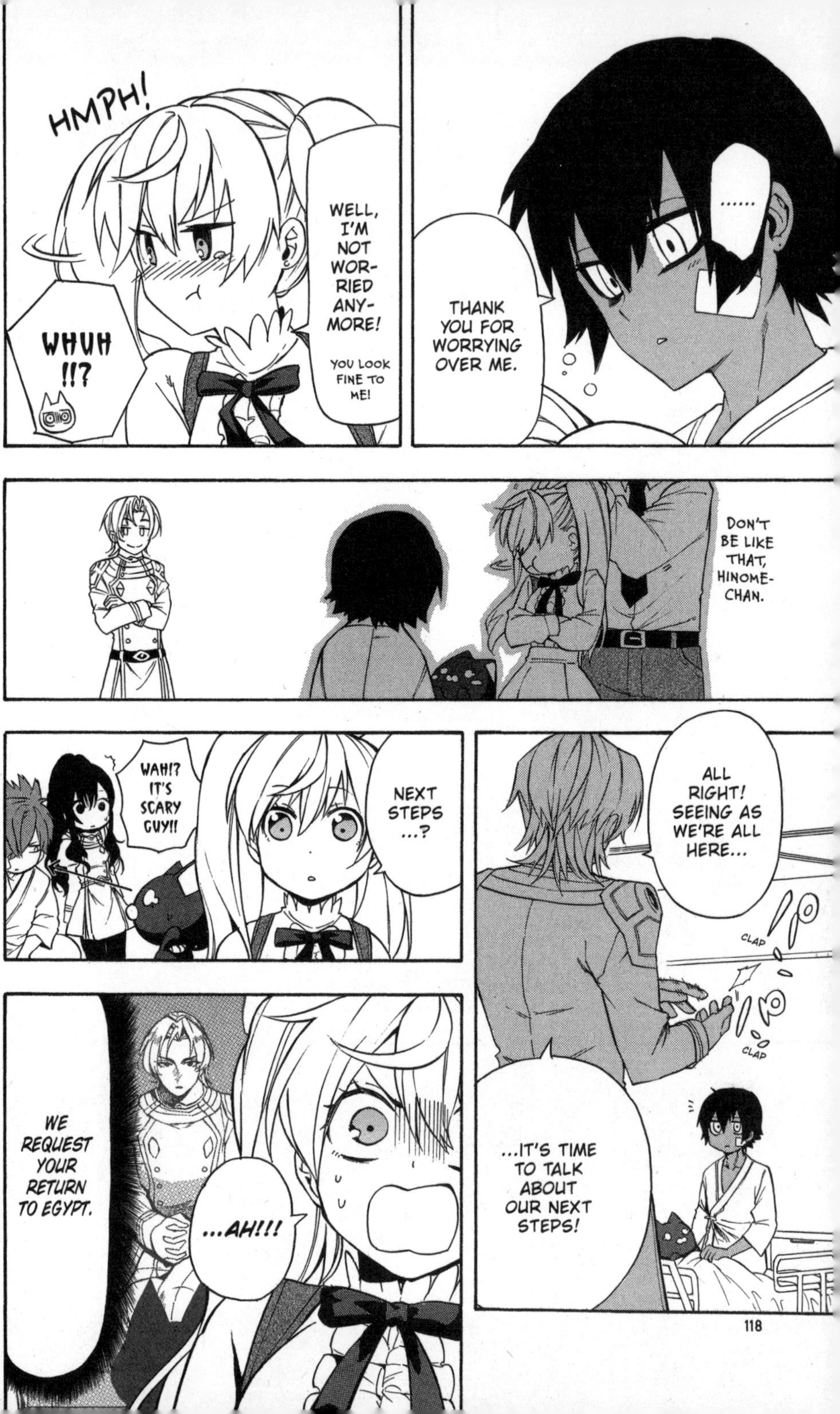
......
THANK YOU FOR WORRYING OVER ME.
HMPH!
WELL, I'M NOT WORRIED ANYMORE!
YOU LOOK FINE TO ME!
WHUH !!?
DON'T BE LIKE THAT, HINOME-CHAN.
ALL RIGHT! SEEING AS WE'RE ALL HERE...
CLAP
CLAP
...IT'S TIME TO TALK ABOUT OUR NEXT STEPS!
NEXT STEPS ...?
WAH!? IT'S SCARY GUY!!
...AH!!!
WE REQUEST YOUR RETURN TO EGYPT.

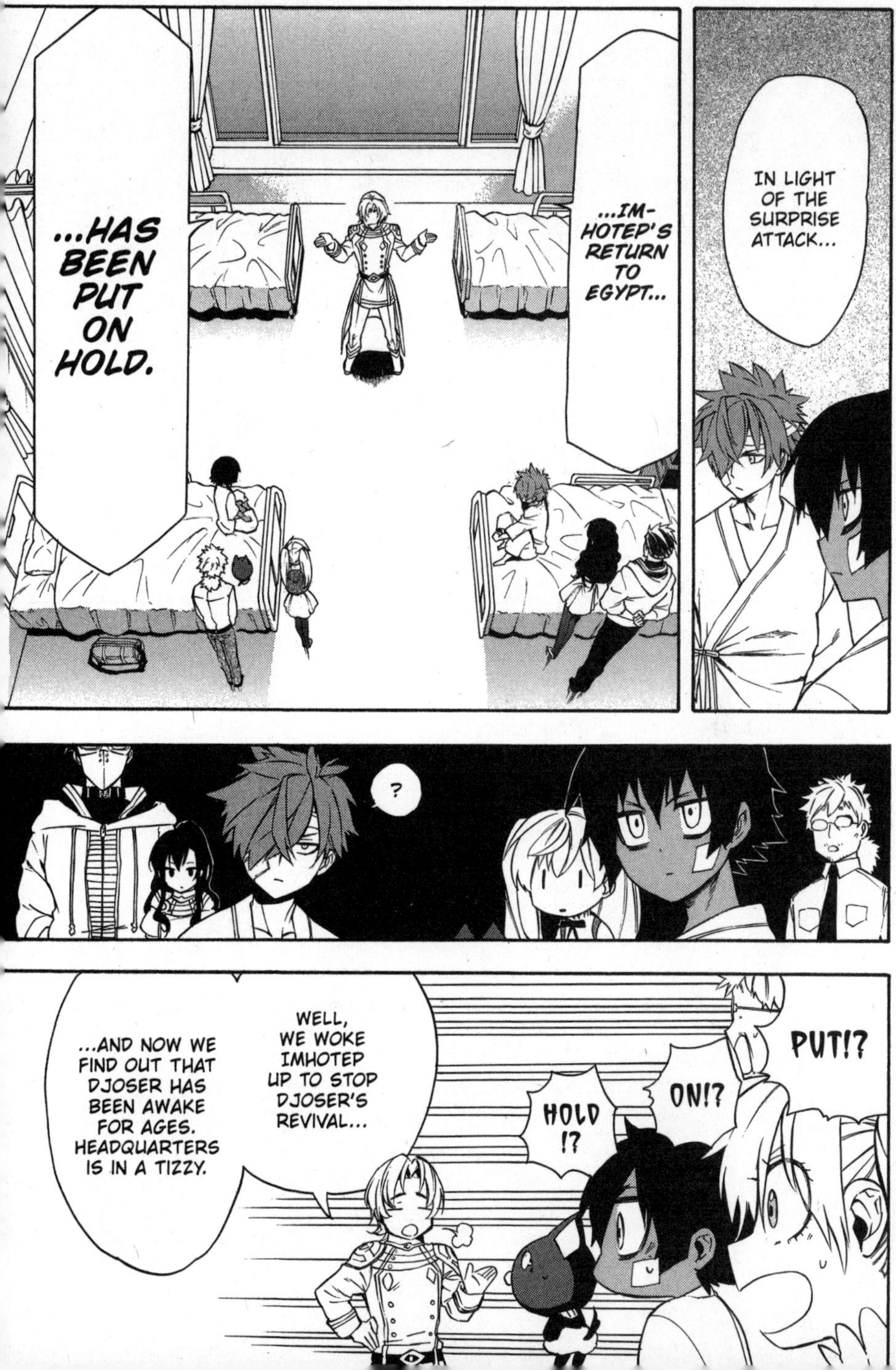
IN LIGHT OF THE SURPRISE ATTACK...
...IM-HOTEP'S RETURN TO EGYPT...
...HAS BEEN PUT ON HOLD.
?
PUT!?
ON!?
HOLD!?
WELL, WE WOKE IMHOTEP UP TO STOP DJOSER'S REVIVAL...
...AND NOW WE FIND OUT THAT DJOSER HAS BEEN AWAKE FOR AGES. HEADQUARTERS IS IN A TIZZY.

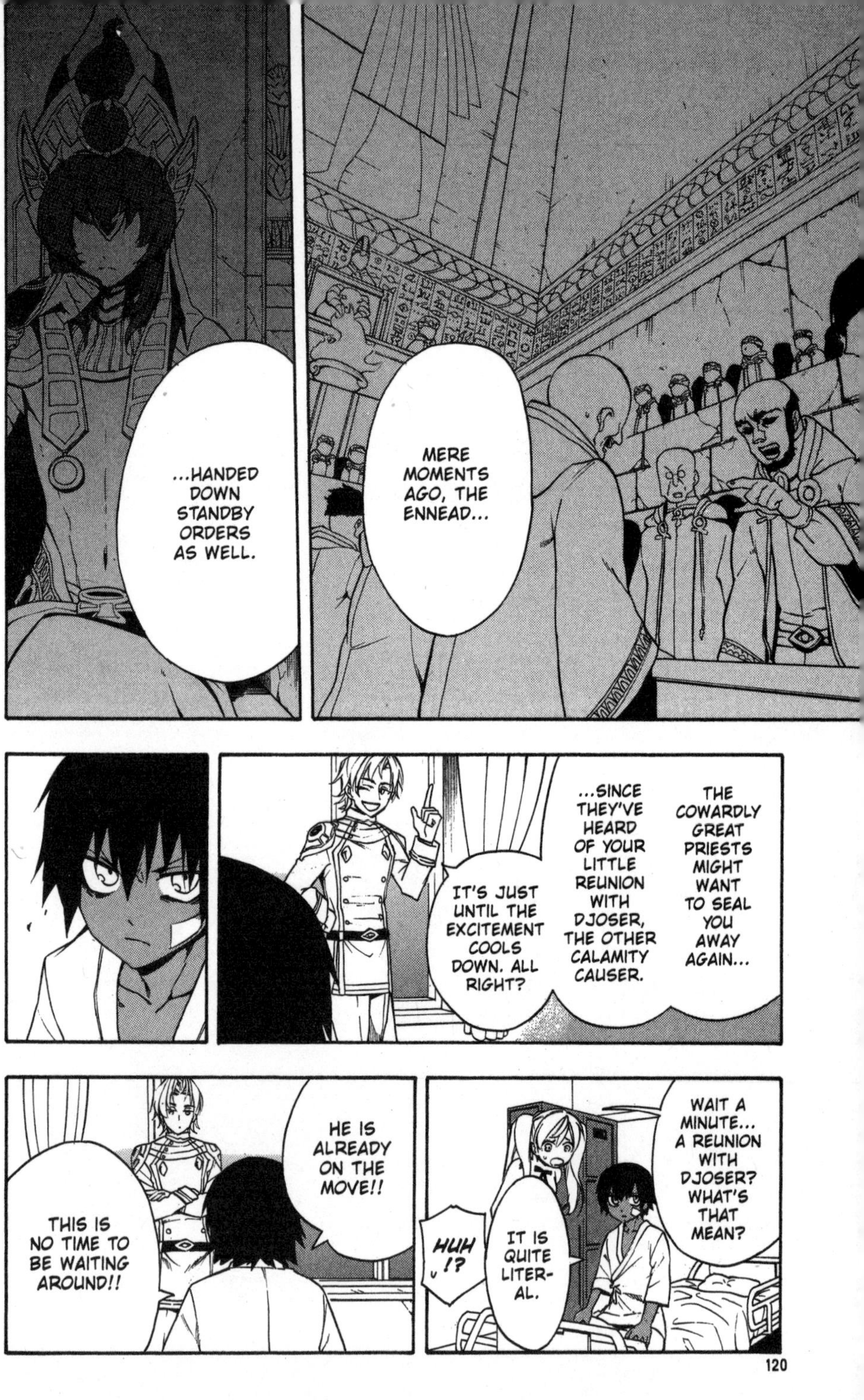
MERE MOMENTS AGO, THE ENNEAD...
...HANDED DOWN STANDBY ORDERS AS WELL.
THE COWARDLY GREAT PRIESTS MIGHT WANT TO SEAL YOU AWAY AGAIN...
...SINCE THEY'VE HEARD OF YOUR LITTLE REUNION WITH DJOSER, THE OTHER CALAMITY CAUSER.
IT'S JUST UNTIL THE EXCITEMENT COOLS DOWN. ALL RIGHT?
WAIT A MINUTE... A REUNION WITH DJOSER? WHAT'S THAT MEAN?
IT IS QUITE LITERAL.
HUH!?
HE IS ALREADY ON THE MOVE!!
THIS IS NO TIME TO BE WAITING AROUND!!

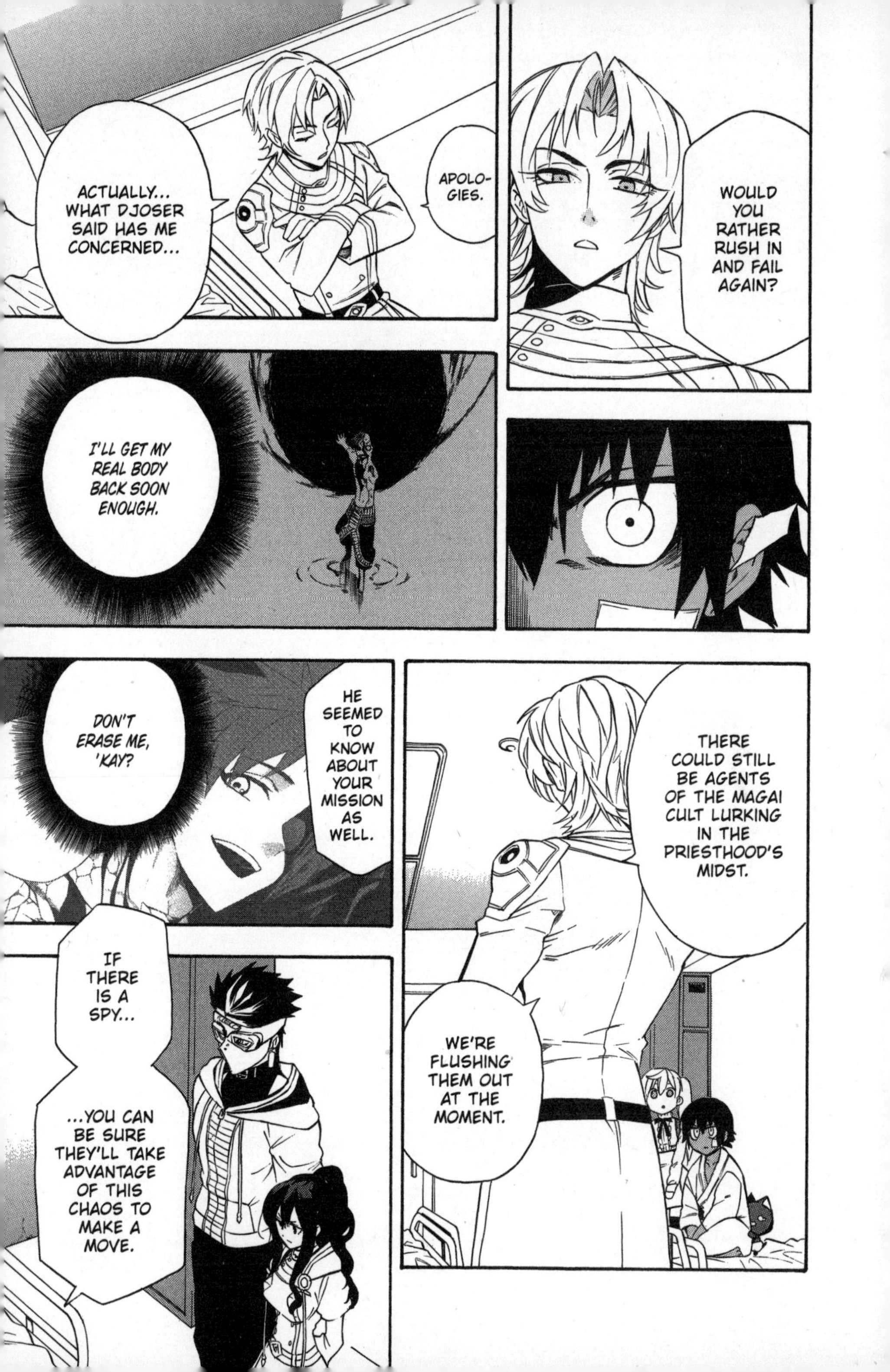
WOULD YOU RATHER RUSH IN AND FAIL AGAIN?
APOLOGIES.
ACTUALLY... WHAT DJOSER SAID HAS ME CONCERNED...
I'LL GET MY REAL BODY BACK SOON ENOUGH.
THERE COULD STILL BE AGENTS OF THE MAGAI CULT LURKING IN THE PRIESTHOOD'S MIDST.
WE'RE FLUSHING THEM OUT AT THE MOMENT.
HE SEEMED TO KNOW ABOUT YOUR MISSION AS WELL.
DON'T ERASE ME, 'KAY?
IF THERE IS A SPY...
...YOU CAN BE SURE THEY'LL TAKE ADVANTAGE OF THIS CHAOS TO MAKE A MOVE.

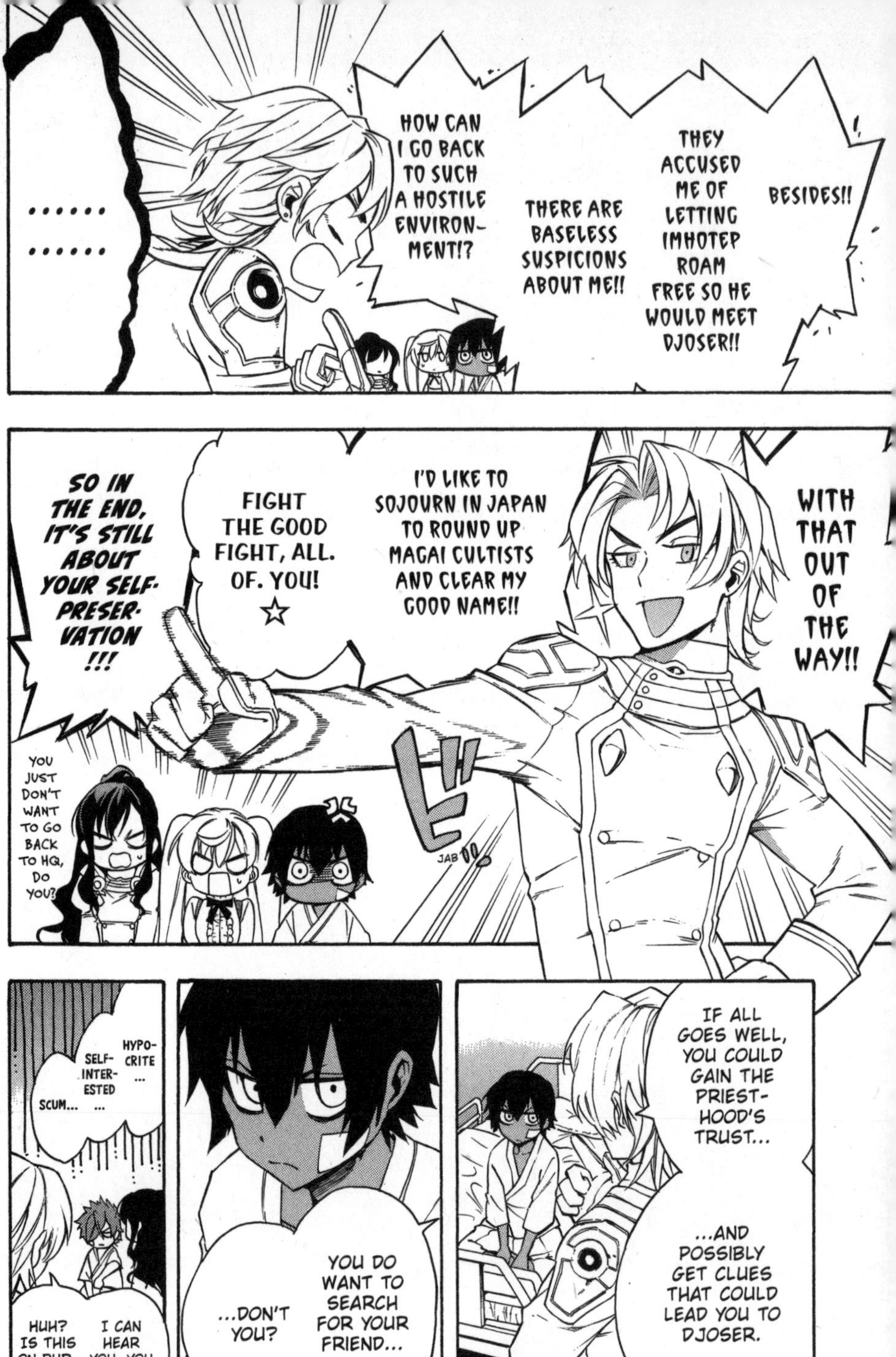
BESIDES!!
THEY ACCUSED ME OF LETTING IMHOTEP ROAM FREE SO HE WOULD MEET DJOSER!!
THERE ARE BASELESS SUSPICIONS ABOUT ME!!
HOW CAN I GO BACK TO SUCH A HOSTILE ENVIRON-MENT!?
......
......
WITH THAT OUT OF THE WAY!!
I'D LIKE TO SOJOURN IN JAPAN TO ROUND UP MAGAI CULTISTS AND CLEAR MY GOOD NAME!!
FIGHT THE GOOD FIGHT, ALL. OF. YOU! ☆
JAB
SO IN THE END, IT'S STILL ABOUT YOUR SELF-PRESER-VATION!!!
YOU JUST DON'T WANT TO GO BACK TO HQ, DO YOU?
IF ALL GOES WELL, YOU COULD GAIN THE PRIEST-HOOD'S TRUST...
...AND POSSIBLY GET CLUES THAT COULD LEAD YOU TO DJOSER.
YOU DO WANT TO SEARCH FOR YOUR FRIEND...
...DON'T YOU?
HYPO-CRITE...
SELF-INTER-ESTED...
SCUM...
I CAN HEAR YOU, YOU KNOW.
HUH? IS THIS ON PUR-POSE??

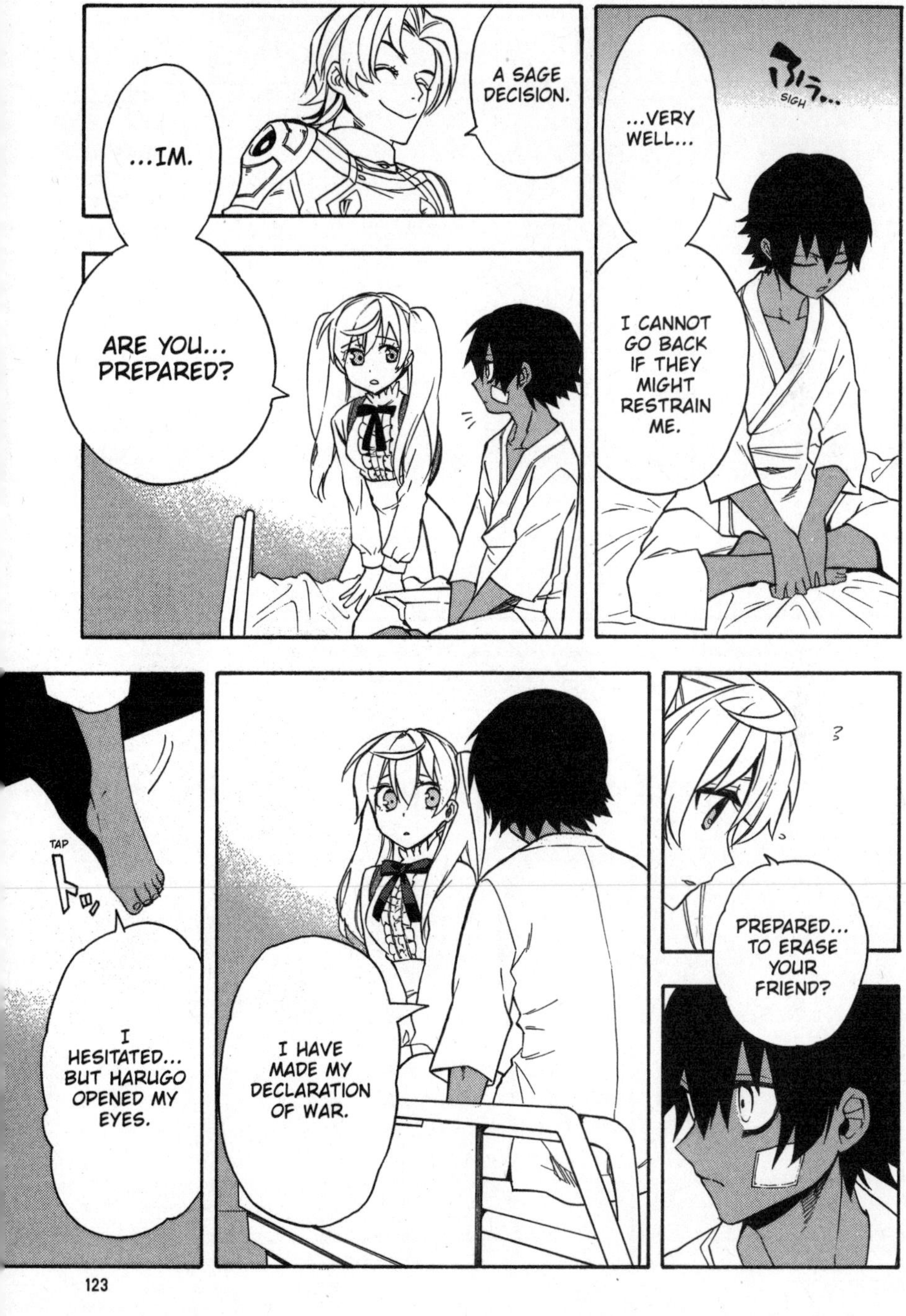

SIGH
...VERY WELL...
I CANNOT GO BACK IF THEY MIGHT RESTRAIN ME.
A SAGE DECISION.
...IM.
ARE YOU... PREPARED?
?
PREPARED... TO ERASE YOUR FRIEND?
I HAVE MADE MY DECLARATION OF WAR.
TAP
I HESITATED... BUT HARUGO OPENED MY EYES.

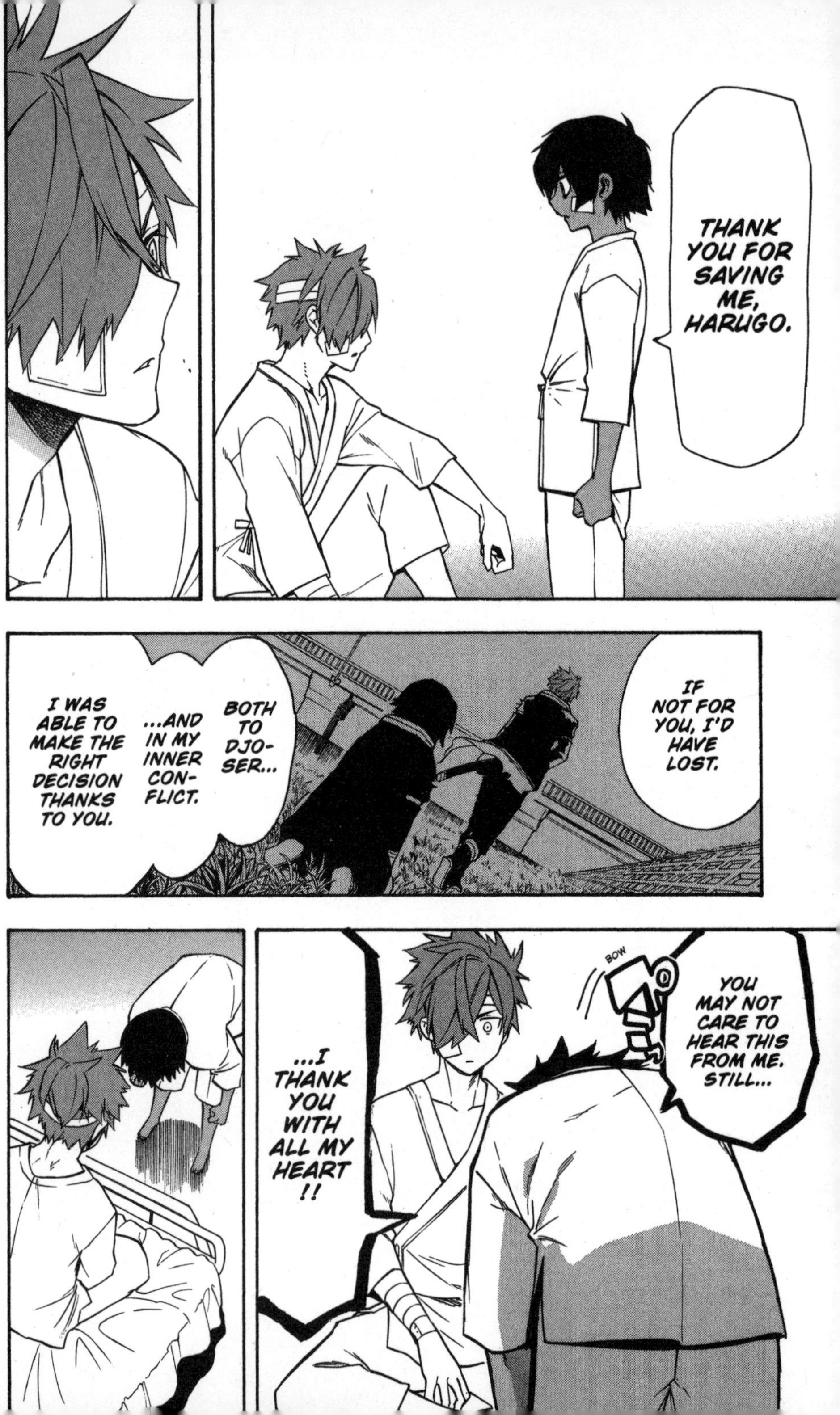
THANK YOU FOR SAVING ME, HARUGO.
IF NOT FOR YOU, I'D HAVE LOST.
BOTH TO DJOSER...
...AND IN MY INNER CONFLICT.
I WAS ABLE TO MAKE THE RIGHT DECISION THANKS TO YOU.
BOW
YOU MAY NOT CARE TO HEAR THIS FROM ME. STILL...
...I THANK YOU WITH ALL MY HEART!!

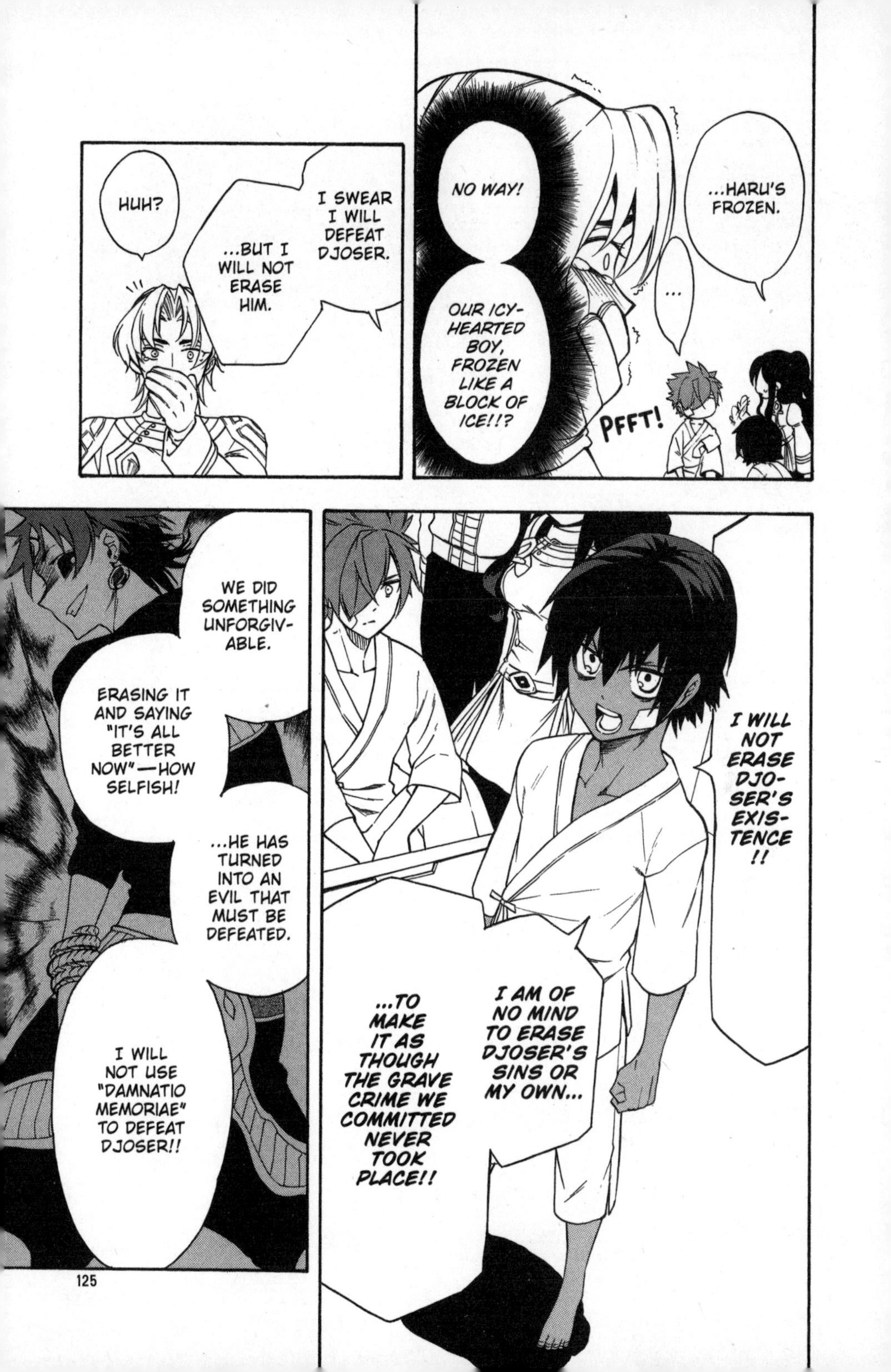

...HARU'S FROZEN.
...
NO WAY!
OUR ICY-HEARTED BOY, FROZEN LIKE A BLOCK OF ICE!!?
PFFT!
I SWEAR I WILL DEFEAT DJOSER.
...BUT I WILL NOT ERASE HIM.
HUH?
I WILL NOT ERASE DJOSER'S EXISTENCE!!
I AM OF NO MIND TO ERASE DJOSER'S SINS OR MY OWN...
...TO MAKE IT AS THOUGH THE GRAVE CRIME WE COMMITTED NEVER TOOK PLACE!!
WE DID SOMETHING UNFORGIVABLE.
ERASING IT AND SAYING "IT'S ALL BETTER NOW"—HOW SELFISH!
...HE HAS TURNED INTO AN EVIL THAT MUST BE DEFEATED.
I WILL NOT USE "DAMNATIO MEMORIAE" TO DEFEAT DJOSER!!

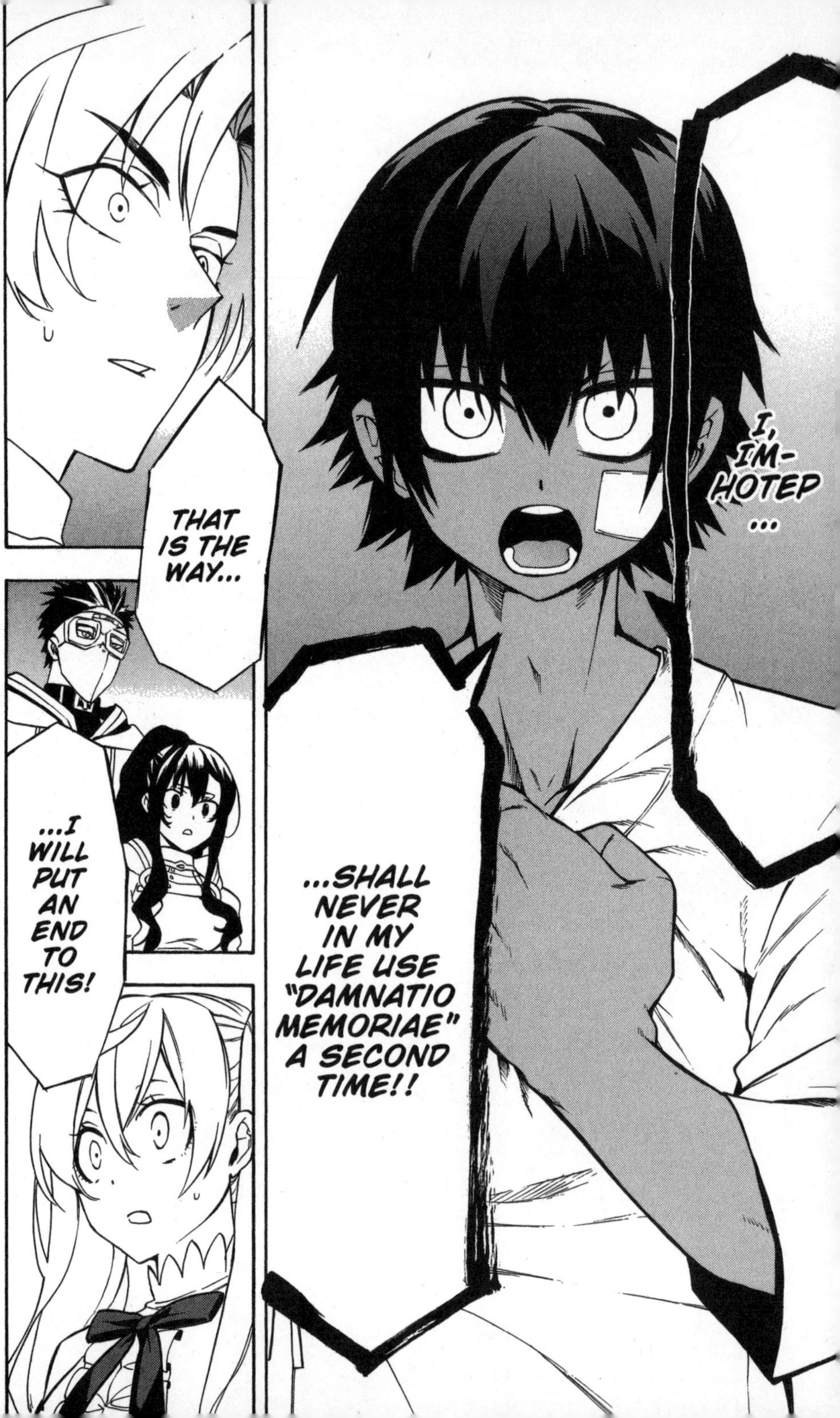

I, IM-HOTEP...
...SHALL NEVER IN MY LIFE USE "DAMNATIO MEMORIAE" A SECOND TIME!!
THAT IS THE WAY...
...I WILL PUT AN END TO THIS!

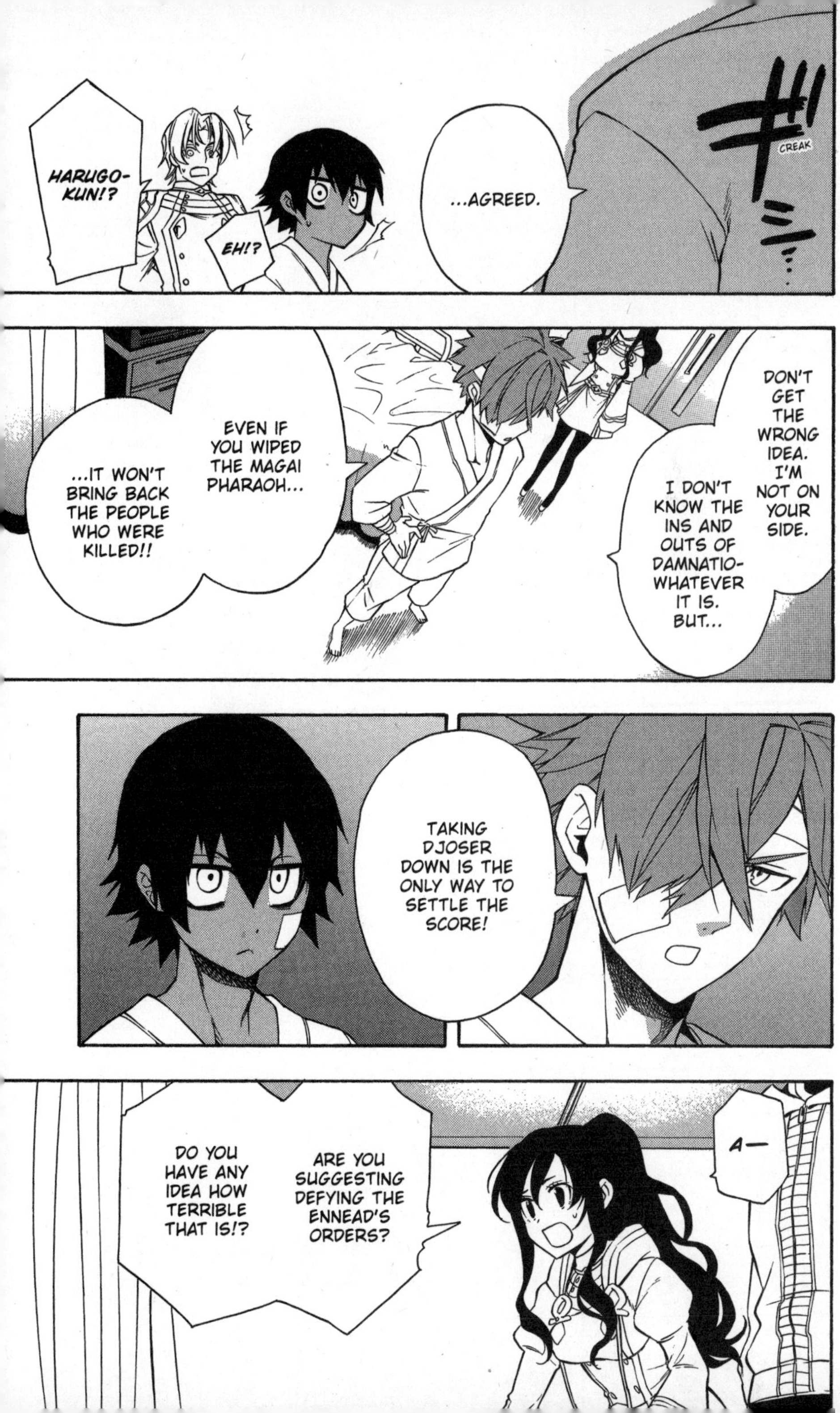
CREAK
...AGREED.
EH!?
HARUGO-KUN!?
DON'T GET THE WRONG IDEA. I'M NOT ON YOUR SIDE.
I DON'T KNOW THE INS AND OUTS OF DAMNATIO-WHATEVER IT IS. BUT...
EVEN IF YOU WIPED THE MAGAI PHARAOH...
...IT WON'T BRING BACK THE PEOPLE WHO WERE KILLED!!
TAKING DJOSER DOWN IS THE ONLY WAY TO SETTLE THE SCORE!
A—
ARE YOU SUGGESTING DEFYING THE ENNEAD'S ORDERS?
DO YOU HAVE ANY IDEA HOW TERRIBLE THAT IS!?

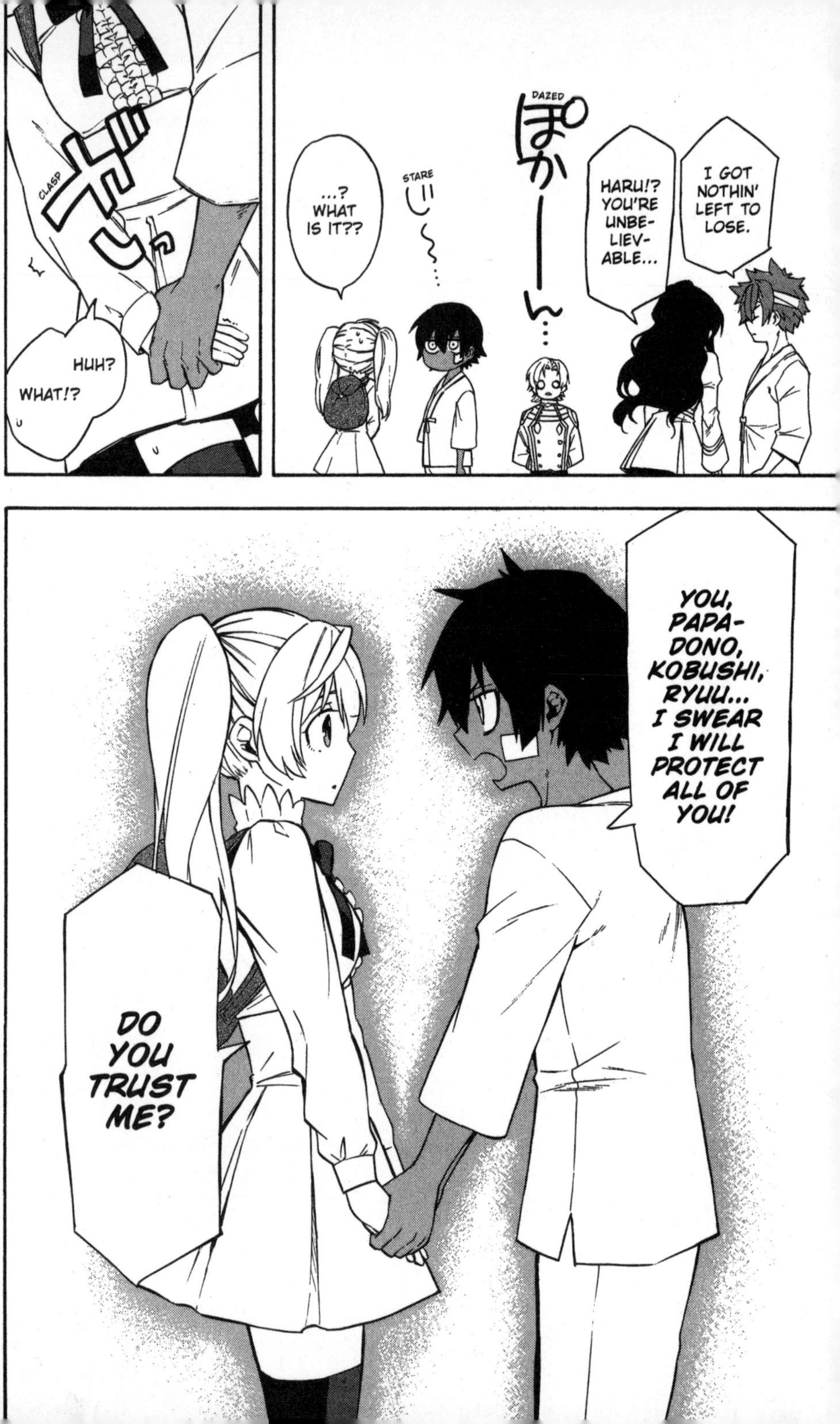
I GOT NOTHIN' LEFT TO LOSE.
HARU!? YOU'RE UNBE-LIEV-ABLE...
DAZED
ぽかーーん…
STARE
じ～…
...? WHAT IS IT??
CLASP
ギュッ
HUH? WHAT!?
YOU, PAPA-DONO, KOBUSHI, RYUU... I SWEAR I WILL PROTECT ALL OF YOU!
DO YOU TRUST ME?

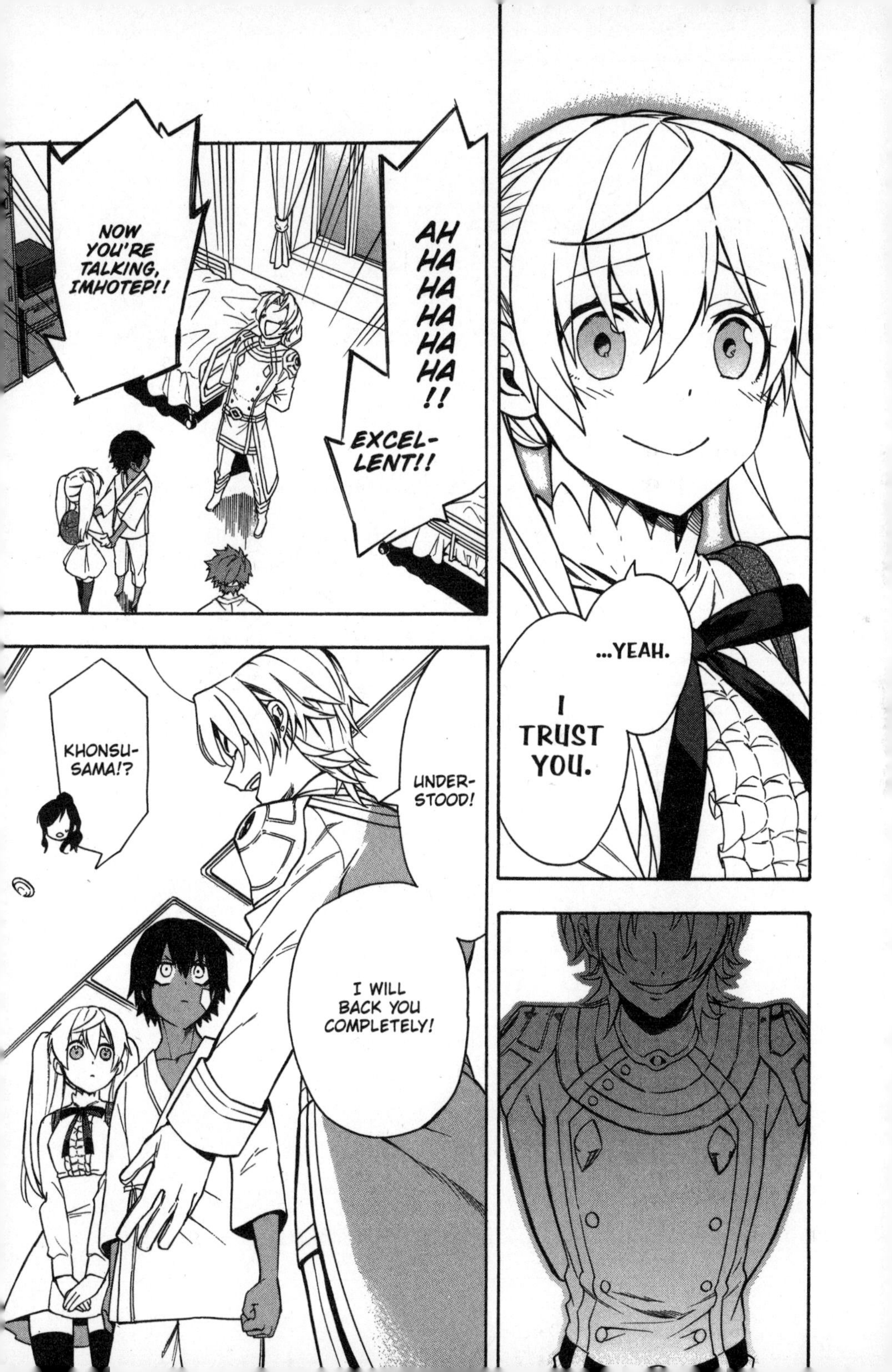
...YEAH.
I TRUST YOU.
AH HA HA HA HA HA HA!!
EXCEL-LENT!!
NOW YOU'RE TALKING, IMHOTEP!!
UNDER-STOOD!
I WILL BACK YOU COMPLETELY!
KHONSU-SAMA!?

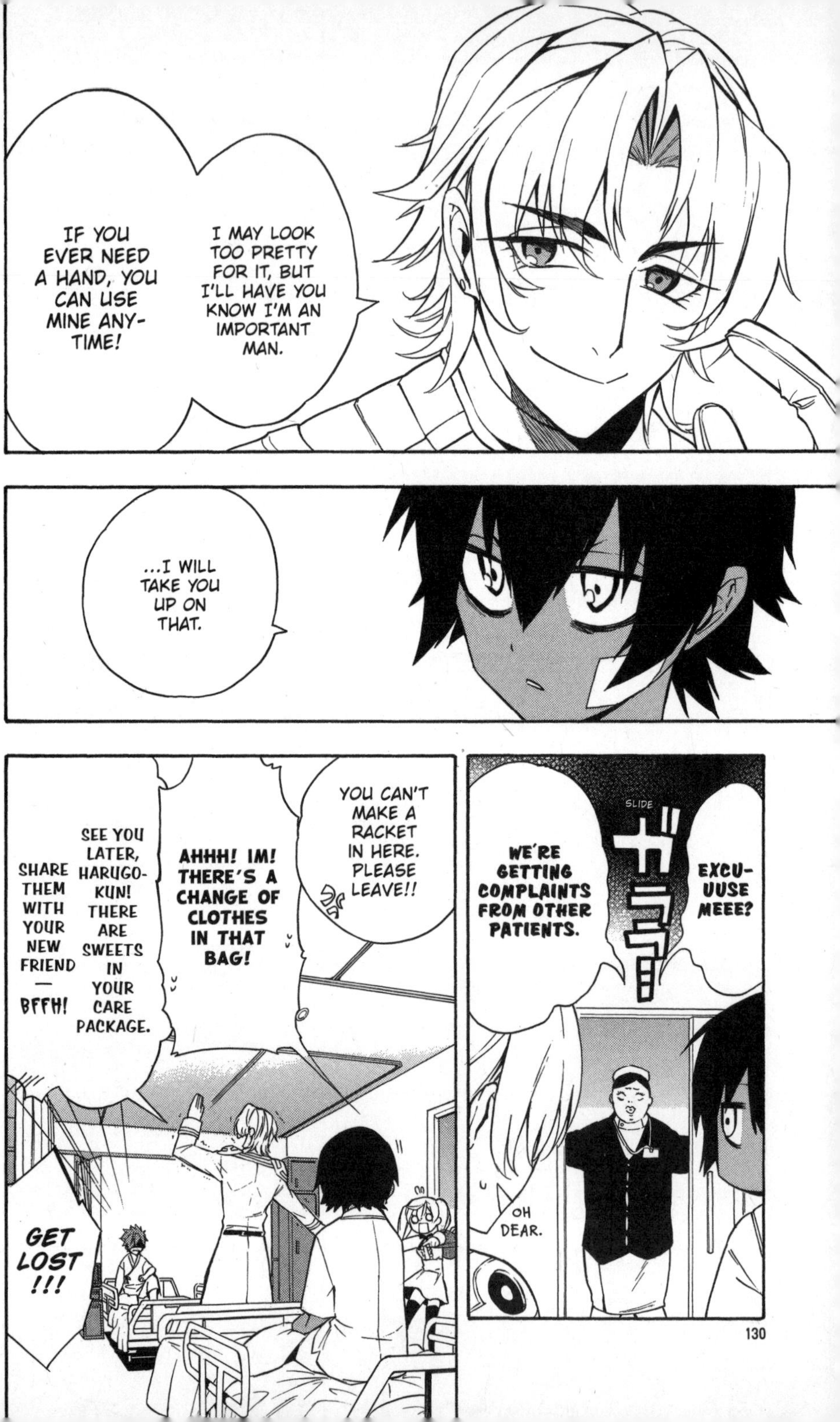

I MAY LOOK TOO PRETTY FOR IT, BUT I'LL HAVE YOU KNOW I'M AN IMPORTANT MAN.
IF YOU EVER NEED A HAND, YOU CAN USE MINE ANY-TIME!
...I WILL TAKE YOU UP ON THAT.
EXCU-UUSE MEEE?
SLIDE
ガラ
WE'RE GETTING COMPLAINTS FROM OTHER PATIENTS.
OH DEAR.
YOU CAN'T MAKE A RACKET IN HERE. PLEASE LEAVE!!
AHHH! IM! THERE'S A CHANGE OF CLOTHES IN THAT BAG!
SEE YOU LATER, HARUGO-KUN! THERE ARE SWEETS IN YOUR CARE PACKAGE.
SHARE THEM WITH YOUR NEW FRIEND — BFFH!
GET LOST !!!

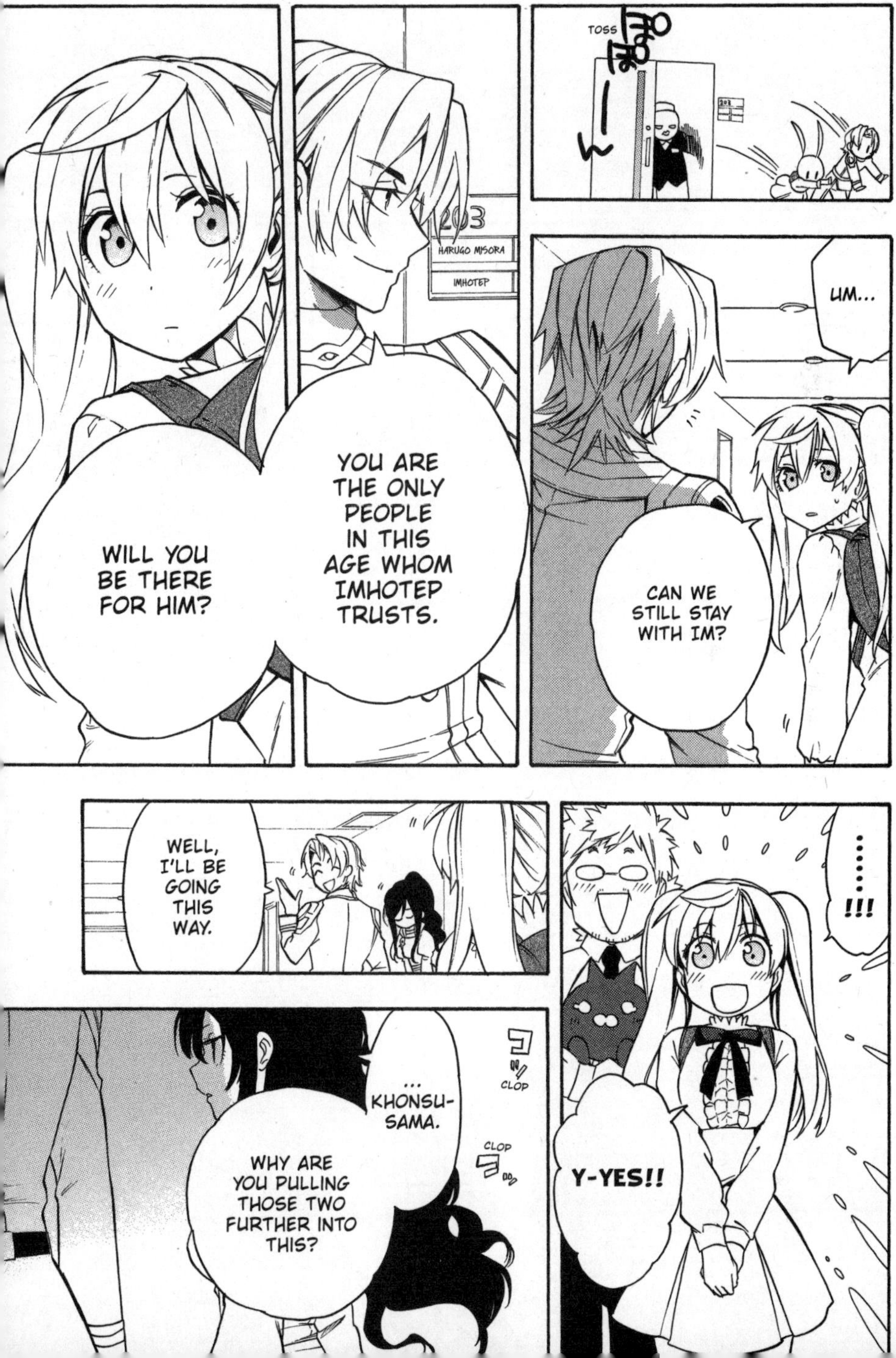
TOSS
ぽぽーん
UM...
CAN WE STILL STAY WITH IM?
HARUGO MISORA
IMHOTEP
YOU ARE THE ONLY PEOPLE IN THIS AGE WHOM IMHOTEP TRUSTS.
WILL YOU BE THERE FOR HIM?
......!!!
Y-YES!!
WELL, I'LL BE GOING THIS WAY.
CLOP
... KHONSU-SAMA.
CLOP
WHY ARE YOU PULLING THOSE TWO FURTHER INTO THIS?

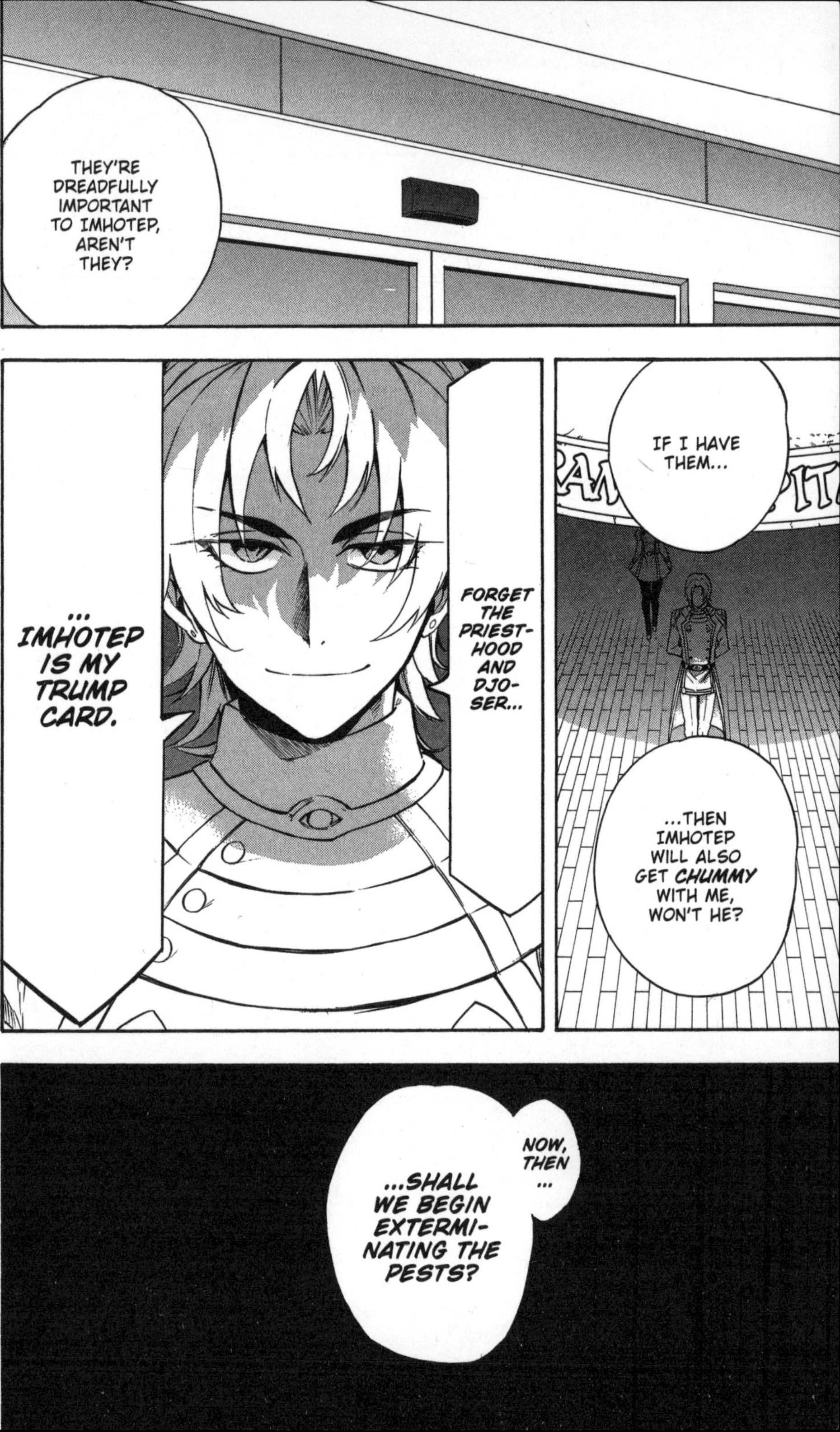
THEY'RE DREADFULLY IMPORTANT TO IMHOTEP, AREN'T THEY?
IF I HAVE THEM...
...THEN IMHOTEP WILL ALSO GET CHUMMY WITH ME, WON'T HE?
FORGET THE PRIEST-HOOD AND DJO-SER...
... IMHOTEP IS MY TRUMP CARD.
NOW, THEN ...
...SHALL WE BEGIN EXTERMI-NATING THE PESTS?

TRANSLATION NOTES

Common Honorifics

no honorific: Indicates familiarity or closeness; if used without permission or reason, addressing someone in this manner would constitute an insult.

-san: The Japanese equivalent of Mr./Mrs./Miss. If a situation calls for politeness, this is the fail-safe honorific.

-sama: Conveys great respect; may also indicate the social status of the speaker is lower than that of the addressee.

-kun: Used most often when referring to boys, this honorific indicates affection or familiarity. Occasionally used by older men among their peers, but it may also be used by anyone referring to a person of lower standing.

-chan: An affectionate honorific indicating familiarity used mostly in reference to girls; also used in reference to cute persons or animals of either gender.

-dono: A respectful term typically equated with "lord" or "master," this honorific has an archaic spin to it when used in colloquial parlance.

-senpai: A respectful term for someone of higher rank or seniority, such as a student in a higher year or a co-worker who has been in their position longer.

-sensei: A respectful term for teachers, artists, or high-level professionals.

-oniisan, nii-san, aniki, etc.: A term of endearment meaning "big brother" that may be more widely used to address any young man who is like a brother, regardless of whether he is related or not.

-oneesan, nee-san, aneki, etc.: The female counterpart of the above, nee-san means "big sister."

Page 149
The classic Japanese literature excerpt on the blackboard is from ***The Pillow Book*** by Sei Shonagon.

Page 158
Hiroshi Inui: a character played by comedian Shigeo Takahashi. Hiroshi's first appearance was in 2002. His bits are "blues songs" in which the line "XX is freedom!" is always repeated (XX being whatever topic the particular bit is about).

Great Priest Imhotep

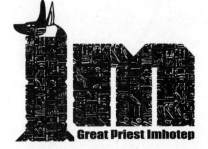

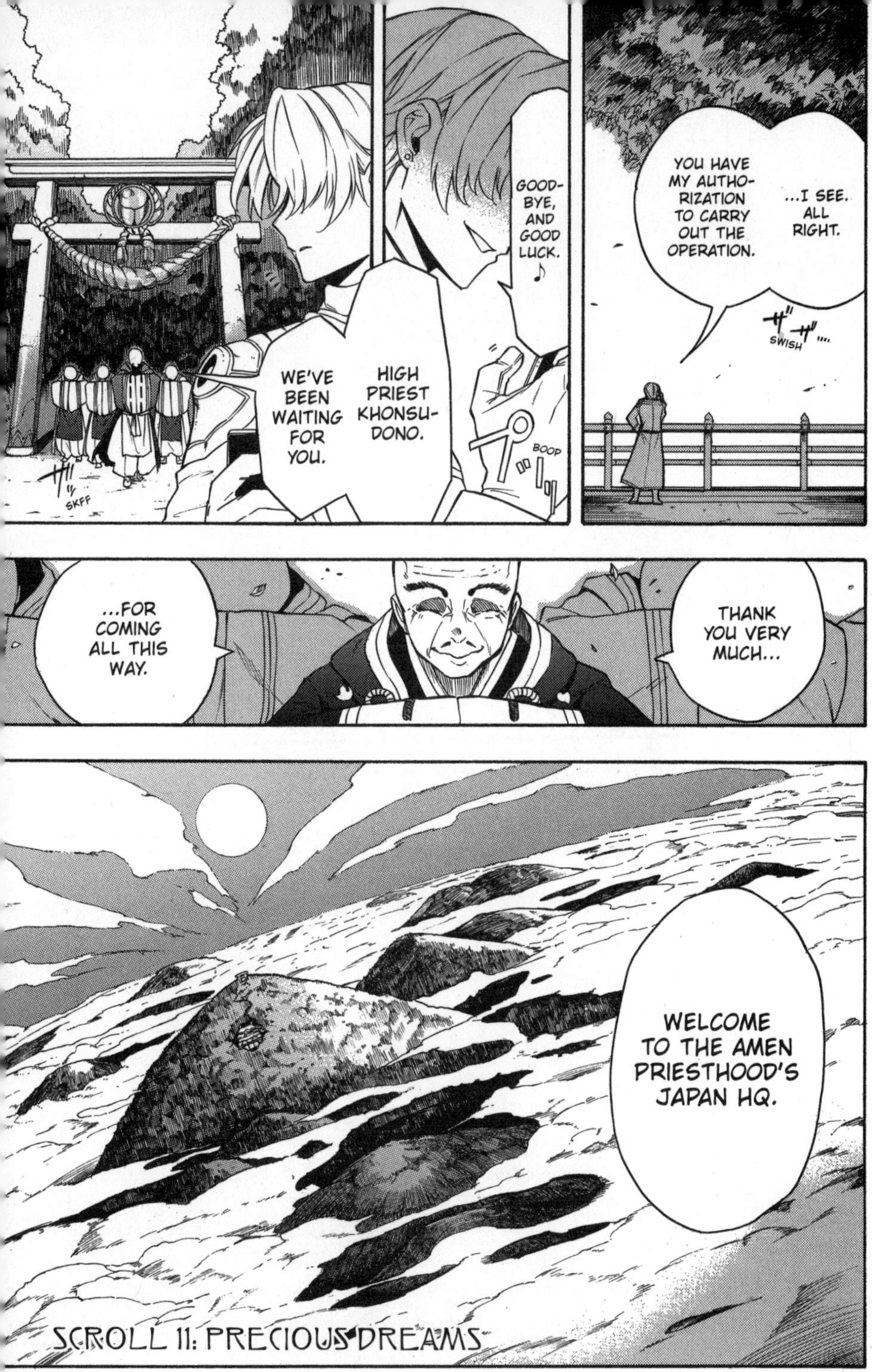

...I SEE. ALL RIGHT.
YOU HAVE MY AUTHORIZATION TO CARRY OUT THE OPERATION.
SWISH
GOOD-BYE, AND GOOD LUCK. ♪
BOOP
HIGH PRIEST KHONSU-DONO.
WE'VE BEEN WAITING FOR YOU.
SKFF
THANK YOU VERY MUCH...
...FOR COMING ALL THIS WAY.
WELCOME TO THE AMEN PRIESTHOOD'S JAPAN HQ.
SCROLL 11: PRECIOUS DREAMS

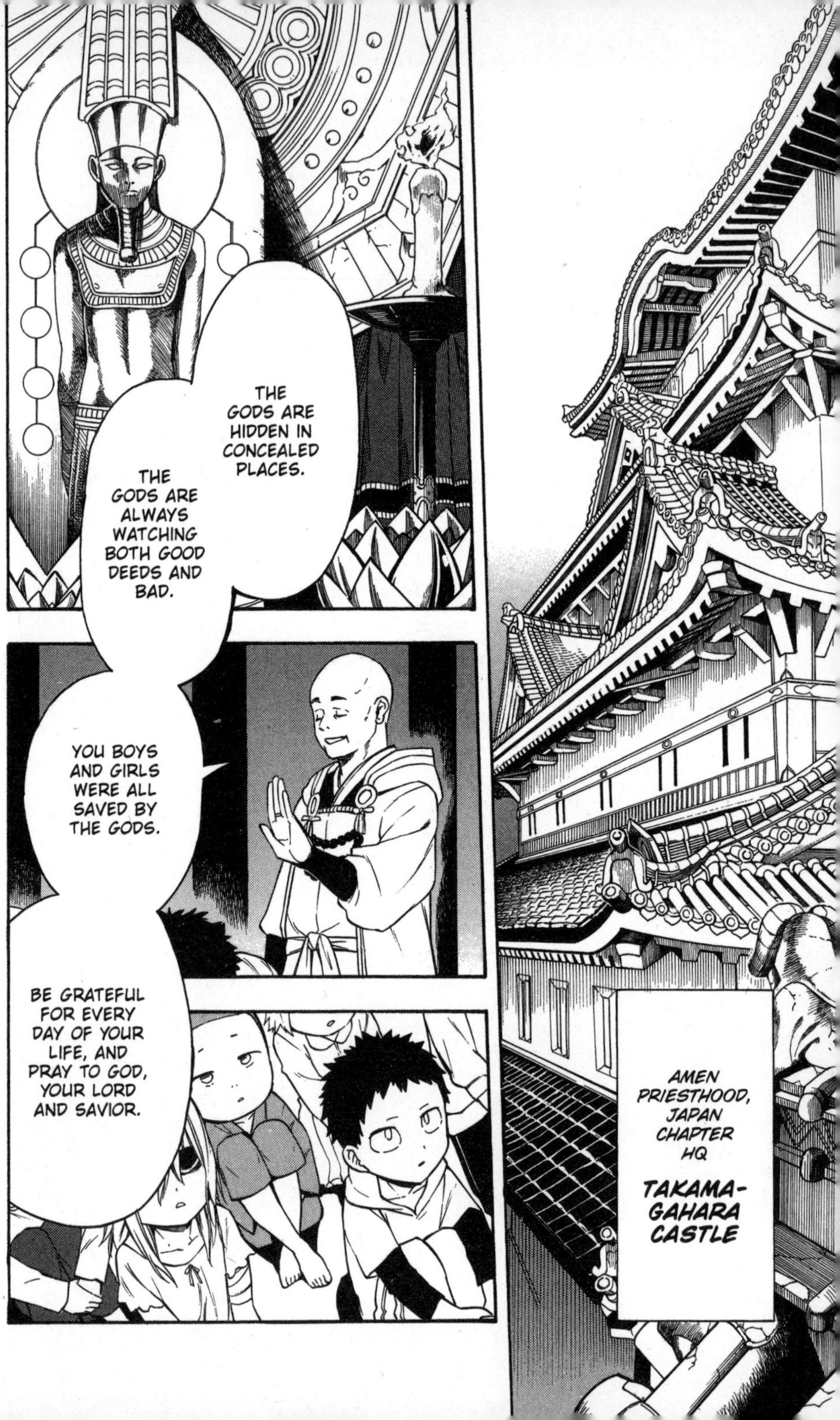
AMEN PRIESTHOOD, JAPAN CHAPTER HQ
TAKAMA-GAHARA CASTLE
THE GODS ARE HIDDEN IN CONCEALED PLACES.
THE GODS ARE ALWAYS WATCHING BOTH GOOD DEEDS AND BAD.
YOU BOYS AND GIRLS WERE ALL SAVED BY THE GODS.
BE GRATEFUL FOR EVERY DAY OF YOUR LIFE, AND PRAY TO GOD, YOUR LORD AND SAVIOR.

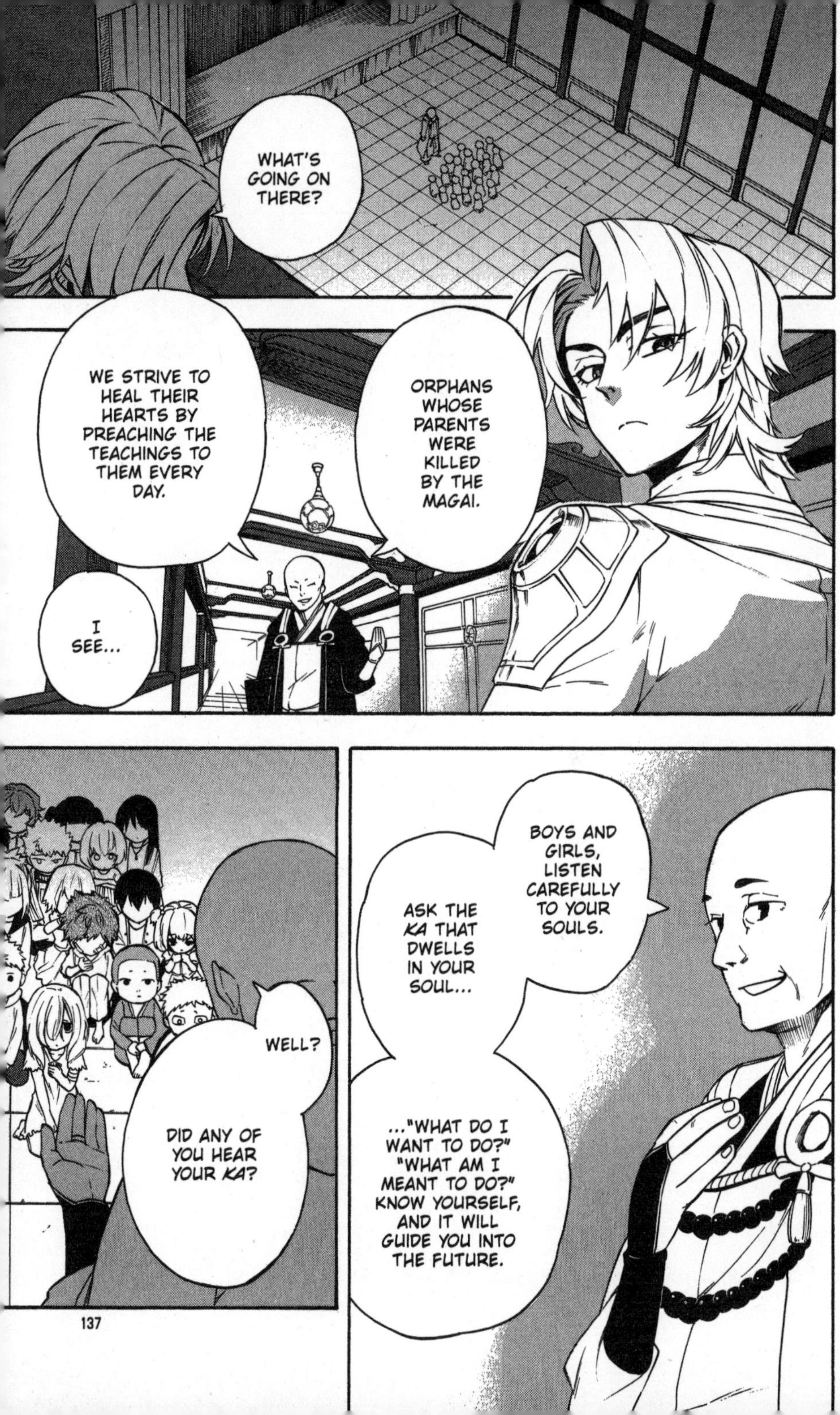
WHAT'S GOING ON THERE?
ORPHANS WHOSE PARENTS WERE KILLED BY THE MAGAI.
WE STRIVE TO HEAL THEIR HEARTS BY PREACHING THE TEACHINGS TO THEM EVERY DAY.
I SEE...
BOYS AND GIRLS, LISTEN CAREFULLY TO YOUR SOULS.
ASK THE *KA* THAT DWELLS IN YOUR SOUL...
..."WHAT DO I WANT TO DO?" "WHAT AM I MEANT TO DO?" KNOW YOURSELF, AND IT WILL GUIDE YOU INTO THE FUTURE.
WELL?
DID ANY OF YOU HEAR YOUR *KA*?

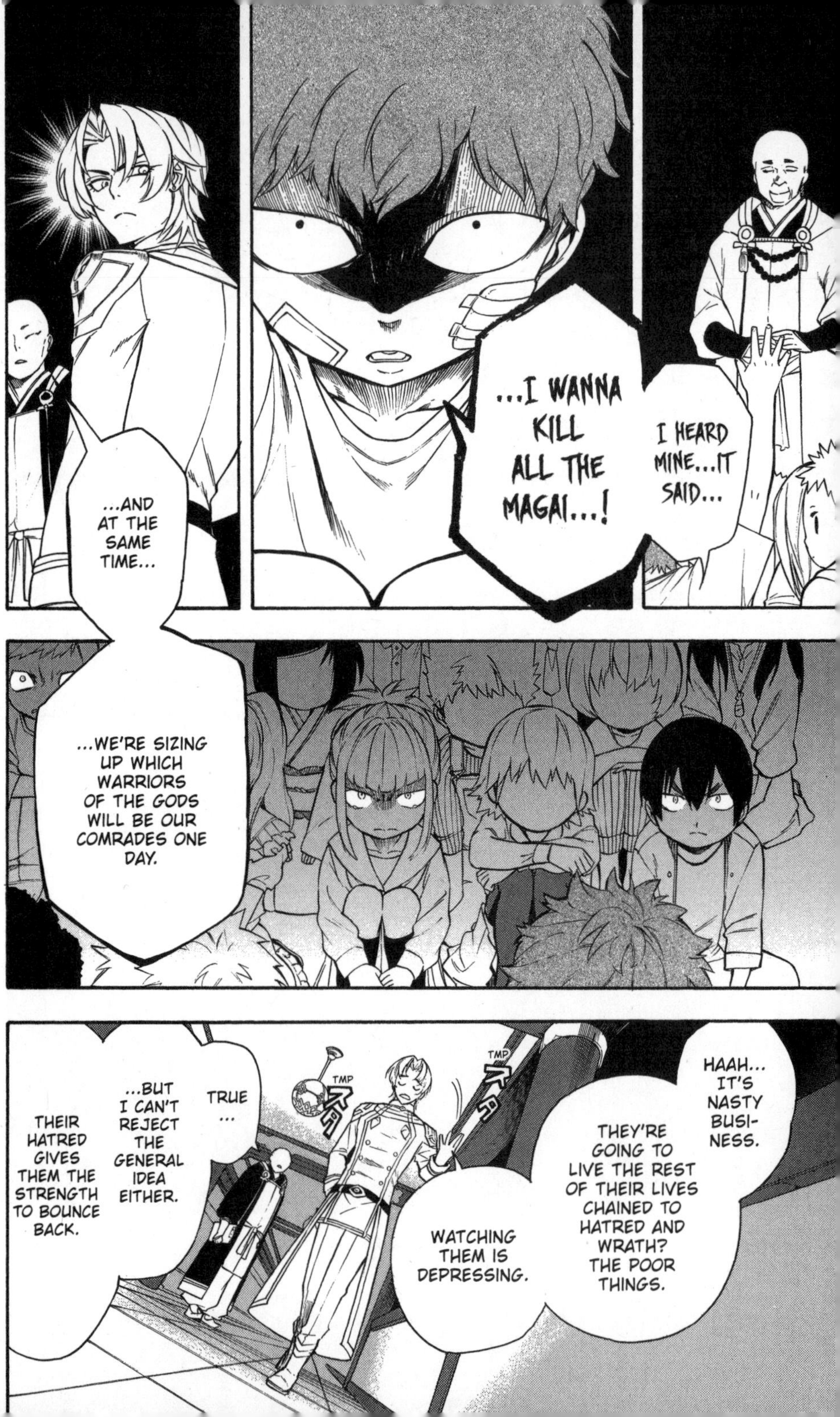
I HEARD MINE...IT SAID...
...I WANNA KILL ALL THE MAGAI...!
...AND AT THE SAME TIME...
...WE'RE SIZING UP WHICH WARRIORS OF THE GODS WILL BE OUR COMRADES ONE DAY.
HAAH... IT'S NASTY BUSI-NESS.
THEY'RE GOING TO LIVE THE REST OF THEIR LIVES CHAINED TO HATRED AND WRATH? THE POOR THINGS.
TMP
WATCHING THEM IS DEPRESSING.
TMP
TRUE...
...BUT I CAN'T REJECT THE GENERAL IDEA EITHER.
THEIR HATRED GIVES THEM THE STRENGTH TO BOUNCE BACK.

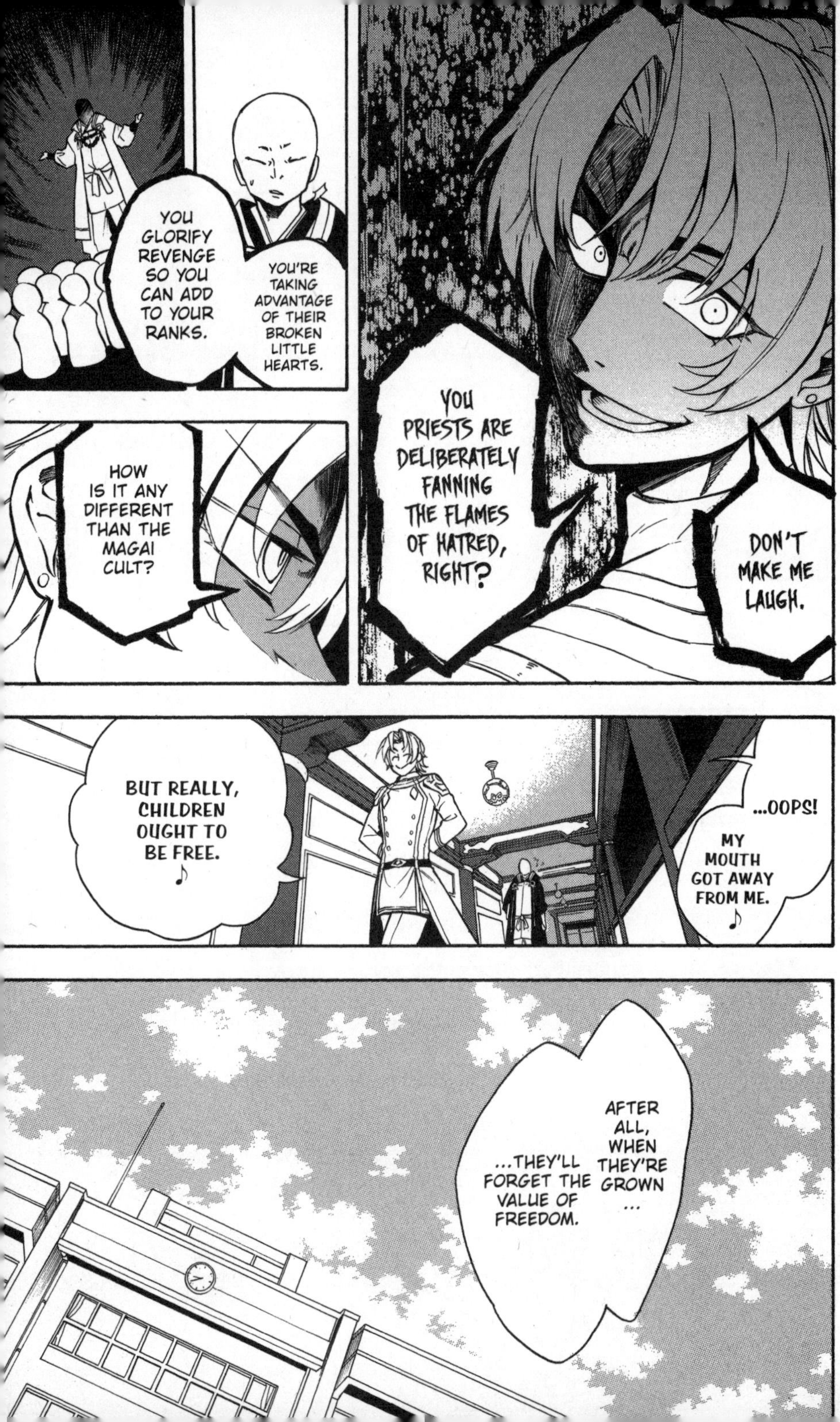
YOU PRIESTS ARE DELIBERATELY FANNING THE FLAMES OF HATRED, RIGHT?
DON'T MAKE ME LAUGH.
YOU GLORIFY REVENGE SO YOU CAN ADD TO YOUR RANKS.
YOU'RE TAKING ADVANTAGE OF THEIR BROKEN LITTLE HEARTS.
HOW IS IT ANY DIFFERENT THAN THE MAGAI CULT?
...OOPS!
MY MOUTH GOT AWAY FROM ME. ♪
BUT REALLY, CHILDREN OUGHT TO BE FREE. ♪
AFTER ALL, WHEN THEY'RE GROWN...
...THEY'LL FORGET THE VALUE OF FREEDOM.

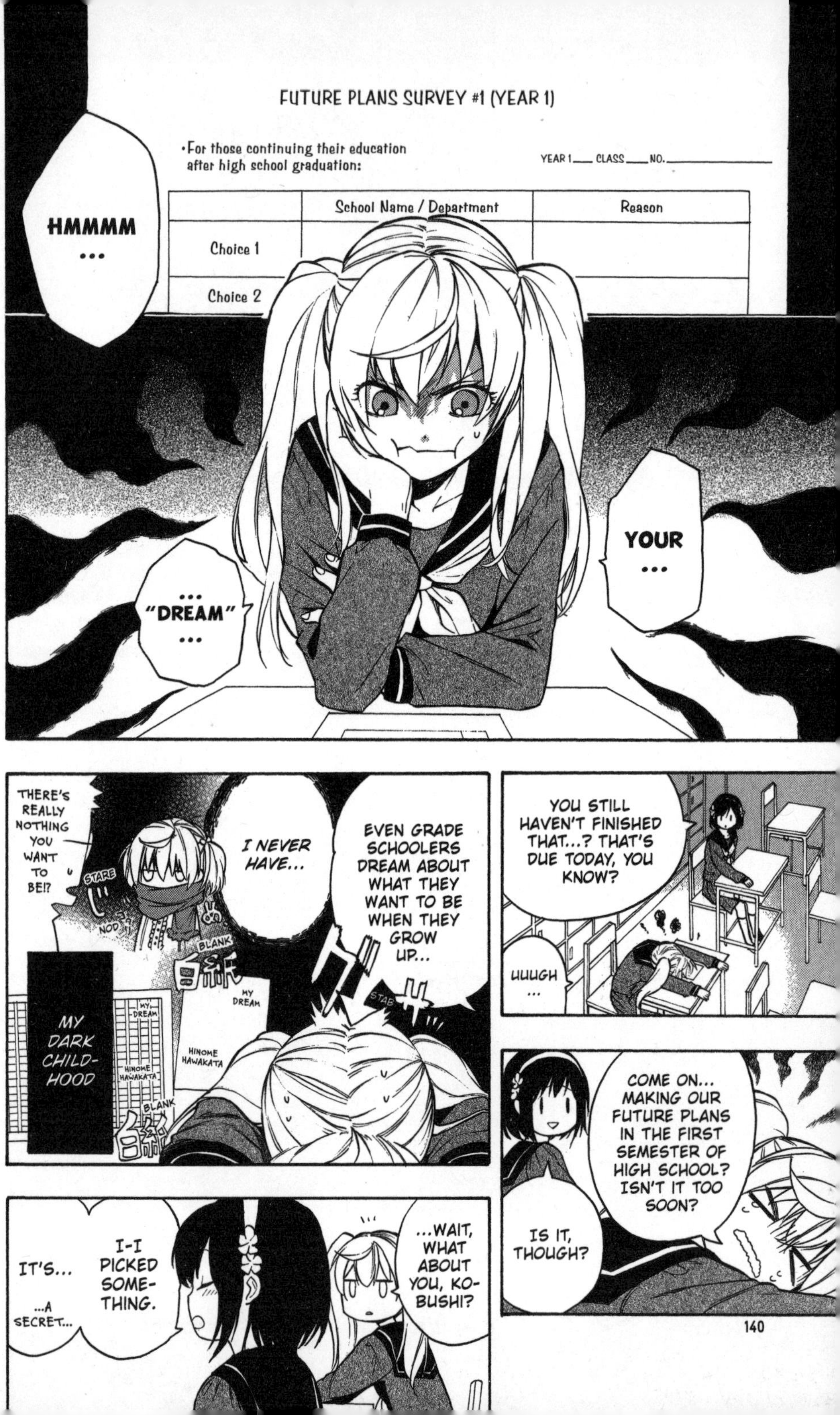
FUTURE PLANS SURVEY #1 (YEAR 1)
•For those continuing their education after high school graduation:
YEAR 1___ CLASS___ NO.___
School Name / Department
Reason
Choice 1
Choice 2
HMMMM...
YOUR...
..."DREAM"...
YOU STILL HAVEN'T FINISHED THAT...? THAT'S DUE TODAY, YOU KNOW?
UUUGH...
EVEN GRADE SCHOOLERS DREAM ABOUT WHAT THEY WANT TO BE WHEN THEY GROW UP...
I NEVER HAVE...
THERE'S REALLY NOTHING YOU WANT TO BE!?
STARE
NOD
BLANK
MY DREAM
HINOME HAWAKATA
STAB
MY DREAM
HINOME HAWAKATA
BLANK
MY DARK CHILDHOOD
COME ON... MAKING OUR FUTURE PLANS IN THE FIRST SEMESTER OF HIGH SCHOOL? ISN'T IT TOO SOON?
IS IT, THOUGH?
...WAIT, WHAT ABOUT YOU, KOBUSHI?
I-I PICKED SOMETHING.
IT'S...
...A SECRET...

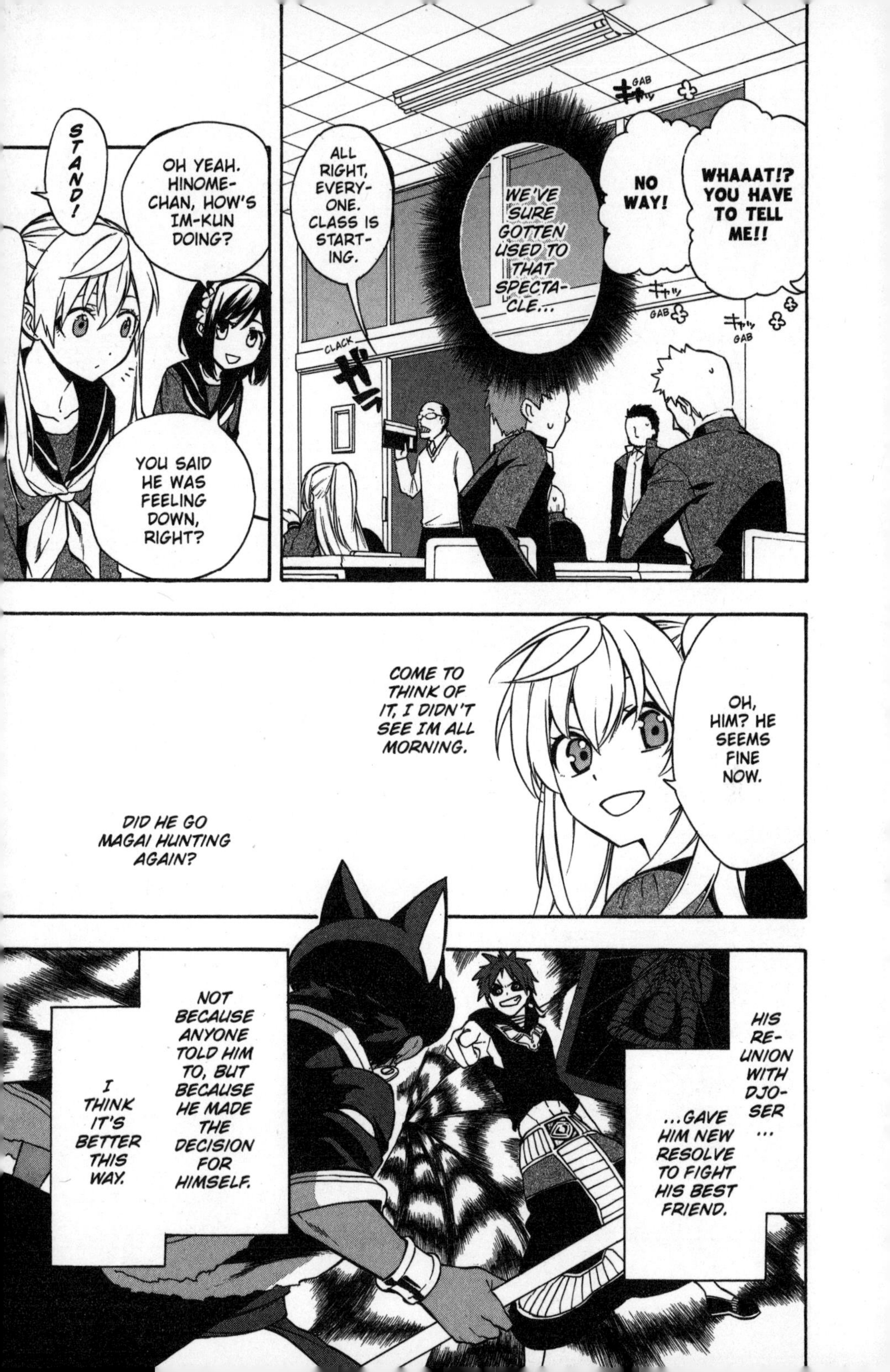
GAB
WHAAAT!? YOU HAVE TO TELL ME!!
NO WAY!
GAB
GAB
WE'VE SURE GOTTEN USED TO THAT SPECTACLE...
ALL RIGHT, EVERYONE. CLASS IS STARTING.
CLACK
STAND!
OH YEAH. HINOME-CHAN, HOW'S IM-KUN DOING?
YOU SAID HE WAS FEELING DOWN, RIGHT?
OH, HIM? HE SEEMS FINE NOW.
COME TO THINK OF IT, I DIDN'T SEE IM ALL MORNING.
DID HE GO MAGAI HUNTING AGAIN?
HIS REUNION WITH DJOSER...
...GAVE HIM NEW RESOLVE TO FIGHT HIS BEST FRIEND.
NOT BECAUSE ANYONE TOLD HIM TO, BUT BECAUSE HE MADE THE DECISION FOR HIMSELF.
I THINK IT'S BETTER THIS WAY.

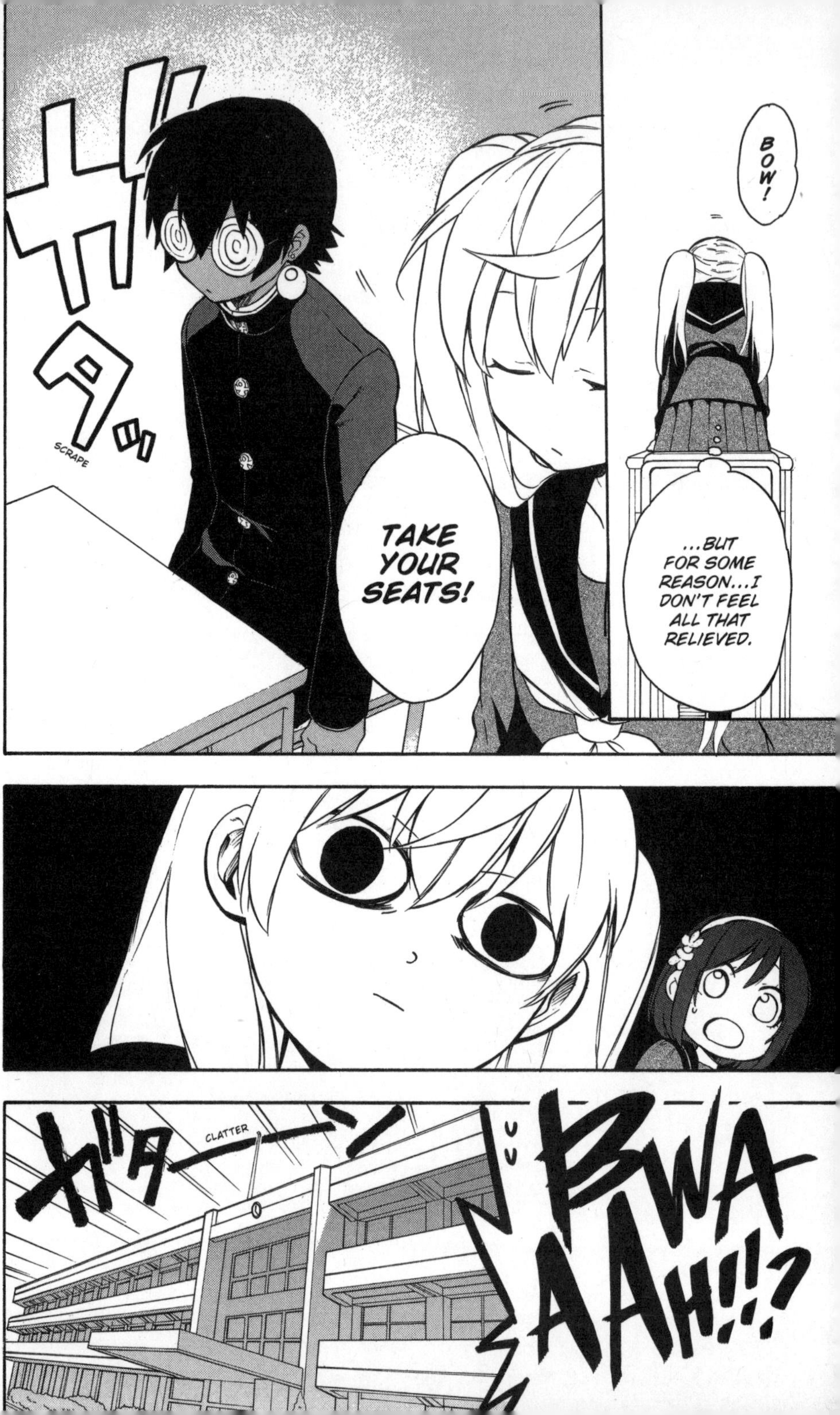
BOW!
...BUT FOR SOME REASON...I DON'T FEEL ALL THAT RELIEVED.
TAKE YOUR SEATS!
SCRAPE
CLATTER
BWAAAH!!?

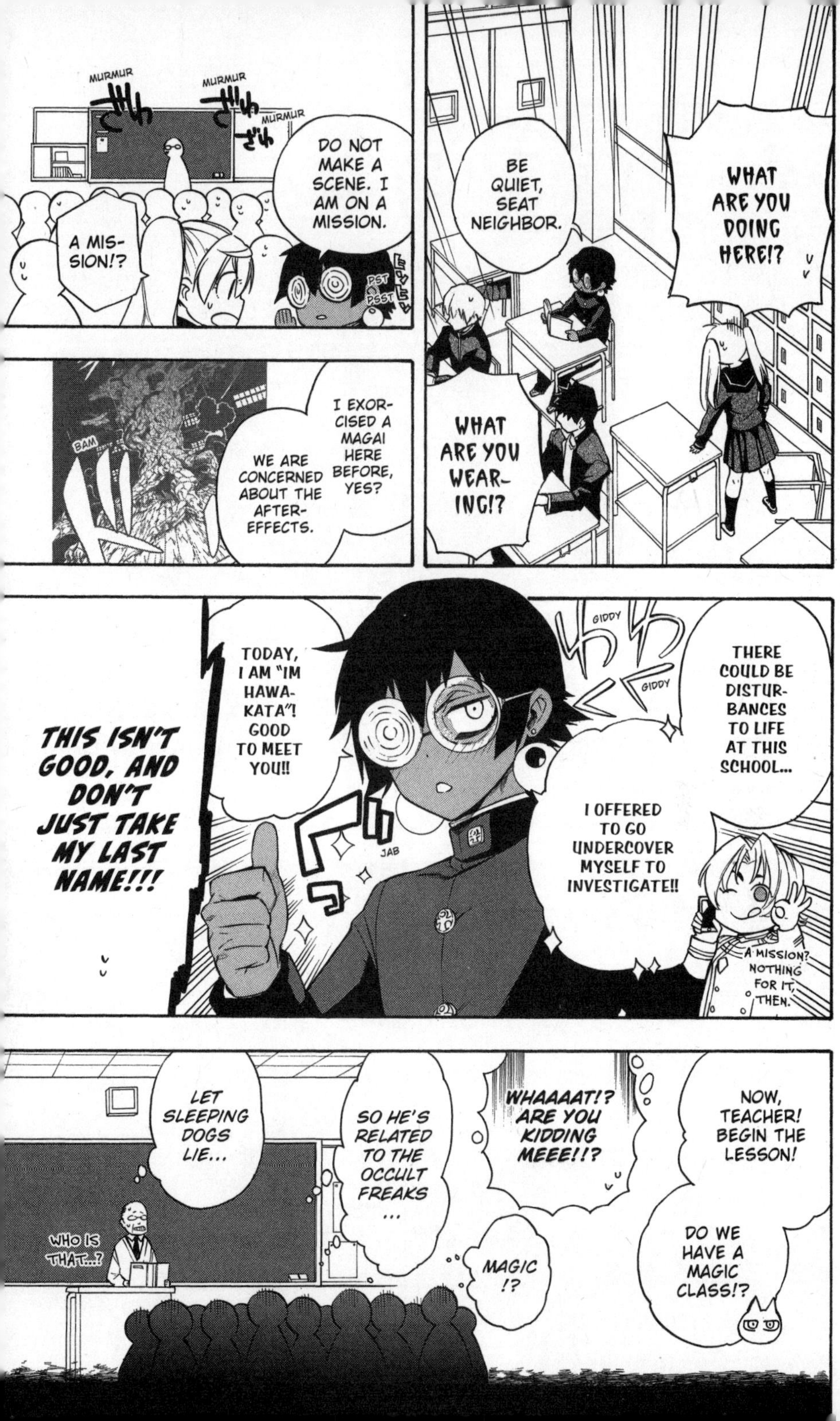
WHAT ARE YOU DOING HERE!?
BE QUIET, SEAT NEIGHBOR.
WHAT ARE YOU WEARING!?
MURMUR
MURMUR
MURMUR
DO NOT MAKE A SCENE. I AM ON A MISSION.
A MISSION!?
PST PSST
I EXORCISED A MAGAI HERE BEFORE, YES?
WE ARE CONCERNED ABOUT THE AFTER-EFFECTS.
BAM
GIDDY GIDDY
THERE COULD BE DISTURBANCES TO LIFE AT THIS SCHOOL...
I OFFERED TO GO UNDERCOVER MYSELF TO INVESTIGATE!!
A MISSION? NOTHING FOR IT, THEN.
TODAY, I AM "IM HAWAKATA"! GOOD TO MEET YOU!!
JAB
THIS ISN'T GOOD, AND DON'T JUST TAKE MY LAST NAME!!!
NOW, TEACHER! BEGIN THE LESSON!
DO WE HAVE A MAGIC CLASS!?
WHAAAAT!? ARE YOU KIDDING MEEE!!?
MAGIC!?
SO HE'S RELATED TO THE OCCULT FREAKS...
LET SLEEPING DOGS LIE...
WHO IS THAT...?

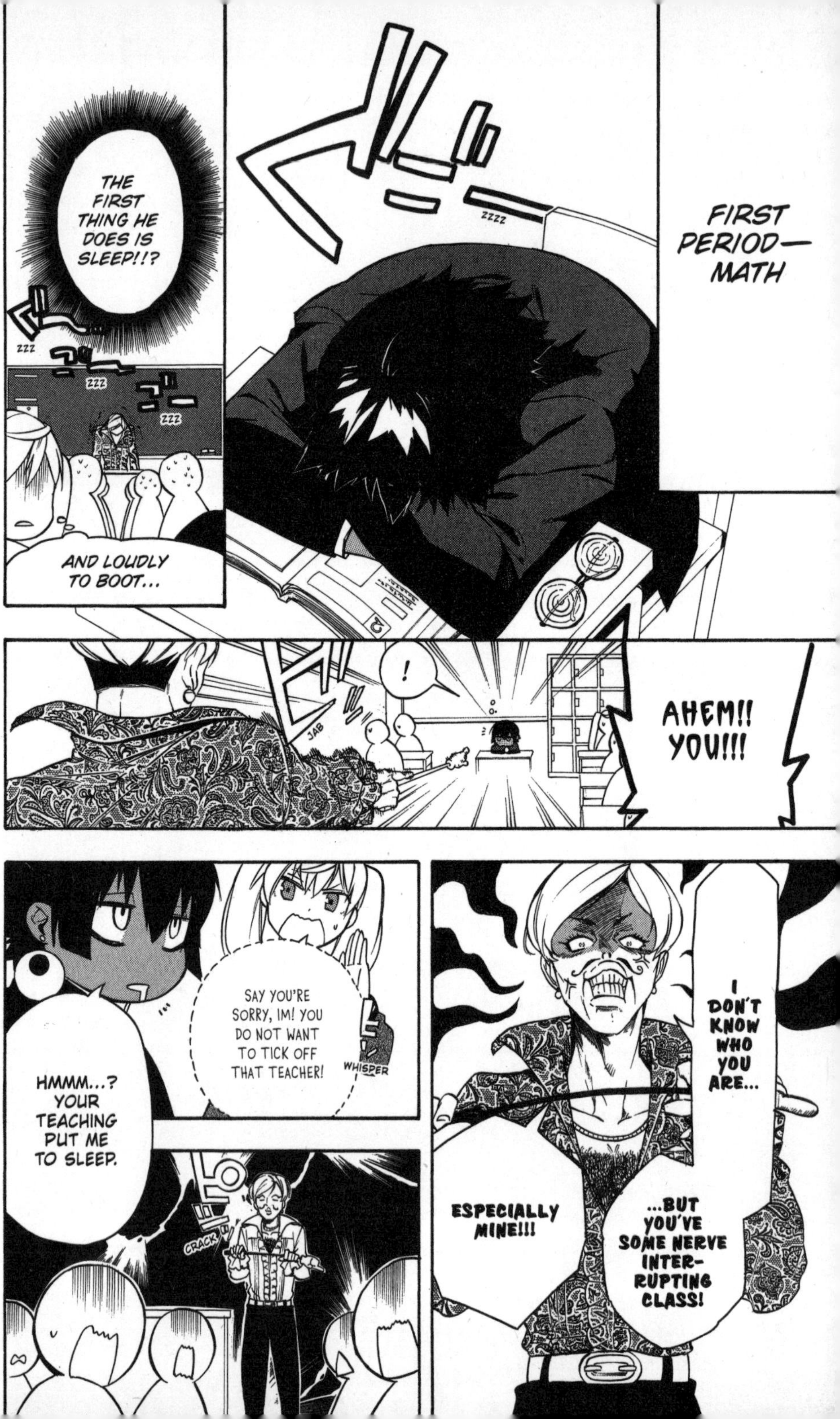

FIRST PERIOD—MATH
ZZZZ
THE FIRST THING HE DOES IS SLEEP!!?
ZZZ
ZZZ
ZZZ
AND LOUDLY TO BOOT...
AHEM!! YOU!!!
!
JAB
I DON'T KNOW WHO YOU ARE...
...BUT YOU'VE SOME NERVE INTER-RUPTING CLASS!
ESPECIALLY MINE!!!
SAY YOU'RE SORRY, IM! YOU DO NOT WANT TO TICK OFF THAT TEACHER!
WHISPER
HMMM...? YOUR TEACHING PUT ME TO SLEEP.
CRACK

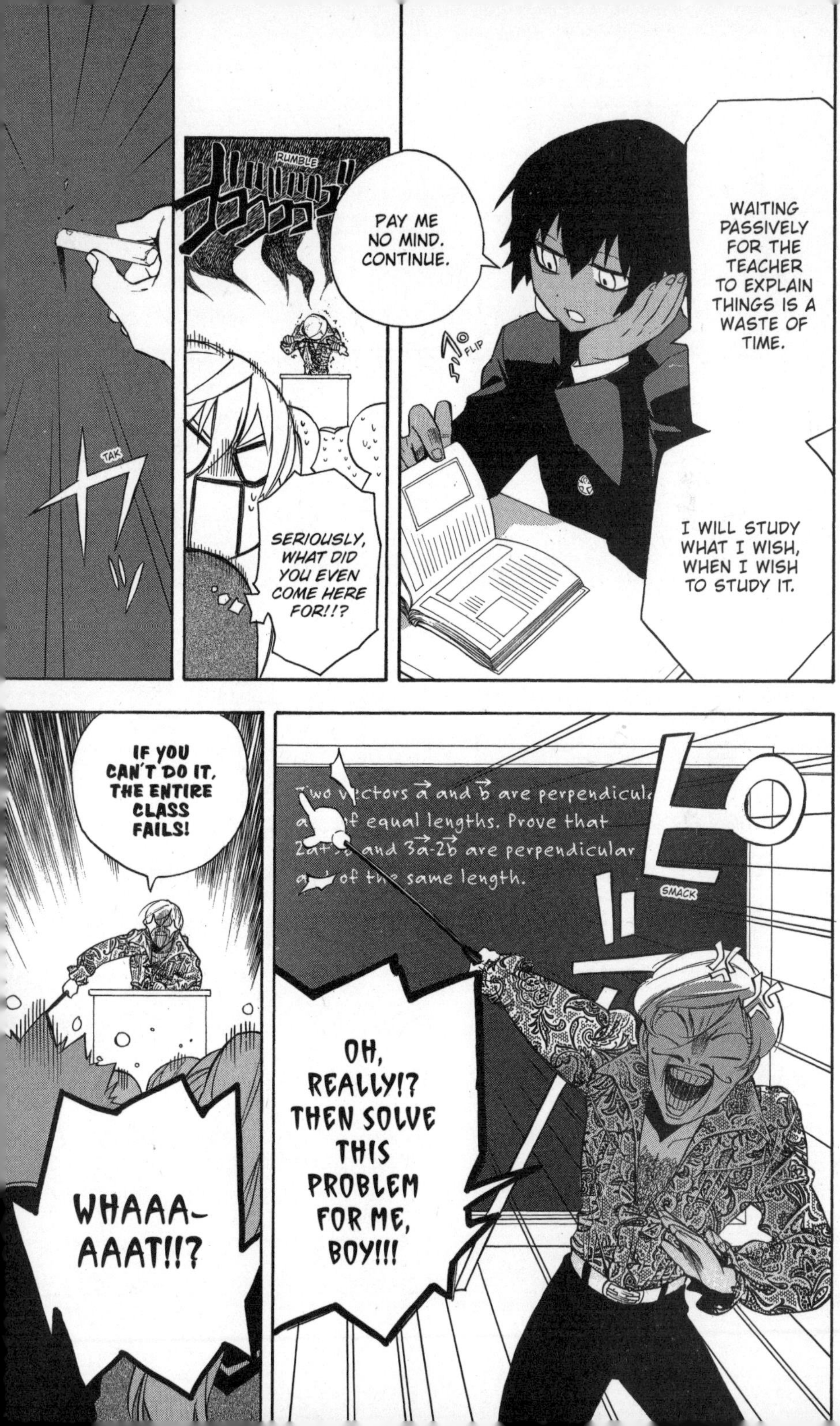
WAITING PASSIVELY FOR THE TEACHER TO EXPLAIN THINGS IS A WASTE OF TIME.
FLIP
I WILL STUDY WHAT I WISH, WHEN I WISH TO STUDY IT.
PAY ME NO MIND. CONTINUE.
RUMBLE
SERIOUSLY, WHAT DID YOU EVEN COME HERE FOR!!?
TAK
SMACK
wo v ctors $\vec{a}$ and $\vec{b}$ are perpendicul
f equal lengths. Prove that
$2\vec{a}+$ and $3\vec{a}-2\vec{b}$ are perpendicular
of th same length.
OH, REALLY!? THEN SOLVE THIS PROBLEM FOR ME, BOY!!!
IF YOU CAN'T DO IT, THE ENTIRE CLASS FAILS!
WHAAA-AAAT!!?

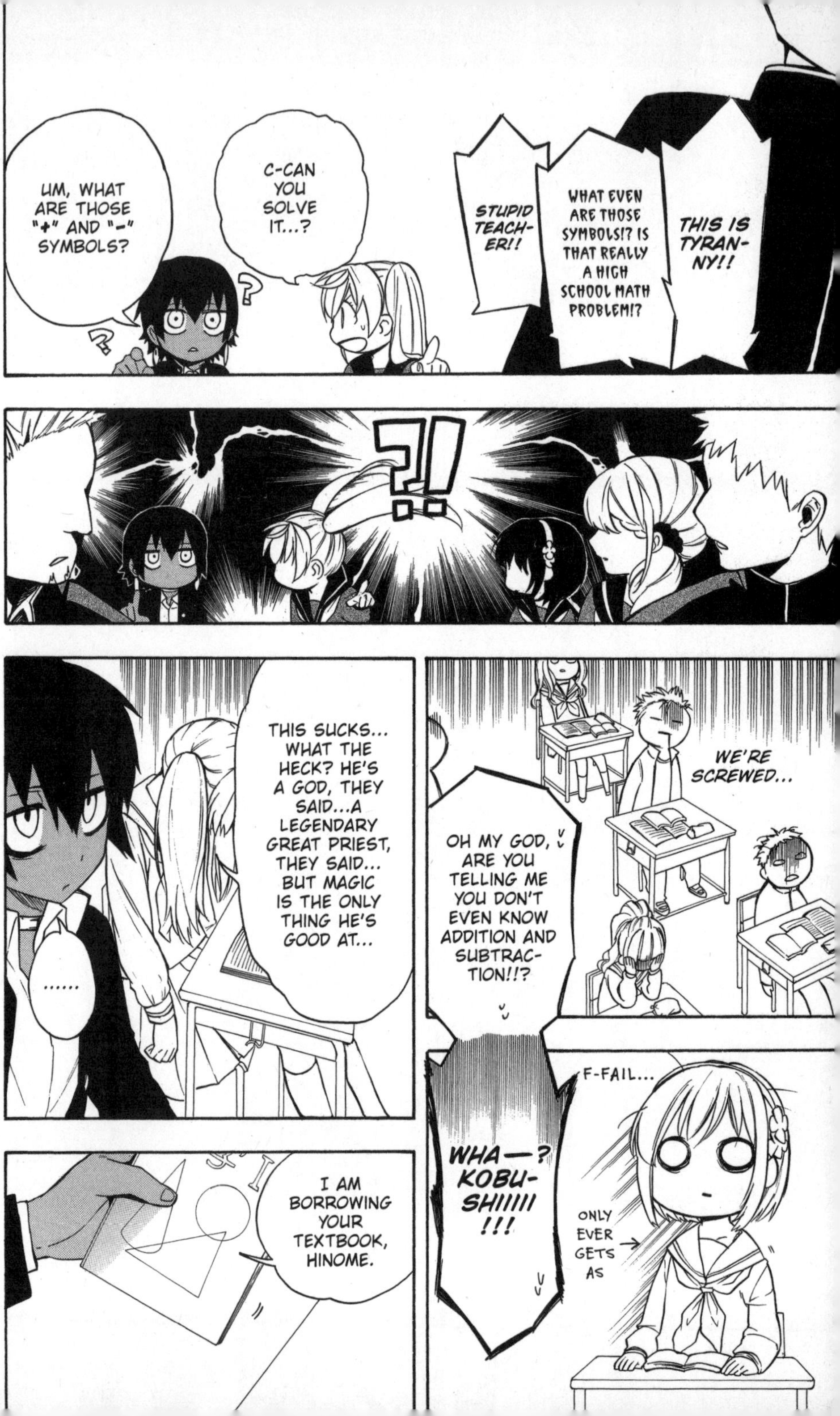
THIS IS TYRANNY!!
WHAT EVEN ARE THOSE SYMBOLS!? IS THAT REALLY A HIGH SCHOOL MATH PROBLEM!?
STUPID TEACHER!!
C-CAN YOU SOLVE IT...?
UM, WHAT ARE THOSE "+" AND "–" SYMBOLS?
?!
WE'RE SCREWED...
OH MY GOD, ARE YOU TELLING ME YOU DON'T EVEN KNOW ADDITION AND SUBTRACTION!!?
F-FAIL...
ONLY EVER GETS AS
WHA—? KOBUSHI!!!!!!!!!
THIS SUCKS... WHAT THE HECK? HE'S A GOD, THEY SAID...A LEGENDARY GREAT PRIEST, THEY SAID... BUT MAGIC IS THE ONLY THING HE'S GOOD AT...
......
I AM BORROWING YOUR TEXTBOOK, HINOME.

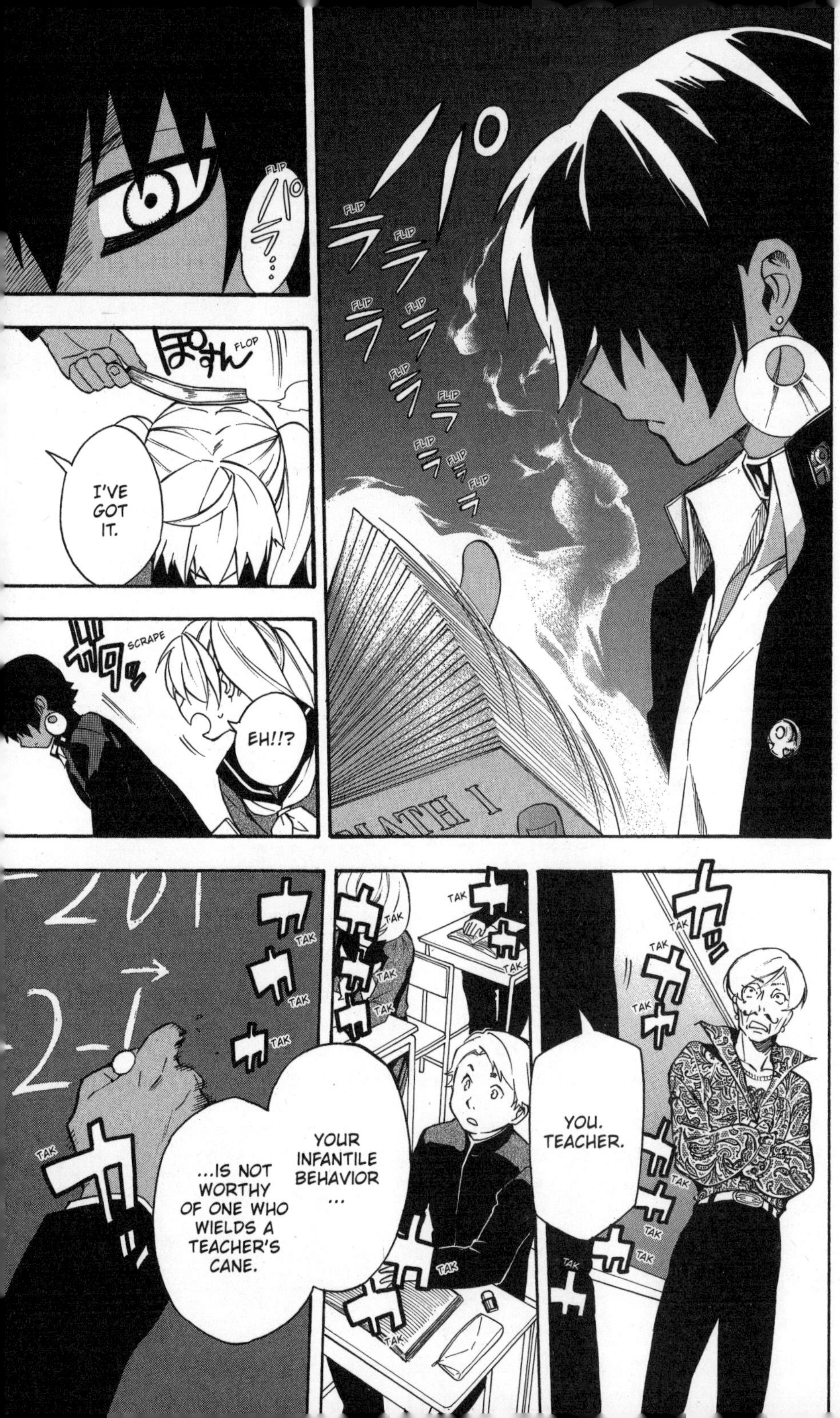
FLIP
FLIP
FLIP
FLIP
FLIP
FLIP
FLIP
FLIP
FLIP
MATH I
FLIP
ぽすん FLOP
I'VE GOT IT.
SCRAPE
EH!!?
TAK
TAK
TAK
YOU. TEACHER.
TAK
TAK
TAK
TAK
TAK
YOUR INFANTILE BEHAVIOR ...
...IS NOT WORTHY OF ONE WHO WIELDS A TEACHER'S CANE.
TAK

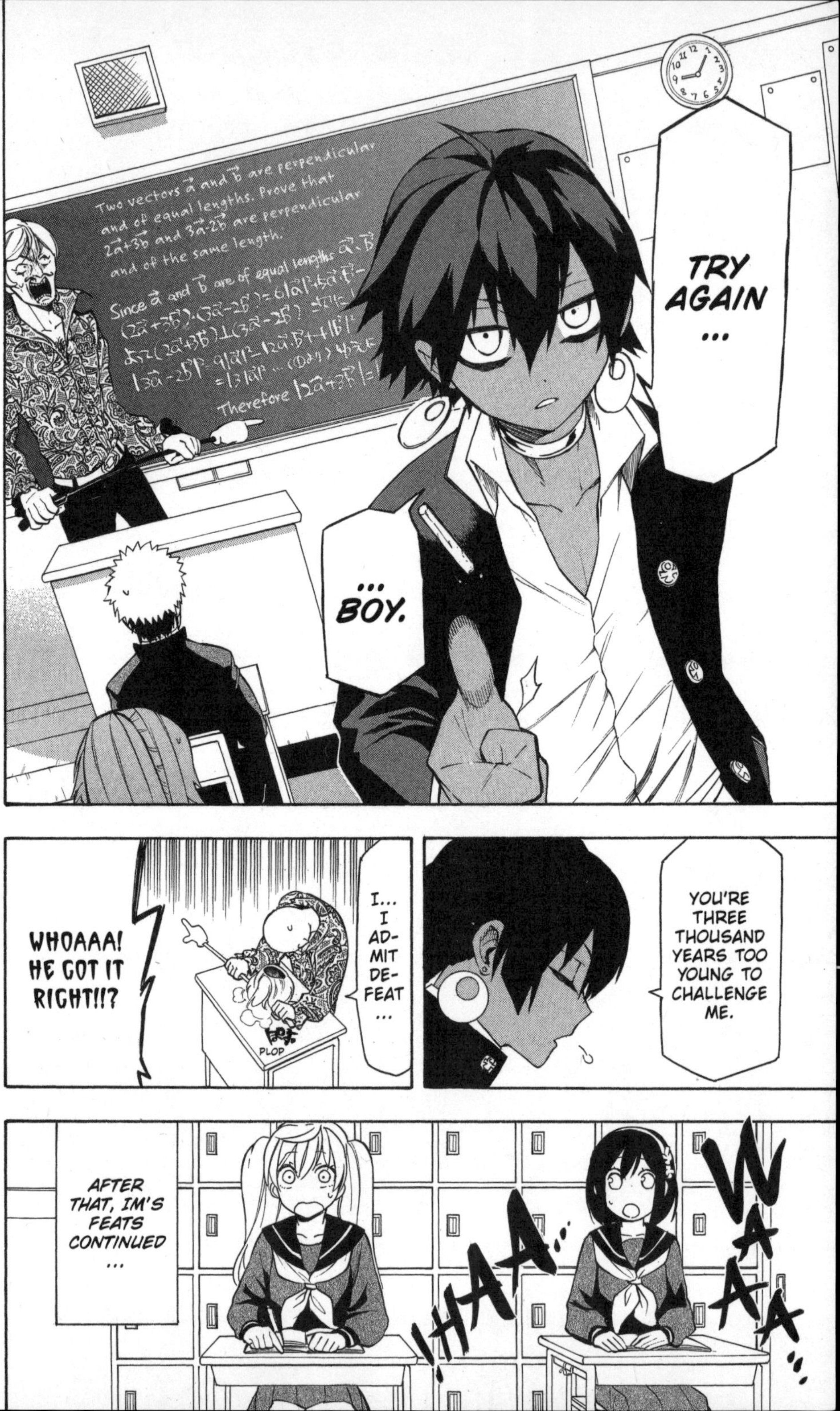
Two vectors a and b are perpendicular and of equal lengths. Prove that 2a+3b and 3a-2b are perpendicular and of the same length.
Therefore
TRY AGAIN ...
... BOY.
YOU'RE THREE THOUSAND YEARS TOO YOUNG TO CHALLENGE ME.
I... I ADMIT DEFEAT ...
WHOAAA! HE GOT IT RIGHT!!?
PLOP
WAAAA...
HAA...!
AFTER THAT, IM'S FEATS CONTINUED ...

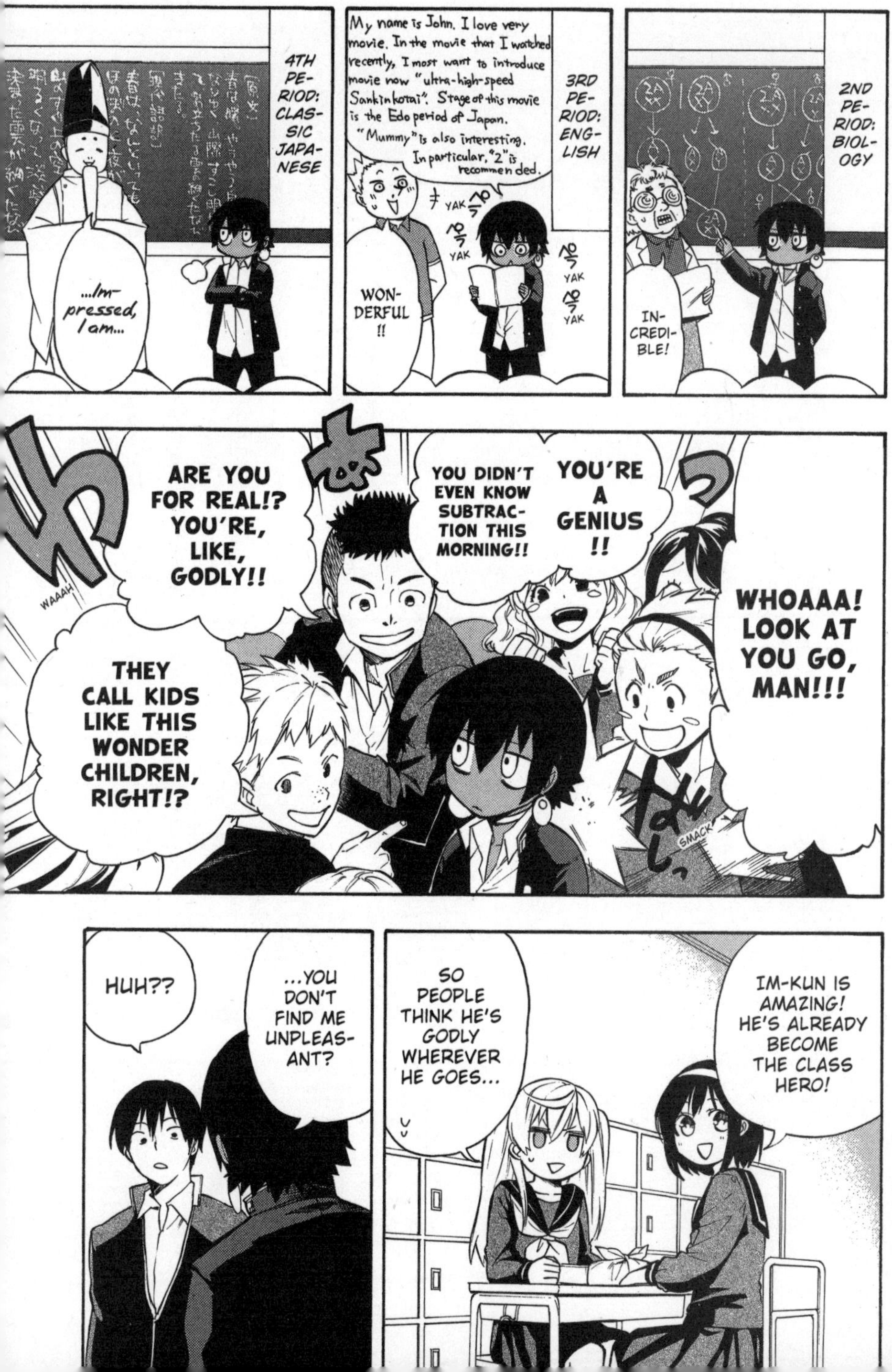
2ND PERIOD: BIOLOGY
INCREDIBLE!
3RD PERIOD: ENGLISH
My name is John. I love very movie. In the movie that I watched recently, I most want to introduce movie now "ultra-high-speed Sankinkotai". Stage of this movie is the Edo period of Japan. "Mummy" is also interesting. In particular, "2" is recommended.
YAK YAK YAK YAK
WONDERFUL!!
4TH PERIOD: CLASSIC JAPANESE
...Impressed, I am...
WHOAAA! LOOK AT YOU GO, MAN!!!
YOU'RE A GENIUS!!
YOU DIDN'T EVEN KNOW SUBTRACTION THIS MORNING!!
ARE YOU FOR REAL!? YOU'RE, LIKE, GODLY!!
WAAAH
THEY CALL KIDS LIKE THIS WONDER CHILDREN, RIGHT!?
SMACK
IM-KUN IS AMAZING! HE'S ALREADY BECOME THE CLASS HERO!
SO PEOPLE THINK HE'S GODLY WHEREVER HE GOES...
...YOU DON'T FIND ME UNPLEASANT?
HUH??

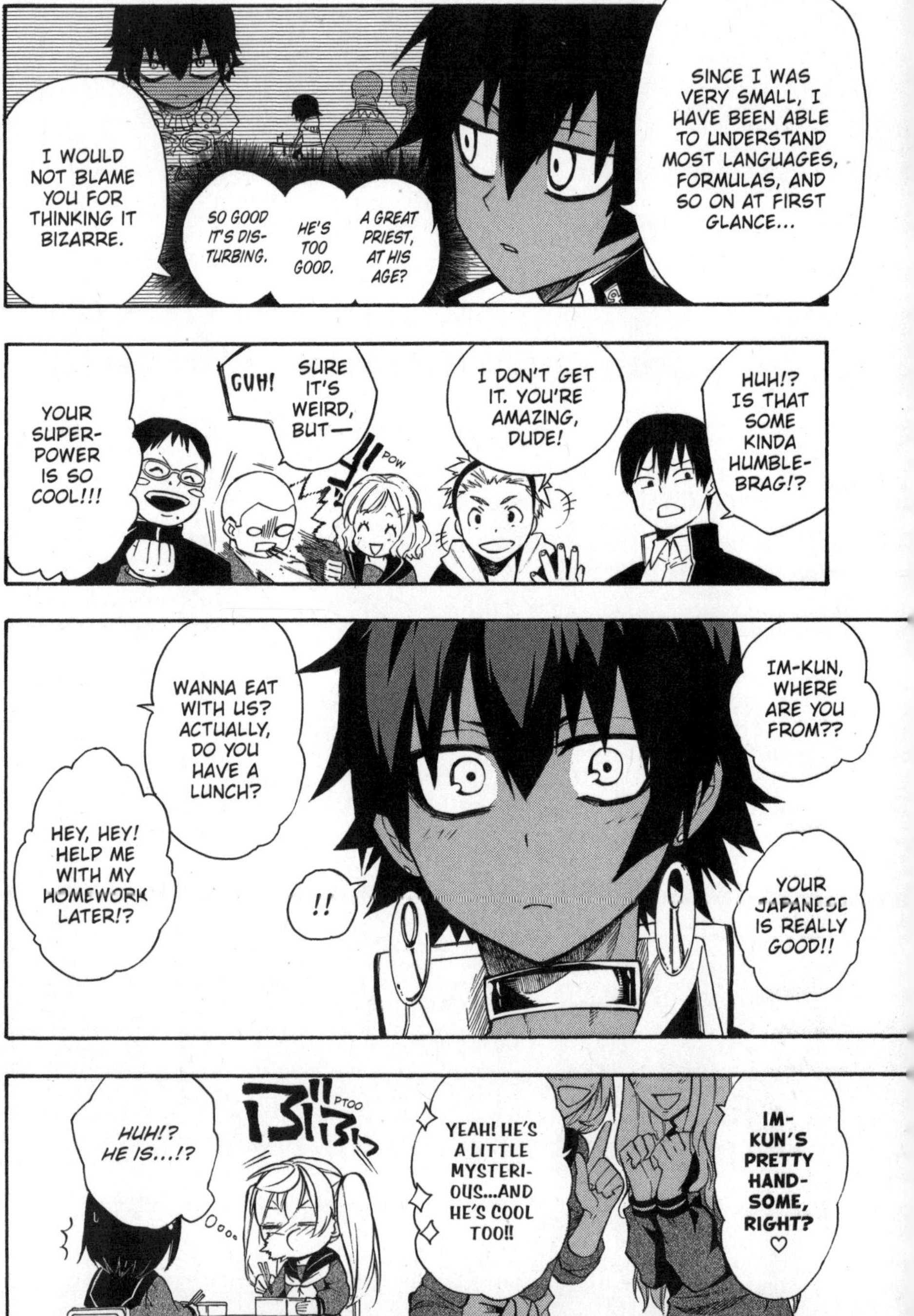
SINCE I WAS VERY SMALL, I HAVE BEEN ABLE TO UNDERSTAND MOST LANGUAGES, FORMULAS, AND SO ON AT FIRST GLANCE...
A GREAT PRIEST, AT HIS AGE?
HE'S TOO GOOD.
SO GOOD IT'S DISTURBING.
I WOULD NOT BLAME YOU FOR THINKING IT BIZARRE.
HUH!? IS THAT SOME KINDA HUMBLE-BRAG!?
I DON'T GET IT. YOU'RE AMAZING, DUDE!
SURE IT'S WEIRD, BUT—
GUH!
POW
YOUR SUPER-POWER IS SO COOL!!!
IM-KUN, WHERE ARE YOU FROM??
YOUR JAPANESE IS REALLY GOOD!!
WANNA EAT WITH US? ACTUALLY, DO YOU HAVE A LUNCH?
HEY, HEY! HELP ME WITH MY HOMEWORK LATER!?
!!
IM-KUN'S PRETTY HANDSOME, RIGHT? ♡
YEAH! HE'S A LITTLE MYSTERIOUS...AND HE'S COOL TOO!!
PTOO
HUH!? HE IS...!?

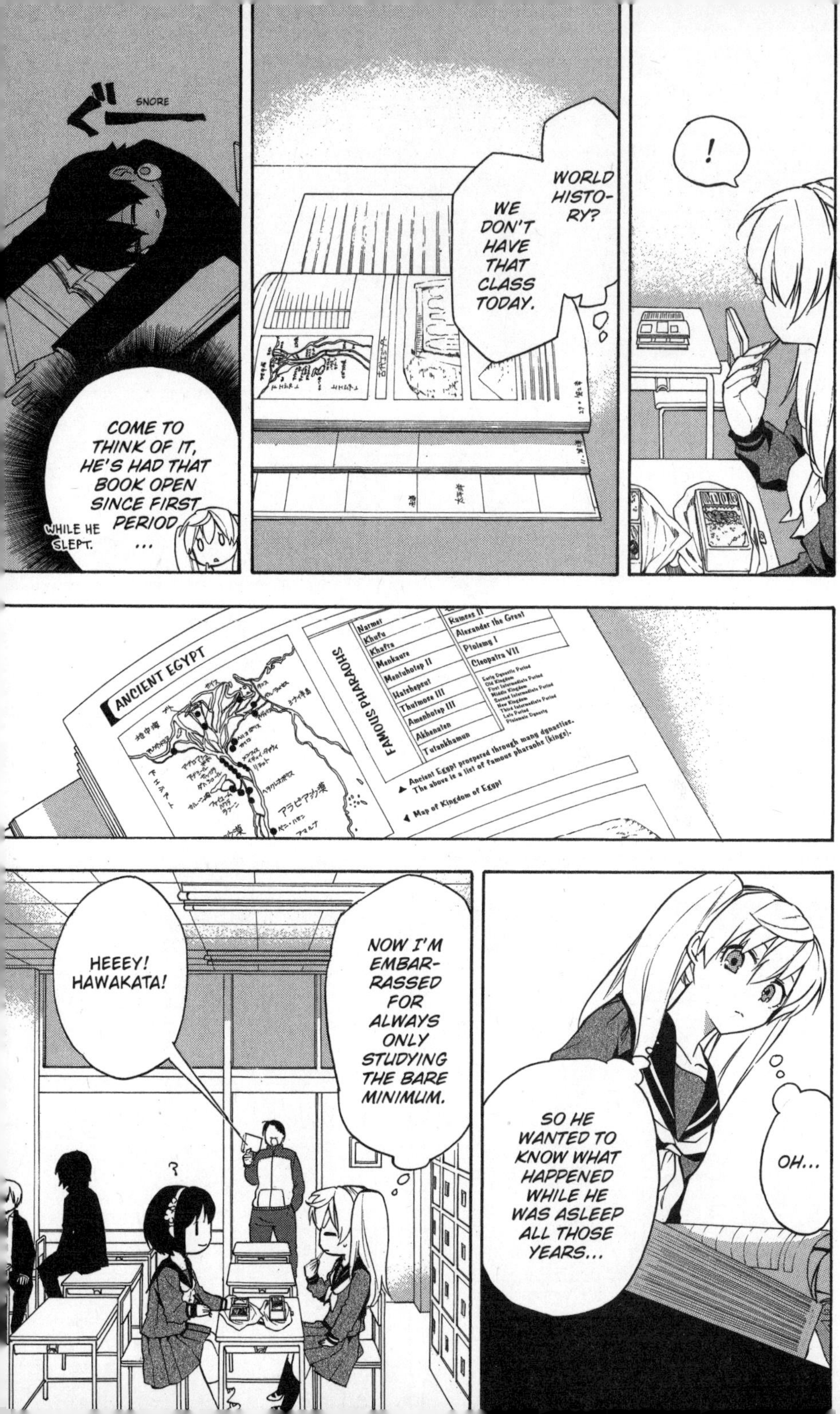
!
WORLD HISTORY?
WE DON'T HAVE THAT CLASS TODAY.
SNORE
COME TO THINK OF IT, HE'S HAD THAT BOOK OPEN SINCE FIRST PERIOD
WHILE HE SLEPT.
...
ANCIENT EGYPT
FAMOUS PHARAOHS
Narmer
Khufu
Khafra
Menkaure
Mentuhotep II
Hatshepsut
Thutmose III
Amenhotep III
Akhenaten
Tutankhamun
Ramses II
Alexander the Great
Ptolemy I
Cleopatra VII
Early Dynastic Period
Old Kingdom
First Intermediate Period
Middle Kingdom
Second Intermediate Period
New Kingdom
Third Intermediate Period
Late Period
Ptolemaic Dynasty
Ancient Egypt prospered through many dynasties. The above is a list of famous pharaohs (kings).
Map of Kingdom of Egypt
OH...
SO HE WANTED TO KNOW WHAT HAPPENED WHILE HE WAS ASLEEP ALL THOSE YEARS...
NOW I'M EMBARRASSED FOR ALWAYS ONLY STUDYING THE BARE MINIMUM.
HEEEY! HAWAKATA!
?

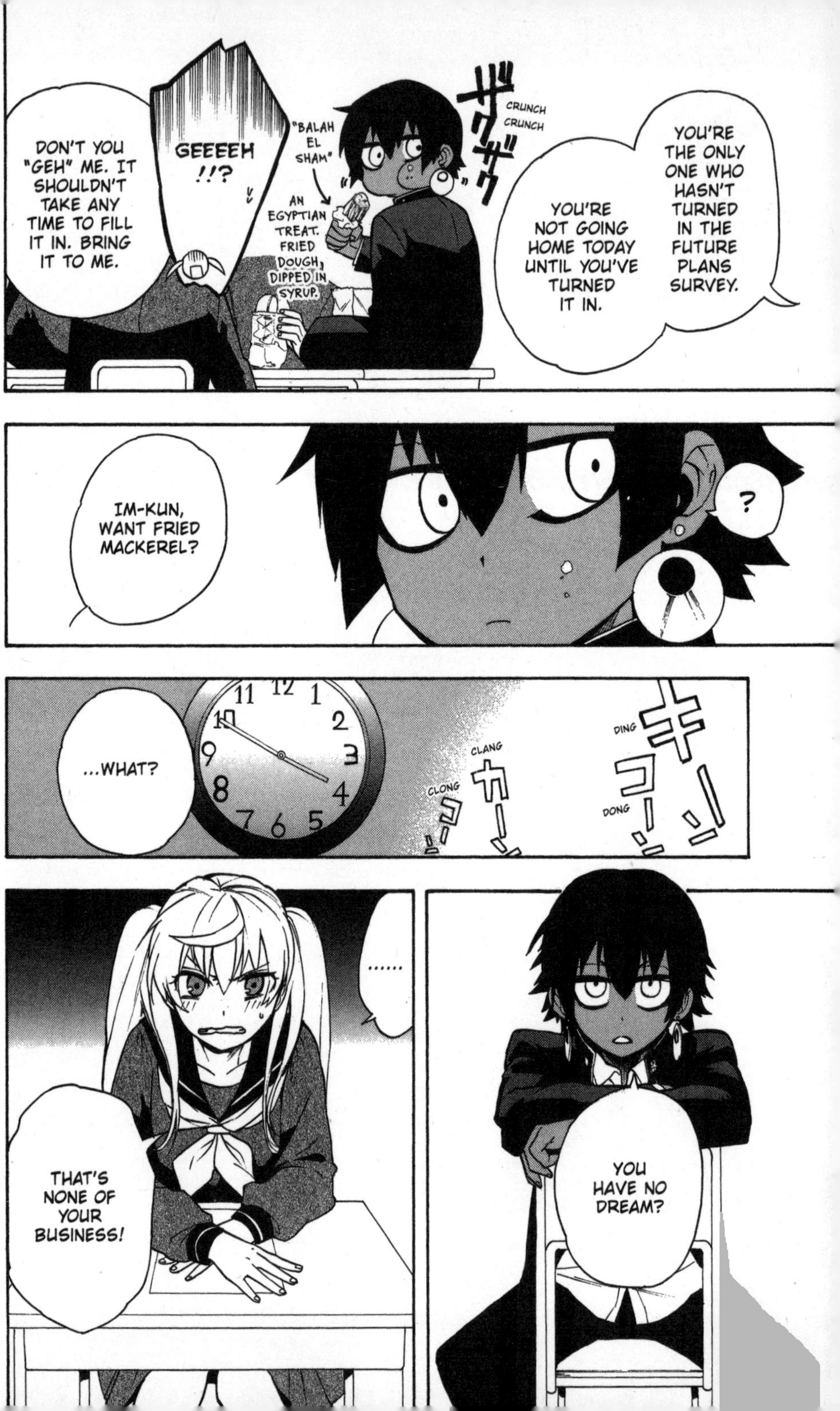
YOU'RE THE ONLY ONE WHO HASN'T TURNED IN THE FUTURE PLANS SURVEY.
YOU'RE NOT GOING HOME TODAY UNTIL YOU'VE TURNED IT IN.
CRUNCH CRUNCH
"BALAH EL SHAM"
AN EGYPTIAN TREAT. FRIED DOUGH DIPPED IN SYRUP.
GEEEEH!!?
DON'T YOU "GEH" ME. IT SHOULDN'T TAKE ANY TIME TO FILL IT IN. BRING IT TO ME.
?
IM-KUN, WANT FRIED MACKEREL?
DING DONG
CLANG CLONG
...WHAT?
YOU HAVE NO DREAM?
......
THAT'S NONE OF YOUR BUSINESS!

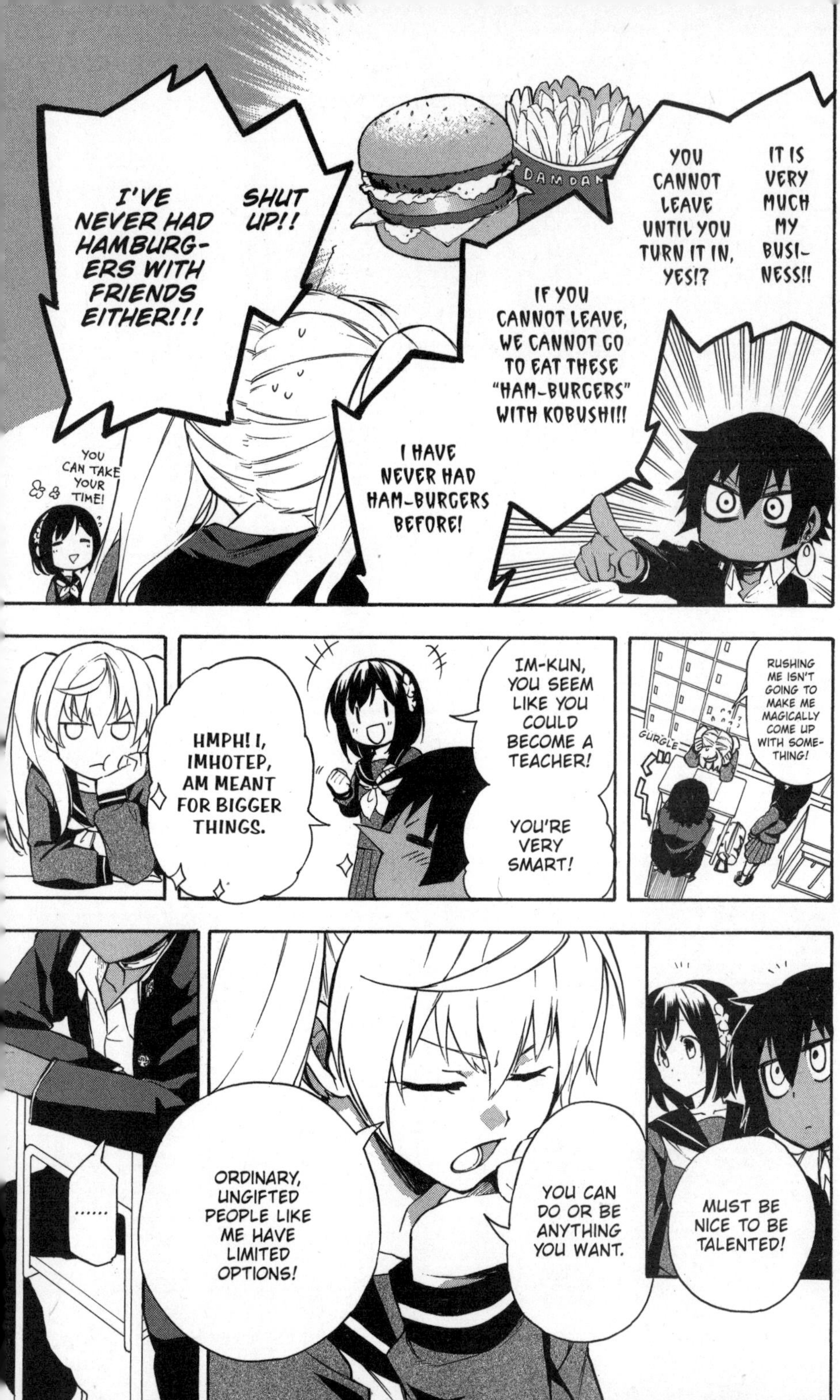
IT IS VERY MUCH MY BUSI-NESS!!
YOU CANNOT LEAVE UNTIL YOU TURN IT IN, YES!?
IF YOU CANNOT LEAVE, WE CANNOT GO TO EAT THESE "HAM-BURGERS" WITH KOBUSHI!!!
DAM DAM
I HAVE NEVER HAD HAM-BURGERS BEFORE!
SHUT UP!!
I'VE NEVER HAD HAMBURG-ERS WITH FRIENDS EITHER!!!
YOU CAN TAKE YOUR TIME!
RUSHING ME ISN'T GOING TO MAKE ME MAGICALLY COME UP WITH SOME-THING!
GURGLE
IM-KUN, YOU SEEM LIKE YOU COULD BECOME A TEACHER!
YOU'RE VERY SMART!
HMPH! I, IMHOTEP, AM MEANT FOR BIGGER THINGS.
MUST BE NICE TO BE TALENTED!
YOU CAN DO OR BE ANYTHING YOU WANT.
ORDINARY, UNGIFTED PEOPLE LIKE ME HAVE LIMITED OPTIONS!
......

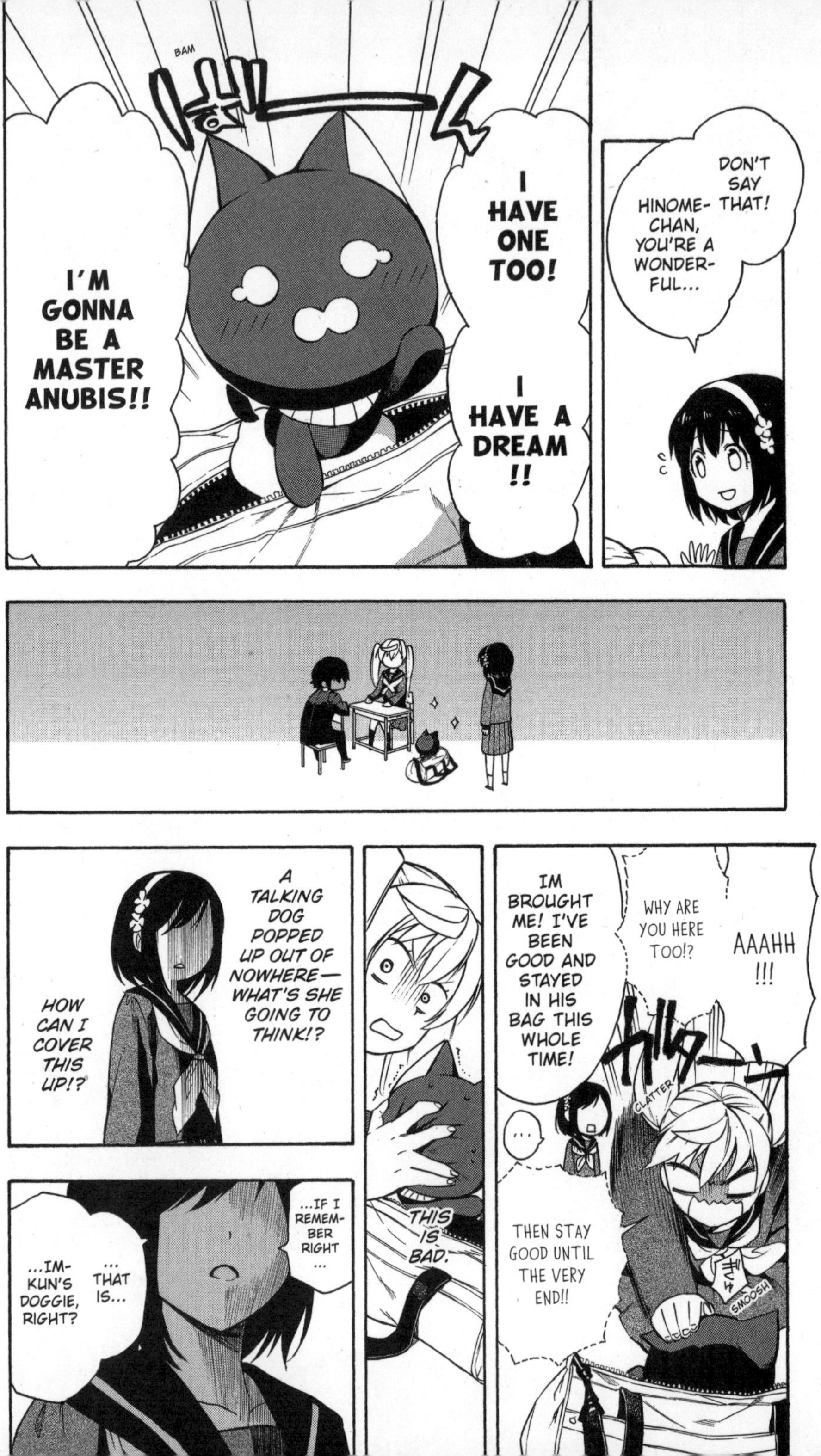
DON'T SAY THAT! HINOME-CHAN, YOU'RE A WONDERFUL...
BAM
I HAVE ONE TOO!
I HAVE A DREAM!!
I'M GONNA BE A MASTER ANUBIS!!
WHY ARE YOU HERE TOO!?
AAAHH!!!
IM BROUGHT ME! I'VE BEEN GOOD AND STAYED IN HIS BAG THIS WHOLE TIME!
CLATTER
...
THEN STAY GOOD UNTIL THE VERY END!!
SMOOSH
THIS IS BAD.
A TALKING DOG POPPED UP OUT OF NOWHERE—WHAT'S SHE GOING TO THINK!?
HOW CAN I COVER THIS UP!?
...IF I REMEMBER RIGHT...
...THAT IS...
...IM-KUN'S DOGGIE, RIGHT?

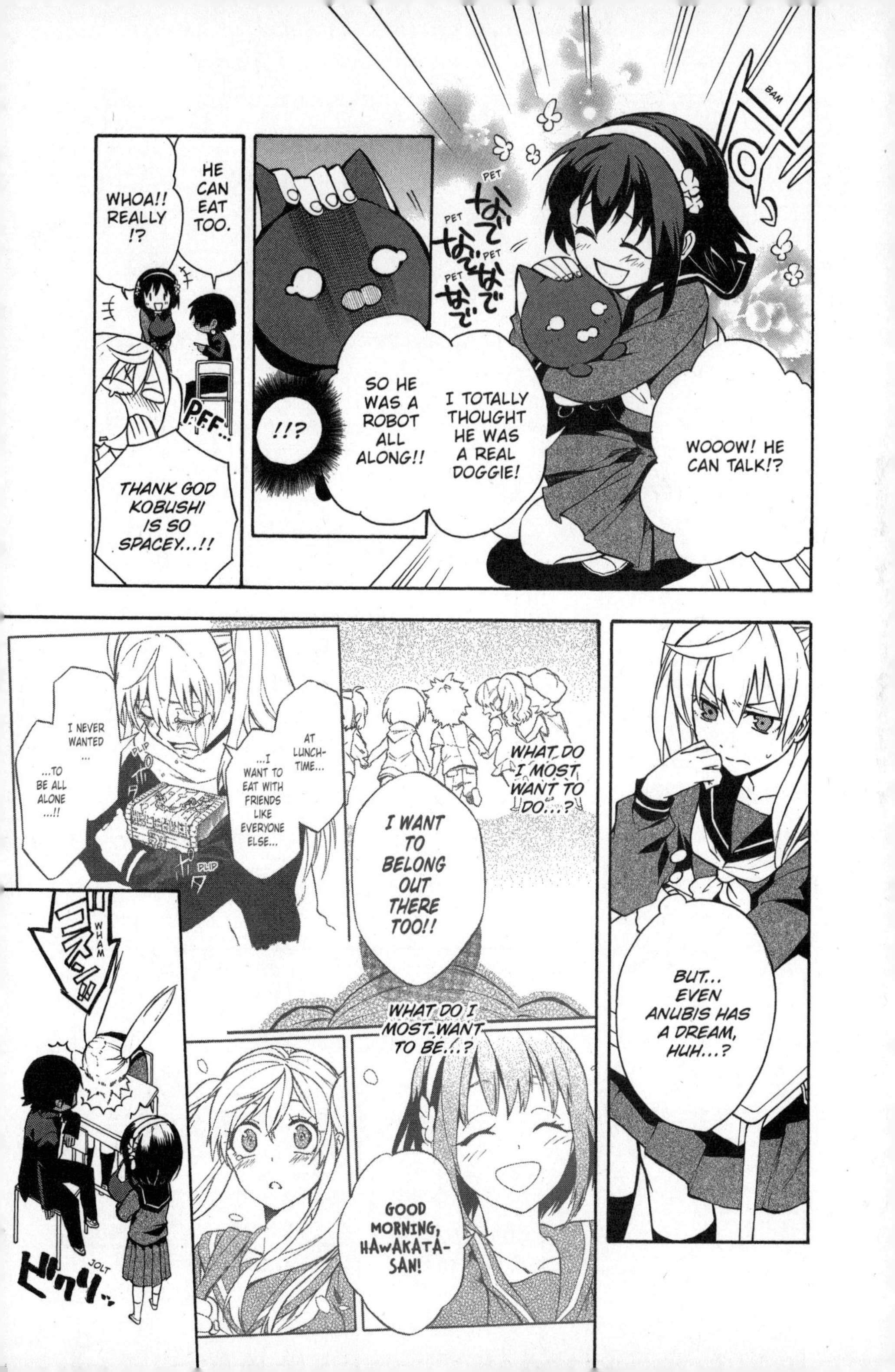
BAM
PET PET PET PET
WOOOW! HE CAN TALK!?
I TOTALLY THOUGHT HE WAS A REAL DOGGIE!
SO HE WAS A ROBOT ALL ALONG!!
!!?
HE CAN EAT TOO.
WHOA!! REALLY!?
PFF...
THANK GOD KOBUSHI IS SO SPACEY...!!
BUT... EVEN ANUBIS HAS A DREAM, HUH...?
WHAT DO I MOST WANT TO DO...?
I WANT TO BELONG OUT THERE TOO!!
AT LUNCH-TIME...
...I WANT TO EAT WITH FRIENDS LIKE EVERYONE ELSE...
I NEVER WANTED...
...TO BE ALL ALONE...!!
PLIP
PLIP
WHAT DO I MOST WANT TO BE...?
GOOD MORNING, HAWAKATA-SAN!
WHAM
JOLT

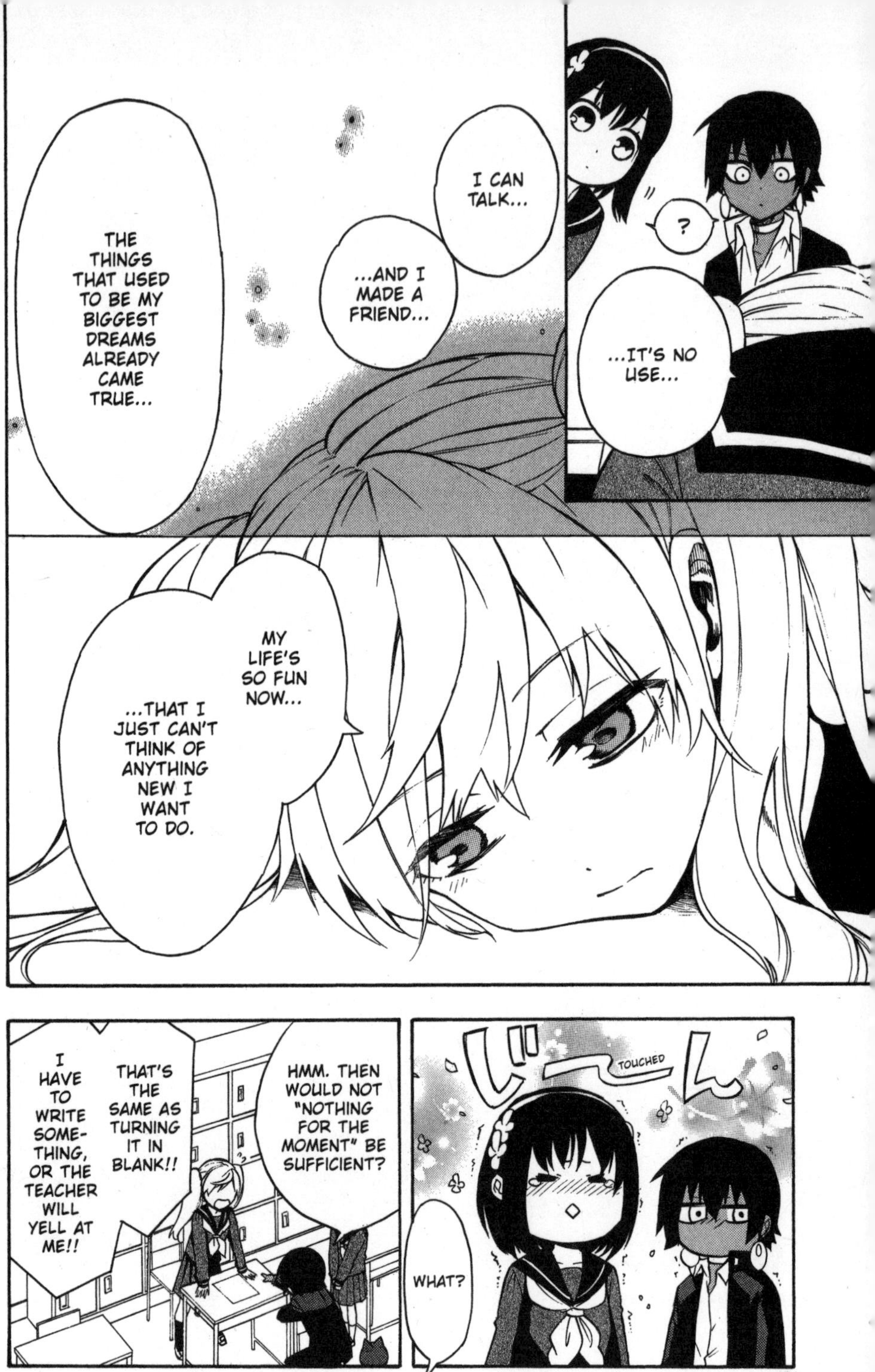
I CAN TALK...
...AND I MADE A FRIEND...
THE THINGS THAT USED TO BE MY BIGGEST DREAMS ALREADY CAME TRUE...
?
...IT'S NO USE...
MY LIFE'S SO FUN NOW...
...THAT I JUST CAN'T THINK OF ANYTHING NEW I WANT TO DO.
じーん
TOUCHED
WHAT?
HMM. THEN WOULD NOT "NOTHING FOR THE MOMENT" BE SUFFICIENT?
THAT'S THE SAME AS TURNING IT IN BLANK!!
I HAVE TO WRITE SOME-THING, OR THE TEACHER WILL YELL AT ME!!

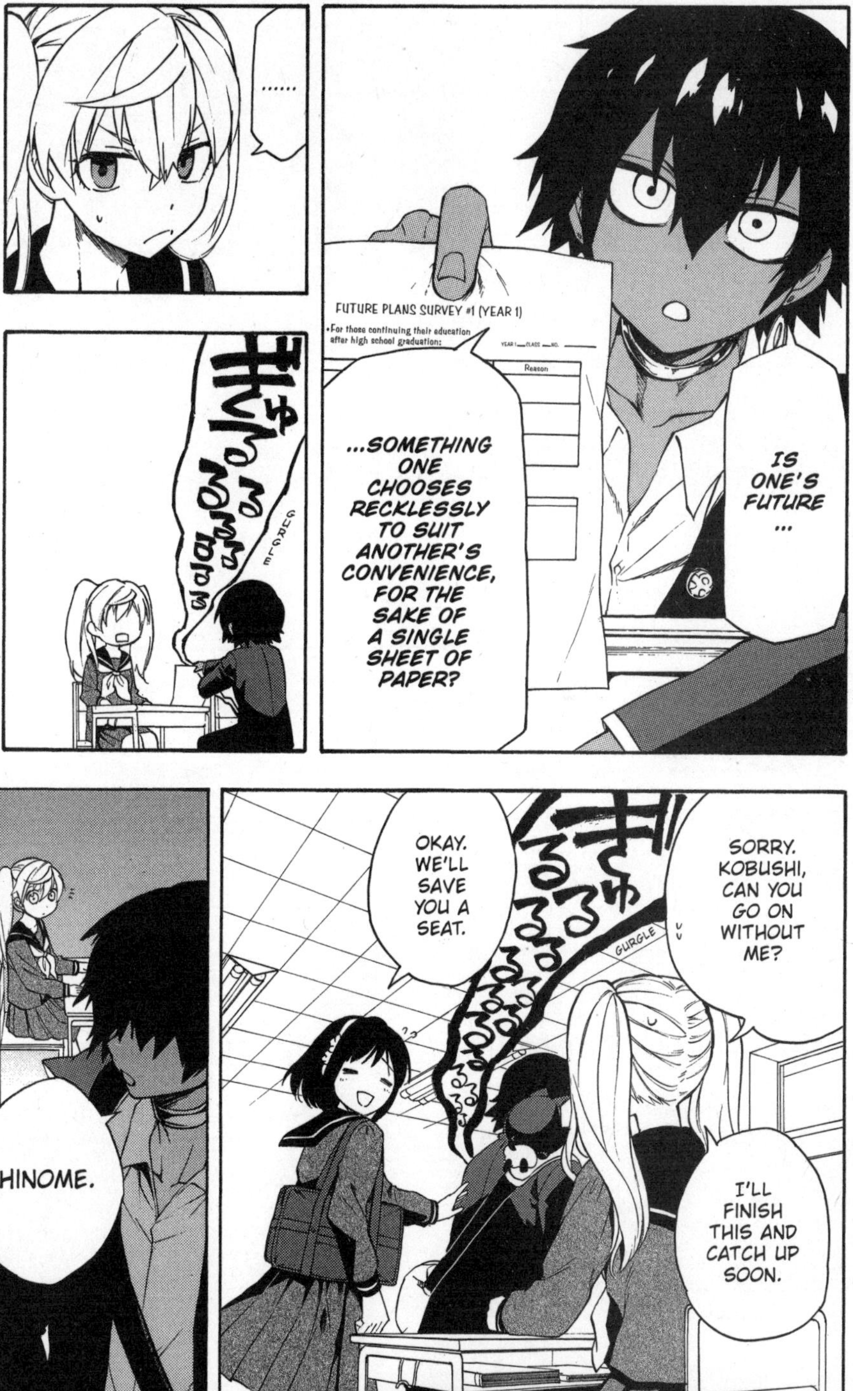
FUTURE PLANS SURVEY #1 (YEAR 1)
•For those continuing their education after high school graduation:
Reason
IS ONE'S FUTURE ...
...SOMETHING ONE CHOOSES RECKLESSLY TO SUIT ANOTHER'S CONVENIENCE, FOR THE SAKE OF A SINGLE SHEET OF PAPER?
......
ぎゅるるるる
GURGLE
SORRY. KOBUSHI, CAN YOU GO ON WITHOUT ME?
ぎゅるるるる
GURGLE
OKAY. WE'LL SAVE YOU A SEAT.
I'LL FINISH THIS AND CATCH UP SOON.
HINOME.

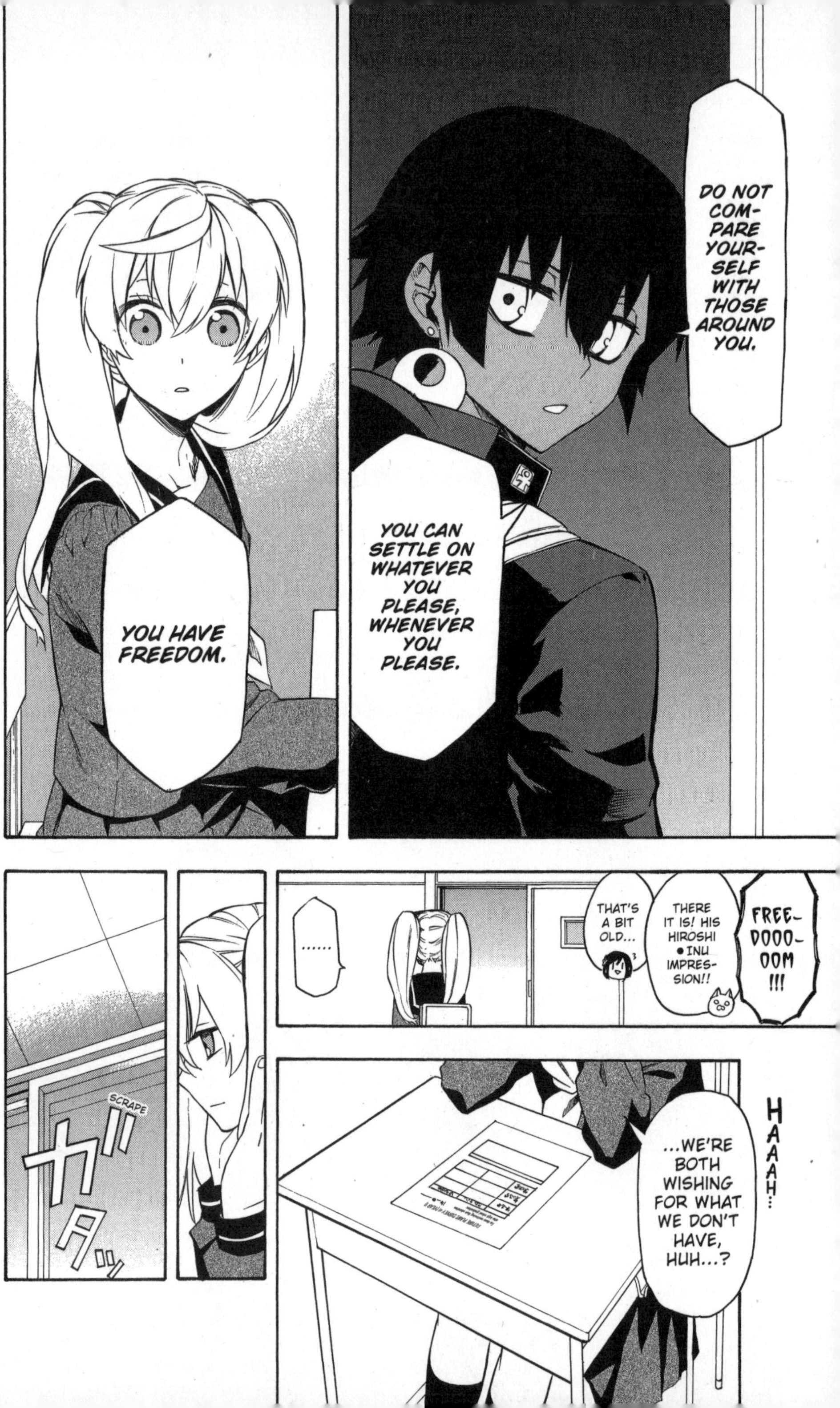
DO NOT COM-PARE YOUR-SELF WITH THOSE AROUND YOU.
YOU CAN SETTLE ON WHATEVER YOU PLEASE, WHENEVER YOU PLEASE.
YOU HAVE FREEDOM.
FREE-DOOO-OOM !!!
THERE IT IS! HIS HIROSHI ●INU IMPRES-SION!!
THAT'S A BIT OLD...
......
HAAAAH...
...WE'RE BOTH WISHING FOR WHAT WE DON'T HAVE, HUH...?
SCRAPE
ガタッ

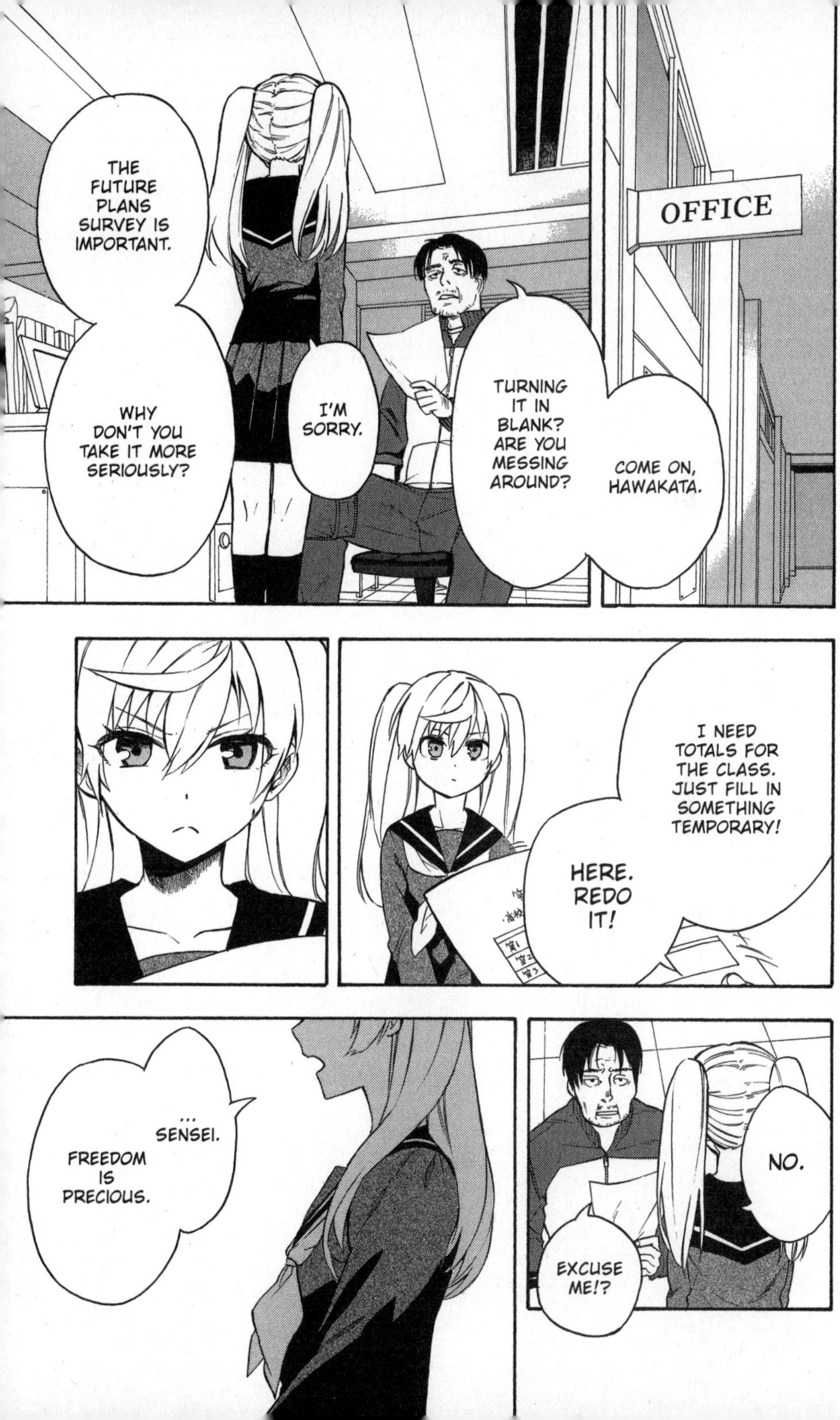
OFFICE
COME ON, HAWAKATA.
TURNING IT IN BLANK? ARE YOU MESSING AROUND?
I'M SORRY.
THE FUTURE PLANS SURVEY IS IMPORTANT.
WHY DON'T YOU TAKE IT MORE SERIOUSLY?
I NEED TOTALS FOR THE CLASS. JUST FILL IN SOMETHING TEMPORARY!
HERE. REDO IT!
NO.
EXCUSE ME!?
... SENSEI.
FREEDOM IS PRECIOUS.

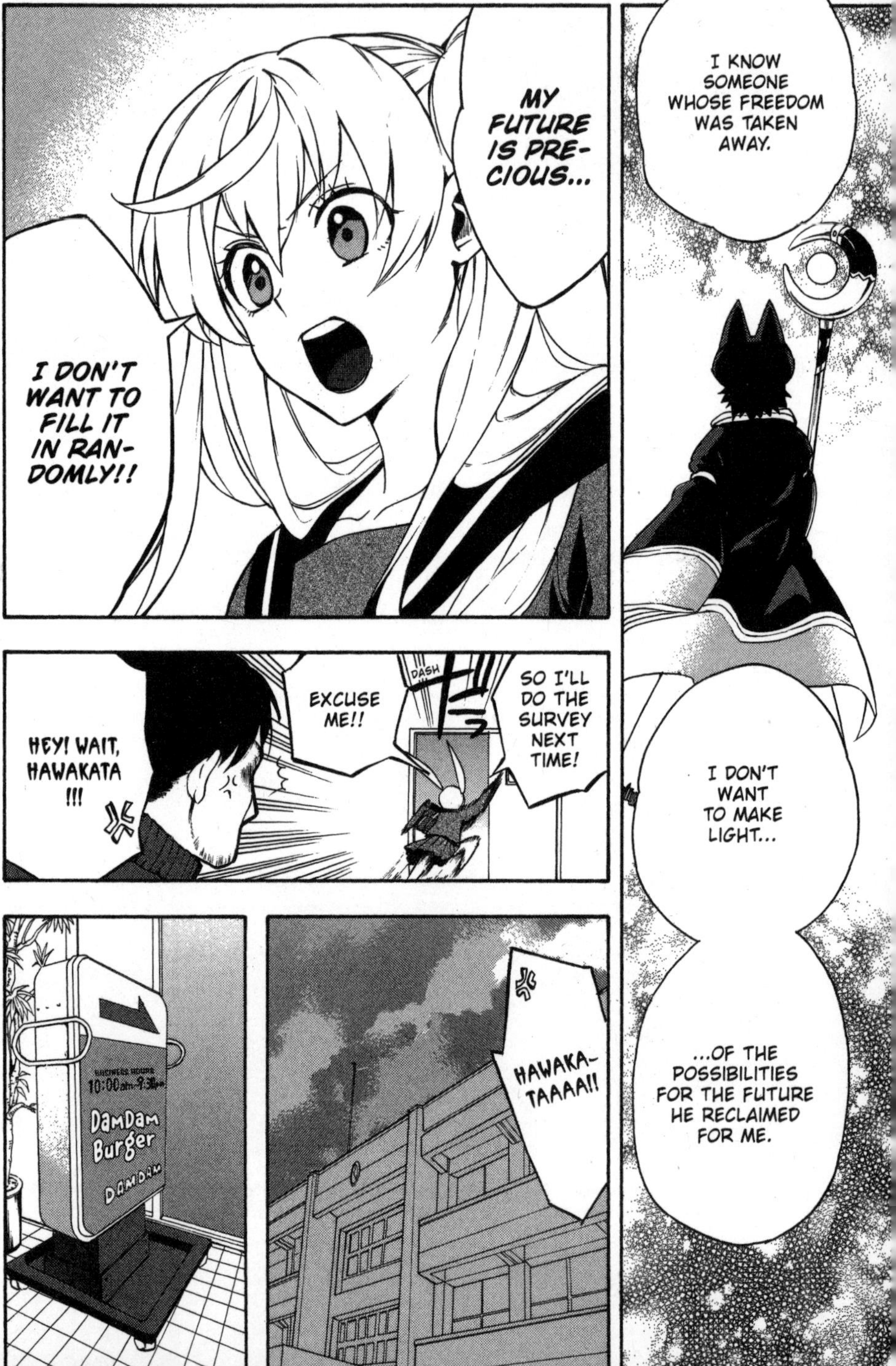
I KNOW SOMEONE WHOSE FREEDOM WAS TAKEN AWAY.
I DON'T WANT TO MAKE LIGHT...
...OF THE POSSIBILITIES FOR THE FUTURE HE RECLAIMED FOR ME.
MY FUTURE IS PRE-CIOUS...
I DON'T WANT TO FILL IT IN RAN-DOMLY!!
SO I'LL DO THE SURVEY NEXT TIME!
DASH
EXCUSE ME!!
HEY! WAIT, HAWAKATA!!!
HAWAKA-TAAAA!!
BUSINESS HOURS
10:00am-9:30pm
DamDam Burger
DAMDAM

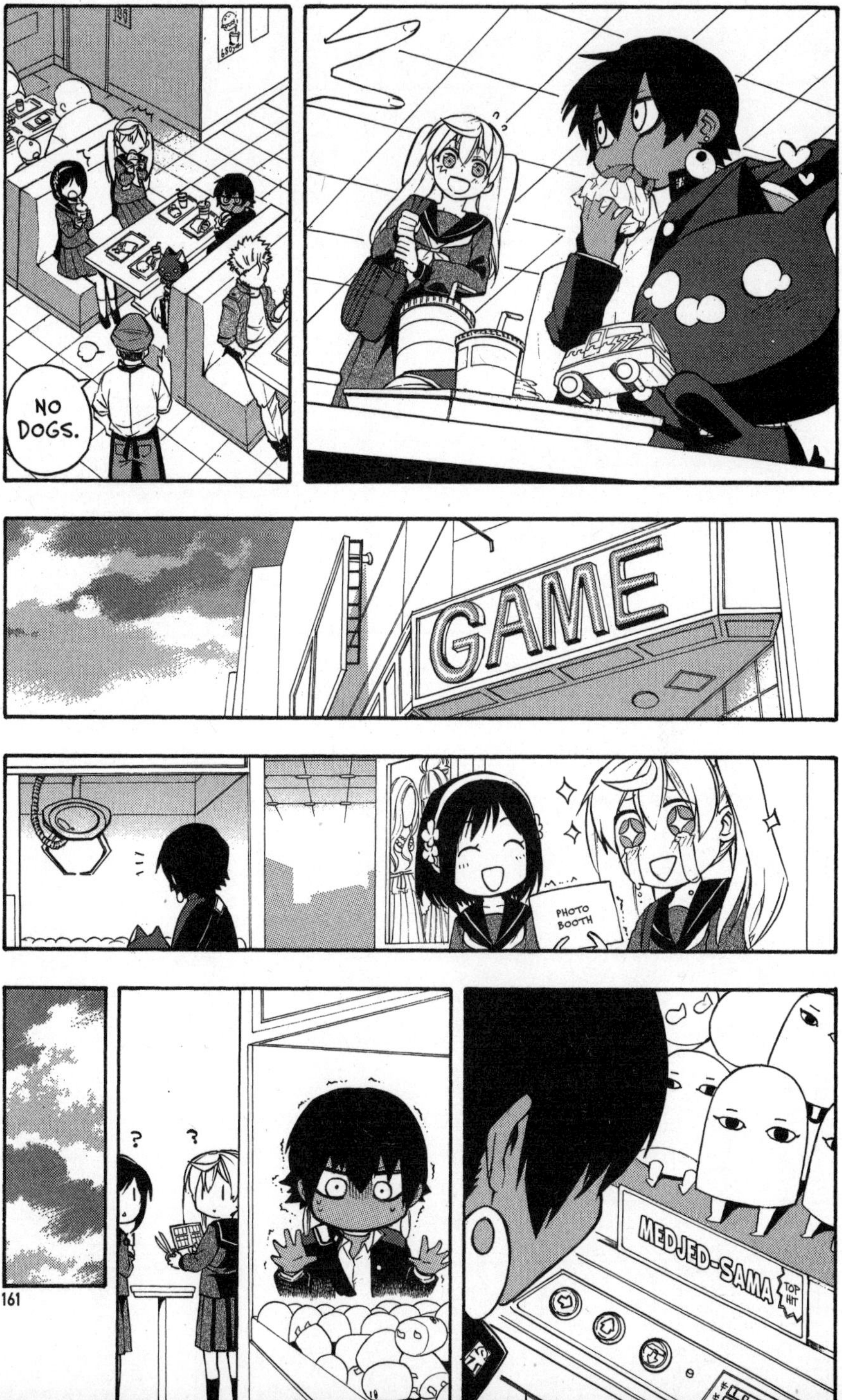
NO DOGS.
GAME
PHOTO BOOTH
MEDJED-SAMA
TOP HIT

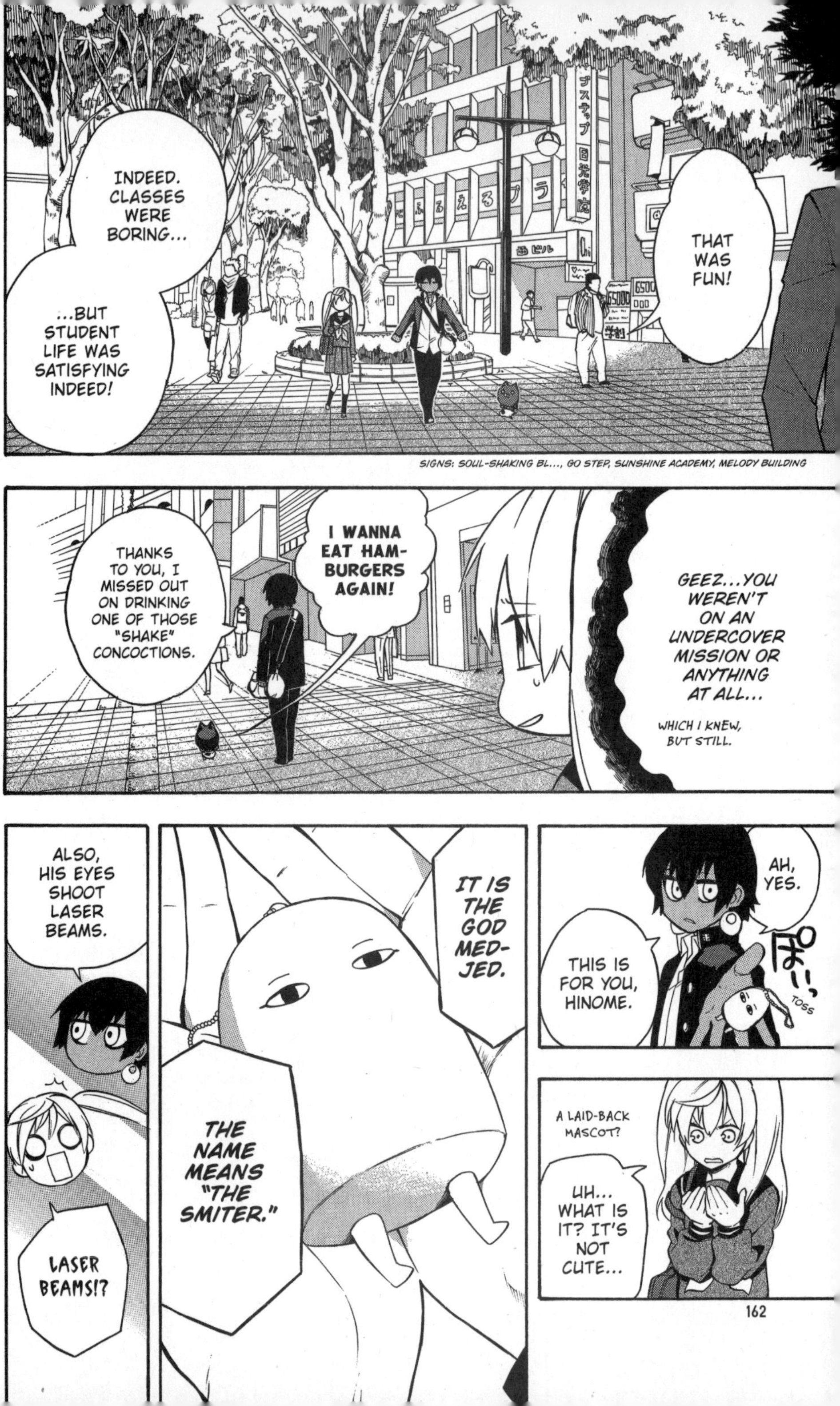
THAT WAS FUN!
INDEED. CLASSES WERE BORING...
...BUT STUDENT LIFE WAS SATISFYING INDEED!
SIGNS: SOUL-SHAKING BL..., GO STEP, SUNSHINE ACADEMY, MELODY BUILDING
GEEZ...YOU WEREN'T ON AN UNDERCOVER MISSION OR ANYTHING AT ALL...
WHICH I KNEW, BUT STILL.
I WANNA EAT HAMBURGERS AGAIN!
THANKS TO YOU, I MISSED OUT ON DRINKING ONE OF THOSE "SHAKE" CONCOCTIONS.
AH, YES.
THIS IS FOR YOU, HINOME.
ぽいっ
TOSS
A LAID-BACK MASCOT?
UH... WHAT IS IT? IT'S NOT CUTE...
IT IS THE GOD MEDJED.
THE NAME MEANS "THE SMITER."
ALSO, HIS EYES SHOOT LASER BEAMS.
LASER BEAMS!?

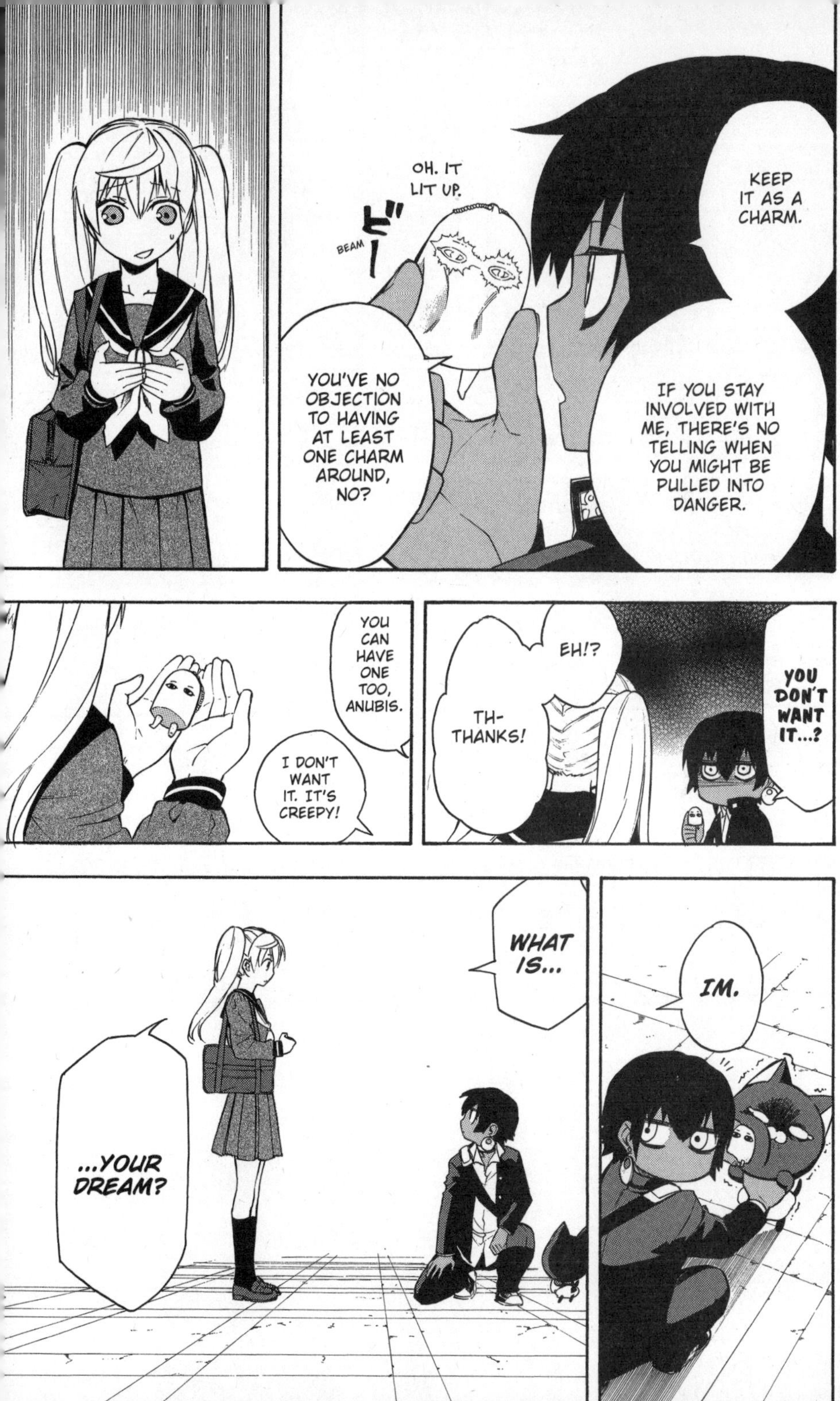
KEEP IT AS A CHARM.
IF YOU STAY INVOLVED WITH ME, THERE'S NO TELLING WHEN YOU MIGHT BE PULLED INTO DANGER.
OH. IT LIT UP.
ビー
BEAM
YOU'VE NO OBJECTION TO HAVING AT LEAST ONE CHARM AROUND, NO?
YOU DON'T WANT IT...?
EH!?
TH-THANKS!
YOU CAN HAVE ONE TOO, ANUBIS.
I DON'T WANT IT. IT'S CREEPY!
IM.
WHAT IS...
...YOUR DREAM?

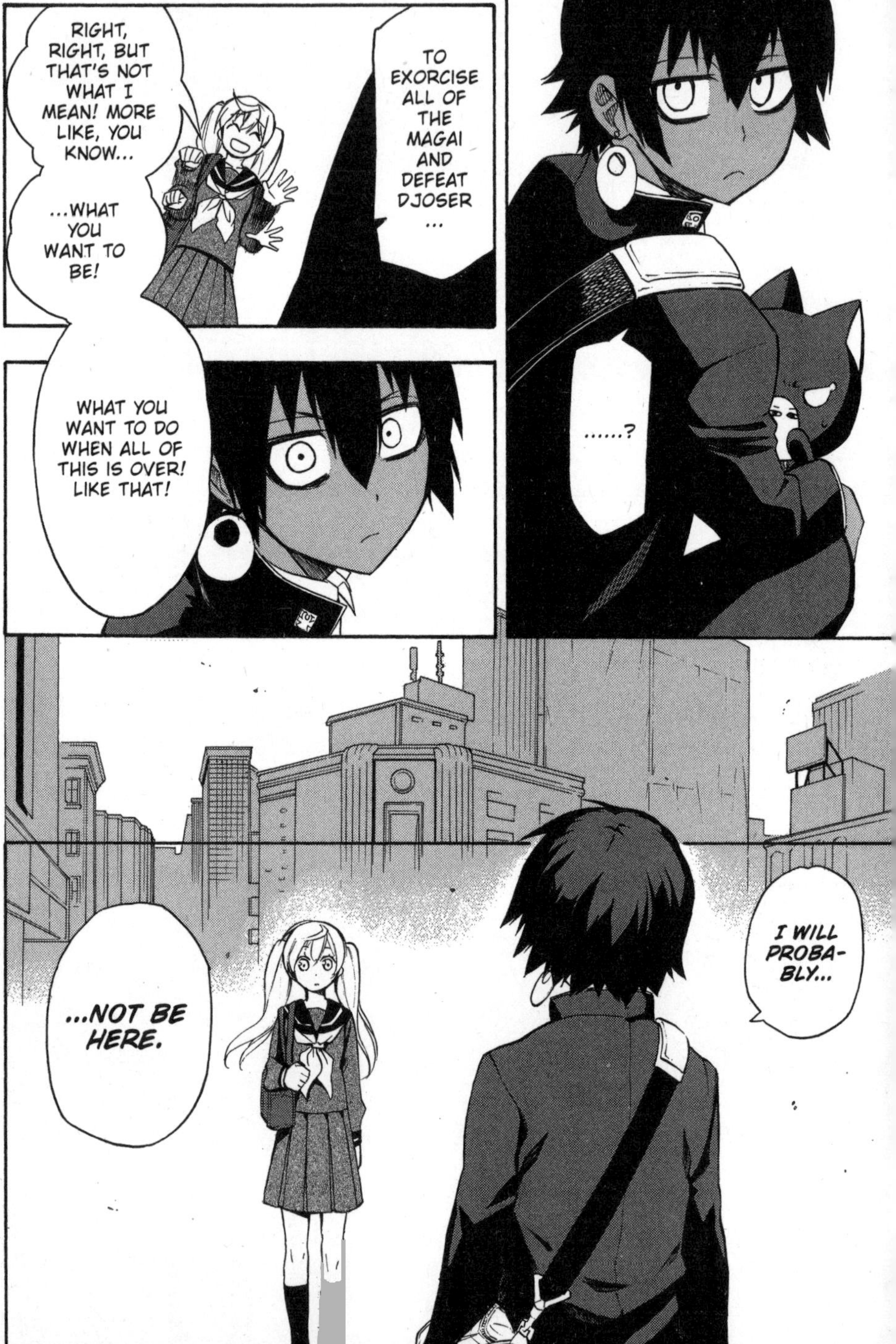
......?
TO EXORCISE ALL OF THE MAGAI AND DEFEAT DJOSER...
RIGHT, RIGHT, BUT THAT'S NOT WHAT I MEAN! MORE LIKE, YOU KNOW...
...WHAT YOU WANT TO BE!
WHAT YOU WANT TO DO WHEN ALL OF THIS IS OVER! LIKE THAT!
I WILL PROBA-BLY...
...NOT BE HERE.

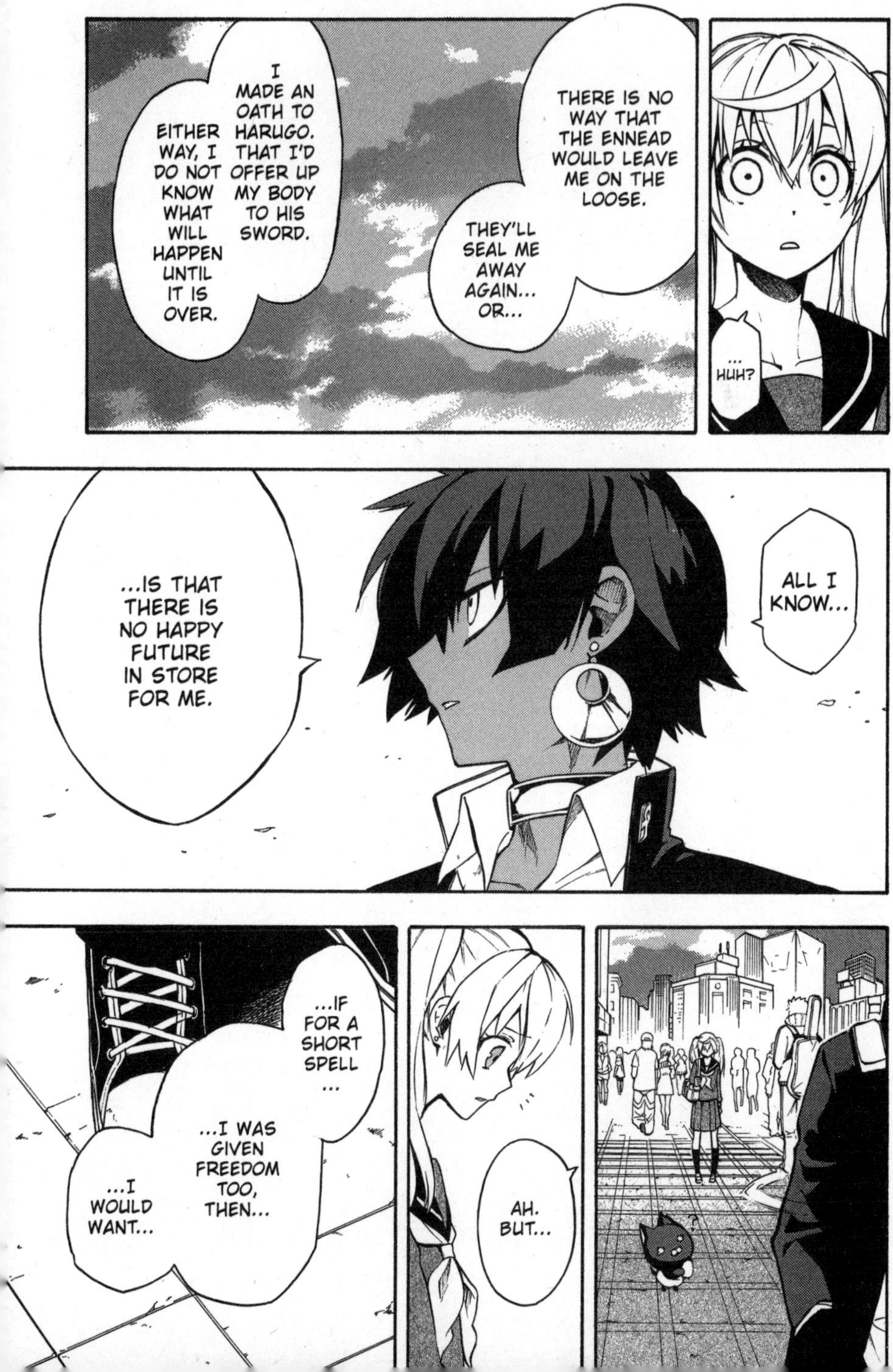
... HUH?
THERE IS NO WAY THAT THE ENNEAD WOULD LEAVE ME ON THE LOOSE.
THEY'LL SEAL ME AWAY AGAIN... OR...
I MADE AN OATH TO HARUGO. THAT I'D OFFER UP MY BODY TO HIS SWORD.
EITHER WAY, I DO NOT KNOW WHAT WILL HAPPEN UNTIL IT IS OVER.
ALL I KNOW...
...IS THAT THERE IS NO HAPPY FUTURE IN STORE FOR ME.
AH. BUT...
...IF FOR A SHORT SPELL...
...I WAS GIVEN FREEDOM TOO, THEN...
...I WOULD WANT...

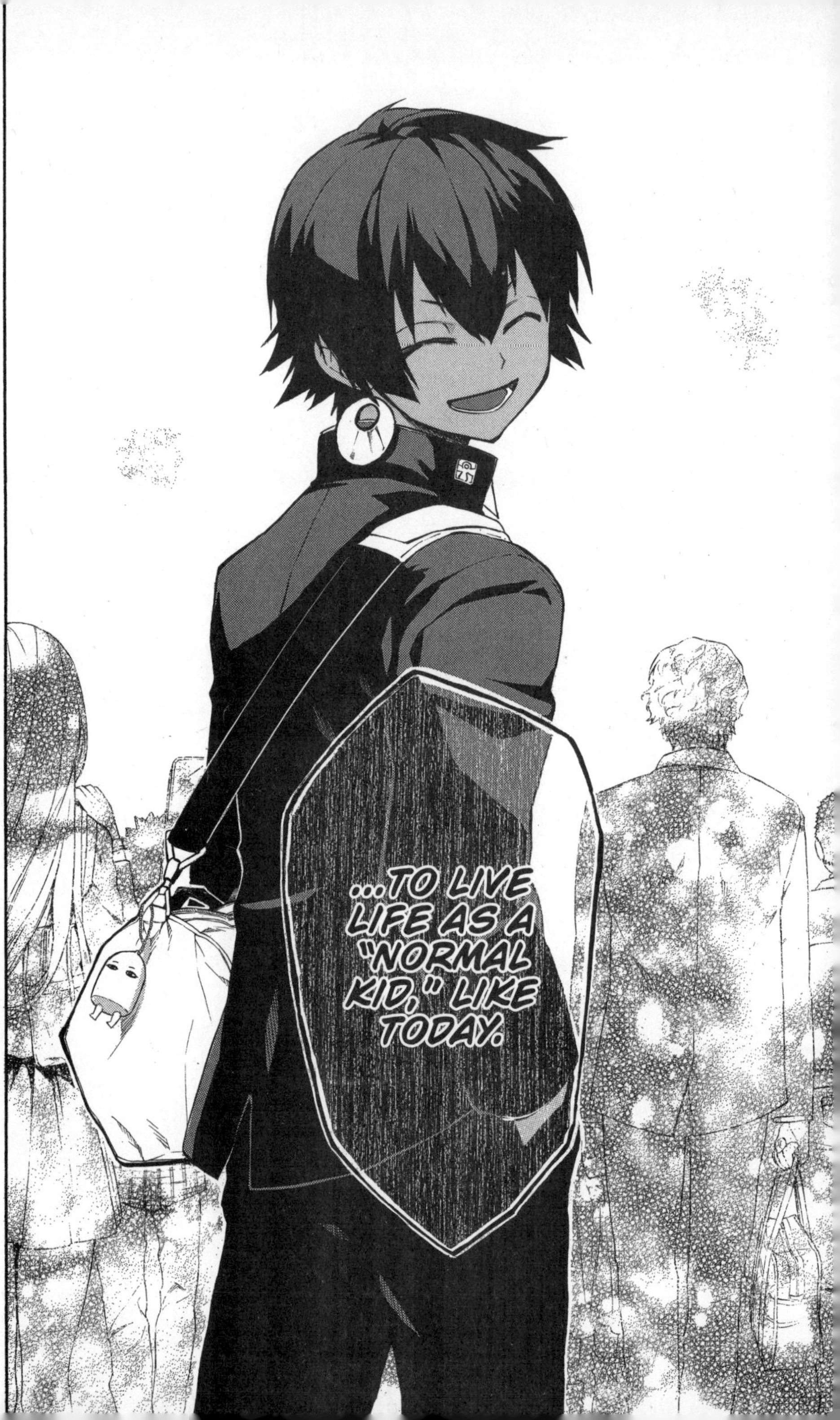
...TO LIVE LIFE AS A "NORMAL KID," LIKE TODAY.

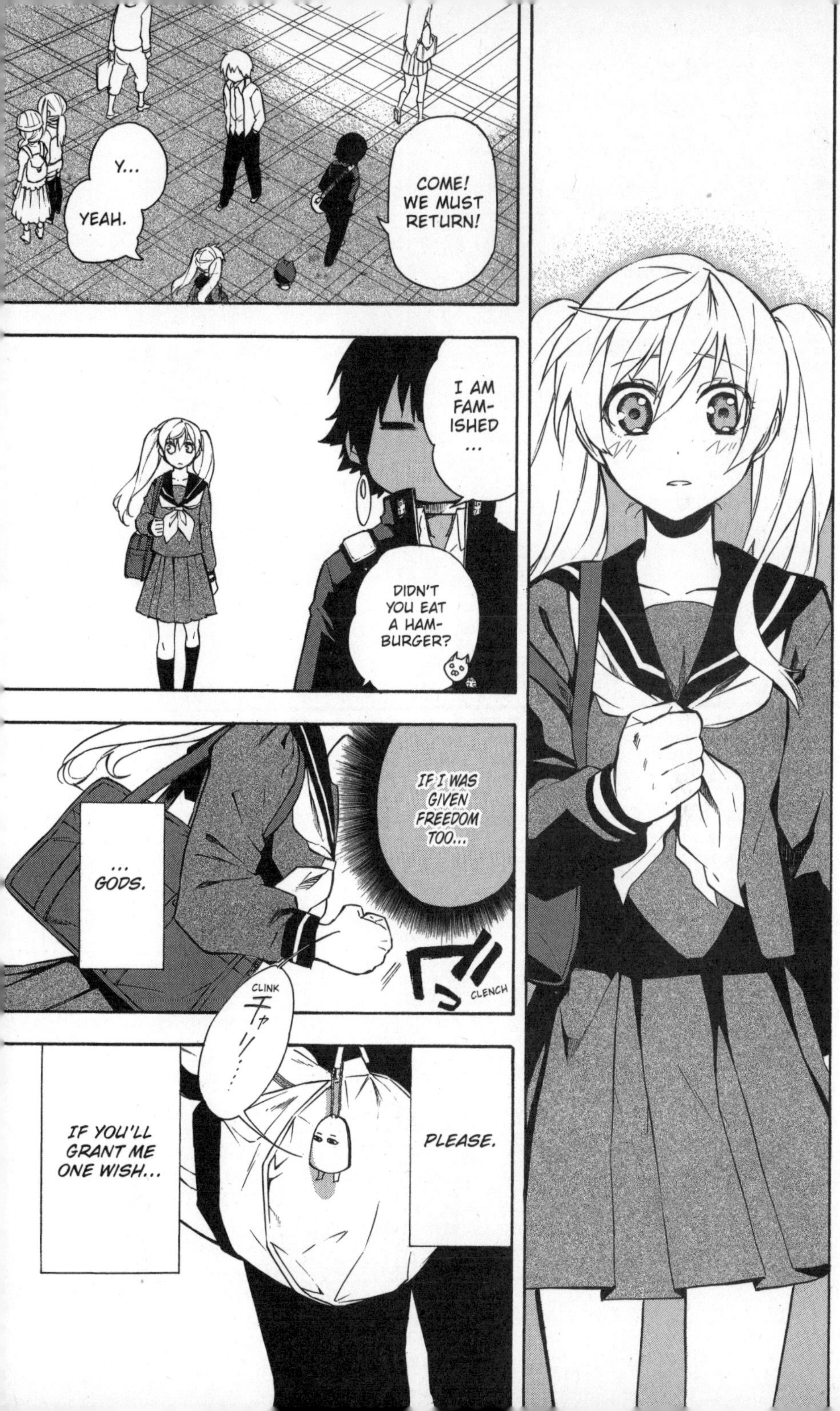
COME! WE MUST RETURN!
Y...
YEAH.
I AM FAM-ISHED ...
DIDN'T YOU EAT A HAM-BURGER?
IF I WAS GIVEN FREEDOM TOO...
... GODS.
CLENCH
CLINK
チャリ…
PLEASE.
IF YOU'LL GRANT ME ONE WISH...

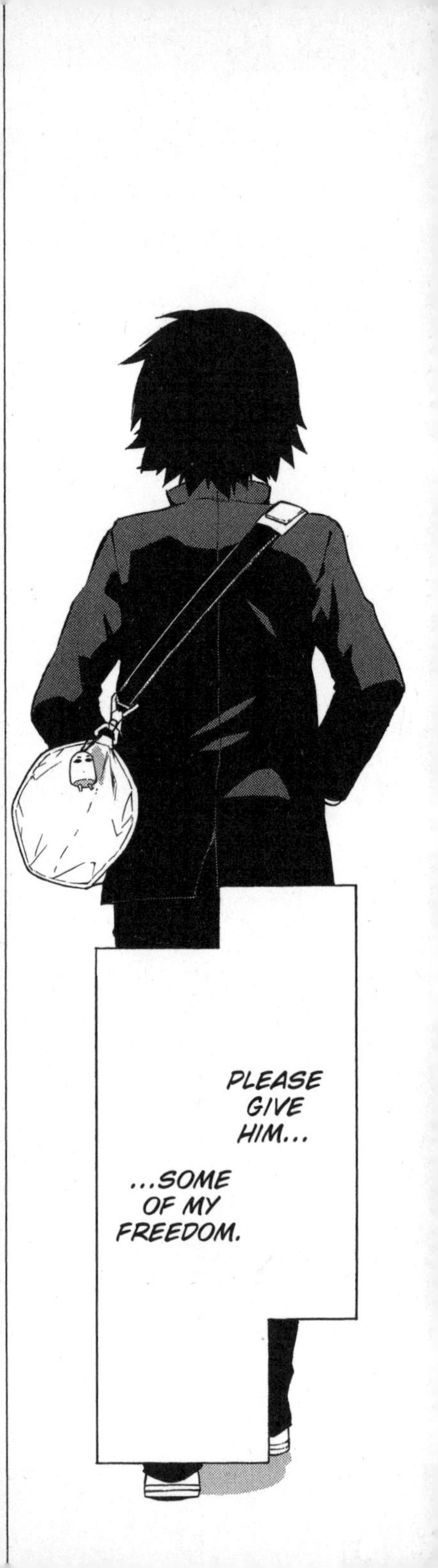
PLEASE GIVE HIM...
...SOME OF MY FREEDOM.

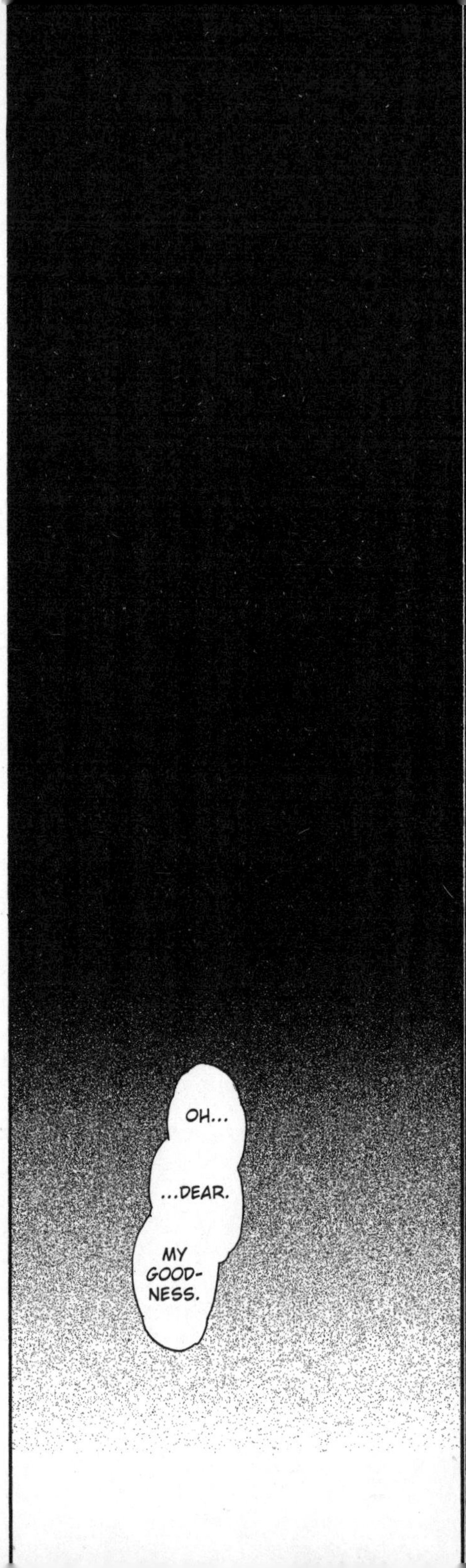
OH...
...DEAR.
MY GOODNESS.

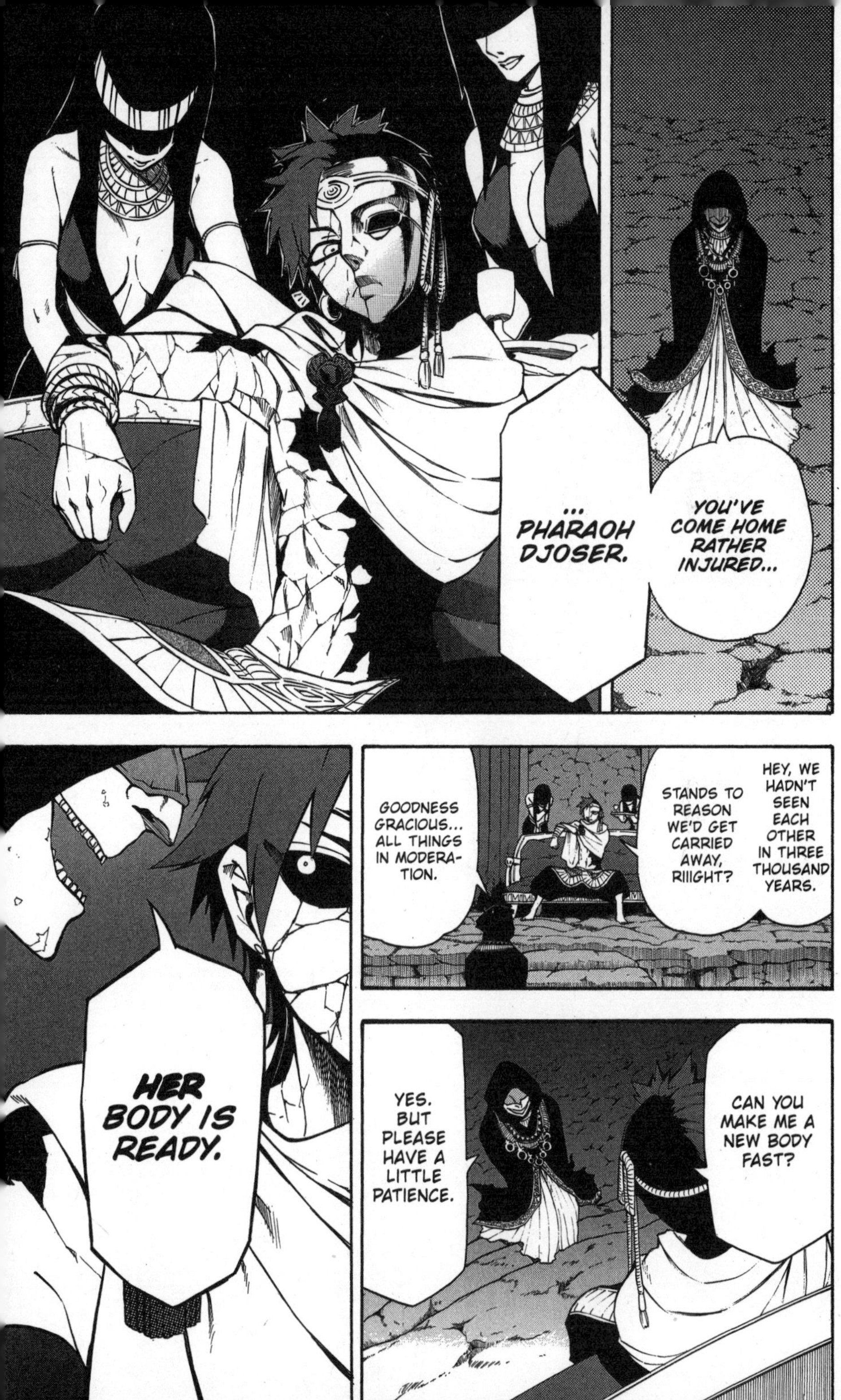
YOU'VE COME HOME RATHER INJURED...
... PHARAOH DJOSER.
HEY, WE HADN'T SEEN EACH OTHER IN THREE THOUSAND YEARS.
STANDS TO REASON WE'D GET CARRIED AWAY, RIIIGHT?
GOODNESS GRACIOUS... ALL THINGS IN MODERA-TION.
CAN YOU MAKE ME A NEW BODY FAST?
YES. BUT PLEASE HAVE A LITTLE PATIENCE.
HER BODY IS READY.

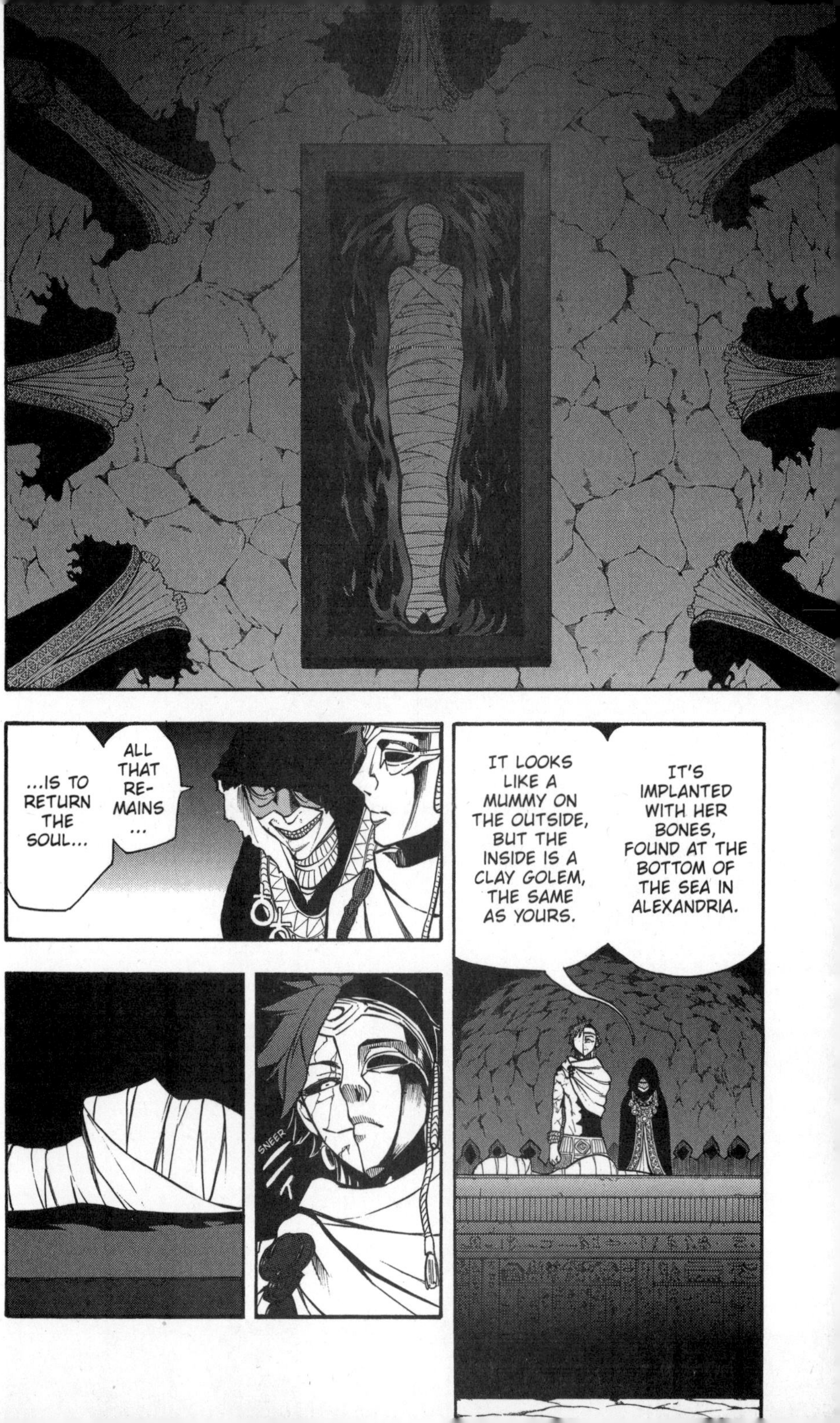

IT'S IMPLANTED WITH HER BONES, FOUND AT THE BOTTOM OF THE SEA IN ALEXANDRIA.
IT LOOKS LIKE A MUMMY ON THE OUTSIDE, BUT THE INSIDE IS A CLAY GOLEM, THE SAME AS YOURS.
ALL THAT RE-MAINS ...
...IS TO RETURN THE SOUL...
SNEER

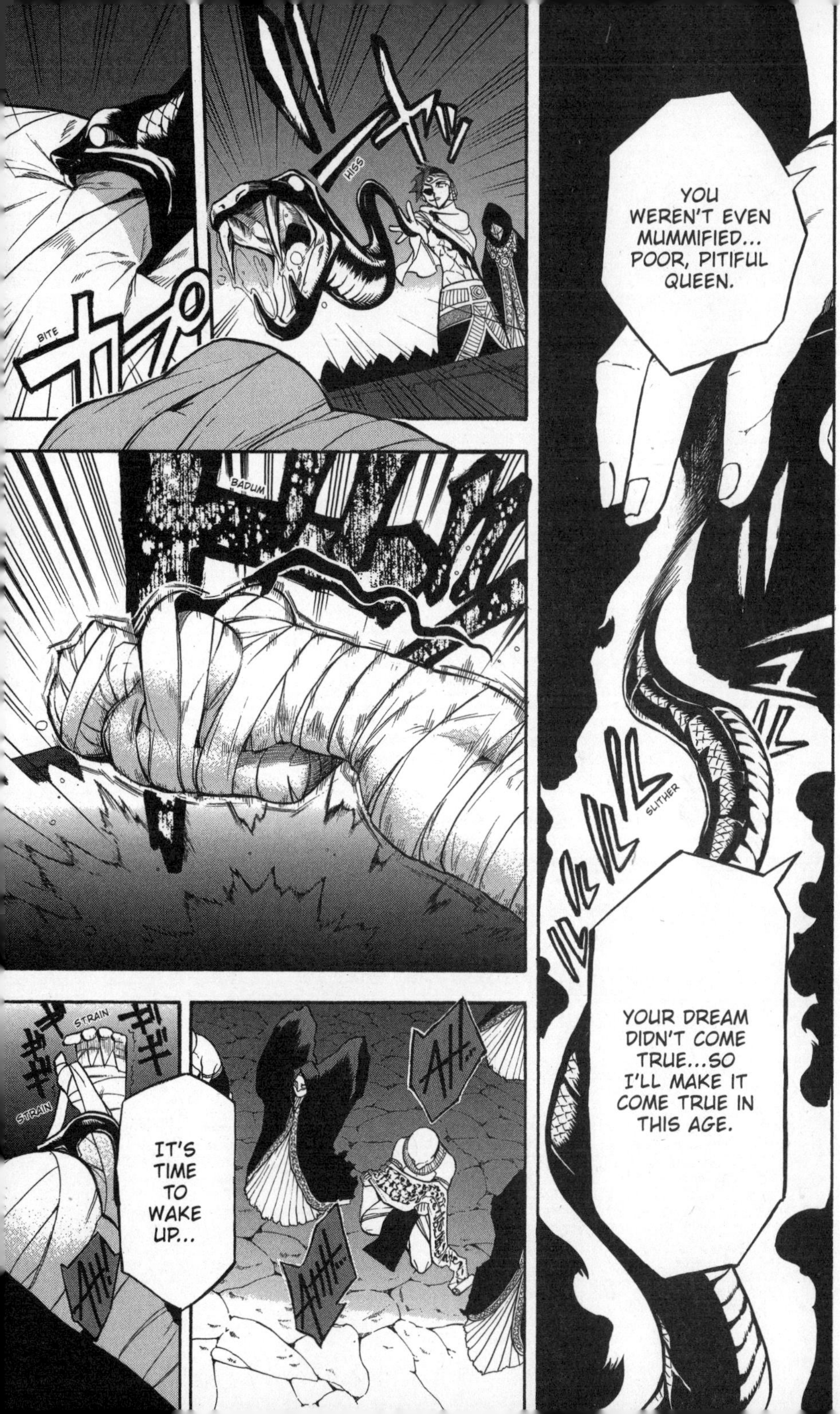
YOU WEREN'T EVEN MUMMIFIED... POOR, PITIFUL QUEEN.
SLITHER
YOUR DREAM DIDN'T COME TRUE...SO I'LL MAKE IT COME TRUE IN THIS AGE.
HISS
BITE
BADUM
AH!
AHH...
STRAIN
STRAIN
IT'S TIME TO WAKE UP...
AH!

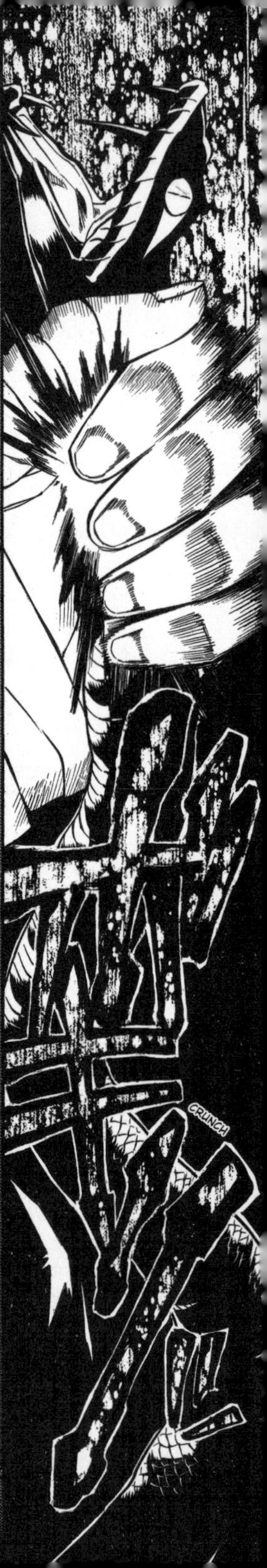
CRUNCH
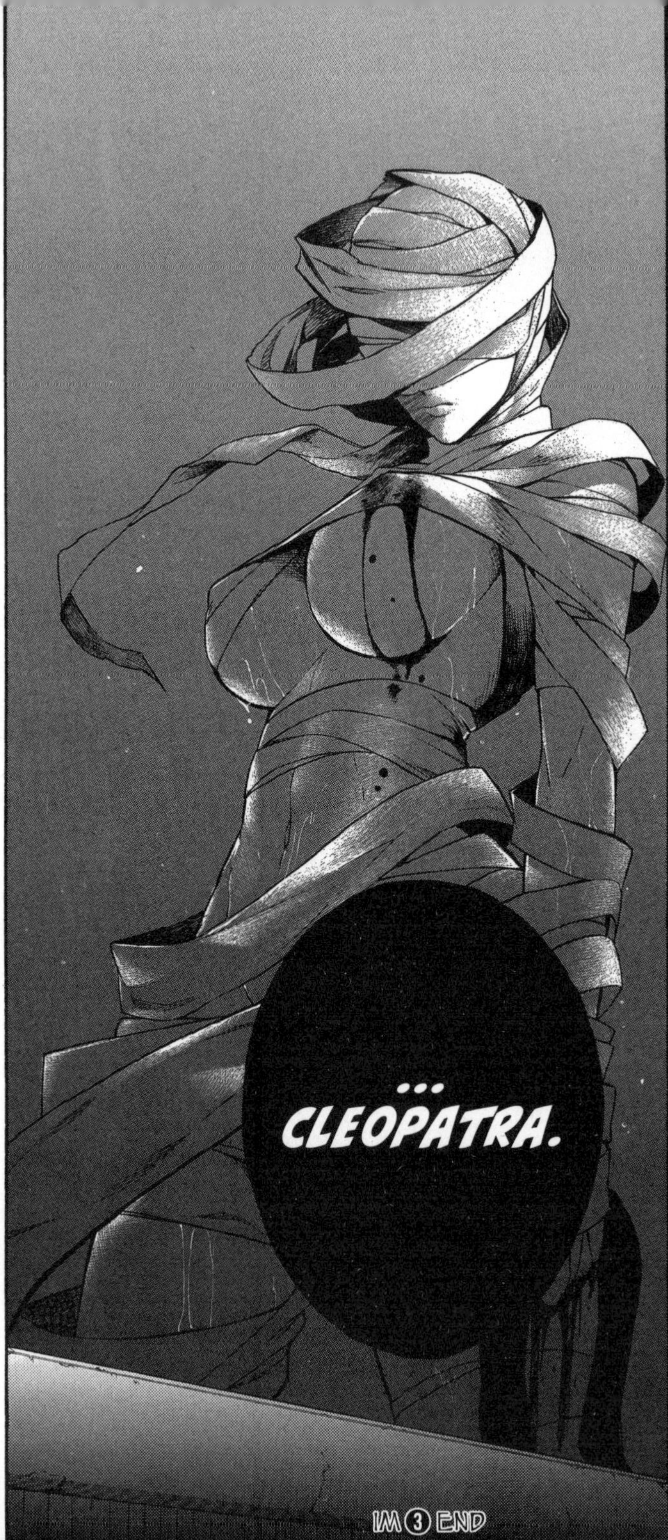
...
CLEOPATRA.

IM 3 END

BEAN-JAM BUNS

THERE IS NO CONVERSATION NOW THAT IT IS ONLY US TWO IN THE HOSPITAL ROOM. HOW BORING.
CHEW CHEW
EATING THE GET-WELL SNACK KHONSU BROUGHT
NUM NUM NUM
THAT REMINDS ME. I WAS WATCHING A SCARY TELEVISION PROGRAM...
CHEW CHEW
RIP
GLUG GLUG
...AND THEY SAID THAT IF THERE IS A TALISMAN STUCK TO A HOSPITAL BED, IT MEANS THE BED IS HAUNTED BY A DANGEROUS GHOST.
HA HA HA!
WHAT'S THAT PAPER STICKIN' OUT FROM YOUR BED?
SIP
?!
WHAP
AHHH...

HARUGO: "FOOLED YOU."

VOLUMES 2 & 3

Special Thanks

- Arisa Yukimiya
- Ui Kizuki
- Mai Ishiguro

SPECIAL HELP FROM:

- You Omura-sensei (volume 2)
- Riko-san (volume 2)
- Chiinyo-san
- Bechika Hatoya-san

My editor, SHIMOMURA-SAN

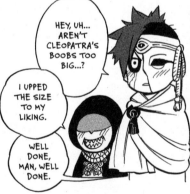

HEY, UH... AREN'T CLEOPATRA'S BOOBS TOO BIG...?
I UPPED THE SIZE TO MY LIKING.
WELL DONE, MAN, WELL DONE.

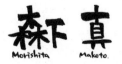

森下 真

Morishita Makoto.

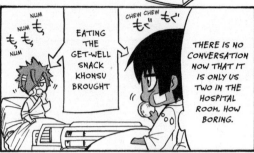

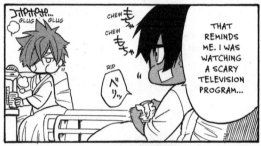

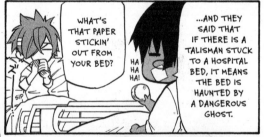

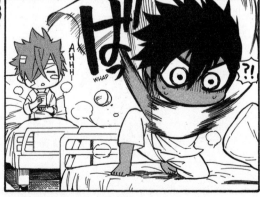

DJOSER VS HARUGO

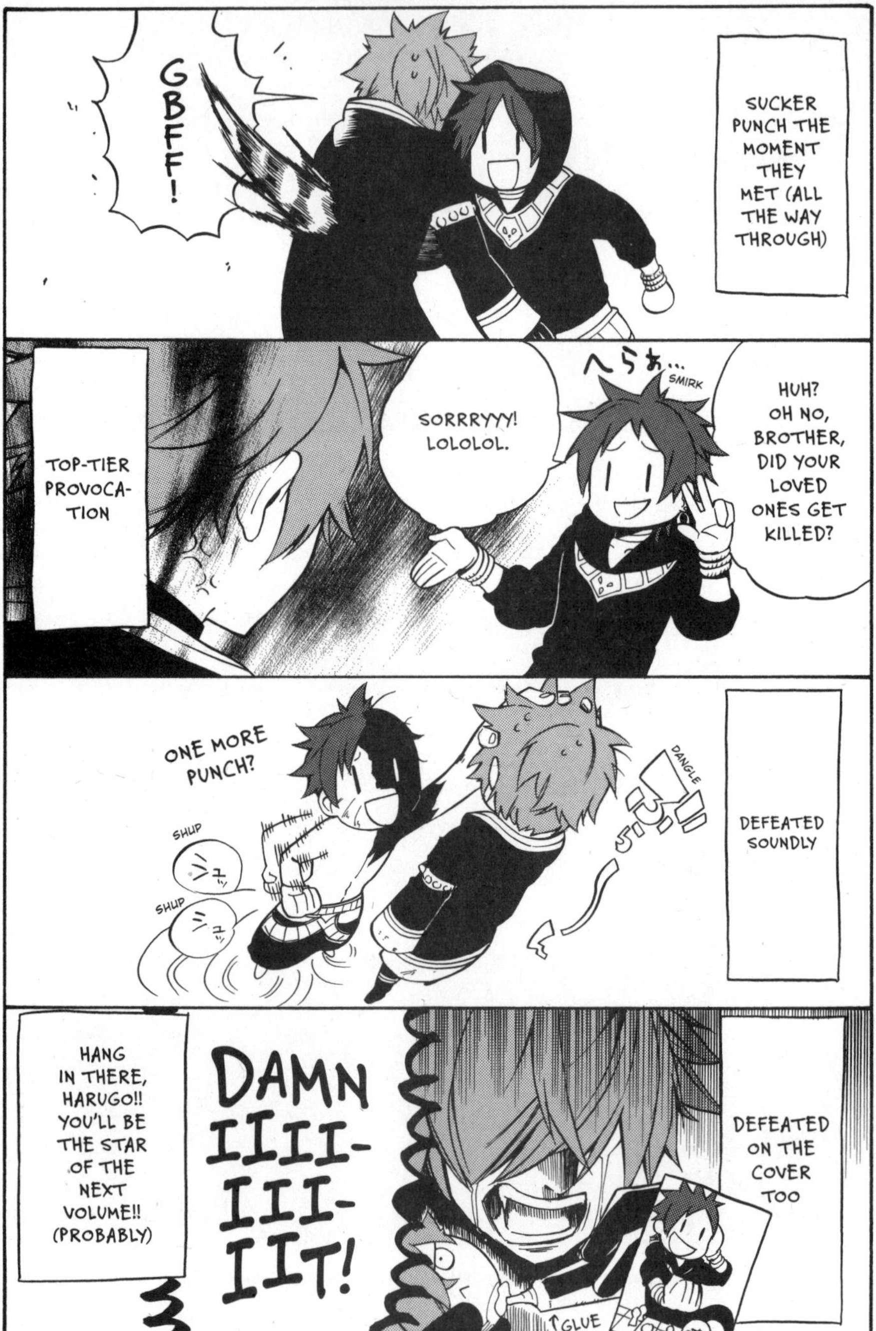
SUCKER PUNCH THE MOMENT THEY MET (ALL THE WAY THROUGH)
GBFF!
HUH? OH NO, BROTHER, DID YOUR LOVED ONES GET KILLED?
へらぁ…
SMIRK
SORRRYYY! LOLOLOL.
TOP-TIER PROVOCA-TION
DEFEATED SOUNDLY
DANGLE
ONE MORE PUNCH?
SHUP
SHUP
DEFEATED ON THE COVER TOO
DAMN IIII-III-IIT!
HANG IN THERE, HARUGO!! YOU'LL BE THE STAR OF THE NEXT VOLUME!! (PROBABLY)
↑GLUE

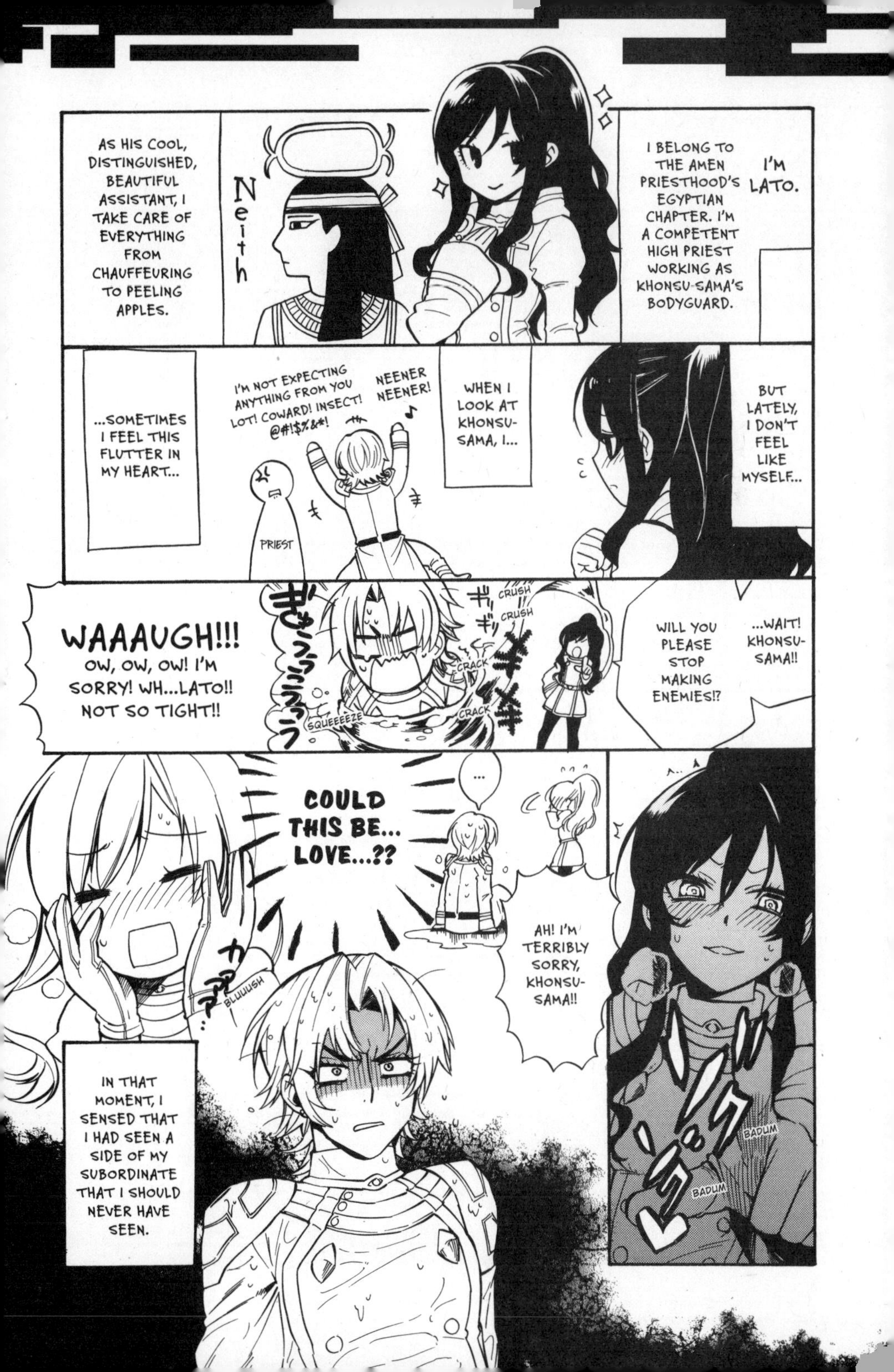
I'M LATO.
I BELONG TO THE AMEN PRIESTHOOD'S EGYPTIAN CHAPTER. I'M A COMPETENT HIGH PRIEST WORKING AS KHONSU-SAMA'S BODYGUARD.
Neith
AS HIS COOL, DISTINGUISHED, BEAUTIFUL ASSISTANT, I TAKE CARE OF EVERYTHING FROM CHAUFFEURING TO PEELING APPLES.
BUT LATELY, I DON'T FEEL LIKE MYSELF...
WHEN I LOOK AT KHONSU-SAMA, I...
NEENER NEENER!
I'M NOT EXPECTING ANYTHING FROM YOU LOT! COWARD! INSECT! @#!$%&*!
PRIEST
...SOMETIMES I FEEL THIS FLUTTER IN MY HEART...
...WAIT! KHONSU-SAMA!!
WILL YOU PLEASE STOP MAKING ENEMIES!?
CRUSH
CRUSH
CRACK
CRACK
SQUEEEEZE
WAAAUGH!!! OW, OW, OW! I'M SORRY! WH...LATO!! NOT SO TIGHT!!
BADUM
BADUM
AH! I'M TERRIBLY SORRY, KHONSU-SAMA!!
...
COULD THIS BE... LOVE...??
BLUUUSH
IN THAT MOMENT, I SENSED THAT I HAD SEEN A SIDE OF MY SUBORDINATE THAT I SHOULD NEVER HAVE SEEN.

Great Priest Imhotep 3

by MAKOTO MORISHITA

Translation: Amanda Haley
Lettering: Rochelle Gancio

This book is a work of fiction. Names, characters, places, and incidents are the product of the author's imagination or are used fictitiously. Any resemblance to actual events, locales, or persons, living or dead, is coincidental.

IM Vol. 3 ©2016 Makoto Morishita/SQUARE ENIX CO., LTD.
First published in Japan in 2016 by SQUARE ENIX CO., LTD. English translation rights arranged with SQUARE ENIX CO., LTD. and Yen Press, LLC through Tuttle-Mori Agency, Inc., Tokyo.

English translation ©2017 by SQUARE ENIX CO., LTD.

Yen Press
150 West 30th Street, 19th Floor
New York, NY 10001

Visit us at yenpress.com & facebook.com/yenpress
twitter.com/yenpress yenpress.tumblr.com
instagram.com/yenpress

First Yen Press Print Edition: May 2020
Originally published as an ebook in August 2017 by Yen Press.

Yen Press is an imprint of Yen Press, LLC.
The Yen Press name and logo are trademarks of Yen Press, LLC.

The publisher is not responsible for websites (or their content) that are not owned by the publisher.

Library of Congress Control Number: 2019953326

ISBN: 978-1-9753-1144-5 (paperback)

10 9 8 7 6 5 4 3 2 1

WOR

Printed in the United States of America